The Making of a European Public Sphere
Media Discourse and Political Contention

D1383191

This book investigates an important source of th‌[...] macy problems. It shows how European integration is debated in mass m‌[...], [...] how this affects democratic inclusiveness. Advancing integration implies a shift in power between governments, parliaments, and civil society. Behind debates over Europe's "democratic deficit" is a deeper concern: whether democratic politics can perform effectively under conditions of Europeanization and globalization. This study is based on a wealth of unique data from seven European countries, combining newspaper content analyses, an innovative study of Internet communication structures, and hundreds of interviews with leading political and media representatives across Europe. It is by far the most far-reaching and empirically grounded study on the Europeanization of media discourse and political contention to date, and it is a must-read for anyone interested in how European integration changes democratic politics and why European integration has become increasingly contested.

Ruud Koopmans is Director of the Migration, Integration, and Transnationalization research unit at the Wissenschaftszentrum Berlin für Sozialforschung (WZB) and Professor of Sociology at the Vrije Universiteit Amsterdam. His research focuses on citizenship and immigration, European integration, social movements and collective action, and evolutionary sociology. He has authored and co-authored ten books, including *Democracy from Below, New Social Movements in Western Europe, Challenging Immigration and Ethnic Relations Politics*, and *Contested Citizenship*. His work has been published in leading journals such as *American Journal of Sociology, American Sociological Review, European Journal of Political Research, Evolution and Human Behavior, Journal of Ethnic and Migration Studies, Mobilization, Social Problems, Theory and Society*, and *West European Politics*. He is a member of the Scientific Advisory Councils of the Institute for German Studies and the Institute for Migration and Ethnic Studies, both in Amsterdam, and in 2004–2005 he was an invited Fellow at the Center for Advanced Studies in the Behavioral Sciences at Stanford University.

Paul Statham is Professor of Political Sociology and Director of EurPolCom, the Centre for European Political Communications, hosted by the School of Sociology, Politics and International Studies at the University of Bristol. He was formerly a professor at the University of Leeds and a researcher at the Wissenschaftszentrum für Sozialforschung Berlin. His research focuses on political contention, media, and citizenship with regard to Europe, immigration, and ethnic minorities. He has published more than fifty articles in volumes and international scholarly journals, including the *American Journal of Sociology, Western European Politics, Journal of Common Market Studies, Harvard Journal of Press/Politics, European Journal of Communication, Ethnicities, Journalism, Mobilization*, and the *European Political Science Review*. He is co-author of *Contested Citizenship: Immigration and Cultural Diversity in Europe* and co-edited *Challenging Immigration and Ethnic Relations Politics*. His research has been supported by six major grant awards from the European Framework Programme and two from the British Economic and Social Research Council.

Communication, Society and Politics

Politics and relations among individuals in societies across the world are being transformed by new technologies for targeting individuals and sophisticated methods for shaping personalized messages. The new technologies challenge boundaries of many kinds – between news, information, entertainment, and advertising; between media, with the arrival of the World Wide Web; and even between nations. The Communication, Society and Politics series probes the political and social impacts of these new communication systems in national, comparative, and global perspectives.

Titles in the series:

Continued after the Index

The Making of a European Public Sphere

Media Discourse and Political Contention

Edited by

RUUD KOOPMANS
Wissenschaftszentrum Berlin für Sozialforschung

PAUL STATHAM
University of Bristol

CAMBRIDGE
UNIVERSITY PRESS

CAMBRIDGE UNIVERSITY PRESS
Cambridge, New York, Melbourne, Madrid, Cape Town, Singapore,
São Paulo, Delhi, Dubai, Tokyo, Mexico City

Cambridge University Press
32 Avenue of the Americas, New York, NY 10013-2473, USA

www.cambridge.org
Information on this title: www.cambridge.org/9780521138253

© Cambridge University Press 2010

First published 2010

Printed in the United States of America

A catalog record for this publication is available from the British Library.

Library of Congress Cataloging in Publication data

The making of a European public sphere: media discourse and political contention / edited by
Ruud Koopmans, Paul Statham.
   p.   cm. – (Communication, society and politics)
Includes bibliographical references and index.
ISBN 978-0-521-19090-9 (hardback) – 978-0-521-13825-3 (pbk.)
1. European Union – Press coverage.   2. Legitimacy of governments – European Union
countries.   3. Europe – Economic integration – Political aspects.   4. Press and politics –
European Union countries.   5. Mass media – Political aspects – European Union countries.
I. Koopmans, Ruud.   II. Statham, Paul.   III. Title.   IV. Series.
JN30.M2835   2010
341.242'2 – dc22   2010006773

ISBN 978-0-521-19090-9 Hardback
ISBN 978-0-521-13825-3 Paperback

Contents

Tables

Figures

Contributors

Prof. Dr. Silke Adam, University of Bern, Department of Social Sciences (Switzerland)

Prof. Dr. Jos de Beus, University of Amsterdam, Department of Political Science (The Netherlands)

Jessica Erbe, Federal Institute for Vocational Training and Education, Bonn (Germany)

Barbara Eschner, TNS Infratest GmbH, Munich (Germany)

Dr. Julie Firmstone, University of Leeds, Institute of Communications Studies (Great Britain)

Dr. Emily Gray, Ipsos MORI Social Research Institute, London (Great Britain)

Margit Jochum, Hôpital fribourgeois, direction médicale, Fribourg (Switzerland), formerly, University of Zurich, Department of Political Science

Prof. Dr. Ruud Koopmans, Wissenschaftszentrum Berlin, Department of Migration, Integration, Transnationalization, Berlin (Germany)

Prof. Dr. Hanspeter Kriesi, University of Zurich, Department for Political Science (Switzerland)

Prof. Dr. Juan Díez Medrano, Institut Barcelona d'Estudis Internacionals, Barcelona (Spain)

Dr. Martin F. Meyer, University of Cambridge, Pembroke College (Great Britain)

Prof. Dr. Barbara Pfetsch, Free University Berlin, Institute for Media and Communication Studies (Germany)

Prof. Dr. Paul Statham, University of Bristol, Department of Sociology (Great Britain)

Dr. Anke Tresch, University of Geneva, Department of Political Science (Switzerland)

Dr. Ann Zimmermann, Aarhus University, Aarhus School of Business (Denmark)

Acknowledgments

This book is the culmination of a large cooperative research project titled "The Europeanisation of Political Communication and Mobilisation in European Public Spheres" (europub.com), which was funded by an award of the European Commission in the context of its Fifth Framework Programme (project number HPSE-CT2001-00046). We gratefully acknowledge this support, without which a research undertaking of this size and international scope would simply not have been possible.

Although it is nominally an edited volume, from the outset our aim in writing this book was to produce a collective statement that integrates the insights and findings derived from the discrete parts of the project. This has not always been an easy task. In some ways, our endeavor has mirrored the trials and tribulations but also some of the achievements of European integration. Along the way, we witnessed interdisciplinary learning processes and disagreements; national team differences and cross-country collaborations; supranational, intergovernmental and federal leadership models; a Europe of different speeds; and even on the odd occasion an "empty chair" policy. At the same time, we were able to collectively benefit as researchers by having access to a large body of original empirical evidence that none of us would have been able to produce alone. In the final analysis, like Europe, it will be for the public to judge whether it was worth the effort.

The production from the project has been prodigious and collective. Prior to this book, it has produced individual country case monographs and numerous scholarly articles and has provided the basis for several doctoral dissertations. There was a social side too: It launched new friendships and collegiate networks and in one case provided the opportunity for a now-married couple to meet. None of the research would have been possible without the support and commitment of the national team leaders: Jos de Beus, Donatella Della Porta, Juan Díez Medrano, Virginie Guiraudon, Hanspeter Kriesi, and Barbara Pfetsch. A significant acknowledgment is due also to the insight and dedication of the junior researchers, postdocs, and student assistants who coded the data, conducted the interviews, and engaged in active discussions on all aspects of the research, many of whom have since moved on to bigger things: Silke Adam, Massimo Andretta, Olivier Baisnée, Jovanka Boerefijn, Manuela Caiani, Manlio Cinalli, Corinne Dönges, Jessica Erbe, Barbara Eschner, Julie Firmstone, Elisa González Galán, Emily Gray, Olivier Grojean, Valentin Henzler, Margit Jochum, Yuki Kobler, Jeannette Mak, Martin Federico Meyer, Carolina de Miguel, Lorenzo Mosca, Jillian Reynolds, Tobias Schlecht, Anke Tresch, Sara Valenza, Mattias Voigt, Tijmen de Vries, and Ann Zimmermann. If the rigorous application of our claim-making method has ruined their pleasure in reading the morning newspaper for a number of years, we offer a belated apology.

Bringing this book together has been no small task. We much appreciate the support throughout of the series editors, Lance Bennett and Bob Entman, and the sterling efforts of Lew Bateman and his team at Cambridge University Press. The Wissenschaftszentrum Berlin für Sozialforschung (WZB) provided a grant, which is gratefully acknowledged, for Paul Statham to spend a couple of months in Berlin in 2009. This helped to facilitate the final push of bringing the manuscript together as a book. Last, but by no means least, we offer our thanks and appreciation to Jutta Höhne at the WZB, who has made an important contribution by formatting, reading, rereading, and integrating the various chapters into a single book text as well as compiling the index. Her dedication to these tasks deserves special mention.

Finally, there have been many colleagues along the way, too numerous to mention by name, who have shared thoughts, comments, criticisms, and moral support at formative stages of the project.

Ruud and Paul, March 2010

Introduction

Europe's Search for a Public

Paul Statham

Today the European Union is visible most days to most Europeans, should they care to glance at their driving licenses, passports, or the coins in their pockets. There are plenty of reminders for ordinary people that they live in an age of political globalization, and that as inhabitants of the European region they are part of its largest experiment so far: the European Union (EU). At the end of the first decade of the new millennium, the EU is a regional order of twenty-seven countries. It is the world's most advanced institutional coopera-tion and a close interpenetration of societies, markets, and governments, both across borders and between supranational and national actors. Its multileveled political architecture is historically unprecedented and over time its power has grown beyond recognition. However, this substantial advancement of Euro-pean integration over the past 50 years has been driven by political elites and, at least for the period of so-called "permissive consensus,"[1] has largely been out of the public eye. Over the past decade the political channels from the executive to the governed have been increasingly seen as inadequate, result-ing in prominent debates about the EU's perceived democratic and legitimacy "deficits" in policy, academic, and public circles. The watershed moment came in the rejection of Europe's constitutional efforts by the French and Dutch peoples in the 2005 referenda. Taken against the expressed wishes of all main political parties, and all mainstream mass media, these popular rejections in usually supportive countries underlined the passing of the age of "permissive consensus."

Even if it did not occur in the supranational top-down way that the archi-tects of the Constitution intended, the debates after the failure of the con-stitutional project have nonetheless brought the public back into all consid-erations of the European Union. In 2006, the Commission embarked on a

---

[1] Under conditions of "permissive consensus," a positive or neutral majority of public opinion allows for elite autonomy and imagination in managing foreign affairs (Lindberg and Scheingold 1970).

public communications charm offensive, adopting a new rhetoric and policy thinking on public engagement with its citizens, invigorated partly by a media-savvy Commissioner for Institutional Relations and Communication Strategy, Margot Wallström, who "blogged" on the Internet. National governments were also less confident that their ratification of the Constitution's less pretentious successor, the depoliticized Lisbon Treaty (2007), would automatically receive public support or quiescence. Where possible they tried to manage ratification decisions away from the public domain. Nonetheless, even when stripped of constitutionalist aspirations and rhetoric, the Lisbon Treaty was rejected by an Irish referendum in 2008. Finally, after much uncertainty, the Lisbon Treaty was adopted by all member states and came into force on December 1, 2009. On November 19, 2009, the European Council agreed that its first president under the Lisbon Treaty would be Herman Van Rompuy. This decision was reached unanimously at an informal meeting in Brussels by the heads of state and governments of the member states, and it was the result of executive-level insider bargaining and private negotiations. Generally, Van Rompuy was considered by the media to be an underwhelming choice as the first full-time President of the European Council and one who would be unlikely to challenge the authority of national leaders in Europe or on the world stage. This apparently low key outcome, reinforcing nation-state power, contrasts starkly to the initial aspirations expressed in the process of the European Convention (2001–2003). Overall, the difficult passage of Europe's attempted Constitutionalization makes further immediate advances for European integration unlikely and has arguably brought the project into question. What is clear, is that now the European project can no longer avoid having a public face, the way that it is seen publicly, is somewhat different from the benevolent image that its elite advocates continue to promote.

Another event that brought globalization prominently to public attention, and arguably into public disrepute, was the onset of a global financial banking crisis toward the end of 2008. The fallout from the banking crisis has led to economic recession, rising unemployment, and national debt burdens that will have to be met by service cuts and higher public taxation for generations across all countries. As the pioneer for common market integration across the European region and the standard bearer for free market competition, the European Union is a potential target for the fallout from the shift in politics that is likely to result. In 2009 the government responses of EU member states were largely to defend their own financial sectors, national debts, and workforces first, often competitively, rather than seek a cooperative framework with their EU colleagues. It is too early to assess the depth and degree of this renationalization shift. What is clear, however, is that within this era of austerity it will be harder for governments to politically sell the argument to their electorates that everyone wins from free-market-driven globalization. Of course, globalization is not restricted to Europe, but the consequences of globalization are increasingly likely to shape politics and in the European region this inevitably places the future and substance of the European Union at center stage.

The examples show that we increasingly live in a world shaped by advancing globalization (e.g., Held et al. 1999) or "de-nationalization" (e.g., Zürn 1998) processes, the benefits and consequences of which are increasingly visible and real for people. It is not disputed that European society has transformed remarkably over the past fifty years. In a recent contribution, Neil Fligstein (2008) documented how the expansion of markets and economic growth has produced Europe-wide economic, social, and political fields, for example, ranging across the telecommunications and football industries. According to Fligstein, this has led to an increasing density of social interaction and a willingness of people to sometimes identify themselves as Europeans, so that "it is possible to say that there now exists a European society" (2008, p. 244). It is certainly clear that increasing trans-European social interaction has made Europe a common reference point and shared location of interests and power, at least for the minority of people who are its pioneers and beneficiaries. However, the degree and form of the Europeanization of national societies, the system of European multilevel governance that has emerged to sustain it, and the extent to which it is visible, salient, and meaningful to general publics are much disputed. On the last point, even Fligstein, who emphasizes the depth of transnational transformation, concedes that a gap remains between structural change and public perceptions (2008, p. 2): "What has struck me most about the creation of a European society is the degree to which people in Europe are unaware of it." Communication is vital for Europeanization. As Craig Calhoun (2003, p. 243) points out, "If Europe is not only a place but a space in which distinctively European relations are forged and European visions of the future enacted, then it depends on communication in public, as much as on a distinctively European culture, or political institution, or economy, or social networks." Applying a general stance on Europeanization through communication that is broadly compatible to that of Fligstein and Calhoun, we focus explicitly on the transformation of media and political systems that supply information about European actors, policies, and issues to general publics. In this way, the research presented in the following chapters aims to provide empirically informed answers to some of the important questions about Europe's ongoing search for its public.

A common starting point for debates about the performance of the European Union is the perceived existence of a "democratic deficit," or even multiple "deficits." Many scholars see a lack of communication to be part of Europe's perceived democratic deficit and emphasize the need for mass-mediated coverage and public visibility for European policy making as a requirement for a legitimate politics (e.g., Habermas 2005, 2006). The future of European politics, and the form that it takes, depends on the performance of polities and media systems, and what type of choices they supply to the voters, citizens, and peoples of Europe. It is still an open question whether these choices will remain largely nationally defined or alternatively whether cleavages will emerge over issues that cross-cut national boundaries, such as preferences for a more social or market-driven Europe. Now that we live in an era of European multilevel governance, however, the development of a politically mature Europe requires a Europe-wide public discourse of some sort. A seasoned observer, Loukas Tsoukalis, flagged up precisely the need for this European conversation in the final paragraph of his *What Kind of Europe?* (2003, p. 222): "Europeans will surely not agree themselves on the choices they make.... This is, after all, the essence of democracy. But they need to become more aware of those issues and the choices they imply. They need a European public space in which to debate what they want to do together and how." Neil Fligstein further points out that this conversation is likely to become argumentative and holds substantive consequences for social relationships and politics across the region: "The main source of tension and conflict over what might happen next in Europe is the gap between those who participate and benefit from Europe directly and those who do not" (2008, p. 4). In this book, we take the emergence of a multilevel system of governance in the European Union (see, e.g., Kohler-Koch 2003) as a case for examining the performance of media and political communication in an era of advancing globalization. Although ours is a Europe-centric focus, we consider our findings on the transformation of media discourse and political contention in response to advancing European integration also to have general relevance for the debates about the capacity of media and political systems to respond to the challenges of globalization, by providing adequate links between polities and citizens, or not.

An impetus for the study is the common stance within communication and political science literatures on the increasing importance of "mediated politics" (Bennett and Entman 2001) and "audience democracy" (Manin 1997) in liberal democracies, where traditional forms of party politics are replaced by a more direct relationship between governments and citizens through mediated political discourses. The case of a possible European public sphere of communication and collective action allows for an empirical investigation of this mediated politics. Media performance is central to any debate about a European public sphere, since media actors are entrusted with making the European level visible and accessible to citizens. Without an effective media providing a supply line of political information, which allows people the opportunity to see, think, and make decisions about the European level, it would matter relatively little if institutional-fix solutions were applied to strengthen the link between the supranational level of governance and citizens.

News coverage is the best resource available for ordinary citizens to see political debates and the efforts by governments to address perceived problems. Conversely, elite and political actors use the news to monitor public understandings of issues and reactions to their policy decisions and actions (Almond 1960; Entman 2004). There are competing views on adequate media performance in liberal democracies (Ferree et al. 2002a; Patterson 1998). In one, the media largely limits itself to providing the public with reliable and accurate information, exposing the corrupt and incompetent. Its role is to publicize the differences between competing political elites by reporting "objectively." The media supplies the information for the electorate to decide between political parties that compete to represent their interests. The other view depicts a more proactive media role. Here the media opens up policy debates to civil society by enabling collective actors and social movements to voice their demands and challenge executive power. Journalists also enter the political debate as actors by commentating and opinion-leading. Hence mediated political discourse becomes an interface for deliberative exchanges between policy makers and civil society, under the watchful gaze of an attentive public. In sum, mass media performance and the relationship between media and political systems importantly shape the degree to which there is a European public sphere at all, and what type of Europeanized public politics is possible.

We study the transformation of national public spheres. While arenas for public opinion formation, media systems, and channels for access to the polity still predominantly exist at the national level, any European public sphere development will have to be generated by actors from within national public spheres, whose communication leads to increasing mutual interpenetration and references to the EU level. As Habermas puts it (2006, p. 102), "The missing European public sphere should not be imagined as the domestic sphere writ large. It can arise only insofar as the circuits of communication within the national arenas open themselves up to one another while themselves remaining intact." The seven countries in our study are Germany, France, Britain, the Netherlands, Italy, Spain, and Switzerland. We chose "old" Western European democracies, rather than newer ones, since we expect their patterns of communication and interaction will have had more chance to develop in response to institutional and policy integration. The newer democracies of Eastern Europe are likely to have their own distinct trajectory in relation to the European Union. Our country selection nonetheless allows for variations across EU membership, length of membership, depth of integration among members, and big and small countries.

The study examines the supply side of the field of political communication that has emerged in response to advancing European integration and that carries political debates over Europe to general publics. A first important dimension is the *visibility* of the European level to publics. For there to be anything that meaningfully resembles a public sphere at all, European decision making needs to be made visible to citizens. Essential here is the performance of mass media in making Europe visible to people. Second, the degree to which the European level of politics is *inclusive* of publics is also important. This refers to the accessibility of European-level decision making to publics. First, as an electorate, the public have their interests represented by competing political parties; second, through collective action, public groups mobilize their demands and pressure governments. Here it is the democratic performance of the political system that matters and the degree to which the public is able to gain formal access to, and be included within public debates about the decision-making processes of European multilevel governance. A third dimension, which derives from the other two, is *contestation*. The more that the European level of decision making becomes visible and the more it includes nonstate voices, the more it is likely to be subject to dynamics of public contestation, leading to a politicization carried by party competition and challenges by civil society actors. Together, these three dimensions, visibility, inclusiveness, and contestation, structure our inquiry into public sphere development and the type of Europeanized public politics that is on offer to the general public. The debates around these issues, and their specific related literatures, are taken up and discussed substantively in detail in the respective chapters.

The book divides into five parts. Part I addresses theoretical, conceptual, analytical, and methodological issues relating to a European public sphere. Part II presents analyses on the emergent general trends for visibility, inclusiveness, and contestation within Europeanized public debates. In Part III, chapters address different aspects of mass media performance in supplying a European public sphere. Chapters in Part IV assess aspects of democratic performance in more detail, by examining political actors' responses to opportunities for shaping mediated debates. Finally, Part V, the conclusion, draws together the findings from across the study to outline a stance on what type of Europeanized public politics we have, how we reached this point, and where we are likely to go from here.

First, Chapter 1 opens up the debate on the European public sphere. This is where we enter the theoretical and normative debates about the possible emergence of a European public sphere and the implications and consequences for democratic legitimacy of advancing European integration. The story is told of the political transformation of Europe through integration, from the early days to the present, and the dilemmas – practical and ethical – that have accompanied this institutional development and shaped its path, not least of which is the missing public. Chapter 1 unpacks the basic conflict lines and critically examines the disputes within political science and normative theory about the institutional development of the European Union and the available mechanisms for supplying public legitimacy. This chapter serves the book by providing a historical contextual background of the institutional integration that has resulted in the European Union's system of multilevel governance and of the driving processes of Europeanization.

Chapter 2 lays out the theoretical framework that underpins our own view on European public sphere development. It critically describes the evolution of empirical approaches for studying the emergence of a European public sphere, and it locates our own approach in this field. The chapter outlines the general theoretical framework, research design, and methods that inform the detailed empirical analyses of subsequent chapters. Importantly, this involves elaborating a perspective on the transformation of political communication by collective actors, whose communicative acts make links across borders and political levels, leading to a Europeanization of public spheres. This analytic framework allows one to distinguish between the forms of possible Europeanization – vertical, horizontal, supranational – that are subsequently used in the book. Chapter 2 also outlines how we combine perspectives on political mobilization and communication – "opportunity structures" and "mediated politics" – to develop a general model for analyzing public sphere development by linking the opportunities supplied by media and political systems to the acts of public claim making by collective actors. In addition, we specify the general comparative dimensions that structure and run throughout the study: across countries, policy fields, and time. Finally, Chapter 2 provides the reader with information on the claim-making method for retrieving data from newspaper sources, which is our primary data source for five of the chapters, and technical details on newspaper selection and sampling.

Part II addresses the general trends of European public sphere development evident along the dimensions of visibility, inclusiveness, and contestation. Chapters 3 and 4 present general-level empirical analyses of claim making by collective actors across countries, policy fields, and time, on the basis of our data set of more than 20,000 cases. Chapter 3 provides answers to questions about the visibility of Europe in mediated public discourses: How much communication and interaction across borders and political levels is there? What are the prevalent forms of Europeanized communication? Does its emergence vary across policy fields according to the degree and form in which they have been Europeanized? Does it increase over time with advancing integration? Are there cross-national variations in Europeanization trends, and what might explain them? Finally, is there a relationship between public sphere emergence and the type of evaluations – supportive or oppositional – that collective actors mobilize over European integration and EU institutions? The study of actors' evaluations leads into an assessment of the degree, extent, and form of contestation over Europe. This issue is picked up directly in Chapter 4, which addresses claim making by collective actors. The prime focus of Chapter 4 is the inclusiveness of the European public sphere. It addresses the important question of who participates in Europeanized public debates and how actors evaluate European institutions and the integration process when they do so. The findings indicate who wins and who loses as a result of the advancing Europeanization of public debates. A key question is whether civil society actors are able to discursively empower themselves relative to government and executive actors within Europeanized compared with national-level communication. In addition, the relationship between inclusiveness and contestation is tested for specific actors. Together the findings from Chapters 3 and 4 provide an overall empirical picture of the European public sphere and explanations for its development in response to the shift of power within decision making that results from advancing integration. These findings provide the context and reference point for the subsequent detailed studies of specific actors and across different types of claim making and media.

The chapters in Part III address different aspects of mass media performance in supplying a European public sphere. Chapter 5 starts by examining how the press has responded to the challenge of covering the European level of decision making. Its findings are based on a systematic analysis of interviews with more than 100 journalists from the print media in the seven studied countries, plus the transnational press. There are different ways that journalists may view their role in making Europe visible and inclusive. What motivations and norms guide journalists? Is the European level adequately covered? What, in their view, constitutes adequate coverage and media performance? Do journalists report the political world that they see, or do they try and open up a more pluralistic debate, adopting a political advocacy role? Do they adopt a more educational or partisan stance over Europe toward their readers? Are there differences across journalistic practices (reporting and commentating), professional roles (EU correspondents, reporters, and editors), newspaper types, or national press cultures?

Chapter 6 builds on this story by presenting a detailed study of claim making by journalists through editorials and commentaries. It is based on an analysis of the contents of more than 1,400 editorial and commentary articles. Journalists' own claim-making acts indicate how, to what degree, and where the media intervenes as an actor attempting to shape the political discourse over Europe. The study allows empirical purchase on whether media commentating has an Europeanizing impact by opening up national debates through references to Europe. In addition, it allows comparison across countries and newspaper types. Important are the types of issues and interpretations (conflict lines) that journalists apply to depict a country's relationship to the European project. In this way, Chapter 6 not only adds to the stance on media performance from Chapter 5 but also facilitates understanding on the extent to which the Europeanized world views mobilized by journalists replicate those that result from the claim making by collective actors that are reported in the news (Chapter 3). This builds an overall picture on the relationship between media and political systems in supplying political information to the public.

So far, chapters have addressed Europeanization by studying newspaper discourse. However, a salient thesis is that the alternative public space of the Internet and World Wide Web provides an important source of claim making that circumvents conventional media. Of course, the Internet's own ideology – often repeated in cultural studies – is that it stands as a force for a more deliberative, accessible, egalitarian, and transparent public debate when compared with political communication in newspapers. Indeed, a common urban myth is that the French "*non*" to the Constitution in the 2005 referendum was generated by oppositional stances accessible via the Internet and on the "blogosphere." Chapter 7 compares the Europeanization potential of political communication carried by the World Wide Web to newspaper media. It analyzes a data set of claim making from thousands of systematically retrieved search engine results and hyperlink networks among a multitude of national and transnational Web sites. This provides an overall empirical picture of the visibility and inclusiveness of the European public sphere that is produced by the millions of individual decisions by people who place material on the Internet and access it. The findings are compared with newspaper claim making to assess Internet performance alongside that of conventional media in supplying Europeanized public debates.

The next chapter, Chapter 8, turns attention to a feature within claim making, by examining the frames that are mobilized in news discourses by media actors in comparison to collective actors. Chapter 8 studies the different ways that actors depict and symbolically package claims about European integration, such as whether they use identity, instrumental, or historical framing strategies. This allows analytic purchase on whether the European Union may be emerging as a set of countries that share and communicate common values and understandings of the integration project – the possible common building blocks for a shared political culture – or whether national or actor-specific visions and trajectories persist.

Part IV moves the discussion on from media to polity performance. Chapters 9 and 10 look at political actors' responses to the transformed opportunities within Europeanized decision making and public discourses for accessing and influencing the political debate. At stake is the effectiveness of channels and communicative linkages between the executive elites, on one side, and civil society actors and citizens, on the other. Chapter 9 looks at the inclusiveness of Europeanized policy domains toward political parties, social interest groups, nongovernmental organizations (NGOs), and social movements, while Chapter 10 examines party competition through media discourse.

Chapter 9 examines the impact of a political environment transformed by advancing Europeanization and mediatization on collective actors' action repertoires. The study covers state actors, interest groups, parties, and NGOs and social movement organizations and is based on structured responses to several hundred interviews. It assesses how important "going public" actually is for collective actors by examining the action repertoires that different actors use in their attempts to access different levels of the European polity, and whether they use insider or public-oriented strategies to gain policy influence. Chapter 9 builds up a general picture of collective actors' strategic responses to perceived opportunities for gaining access to European policy making. The study allows triangulation with key findings from the claim-making study on inclusiveness to see if the way actors see their own world matches the image produced by their successful claim-making acts. As in Chapter 4, a key concern is the extent to which actors from civil society, especially weaker NGOs and social movement organizations, are able to make their voices heard.

Chapter 10 turns attention to political party competition as a means for representing and mediating choices to voters over European integration and the European Union institutions. It contributes empirically to the debates about the relationship between political parties' alignments over Europe and traditional ones, especially the left–right cleavage. Is party contestation increasing, and to what degree and how do domestic political parties make Europe visible? Does a favorable consensus hold among mainstream left and right parties, or is criticism increasing over Europe at the core of political systems? What is the substance of this criticism? Is it ideological Euroscepticism, or is it a constructive critique of the European project? Do parties mobilize appeals to the "winners" and "losers" of Europeanization? Chapter 10 uses a sample of evaluative claim making by all actors belonging to a national political party. This allows for comparison of party contestation across countries, party families, and time. It also demonstrates that the claim-making approach has the potential to produce systematically linked quantitative and qualitative data analyses.

Finally, Chapter 11 in Part V synthesizes our perspective on visibility, inclusiveness, and contestation into an interpretive framework for different types of emergent Europeanized public politics. First it identifies the possible pathways for a Europeanized public politics. Then it draws together the evidence from across the chapters to outline a coherent stance on public sphere development in response to European integration. Key findings are presented on the dimensions of visibility, inclusiveness, and contestation, drawing on evidence across media, countries, actors, policies, and time. In this way, the concluding chapter answers to what degree – and how, where, when, by whom, and why – a Europeanized public politics has emerged and what it consists of. This returns us to the important questions raised by Chapter 1. Chapter 11 then continues with a discussion of the failed constitutional project, showing how that event may have transformed the situation leading to a possible increase in public attention for European integration. Finally, it proposes a realistic way forward for the European Union's search for public legitimacy, starting out from where we are now.

PART I

A EUROPEAN PUBLIC SPHERE

Questions and Approach

I

The European Union and the Public Sphere

Conceptual Issues, Political Tensions, Moral Concerns, and Empirical Questions

Jos de Beus

> Truly political assembly only prospers under the great protectorate of public
> spirit, as the living prospers only under the protectorate of a clear air.
>
> Karl Marx, *Rheinische Zeitung*, May 1842[1]

A PUBLIC SPHERE DEFICIT OF EUROPE?

In the aftermath of the Treaty of Nice (agreed to by the European Council in December 2000), the leaders of the European Union (EU) decided to promote a debate on the future of European integration. They were worried by a growing alienation among local elites and masses within the member states (Ludlow 2002). They created a public meeting of appointed representatives of national governments, national parliaments, the European Commission, and the European Parliament – next to representatives of candidate countries without a decision-making role. Their Convention on the Future of Europe started in Brussels in February 2002 and ended in June 2003. It conducted broad discussions about basic issues, such as European identity, supranational competence, and the power balance between large and small countries. It produced a draft constitution that provided the framework for a new Treaty of Rome, signed in October 2004 by all members of the European Council (Dinan 2005; Duff 2005; Norman 2003, pp. 173–182).

This experiment in publicity was widely covered by the news media. It was a visible and personalized display of bargaining by national governments and European agencies – just remember Chairman Giscard d'Estaing's stately performances. Nevertheless, it became a double failure (Moravcsik 2006). Its procedure (the convention's working groups and plenary sessions) remained a secluded domain of EU-centric ministers, diplomats, lobbyists, journalists, and experts. It did not draw the attention of wider audiences in the member states, nor did it bring in societal actors, such as political parties, social movements,

---

[1] Quoted by Splichal (1999, p. 67).

13

and public policy advocacy networks. Its substance (a new treaty) was rejected by angry French and Dutch referendum voters in the middle of 2005. This rejection plunged the entire project of reform of European rules and institutions into a crisis. The Reform Treaty of Lisbon (signed in December 2007) did save certain proposals of the convention, such as the permanent presidency of the European Council and the usage of majority rule in the European Council of Ministers. The protracted and difficult process of national ratifications indicates a continuing struggle about the raison d'être and sustainability of European integration (Anderson 2007; Bartolini 2005; Katzenstein 2005; Zielonka 2006).

The example of the failure of the second Treaty of Rome, also compared with the success of the first one in 1957, illustrates a general and urgent phenomenon that is the central topic of this volume. On the one hand, European authorities today welcome and facilitate a public process of European integration. They argue that the legitimacy, effectiveness, and efficiency of far-reaching policies such as liberalization of markets, monetary unification, eastern enlargement, and cooperation in matters of national security depend on public knowledge, opinion, and acceptance, more particularly on the viability of a public sphere in which representative government can work and flourish at two levels (the national level and the European level). On the other hand, most efforts by European authorities to open up a public sphere seem to backfire and in some cases even jeopardize public support of, and state compliance with, the *acquis communautaire* (agricultural, regional, trade, and competition policies). Either the expected rate of mobilization and communication fails to materialize, or the results of the emerging public sphere in terms of public understanding and commitment are poor. This phenomenon may be referred to as the "public sphere dilemma" or the "public sphere deficit of Europe."

Does a public sphere deficit of sorts exist in the EU? That is the leading question of the research presented in this book. We examine the extent of Europeanization of the public sphere and the distribution of public policy access as well as the positioning of political actors (including news media) with respect to the question of European integration within seven democratic societies, namely France, Germany, Italy, the Netherlands, Spain, the United Kingdom, and Switzerland (the European neighbor and nonmember in our sample). The public sphere deficit is an integral part of the topical and controversial issue of the democracy deficit (if any) of the European Union, that is, the systematic lack of authority of national and European parties and parliaments related to European integration and other modes of scale enlargement and scale lifting (Bartolini 2006; Follesdal and Hix 2005; Hix 2006, 2008; Magnette and Papadopoulos 2008; Majone 1998; Moravcsik 2004; Schmidt 2006; Schmitter 2000; Siedentop 2000).

The basic concept warrants clarification from the start. A public sphere is an intermediate sphere of public actions, affiliations, and relations beyond the state and the market, where citizens as relatively free and equal members of society and its polity use many, independent, and partly rival associations and media to learn, discuss, organize collective action, and bargain, among other things, and where such practices of citizenship tend to protect and promote constitutional democracy under preconditions of maturity (state capacity, civic identity of the people, and flexibility of elites; see Habermas 1962; Lipset and Lakin 2004; Snyder 2000).

More concretely, the public sphere implies open struggle between political parties for the votes of those who are governed. It implies parliamentary representation of the people that is publicly recorded in official reports and is, more generally, accessible and perceptible by the senses of citizens on the public tribune, journalists, and all listeners to the radio, watchers of television, and users of the Internet in the case of broadcasts of parliamentary sessions. It also implies accountability of the government in the face of alert activists, journalists, and individual citizens. In a broad sense, the public sphere entails conflict-ridden yet open and peaceful interplay between state and civil society covered by the news media (also similar interplay between different kinds of voluntary associations); coherence of the entire policy process in the legislative, executive, and judicial branches of government (transparency); openness within associations and media themselves; and regular publication of important documents by the government.

Public spheres in national democracies to date are the unintended consequence of histories of influence seeking by outsiders and insiders (Zaret 2000). Outsiders tend to go public to create pressure on the government and vested interests, or to penetrate old bastions of power. Insiders tend to organize publicity and reach their constituencies there to strengthen their institutions (the central state, the national parliament, a specific ministry, and so on) and beat other insiders. In every practical form and meaning of the public sphere, there is always an invisible and rather uncontested part of society and politics, such as "tax collection, census taking, military service, diffusion of information, processing of government-mediated benefits, internal organisational activity of constituted political actors, and related processes" (Tilly 2005, p. 5).

A public sphere may exist or not exist at two levels, that is, the European level of Brussels, Strasburg, and Luxembourg (main sites of European agencies) and the national level of the member states, in particular their capital cities. A European public sphere may be missing when and because there are no EU-relevant associations and media tout court, according to an ambitious standard drawn from the pure democratic ideal (absolute view), or when and because such associations and media are much less developed than those within the polities of the member states (relative view, mostly focused on some domestic or international average of public sphere growth). A European public sphere may be weak when and because there is no EU-relevant mobilization and communication according to some minimal standard (absolute view), or too little of such ongoing processes according to a national or international standard (relative view). A European public sphere may be asymmetric when and because the distribution of associations and media and/or their repertoires of action and interaction are skewed, either absolutely or in comparison with national and international distributions.

For different reasons, the two most important schools of European engineering to date – that is, the realists, alias intergovernmentalists (such as General De Gaulle), and the idealists, alias federalists (such as Senator Spinelli) – argue that the European public sphere is missing or weak. Realists deny the unity and capacity of supranational agencies in relations among states. Idealists criticize everyday nationalism by governments, political associations, news media, and citizens as the root of evil, that is, the technocratic and bureaucratic nature of the European politics of integration. This volume, however, tries to demonstrate some substantive Europeanization of the national public sphere, particularly in certain advanced areas of European integration (such as monetary policy). The real issue lies elsewhere: the continued dominance of representatives of central governments and the continued irrelevance of representatives of social groups in a wide sense.

1951–1989: INVISIBILITY, OR THE SECRET ACCUMULATION OF EU POLITICAL CAPITAL

The first decades of European unification start with the preparation of a coal and steel community in 1950 and end with an agreement on making an internal market (mobility of goods, persons, services, and capital) in the Single European Act (the so-called Europe 1992 campaign of Delors's first presidency). In this period, European policy does not mean much in terms of system capacity (single competence, budget, civil service, and so on), both absolutely and in comparison with the steadily expanding public policy activism in the member states. It revolved around protection of agriculture, the opening of national markets and branches of export on the basis of jurisprudence by the European Court of Justice, and assistance to poor areas as the backdrop to entry of poorer member states in 1973, 1981, and 1986. As a result of French initiatives, unanimity became the conventional rule of decision, while a new body was created (the European Council) to block expansion and usurpation of power by supranational agencies and entrepreneurs.

It would be incorrect to claim that this has been a silent revolution of international politics in Western Europe, unnoticed or taken for granted without much emotion by aloof voters who wait and see, pragmatic industrialists and professions (those that were directly affected by the European project), and a lofty circle of broad-minded journalists. On the one hand, a kind of top-down recognition of Europe occurred because of the perseverance of federalists. Their climax was the introduction of national elections for the selection of members of the European Parliament in 1979. They scored a symbolic success with the broad acceptance by this parliament of a draft constitution in February 1984 (Dinan 2005, p. 92). On the other hand, European planners engendered resistance by the very constituencies they had shaped themselves in the first place. Since 1968 (the Mansholt Plan), efforts were made to diminish the disadvantages of common agricultural policy for consumers, small farmers, the environment, and farmers in poor countries, and to impose certain costs of modernization and free enterprise on European farmers. This unleashed waves of protest action by farmers' associations and unorganized farmers in Brussels and national capitals at the end of the 1960s and the early 1970s, the first expression of recognition of the united Europe from below.

Nevertheless, European unity in the first decades was by and large constructed in a context of closure and secrecy. Indeed, the workshop of Europe was a private sphere of public policy: "The 'Europeanisation' of national political life has largely gone on behind the scenes, but its very invisibility has seen the triumph of a unique political experiment" (Leonard 2005, p. 13). Here are some factors that explain such striking functionality of avoidance and protracted restriction of publicity.

First, European integration was at first seen as a special element of foreign policy. Foreign policy relied on the tradition and norm of diplomacy behind the scenes, informal summit conferences, privileges for heads of state, and state secrets. The primacy of national departments of foreign affairs was a feature of the early politics of European integration.

Second, there was at first broad agreement among leaders of parties in the middle, of local communities, and of public opinion about the necessity of European reconciliation and pacification with American blessing by means of planned modernization and gradual liberalization of national economies on the continent. Such harmony and confidence in state elites were made easier by the start of the Cold War, economic recovery (the German miracle), economic growth with full employment, and the apparently positive consequences of the European Economic Community as a new institution (Milward 1984, 1992; Olson 1982, pp. 118–119, 130–131).

Third, the architects of Europe feared that public federalism with an appeal to supranational sovereignty and postnational identity would only wake up the demons of aggressive nationalism in the countries involved. It would also create unbridgeable distances between negotiators and additional geopolitical instability (weakening of the front against the Soviet Union and its allies). This argument developed into the doctrine of functionalism, that is, interweaving through gradual yet irreversible growth of the role of a European center from sector A to the connected sector B, from country A to neighbor B, and from agency A to the completing agency B. Facelessness and colorlessness of European policy makers and their ways of conduct were the price of business-like cooperation (Duchêne 1994).

Fourth, the periodical deals between Europeanists and traditionalists in the establishment of member states implied that political actions of government with a potential of conflict and mobilization in left–right schemes were fulfilled by national states (social policy) or traditional alliances (defense). European cooperation became nonpolitical, consensual, and technical. It involved administrative actions of government for the sake of simultaneous implementation and enforcement by member states themselves (competition policy, later trade policy, monetary policy, and environmental policy). As the economist Galbraith pointed out a long time ago – and clockwise afterward – with respect to the "mystique of central banking" (Galbraith 1954 [1975], p. 54), these sectors of public policy are incomprehensible and somewhat magical in the eyes of ordinary citizens and members of the public (see Scharpf 1997).

Fifth, the representatives of national governments did not want at the European level the kind of publicity that was customary at the domestic level, or reached full growth there in the 1960s. They discovered the practical advantages of a two-level game, like greater space for bargaining, an information lead with respect to domestic actors with blocking power (including opposition parties), concealment of inner room defeats, blame shifting to Brussels or to certain member states in case of expensive and unpopular deals, and blowup of the national role in case of profitable and popular results of bargaining (natiocentrism; see Evans, Jacobson, and Putnam 1993; Putnam 1988). This double was responded to and reinforced by the double of lobbyists. Those who are the first to start a European lobby or platform on behalf of large corporations, branches of industry, and local layers of government may win durable direct contact with European holders of power and special influence on European policies. The success of most lobbies relies on evasion of the public sphere (Pedler and Van Schendelen 1994).

Sixth, the mixed and often essentially ambiguous nature of the European order may constitute an obstacle for politicians who want to increase the publicity of their own performance, or those of partners and opponents. On the one hand, the EU is an extra large supervisory authority with administrative competences delegated and defined by national states. On the other hand, the EU means continuation of national politics and geopolitics on the scale of a world region. European ministers form a legislative branch, a senate of sorts on a par with the European Parliament (a house of representatives of sorts) that allows for permission of television cameras. But these ministers also belong to the European executive branch, a government on a par with the European Commission that can only work by means of sessions behind closed doors. The European Commission sees itself as an overarching government of governments, which explains its open attitude toward journalists. Nevertheless, the commission is in many ways a higher civil service of the European Council (the body that appoints its president). This official dimension forces the commission to restrain media management and to move in public rather prudently and in the networking spirit of Jean Monnet. The European Parliament would clearly profit from the kind of publicity that surrounds national parliaments. However, it is still street-lengths away from such publicity because of its lack of normal competences versus an executive branch, lack of normal party relations (incumbent parties vs. opposition parties), complex procedures, appeal to corrupt politicians, and reluctant settlement between members from countries with an open political culture and those from countries with a closed one. Strictly speaking, it is only the European Court of Justice and the European Court of First Instance that look like their national equivalents (the European Central Bank has hollowed out its national equivalents and is formally the most autonomous central bank in the world). Nonetheless, these bodies usually operate in their own demarcated area of control, crowded with experts and professional political forces with conflicting interests.

Seventh, the buildup of a public sphere was hampered during the first decades of European integration by general factors such as language barriers; size; the universal dilemma of collective action of, by, and for rational actors; and the ancient diversity of national traditions of the public sphere (see Archibugi 2005; de Swaan 2001; and Wagner 2006 on language barriers).

Finally, some styles of European politics are more conducive to invisibility than others. All governments, whether large or small, long-standing members or new ones, and rich or poor, have an institutional interest in controlling the public sphere with respect to their European agenda. But governments in consensual democracies seem more willing and capable of avoiding broad mobilization and communication in issues of foreign policy than governments in majoritarian democracies (Lijphart 1968 [1975], 1984, 1999, 2008). The pursuit of unanimity and harmony on the European course of the nation, the shared understandings among leaders and elites (sometimes cartels of them), the obedience of constituencies, and the promotion of say in the matter of managers, experts, and spokespersons of minorities are all conducive to avoidance of intractable conflict and vehement debate. If we construct a dichotomy according to the index of Lijphart, then the Netherlands, Germany, and Italy were consensual members of the original European Economic Community; France was a lonely majoritarian member; the new member states – the United Kingdom and Spain – were strengthening the majoritarian ranks; and non-member Switzerland was a consensual democracy with the special feature of referendum-induced consensus (Della Porta 2003; Lijphart 1999). This implies that during the first decades of integration, ceteris paribus, five old member states (Italy, Germany, and the Netherlands, as well as Belgium and Luxembourg, two additional consensual democracies) were leading the depoliticization of Europe in electoral campaigns as well as the creation of consensual institutions and practices at the EU level.

All these factors have contributed to the following stylized fact. The political capital of the EU, that is, its stock of mutual respect, trust, solidarity, and propensity to cooperate, accumulated gradually and implicitly in the period since 1951. Citizens in the member states acted as if the European layer of politics and administration still did not exist, while the network of policy makers on this layer acted as if citizens with overarching national loyalties did not exist anymore.

Such bilateral and symmetric neglect was unavoidable and useful in the first stage of integration. Comparative research about national political systems tells us that incomplete and premature democratization induces internal and external instability because of the impact of untamed nationalism, while democratization after institutionalization of central state authority, the rule of law, regulated markets, professional news media, and organized political parties is conducive to internal and external pacification (Bartolini 2005, 2006; Mansfield and Snyder 2005; Snyder 2000). If we apply this result to the

European case in a counterfactual sense, it implies that early domestic and inter-national politicization of the European question in full publicity would have needlessly jeopardized the stability of European societies and states, already dethroned as hegemonic powers and at first vulnerable after the Second World War. In other words, the first demand of the EU with respect to candidate members, to wit, consolidation of democracy including the public sphere, is, and must be, the last demand that the EU raises with respect to its own work-ing. Thus, the commonplace idea that the EU makes high procedural demands on new entrants, which it cannot meet itself, is a half-truth.

THE EU SINCE 1989: INITIATIVE AND IMPASSE

The EU is a powerful organization with supranational powers that are rather unique in international relations. It is a robust bargaining mechanism of, for, and by twenty-seven national states with a will to mutual commitment, par-ticularly to coordination of national economies. It has a currency (the euro), and it has a budget (of 862 billion euros) until 2013. It strikes trade deals with the United States and its non-Western competitors in the World Trade Organ-isation. It lodges two extremely affluent countries (Luxembourg and Ireland), while it rejoices the regard and awe of numerous candidate member states in the east and south of the European zone. It has a headquarters, namely the Berlaymont Building in Brussels, residence of the European Commission. Last but not least, the EU gives serious consideration to new tasks (such as coun-terterrorism, foreign policy, energy supply, and control of global warming) without giving up old tasks.

Yet the expressions of an impasse of the EU are manifest and manifold. There are recurrent and acrimonious renegotiations about institutional reform (the treaties of Maastricht in 1991, Amsterdam in 1997, Nice in 2000, and Rome in 2004). There is open animosity about crisis management in food security and public health (mad cow disease, foot-and-mouth disease, avian flu), overhaul-ing of redistributive policies (common agricultural policy, regional policy), and international mergers in public utilities and basic industries. There is laborious enforcement of the Stability and Growth Pact. There are claims of a miscarriage of the cautious British strategy of entry into the Economic and Monetary Union by the Labour Party under Blair's premiership, as well as miscarriage of the ambitious Lisbon strategy (2000) of economic recovery, technological innova-tion, and global competitiveness, interwoven with a lack of credibility of its revision by the Barroso Commission since 2004. Rifts exist between supporters and opponents of economic liberalism, national protectionism, and – in the area of foreign policy since 2001 – divisions about the proper response to Ameri-can imperialism, Russian and Chinese authoritarianism, and Turkish Islamism. Confusion and polarization abound in the European response to controversial and symbolic events, such as the rise of politicians suspected of antidemo-cratic schemes (Le Pen, Dewinter, Haider, Berlusconi, Fortuyn, Wilders); acts of terror in Madrid, Amsterdam, and London; the appointment of an orthodox Catholic from Italy in the European Commission; and the publication of cartoons with a satire of Islam in Denmark. There has been a long period of "reflection" concerning the constitutional framework of European society and politics, inserted after the negative referenda in France and the Netherlands in 2005. And, last but not least, there have been frequent European peak conferences and seminars about everything that is fundamental and apparently melting in the air: the European ideal (telos) of civilization and soft power, the democracy deficit of the EU, the European models of welfare, the European enlightenment of ordinary citizens, the European commitment of those citizens, the European approach of Islam (models of pluralism), and the mixed order of the EU (subsidiarity, different speeds of integration, and methods of multilevel administration, such as the open method of coordination).

However, seasoned politicians, commentators, and scholars point out that there is nothing unique about temporary standstill in European unity (Davies 1996; Gillingham 2003; Hitchcock 2003). Since the Second World War the politics of European integration has made unparalleled progress through moments of crisis, intervening periods of muddling through, fluctuating moods of optimism and idealism (Euro entrepreneurship) as well as pessimism and realism (Eurosclerosis), and perpetual negotiations under the shadow of veto power by (alliances of) national governments. Both the 1960s and 1970s can be assessed with some fairness as decades of nondecision and saturation (Dinan 2005; Judt 2005). European integration cannot be linear. It must be cyclic (Hoffmann 1995). Indeed, a simultaneous backlash in two worlds – that of states and administrative elites, that of peoples and social movements – makes a lot of sense after all the sweeping widening and deepening of the EU since the start of Delors's spectacular presidency of the European Commission in 1985 until today (control of the American banking crisis and of imbalances in the world economy).

Nevertheless, in some important ways the present problem of Europe building seems special and quite effective in disqualifying notions of irreversible integration and smooth interdependence. First, there is much more at stake because of the very success of European cooperation and ordering in such divergent areas as competition policy, monetary policy, the natural environment, and the freedoms and rights of workers and immigrants (Hooghe and Marks 2001, pp. 187–189). Popular estrangement and lack of practical compromise among elites are conducive to cutthroat rivalry (between European firms, states, regions, and interest groups of producers and professionals) as well as paralysis of besieged authorities (the European Councils of heads of government and of ministers, the European Commission, the European Central Bank). All this may very well undermine the routine policies of the EU and the twin towers of Europe: the single market and the monetary union.

Second, there is much more at stake because of the growth of the number of states and peoples involved. European procedures of public policy making have deeply penetrated into the working of national political institutions, such as cabinets of ministers, departments, courts, and parliaments. Policy processes in national capitals and the places of residence of European agencies are inter-mingled. Although some political actors, such as Delors (1985–1995), oversold the European origins of national law, the impact of the *acquis communautaire* (the entire set of EU laws, framework laws, regulations, decisions, recom-mendations, and advices) on the legal order of member states can hardly be overrated. Hence, the indirect influence of European rules and policies on the opportunities and prospects of millions of households and persons is larger than ever. If the worse would happen and the sequence of European compromise, general legislation, and decentralized implementation and law enforcement gets stuck, the consequences would be enormous. Policy immobility in the 1960s and 1970s was compensated by the silent activism of the European Court of Justice, which maintained coherence and momentum. A repetition of that inci-dental prominent role for a body of appointed judges who miss the standing and history of many national supreme courts seems unlikely in the present-day climate of aversion against uncontrolled networks of supranational power (Weiler 1999).

Third, public administration within European countries has become more complex and unruly, in comparison with both the official public philosophy of efficient and effective governance of regional public goods and the earlier experience of backlash of European regionalism in the 1960s and 1970s. Then, central governments were facing issues of redistribution of the benefits of eco-nomic growth, catch-up participation of minorities of citizens, and control of the limits and pathologies of economic planning and collectivist social security from cradle to grave.

Today, governments face issues of decline and lagging competitiveness, lack of integration between old and new groups of citizens (migration in West-ern Europe, nation building in Eastern Europe), and control of the limits and pathologies of welfare state reform, liberalization of markets, and multilevel governance. In 2005, only two member states spent more than 3% of their gross national product on research, and only four member states had more than 70% of their workforce employed, while these percentages are official EU targets in 2010 (European Commission 2006a). The gap between European and Ameri-can labor productivity, research and development, and gross domestic product per capita has widened. Such widening brings the postwar catch-up of many national economies in Western Europe under the auspices of the European Eco-nomic Community to a close. Furthermore, the sustainability of the European model of society, a mixture of social protection of workers and cooperative industrial relations, is threatened by external factors – immigration from Africa and Arabia, the rise of Chinese and Indian competitors, and diffusion of the American shareholder model of corporate governance – and internal factors – massive unemployment, rising costs of care for the elderly, and labor immigra-tion from Eastern Europe (Pisani-Ferry and Sapir 2006; Sapir 2004, 2005).

Finally, and most crucial from the perspective of this book and its authors, the conditions for politics have become harder and in some respects more unfa-vorable, as far as European relaunch and democratic resilience are concerned.

The political differences between European stagnation in the 1960s and 1970s and stagnation as it exists today concern both the geopolitical setting and the domestic setting.

In the 1960s and 1970s, European integration as response to the dwarfing of Europe during the century of its self-destruction and the genesis of American hegemony was still driven by the presence of an enemy (the Soviet Union), the steering by an inner center (the axis of France and West Germany), and the diplomatic surveillance of the United States (Lichtheim 1972 [2000]). Today, the geopolitical constellation for further integration is weakened. There is no immediate foreign threat anymore. Southern and Eastern enlargement of the EU has been instrumental to the consolidation of the European zone of perpetual peace – Kant's famous phrase and the goal of generations of European architects and policy makers, together with other major improvements, such as pacification of the Balkans after the Kosovo war, the democratic revolution in countries within the Russian sphere of influence (Ukraine, Georgia), and the rise to power of a democratic Muslim movement in Turkey. The French–German axis does not provide breakthroughs anymore, because of German unification, expansion of EU membership beyond the Western European continent, and protectionist as well as opportunistic leadership in Paris and Berlin after the Mitterrand–Kohl friendship. The United States stopped its active support of European recovery because of an ambivalent assessment of a strong EU as an economic, cultural, and military equal and rival in the Western alliance, while the governing classes of Europe and its public intellectuals disagree about America as counterpart, role model, and partner (Calleo 2001; Garton Ash 2004; Habermas 2004; Kupchan 2002; Levy, Pensky, and Torpey 2005; Münkler 2005).

The domestic setting of European politics is also new and restrictive. The public climate of permissive consensus, in which a positive or neutral majority opinion of the public allows for elite autonomy and imagination in foreign policy, in particular public action toward the objective of European unification, is all but exhausted (Key 1961, pp. 32–35, 552; Lindberg and Scheingold 1970). The current climate is marked by critical support, scepticism, and hostility. The EU has, on purpose and partly behind its own back, shaped a network of constituencies in numerous areas of public policy (for example, agriculture, transport, protection of minority cultures, and promotion of scientific research). There are cases in which winning political parties in the middle and news media with large market shares share diffuse views about the need of new EU policies, the obsoleteness of old ones, and the terms of reform. Even in such cases, constituencies with vested interests of the EU's own making may block or slow down legitimate and potentially effective policy changes (Héritier 1999; Hix 2005; Leibfried and Pierson 1995).

The supporters of federalism are retreating. Federalism in the European context implies active commemoration of world wars, the Holocaust, and decolonization; moral commitment to the European idea and the primacy of European loyalty; steady expansion of European policies; and the building of a quasi-national, constitutional, democratic, and central state in the Brussels District (supranational authority; see Etzioni 2001; Morgan 2005; Rifkin 2004). The strongholds of such federalism used to be the European Parliament, the European Commission and its civil service, European federations of people's parties (in particular Christian Democracy), European federations and lobbies of industrialists and trade unionists, and older generations of idealists, such as those in the European Movement. All these strongholds lost ground or reformulated their respective strategic doctrines in their confrontation with contemporary modes of resounding anti-Europeanism. These are rooted in multiple and partly overlapping traditions, such as patriotism, nationalism, populism, regionalism, conservatism, libertarianism, cosmopolitanism, environmentalism, and realism.

The entry of new member states implies an increasing plurality of passions, interests, ideas, habits, and expectations in what already is "the most formalised and complex set of decision-making rules of any political system in the world" (Hix 2005, p. 3) The new plurality is a trial of all arrangements and practices of politics in the EU. Furthermore, the new plurality entails a plurality of sensible views on institutional design and cultural convergence. The New Europe demands a lot, perhaps the impossible: more power sharing *and* more weight of countries with large populations; more democratic contestation *and* more religious toleration and moderation; more self-protection and expansion as an economic block *and* more goodwill, decency, and cutting power as a geopolitical block.

The final element of hard times in European politics is the lack of recognizable structure in its political space (see Crouch 1999; Hallin and Mancini 2004; Therborn 1995). Democratic solution of conflicts and contradictions requires some clear patterns of organization of distinct collectives: of nations, ethnic minorities, religions, classes, occupations, generations, and communities based on ideological world pictures. After six general elections of the European Parliament since 1979, the European political space is still fuzzy and underpopulated, while the primacy of party politics still remains a promise. On the one hand, the European politicization of issues (if any) had not changed the national party systems of member states, mainly because the European question remains secondary for both politicians and voters in electoral settings (Mair 2000a, 2000b; van der Eijk and Franklin 1996). On the other hand, transnational debates between supporters of liberalization of European capitalism and those of regulation (and a number of other European cleavages) do not engender a pan-European party system, because of the weakness of party federations, the federalist bias of the European Parliament and its scanty popular credibility, and the absence of party politics at the level of European commissioners, leaders of government, and ministers (Blondel, Sinnott, and Swenson 1998; Kreppel 2002; Marks and Steenbergen 2004). Instead, EU promotion of European markets seems to go in tandem with a clash within national party political systems between representatives of winners and losers of globalization (Hooghe and Marks 2005; Kriesi 2007; Kriesi et al. 2006b;

Mair 2007a). Hence, for many ordinary citizens of national states with a touch of political consciousness, Europeanism today is as extraterrestrial as colonialism was yesterday.

THE CALL FOR A EUROPEAN PUBLIC SPHERE: PRACTICAL AND ETHICAL

The EU impasse reinforces an already existing, indeed onrushing call for bringing the public in the politics of integration. This harks back to the justly famous judgment of the German Constitutional Court of October 1993 on the compatibility of the Economic and Monetary Union and the German conception of associational, competitive, deliberative, and steering democracy (van Gerven 2005, pp. 41–43).

Here are some quotations from the Laeken declaration of the European Council (December 2001): "In short, citizens are calling for a clear, open, effective, democratically controlled Community approach, developing a Europe which points ahead for the world.... The Union needs to become more democratic, more transparent and more efficient. It also has to resolve three basic challenges: how to bring citizens, and primarily the young, closer to the European design and the European institutions, how to organise politics and the European political area in an enlarged Union and how to develop the Union into a stabilising factor and a model in the new, multipolar world" (Ludlow 2002, pp. 229–230).

The Laeken declaration was the prelude to the Convention on the Future of Europe. During its proceedings, 160 organized representatives of units of government, organizations of capital and labor, universities and research institutes, and civil movements were informed and were invited to send in suggestions and comments (European Convention Secretariat, Cover note 112/02, June 17, 2002). There was a special meeting with young political activists from both old and new member states. The convention proposed to open up legislative meetings of councils of EU ministers and to introduce Europe-wide popular initiatives and special procedures of review of European Commission plans for clusters of national parliaments (Norman 2003). In June 2006, the European Council decided that all Council deliberations on legislative acts based on codecision with the European Parliament, and all first Council deliberations beyond codecision, shall be open to the public.

The 2004–2009 European Commission included the first commissioner ever charged with institutional relations and communications strategy. The response of Commissioner Margot Wallström to the unexpectedly negative referenda on the European Constitution has been a white paper on communicating European policies, enhancing debate and dialogue, and improving both the EU understanding of public opinion and public understanding of the EU (European Commission 2006b).

This striking call for a European public sphere can be attributed to a number of factors. First, the relative influence of leaders of government and ministers with respect to the European Commission increased after the departure of Delors (Grant 1994; Ross 1995). Such intergovernmentalism became more assertive in the grand spirit of Charles de Gaulle, in the sense that all leaders of government presented themselves as the face of their nation and as cornerstone of democratic mandate in Europe. Their agenda became crowded with strategic items, well suited for salient interpretation in terms of vital national interests and essential international differences. They tried out a set of ways to improve their representational role and reach constituencies on the home front. Many of these involve the public sphere, such as conspicuous meetings in parliament before and after European Council meetings, fringe meetings of sister parties, open articulation of bargaining demands (megaphone diplomacy), public framing of messy bargaining outcomes in natiocentric and leader-centered terms, and public blame shifting to European agencies. Summit fights for public prestige are dubious weapons. On the one hand, political leaders in domestic trouble may lift their standing vis-à-vis their rivals by exhibitionist performances in Brussels. On the other hand, these leaders treat each other rudely and tarnish common positions. (There are extenuating circumstances. The pressure of exhaustive official meetings, numerous assistants inside, and greedy reporters outside may rise so high that rude leaders of government such as the French president Jacques Chirac combine public gallery play with private wheeling and dealing on toilets; see van der Velden 2005, p. 88.)

Second, the European Commission has gradually become proactive in inventing and combining strategies that may shape a public sphere and also promote its own power base and reputation (Mak 2001; Nugent 2001; Smith 2004). These strategies entail consultation of economic associations and regions, promotion of national minority cultures, introduction of symbols of European unity and citizenship, public campaigns (as the campaign for smooth introduction of euro notes and coins), diffusion of information free of charge and in the vernacular of member states, creation of a television channel (Euronews) and Internet sites, and press conferences as well as interviews with journalists. As one observer has noted, "The Commission is a far more transparent body than the Council or most national governments" (Middlemas 1995, p. 225). *Mutatis mutandis*, the European Parliament since 1979, the year of the first general elections of this parliament in the member states, applies similar strategies as the European Commission to reach the largest possible audience beyond the unavoidable lobbyists.

Third, certain strategic choices and policy scandals in a European context trigger domestic and border-crossing unrest. They become events and catalysts with all publicity belonging to them: protest, atmosphere of crisis among policy makers, hasty debates in parliament and on television, and fast journalism (de Vreese 2003; Norris 2000a, pp. 183–207; Peter 2003). Examples include the entry and exit decisions of national governments (the Schengen Agreement on border control, the European Social Charter, the Economic and Monetary Union); European epidemics in which the interests of farmers and consumers clash; the deviant behavior of member states, policy sectors, or ministers (such as illegal outlays of the European Social Fund); and conspicuous corruption of European agencies. Imig and Tarrow register 490 events of protest against European measures in the period 1984–1997. Although this constitutes a meager 5% of all protest, it concerns a shock wave since the Treaty of Maastricht. In the year 2002, twelve protests were signaled in the old Europe of fifteen candidates and seven protests were signaled in the new Europe of thirteen candidates (mainly eastern states), which is 6% altogether (Imig and Tarrow 2001a, pp. 34–35; Trif and Imig 2003).

Fourth, publicity by venerable European policy makers has been forced from below. The most striking example is the growth of referenda. In the period 1972–2003, forty referenda were held on entry (twenty-three cases), ratification of treaties and basic laws (thirteen), start or stop of entry or constitutional amendment (three), and ratification of enlargement (one). Thirty of these referenda were held after 1989. This survey does not include the referenda on the European constitutional treaty in Spain, France, the Netherlands, and Luxembourg (Kaufmann, Lamassoure, and Meyer 2004). A more diffuse example of publicity from below is politicization of European cooperation and membership by political parties, often radical parties on the left (the Dutch Socialist Party) or the right (the French National Front, the Italian Northern League in Berlusconi's House of Freedom alliance), sometimes also parties in the middle (the British Conservatives). The example is diffuse since such politicization is mixed with the issue of immigration, indeed of globalization rather than European integration. Furthermore, these parties exploit elections and sessions of the European Parliament as a platform for Eurosceptic messages.

Finally, there is the legacy of federalism and functionalism (federalism by stealth, that is, gradual expansion of European member states, sectors of public policy, *and* audiences; see Haas 1958; Schmitter 1969). Both groups envisaged the rise of a pan-European public sphere with transnational elites, political parties, interest groups, newspapers, corporations (including broadcasting corporations), and arts and sciences. Their vision of crafting a supernation of citizens with European loyalties is still framing the beliefs, desires, and actions of a part of the EU establishment (Delanty 1995; Delanty and Rumford 2005; Pagden 2002; Shore 2000).

In general, the impressive EU initiatives since the late 1980s, starting with the Single European Act (1986), have turned the question of popular support of further integration into a political agenda piece. When (and because) popular benefits of these initiatives turned out to be mixed or only visible in the future while popular costs (losses of social policy protection, control of national parliament, and so on) were pure and immediate, the centrifugal forces of regionalism, populism, and nationalism became stronger and more manifest in their blocking power. In particular, politicians and policy makers operating at both levels (national and European) have henceforth selfish reasons to come to terms with the democracy deficit: a mixture of incomplete parliamentarism in European affairs, asymmetric access to decision making at national and European levels (in favor of groups with greater resources and skills), EU policy failure and corruption, and underdevelopment of a pan-European public sphere.

Hence, the call for Europeanization of the public sphere cannot only be explained but also justified in terms of arguments concerning the enlightened self-interest, credibility, and effectiveness of the European governing classes, or the "Eurocrats" as Spinelli (1966) called them (he was the Italian leader of the European Movement of federalists during the Cold War and one of the first authors on the democracy deficit of supranational jurisdiction). Furthermore, such justification may be taken one step further. There are also arguments concerning public interest, autonomy of citizens, and legitimacy in an EU setting, derived from the history of political thought with respect to civil society and the public sphere (Cohen and Arato 1992; Splichal 1999). Such arguments focus on the desirability of a vital sphere of associations and media within and across borders. These arguments articulate the promise of the European public. They are mainstream ideas by now in Europe's evolving political tradition, although some of them appeal more to conservatives and others to progressives.[2] A European public sphere may protect and promote (i) the social basis of state authority in modern societies, (ii) the stability and working of parliament and political parties in democratic societies, (iii) moral consensus, the public interest, and organized justice in plural societies, (iv) the competence, knowledge, rationality, decency (including moderation), and commitment of ordinary members of civil societies, (v) voluntary compliance of citizens with laws and public policies in ordered societies, and (vi) the voice of the poor and deprived citizens in dynamic market societies.

It is tempting, then, to make a case for the quasi-universal "optimality," as welfare economists call it, of a European public sphere where self-interest of relevant holders of political power and democratic morality coincide, no one stands to lose, and the last political problem concerns the fair sharing of costs of transition and burdens of publicity. As always in matters of European integration, this case is much more complicated and requires empirical evidence.

RESEARCHING THE EUROPEAN PUBLIC

Europeans are as argumentative as Indians (Sen 2005). Scholars in the area of European integration are no exception here. There seem to be two mainstream positions, namely, those who recognize the factual existence and significance of a European public sphere deficit as part of a general democracy deficit, and those who deny it. Consider first the case of yes-researchers (Hix, 2005, 2008; Schmitter 2000).

First, the EU needs a vital public sphere, because of its intrinsic value for European integration (the public sphere as an end in itself, that is, an integral component of the democratic ideal and its realization since 1945), or its

---

[2] See, for example, Bentham (1830 [1983]) and Habermas (1962).

instrumental value (the public sphere as a means to achieve legitimate public goals in this region of the world, such as peace, prosperity, employment, and protection of nature and the arts). Even minimal cooperation among national governments, as envisaged by radical Eurosceptics, requires a public sphere of sorts. A return to the closed and secret geopolitics of European great powers of the past is impossible, undesirable, or unattainable under modern and postmodern circumstances of democracy.

Second, the European public sphere needs to be dual, in the sense that it entails both the international level of European society and politics (decision making in Brussels) and the national level of the member states (decision making in capitals). For example, important decisions, such as revisions of the Treaty of Rome (1957), the introduction of the euro (the Madrid meeting of the European Council in 1995), or the ban of old member states (Haider's Austria in 2000) and the entry of new ones (Erdogan's Turkey since 2002), need to become the object of public debate in each EU agency – such as the European Parliament – and in each member state as well.

Third, the public sphere needs to develop and stabilize in both a top-down and bottom-up way. Top-down examples are summits of the European Council of leaders of national governments (recurrent media events), the *Official Journal of the European Union* (the official accounts of meetings of the European Parliament) and the State of the European Union, and the annual meeting of members of cabinet and members of national *and* European Parliament in the Netherlands. Bottom-up examples are farmer demonstrations against the Mansholt Plan for reform of the common agricultural policy in 1968 (the oldest example) and, more recently, antifascist street protests against the rise to power of Austrian radical conservatives in 2000, and marches in Berlin, London, Madrid, Paris, and Rome against the American and British intervention in Iraq on Saturday, February 15, 2003 (see respectively Imig and Tarrow 2001a, 2001b; Levy et al. 2005; van der Steeg 2005). Indeed, a famous French politician – Strauss-Kahn – referred to that specific Saturday as the birthday of the European nation, while a famous German philosopher – Habermas – suggested that it constitutes the birthday of a European public sphere, nearly fifty-two years after the treaty on the European Coal and Steel Community signed in Paris in April 1951 (Levy et al. 2005, pp. xvi, xxiii).

Finally, the EU here and now does not have a vital public sphere. Nor does it have a public sphere surplus (excessive mobilization and communication creating public policy overload or worse: civil war in Europe and European aggression abroad; see Huntington 1968; Mansfield and Snyder 2005). Instead, it suffers from a dual public sphere deficit as part and parcel of a general democracy deficit. The latter deficit is a lack of resonance of the EU beyond the public policy sphere, of responsiveness and accountability in the wider public sphere, and of general accessibility and clarity.

The case of the no-researchers can be summarized as follows (Majone 1996, 1998, 2002; Moravcsik 1998, 2004, 2005a, 2005b). First, national governments were, and still are, the main actors driving European integration. The course of such governments is publicly and critically scrutinized by national parties, parliaments, interest groups, and media. Peak conferences of heads of state and ministers have become great media events. In some cases, they give cause to nationalist hype.

Second, the European Parliament creates and reproduces its own publicity by means of its direct elections since 1979, its increased authority and willingness to use power in its relations with the European Commission and the European Council, and its plenary sessions and debates on issues that are crucial to international politics and sensitive to national constituencies (such as European membership of Turkey).

Third, the European Commission has been effective in promoting transparency of European decision making, managing its own public relations, and conquering a prominent place in the daily news, the lobby circuit, the permanent foreign policy debate among democratic societies in the West, and the international debate of public intellectuals. In many ways, the public sphere of European agencies can bear comparison to the public sphere of their functional equivalents at the national level.

Fourth, the optimal public sphere of European integration is special. On the one hand, European integration means delegation of competence to special authorities that are independent of partisan politics and insulated from popular opinion in a reasonably well-defined area of regulation and implementation of technical policy designs: agriculture, regional development, global trade, exchange rates and monetary policy, foreign aid, and trade-related competition, environmental, and consumer policies. The EU does not interfere with taxation and spending in national bread-and-butter issues, such as social security, housing, and health care. On the other hand, European policy making is deeply consensual. Every possible interest, concern, problem, or angle is taken into account in protracted and comprehensive processes of power sharing and accommodation. Although European consensus thrives on a modicum of closure and secrecy (and paternalism), it is practically impossible to limit and control the domain (who?) and scope (what?) of European dossiers as soon as dossiers become fiercely contested, such as the dossier on the liberalization of services (Lijphart 1999, 2008, pp. 156–158).

Finally, the demands of theorists of the democracy and public sphere deficits are supererogatory. No foreign policy and international governance can fulfill the demands of democratic cosmopolitanism with respect to representation and participation in a large denationalized sphere of political parties, news media, and active citizens. Public spheres within the member states themselves are imperfect and liable to depravation. Indeed, most national democracies today wrestle with symptoms of exhaustion, dissatisfaction, and malaise. Furthermore, a swift and radical democratization of European affairs (extending the public sphere) may very well speed up European stagnation, disintegration, and anti-Europeanism in general.

The research in this book treats this academic controversy as an open empirical issue. Both yes-researchers and no-researchers seem to agree that an agonizing reappraisal of apparently illusionary values and norms of democracy and publicity is warranted to stop the unraveling of old EU legitimacy, and to create new legitimacy. The study covers the period 1990–2002. This is a decade of optimism, entrepreneurship, and acceleration in European integration. It is also a period of growing resistance against European dirigisme and lack of digestion of European measures at national levels. Our research draws on the current wisdom of comparative political studies, media studies, and European studies. Nevertheless, a double difference between the standard literature and our approach should be stressed from the start.

The empirical-theoretical literature ignores mutual feedback between European integration and the Europeanization of public spheres within the member states of the EU. Supporters of federalism and constructivism examine the ethical politics of political leaders and the popular reception of their ideals and frames. Supporters of functionalism and governance theory examine the politics of administration of new organs and the augmentation of networks of organized interests, such as lobbies. Supporters of yet another pair of schools – intergovernmentalism, institutionalism – point at the power politics of state elites and EU elites as well as the evolution of institutions in international relations (Wiener and Diez 2004).

The study in this book examines the Europeanization of public spheres in the society and politics of Europe's nation states as domains of debate, collective action, news, democratic governance, and civic commitment. This provides a perspective that has been neglected so far, namely the politics of representation of a clear-cut European public in the making by governments, political parties in parliament, socioeconomic interest groups, other associations in civil society, and news media *together*, albeit against others or divided against themselves, and unintended in many ways. Who is participating in the politics of European integration? What do they claim and frame, as to the conceptions of Europe? When do they represent, where, how, addressing whom, for or against whom, why, and with which lasting impact, if any? The perspective of representation completes the growing contemporary literature on the Europeanization of diplomacy, law, and public administration and its parliamentary control (Featherstone and Radaelli 2003; Green Cowles, Caporaso, and Risse 2001; Radaelli and Schmidt 2005).

Furthermore, the philosophical-historical literature ignores the Europeanization of public spheres within European nation states. It points either at the resilient self-containment of national traditions of political identity and culture (legitimate diversity of political societies in Europe), or at the great invention of transnational (pan-European, cosmopolitan) modes of the public, public activity, publicity, public sphere, and public opinion. The former is deterministic. It denies the possibility of Europeanization of national leadership and citizenship, that is, a certain denationalization of articulation of interests, passions, and reasons (such as making of references). The latter is voluntaristic. It considers the possibility of exhaustion and extinction of national leadership and citizenship in a full process of Europeanization and globalization. This literature is moralized and inclined to either stark pessimism ("no European demos") or stark optimism ("a European demos *sui generis*"; see Gowan and Anderson 1997; Schmitter 2000; Siedentop 2000). The study constructs and assesses the empirical base of such grand forecasts and strong convictions. By means of several methods we try to draw a plausible account of the compound public sphere of Europe.

The research in this volume is comparative in three ways: across seven countries, in the periods of 1990, 1995, and 2000–2002 (the after-Maastricht era), and across seven fields of public policy. The project uses a variety of methods to analyze the Europeanization of public mobilization and communication along these dimensions: content analyses of public statements and demands (claims) as well as newspaper editorials; keyword searches on the Internet as well as a network analysis of connections among Web sites; and interviews with key representatives of collective actors and with media professionals, as well as a network analysis based on such interviews. The overall data-gathering effort in the context of the project deserves some emphasis. We content-coded literally tens of thousands of newspaper articles and editorials, analyzed the Web sites of thousands of collective actors and the network links among them, and interviewed about 500 people. We are quite confident that no other project working in this academic area has ever collected and analyzed data on the Europeanization of mobilization and communication that approaches this effort in its size, qualitative reach, and breadth of different methods and types of data.

But why bother? This research tries to cover a threefold turn that is immediately relevant to the European concerns of politicians, civil servants, activists, journalists, owners of news media, corporate managers, professionals, and ordinary citizens. First, the project suggests that the rise of a European public will not occur at the level of a pan-European society beyond national borders but at the level of social and political life within and across member states. As European power, competence, and action repertoire grows, the EU will become the focal point of domestic and international mobilization and communication. The rate of Europeanization in different countries will differ, of course, depending on temporal developments, issue fields, country differences, and, in particular, differences between national political opportunity structures (Kitschelt 1986; Kriesi 1993; Kriesi et al. 1995; Tarrow 1994). In short, the European public sphere is home grown.

Second, the project suggests that the politicization of European policies in the electoral space of political parties – and beyond the space of national states in international relations – will arise in a process of struggle for access and positioning by old and new actors, that is, a process of public sphere innovation. To date, most policies of the European Council of leaders of government and ministers, the European Parliament, and the European Court of Justice and the European Court of First Instance are impolitic, or political in affairs between governments (traditional foreign policy), or political for the few, that is, for lobbyists. The future EU will house a space for normal partisan representation, participation, division, competition, and compromise as integral part of a possible two-level (European and national) public sphere. In short, first the European public sphere, bottom up, and then the European political space (Blondel et al. 1998; Jönsson, Tägil, and Törnqvist 2000; Marks and Steenbergen 2004; Sbragia et al. 2006 on constitutional referenda; van der Eijk and Franklin 1996).

Third, the emergent public sphere of Europe is not the final stage of a full postnational and federal democracy, the final goal of European integration as envisaged by generations of European architects, but rather an integral part of controversial integration today with an open end as to the size and standing of the EU in terms of members, external frontiers, competences, public policy strategies, budgets, and organizations (Calleo 2001; Delanty and Rumford 2005; Etzioni 2001; Gillingham 2003; Morgan 2005; Rifkin 2004; Tsoukalis 2003; van Gerven 2005). In short, European unity will be the outcome of more or less democratic interplay between the integration of governments and policies and the integration of peoples and public spheres.

2

Theoretical Framework, Research Design, and Methods

Ruud Koopmans and Paul Statham

Chapter 1 has set the scene regarding the normative importance of a public sphere for the future of Europe. In this chapter, we lay out the general theoretical framework and design that informs and unites the chapters of this book into a collective body of research. Subsequent chapters are embedded in their own literatures and address specific research questions relevant to the key debates in their fields. However, such apparent pluralism does not mean that we have come to the table without a clear overall theoretical framework addressing key general research questions.

Important questions guiding our inquiry are as follows. First, to what extent is there a sphere of communication that can be considered a European public sphere? Here we aim to examine the form, type, and extent of communication patterns that are "Europeanized." This addresses the nature, extent, and form of a European public sphere that is created by acts of political communication and mobilization, that is, "claim making." Second, in what ways has the political space been transformed by this Europeanization of communication, and with what consequences? Here we investigate how Europeanized communication transforms politics, or not. This means looking at which political actors gain access to Europeanized politics, and which positions they take up, within this emergent "mediated" field of European multilevel governance. For example, is the participation of elites privileged over civil society actors, or EU actors over national ones? Who wins, who loses? Such questions are recurrent themes throughout the contributions to this book.

In this chapter, we first outline how our theoretical stance evolved in relation to other approaches within the European public sphere literature. Second, we outline our conceptual approach by developing a model for the different possible types of political communication "acts" in a multilevel setting. Third, we offer a general explanatory framework for the processes that shape Europeanized communication, by combining insights from the related fields of political mobilization and social movements, on one side, and media and political communications, on the other. This serves to identify and locate the specific fields and substance of our inquiry relative to one another for the subsequent chapters. Fourth, we discuss the important comparative dimensions of our research design, which runs across countries, time, and policy issue fields. Then we discuss our selection of newspapers as a data source for the study. Finally, the relative empirical emptiness of this field on our arrival required that we engage in significant methodological innovation. This project has led us to develop and refine the "claim-making" method (Koopmans and Statham 1999; Koopmans et al. 2005), which we outline and discuss, since it produces the primary data source for many of our chapters. We now turn to the evolution of research on the European public sphere.

WHAT DO WE MEAN BY EUROPEANIZATION OF PUBLIC SPHERES?

As we witnessed in the Introduction and Chapter 1, the age of the permissive consensus has definitely come to an end. The fallout from the 2005 constitutional referenda made it fully apparent that further advances in the European integration process will be possible only if its proponents succeed in mobilizing the citizenry's support and gaining legitimacy in the public domain. It dealt a possibly fatal blow to an idea that was already in decline: that political elites could simply proceed by building Europe in the absence of Europeans. It is perhaps therefore not surprising that the conditions for the emergence of a European public sphere have come to the foreground of the social-scientific debate about European integration, especially over the past decade.[1] Here we critically discuss how these different perspectives evolved, as a basis for introducing our own approach.

Especially the earlier studies in this tradition (e.g., Erbring 1995; Kielmansegg 1996; Kopper 1997; Schlesinger 1995) focused on the probability of the emergence of transnational mass media on the European level. This way of approaching the problem usually results in a negative answer to the possibility of a European public sphere, and it emphasizes linguistic and cultural boundaries as insurmountable barriers to the Europeanization of public debates, collective identities, and collective action. Although some authors reckon with the possible emergence of English as a true lingua franca in Europe that would allow direct transnational communication on a mass level (de Swaan 1993, 2007), this prospect seems to be very distant, not least because of strong resistance against such cultural homogenization in many non-English-speaking member states. In our view, this perspective on the Europeanization of the

---

[1] Among the many contributions, see, for example, de Vreese (2003), Gerhards (1993, 2000), Kantner (2004), Meyer (2002, 2005), van der Steeg (2002, 2005), Machill, Beiler, and Fischer (2006), and Downey and Koenig (2006); also see chapters in Fossum and Schlesinger (2007). For a critical review of the development of the European public sphere as a research field, see Cristoph Meyer (2007). For studies that, like ours, attempt to provide answers to general trends by recourse to large-scale cross-national data, see especially the research program initially led by Bernhard Peters (Peters et al. 2005; Wessler et al. 2008; Sifft et al. 2007) and that by Hans-Jörg Trenz (2004, 2005).

public sphere is deficient because it views Europeanization as a replication, on a higher level of spatial aggregation, of the type of unified public sphere that we know – or think we know – from the nation-state context. This perspective often presupposes a degree of linguistic and cultural homogeneity and political centralization that cannot be found in many well-functioning democratic nation-states. For instance, the Dutch consociational democracy has proved to be a successful way to politically integrate a population characterized by deep sociocultural cleavages (Lijphart 1968 [1975]). Similarly, Switzerland is one of the most stable and successful Western democracies, despite important cultural differences, not least of which is the existence of four different and persistent language regions (Ernst 1998).

If one looks for a genuinely transnational European public sphere, there is not much to be found (Kevin 2003; Schlesinger 1999). There have been a few attempts to establish European-wide mass media, but most of these have either quickly disappeared (such as the newspaper *The European*) or lead a marginal and often heavily EU-subsidized existence (e.g., the television station Euronews or the weekly *European Voice*, which reaches a limited audience of EU experts, bureaucrats, and lobbying professionals). In as far as transnational media have been able to carve out a niche in the media landscape, the successful examples have a global rather than European profile and audience (e.g., CNN, BBC World, *International Herald Tribune, Le Monde diplomatique, Financial Times*).

Gerhards (1993, 2000) has rightly emphasized that the more realistic scenario is not that of a genuinely supranational European public sphere in the singular, but the Europeanization of the various national public spheres. This view assumes that – also because of the language factor – nationally based mass media are there to stay, but that their content may become less focused on the nation-state context and will increasingly include a European perspective. Gerhards (2000, p. 293) mentions two criteria for such Europeanization of national public spheres: an increased proportion of coverage of European themes and actors, on the one hand, and the evaluation of these themes and actors from a perspective that extends beyond a particular country and its interests, on the other. Using media content data drawn from Kepplinger (1998), he shows that between 1951 and 1995 there has hardly been any growth in European themes in Germany and only a very slight increase – at a very low level – in the coverage of European actors. These data, however, were gathered for other purposes and it is therefore questionable whether they accurately measure the European dimension of themes and actors, let alone the intricacies of multilevel politics that may result in varying mixtures of national and European dimensions in news coverage. These methodological reservations notwithstanding, we agree with Gerhards that an increased presence of European actors and themes in national media would be an important criterion for the Europeanization of public spheres. However, Gerhards's second criterion seems unnecessarily restrictive in that it demands an orientation on a European common good in order for an act of public communication to qualify as "Europeanized" (for this criticism see also Trenz 2000). If we use this common good criterion, we should also exclude much of the routine national claim making (e.g., of many socioeconomic special interest groups) from the national public sphere.

Even though Europeanization in Gerhards's view does not require supranational mass media, it does presuppose a form of Europeanization of policies and politics along similar lines as that of the traditional nation-state. It is not surprising therefore that Gerhards (2000) arrives at the conclusion that the European public sphere deficit is a direct consequence of the democratic deficit, which he sees in the lack of the kind of government–opposition dynamics, and the direct accountability of office holders to the electorate that we know from the national level. This position has been criticized by Eder, Kantner, and Trenz (2000) as too restrictive. They assume that because of the complex nature of multilevel politics, we will not necessarily find a strong orientation of public communication on European institutions. In their view, the Europeanization of policies and regulations may instead lead to a parallelization of national public spheres in the sense that increasingly the same themes are discussed at the same time under similar criteria of relevance. An example is the debates on asylum policies in different European countries during the 1990s, following European-level discussions and the Dublin Convention. National political actors carried the ideas developed here into their national public spheres, and as a result discussions started more or less simultaneously in several member states about establishing lists of "safe third countries," a notion that was developed in Dublin. The fact that such policies had a European-level origin was hardly mentioned in the coverage of these debates on the national level. Although what we see in such cases is certainly a consequence of the Europeanization of *policy making*, it does not in our view constitute Europeanization of the *public sphere*. As long as the European dimension remains hidden from the public's view, one cannot call such debates "Europeanized." For the citizen, unaware of what was discussed in Dublin or of the similar discussions in other member states, these appear to be purely national debates. If anything, such examples illustrate the nature of the public sphere deficit rather than being a solution to it.

Nonetheless, Eder et al. (2000) are on the right track in insisting that direct references to the EU or other European-level institutions and legal frameworks are not a necessary precondition for the Europeanization of public spheres. What Gerhards's perspective forgets is namely that although, particularly in the first pillar, the EU has some supranational features, much of its policies, and even more so those of non-EU European institutions such as the Council of Europe, have an intergovernmental basis. These intergovernmental features of the European polity are more likely to be expressed in an alternative form of Europeanization of public spheres, which has thus far received little attention in the literature (a partial exception is Risse 2002).

This type of Europeanization does not consist of direct references to European actors and themes, but of increased attention for public debates and mobilization in other member states. In an intergovernmental polity, other European states can no longer be treated as foreign countries whose internal politics are not really relevant for one's own country. To the contrary, in such a polity, it may matter a great deal who wins the elections in another EU member state, or what kind of new policy another member state develops in a particular field. Such tendencies are reinforced by the interdependencies created by common market policies and the freedom of movement within the EU. Under such conditions, policies in one country may become directly relevant for one's own country in a way that goes far beyond traditional international relations. For instance, if Germany liberalizes its naturalization policies, this is immediately relevant for other member states – because, once naturalized, immigrants from Germany can freely travel to and take up work in another EU country. Similarly, the Northern EU countries watch closely what measures countries such as Italy, Greece, and Spain undertake to prevent undocumented immigration from Africa and the Middle East, which under the Schengen Agreement is no longer just "their" problem.

We thus arrive at three theoretically possible forms of Europeanization of public communication and mobilization (Koopmans and Erbe 2004):

1. The first form is the emergence of a *supranational European public sphere* constituted by the interaction among European-level institutions and collective actors around European themes, ideally accompanied by (and creating the basis for) the development of European-wide mass media.

2. The second is *vertical Europeanization*, which consists of communicative linkages between the national and the European level. There are two basic variants of this pattern: a bottom-up one, in which national actors address European actors, make claims on European issues, or both; and a top-down one, in which European actors intervene in national public debates in the name of European regulations and common interests.

3. The third is *horizontal Europeanization*, which consists of communicative linkages between different European countries. We may distinguish a weak and a strong variant. In the weak variant, the media in one country cover debates and contestation in another country, but there is no communicative link in the structure of claim making between actors in different countries. In the stronger variant, there is such a communicative link, and actors from one country explicitly address or refer to actors or policies in another European country.

It is important to note that we can only speak of "European," "global," "national," or "local" public spheres in a relative sense. Following the classic work on nationalism and social communication of Karl W. Deutsch (1953), we propose that the spatial reach and boundaries of public communication can be determined by investigating patterns of *communicative flows* and assessing the *relative density of public communication* within and between different political spaces (see Koopmans and Erbe 2004). In Figure 2.1, we have drawn a set of concentric spheres delimiting different political spaces that are of interest

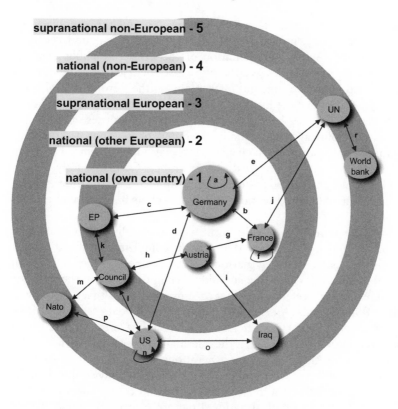

Areas mark the political spheres in which actors are situated. In this example, Germany has been taken as the national point of reference, and thus Sphere 1 "national (own country)" corresponds to German actors. Each **arrow** represents possible communication linkages between actors, as explained in the text.

FIGURE 2.1. Political spaces and communicative links in a multilevel setting (EP = European Parliament; NATO = North Atlantic Treaty Organization).

to us in this study.[2] At the center, we find the national political space of a particular country (Sphere 1; for illustrative purposes, we take the German political space as an example here). In the sphere around it (Sphere 2) are the respective national political spaces of other European countries. In this study, we do not limit Europeanization to "EU-ization." Therefore, we use an inclusive definition of Europe that includes not just the EU member states plus all applicants including Turkey, but also other European countries such as Norway, Switzerland, and the Balkan States. We excluded Russia and other countries of the former Soviet Union (except of course the three Baltic EU

---

[2] We thank Jessica Erbe for adapting the original figure from Koopmans and Erbe (2004) for the purpose of this chapter.

member states).[3] In the next sphere (Sphere 3), we find the supranational European political space, in which the European institutions and common policies are situated. Again, our definition of the European public space is more inclusive than just the EU. We therefore also include claims by non-EU supranational and intergovernmental institutions on the European level, such as the Council of Europe or the European Free Trade Association. Beyond that, the next concentric circle (Sphere 4) contains all other countries of the world and their national political spaces. Finally, the outer sphere (Sphere 5) contains global supranational institutions such as the International Monetary Fund, the G-8 (the Group of Eight forum, consisting of France, Germany, Italy, Japan, the United Kingdom, the United States, Canada, and Russia), the International Court of Justice or the United Nations (UN), as well as international treaties and conventions.

In terms of our model, the ideal-typical national public sphere is characterized by communicative linkages that remain completely confined to one national political space. A purely national claim is one in which a German claimant makes demands on a German addressee in the name of the interests of a German beneficiary, referring to a set of aims and frames that refer only to the German political space. An example drawn from our data set is a German media report on a call by the German government on the German Trade Union Federation to cooperate in a reform of the (German) retirement system in order to secure pensions for future (German) generations (corresponding to Arrow a in Figure 2.1). The degree to which we can speak of a nationally confined public sphere is then measured by the relative amount of all communicative action that conforms to this ideal-typical national pattern of claim making. A fully nationalized public sphere would have a density of 100% of such nationally confined communicative linkages. In a fully denationalized public sphere the density of purely national communicative linkages would be 0%. This would not imply that national actors, addressees, interests, and issues do not play a role any more, but that these always appear in combination with some sort of reference to political spaces beyond the country in question.

Along similar lines, we may speak of the emergence of a *supranational European public sphere* to the extent that we find claims that link European claimants to European addressees in the name of European interests, without referring to any other level of political space. An example is a motion passed by the European Parliament urging the Commission to undertake institutional reforms in the context of the enlargement of the Union (Arrow k). Similar to the density scores for nationally confined political communication, we can conceptualize a supranational European public sphere as the percentage of all communicative action in which European actors refer to European addressees, interests, and issues.

[3] Admittedly it is debatable where exactly to draw the line between Europe and non-Europe. However, an alternative operationalization that does include the former Soviet Union leads to virtually the same empirical results as those reported in this book.

Such a supranational European public sphere would be the replication of the classical pattern of the national public sphere on the level of the European Union. However, if Europe is indeed a new type of multilevel polity, this will probably not be the most frequent type of Europeanized communication. Within the model of *vertical Europeanization*, we may distinguish a number of varieties in which vertical communicative linkages between the national and the European political space can be made (represented in the figure by Arrow c). In the *bottom-up variant*, the simplest form is when national actors directly address European institutions, such as when a national actor brings a case before the European Court of Justice, or when German foreign minister Fischer demands that the European Parliament be strengthened in the next treaty revision. However, there are also more complex patterns in which national actors address national authorities, asking them to promote the group's interests on the European level (a case with a national claimant, addressee, and beneficiary, but an issue with a European scope). The *top-down variant* of vertical Europeanization occurs when European actors address national actors, usually regarding common European issues and interests, such as when the European Commission threatens sanctions against governments that do not meet the criteria of the stability pact.

The *weak variant of horizontal Europeanization* occurs when media report on what happens within the national political spaces of other European countries, for instance if a German newspaper reports that the French National Assembly has adopted a new immigration law (Arrow f). In terms of the structure of claim making, this case is similar to the purely German claims, but the difference is that in this case German media bring foreign claims to the attention of the German public. The degree to which such coverage represents a form of Europeanization of the German public sphere can only be evaluated in a relative sense. Horizontal Europeanization occurs if coverage of other European countries is increasingly overrepresented in comparison to that of non-European countries. If, on the other hand, references to France and Italy are not more frequent in the German public sphere than, say, to Japan or Mexico, we may perhaps still speak of a transnationalization of the German public sphere in a wider sense but not of a more specific Europeanization of public communication.

The *stronger variant of horizontal Europeanization* is characterized by direct communicative linkages between actors in two or more European countries (Arrow b). Examples are when Prime Minister Tony Blair issued a statement in support of Gerhard Schröder's bid for the Chancellorship, or when the German government criticized the French government's handling of the bovine spongiform encephalopathy (BSE) epidemic. As in the case of vertical Europeanization, there may be cases in which all actors involved remain national (German) ones, but the issue is framed in a comparative way with one or more other member states, such as when the German opposition criticizes the government's economic policies, pointing out that Germany has the worst performance of all EU countries. In such a case, the policies and performances of other EU countries are deemed relevant as benchmarks for German policies, thereby inserting a European dimension into the German public debate.

Of course, there can also be mixtures of horizontal and vertical Europeanization. A common example is when government representatives of several member states issue a common statement on some European issue, such as when the Spanish, British, and Italian governments presented common proposals for institutional reform of the EU. Another common combination of vertical and horizontal dimensions occurs when the media of one country report on interactions between the EU and another member state, such as when the German media report about the FPÖ's[4] warning that Austria can veto decisions in the Council of Ministers (Arrow h).

All these forms of Europeanization of public communication must carve out a communicative niche not only in competition with purely national public communication, but also relative to transnational communicative interaction that extends beyond Europe. It is, after all, possible that a denationalization of public communication and mobilization occurs, but that most of the resulting transnational linkages refer to supranational institutions and regulations with a wider scope than Europe (e.g., the UN; see Arrow e), or to national political spaces outside of the European Union, (e.g., to the United States, Russia, or Japan; Arrow d). However, claim making that links European institutions to non-European countries or to global supranational organizations does qualify as a form of Europeanization, of the supranational variant to be more precise. Such claims constitute the foreign political dimension of the European polity, such as when the EU and the United States criticize each other's positions in the General Agreement on Tariffs and Trade negotiations (Arrow l), or when the EU General Affairs Council agrees on embedding the Western European Union in the North Atlantic Treaty Organization structures (Arrow m).

Another form of communicative interaction involving supranational political spaces or countries beyond Europe that can constitute a form of Europeanization is when national media report on interactions between actors from other European countries, on the one hand, and supranational institutions or non-European countries, on the other. Examples include German media reports about the visit of Austrian extreme right leader Jörg Haider to Saddam Hussein in Iraq (Arrow i), or French human rights nongovernmental organizations calling on the UN High Commissioner for Refugees to improve protection for female refugees (Arrow j). As in the case of coverage about other member states' internal affairs, the coverage of such claims in the German media might indicate a growing awareness of the relevance of other European countries' foreign relations to one's own country's (or Europe's) position in the world. Of course, a precondition would again be that such coverage of other European states' foreign politics would be overrepresented compared to coverage of international and supranational politics in which other European countries do not play a role.

---

4 FPÖ stands for Freiheitliche Partei Österreichs (the Freedom Party of Austria).

Finally, there are two types of communicative linkages that – like the purely nationally confined claims that we began with – clearly constitute non-Europeanized political communication. The first type consists of communications that link a particular national political space to non-European countries or to supranational institutions, and that bypass the European level. Examples are the debate about United States–German relations in the context of the Iraq conflict (Arrow d), or the German government asking the UN Secretary General to mediate in a conflict outside Europe (Arrow e). Second, a substantial part of foreign political coverage consists of the internal affairs of non-European countries (Arrow n), relations between such countries (such as President Bush's claims on the situation in Iraq, Arrow o), between them and supranational institutions (e.g., the United States asking the North Atlantic Treaty Organization for support after September 11, Arrow p), or among supranational institutions (the UN, for instance, calling on the World Bank to include poverty reduction in its funding criteria, Arrow r).

Summing up, we can speak of a Europeanized public sphere to the extent that a substantial – and, over time, increasing – part of public contestation goes beyond a particular national political space (the European public sphere's inner boundary), and does not bypass Europe by referring only to non-European supranational and transnational spaces (the outer boundary of the European public sphere). Coverage of other member states' internal and foreign affairs constitutes a borderline case and can only be interpreted as a form of Europeanization if such coverage is overrepresented (and over time increasingly so) compared to the coverage of the internal and foreign affairs of non-European countries.

EXPLANATORY FRAMEWORK: POLITICAL OPPORTUNITIES,
MEDIATED POLITICS, AND CLAIM MAKING

To explain differences over time and across countries and policy fields in degrees and types of Europeanization, we use a theoretical framework that combines insights from research on political mobilization and social movements, on the one hand, and media and political communications research, on the other.

Our general approach follows insights from social movement research (e.g., Kitschelt 1986; Kriesi et al. 1995; McAdam, McCarthy, and Zald 1996; Tarrow 1994) on political opportunities, which Tarrow (1994, p. 85) defines as "consistent – but not necessarily formal or permanent – dimensions of the political environment that provide incentives for people to undertake collective action by affecting their expectations of success or failure." This literature emphasizes that levels and forms of mobilization by social movements, interest groups, and citizens' initiatives are strongly influenced by the institutional structure and public discourses of the political systems in which these groups operate. Such approaches have been applied to Europeanized multilevel governance, but so far in a limited way that focuses only on one type of collective actor (e.g., Marks and McAdam 1996 on social movements), or on one type of action form, the actually quite rare examples of European protest (e.g., Imig and Tarrow 2001a). We examine public acts of political communication by a full range of collective actors, including elites, which is necessary for the general level of explanation that we are aiming for.

In general, a political opportunity perspective leads us to expect increased levels of Europeanization of political communication and mobilization as a result of advancing European integration. However, different from the functionalist perspective, this connection between European integration and patterns of mobilization and communication is not seen merely as a process of adaptation, but as depending crucially on the mediating role of political institutions and power configurations. Moreover, unlike the predominant view within the intergovernmental perspective on European integration, a political opportunity approach does not focus primarily on states as the crucial actors within the European policy process; instead it focuses on collective actors *within states* – governments, political parties, interest groups, social movements, national and regional actors, and so on – and analyzes their responses to European integration by asking how the integration process alters the set of opportunities and constraints for each of these collective actors.[5]

The increased competences of European institutions and reach of European policies may imply new opportunities for certain collective actors to influence the policy process. For example, on several occasions, actors have successfully appealed to the European Court of Justice to overturn national policies and regulations. However, the increasing importance of the EU may also impose new constraints that make it more difficult for collective actors to exert influence on the policy process. Unitary regulations on the European level limit the latitude of national policies and may thereby constrain the mobilization opportunities of groups that were traditionally well connected in their national policy arenas (e.g., labor unions). Thus, while for some contenders "Europe" may on balance imply a more favorable set of opportunities, other actors may stand to lose influence.

Another important source for our general approach comes from the political communications literature that emphasizes the central role of "mediated political communication" (Bennett and Entman 2001) in modern democracies (e.g., Mazzoleni and Schulz 1999; Norris 2000a; Swanson and Mancini 1996). It is not enough that political opportunities simply "exist"; to be accessible to collective actors they need to be made visible and meaningful in the public domain. In modern democracies the media has become the prominent player informing the public about political processes, and is increasingly indispensable

---

[5] Importantly, this shifts the emphasis onto collective actors as the drivers for Europeanization through their increasing interactions across national borders and political levels, in contrast to much of the literature (e.g., Wessler et al. 2008) which remains fixated on states and studies Europeanization on the basis of state interaction. In this sense, our focus on collective actors is compatible with that of Fligstein (2008), who like us draws inspiration from Karl W. Deutsch (1953).

to the political communication efforts of social organizations. At the same time, political actors have had to adapt to the requirements of an environment shaped by the mass media. For example, the mass media has developed in a way that allows political party leaders to appeal directly to voters, thereby undermining the need for parties' organizational networks (Mair 1997, p. 39). Some argue that "mediated political communication" increasingly takes center stage, so that such processes "have made the media an increasingly central social institution, to a significant extent displacing churches, parties, trade unions, and other traditional organisations of 'civil society' as the central means by which individuals are connected to the wider social and political world" (Hallin and Mancini 2004, pp. 33–34).

From this perspective, we consider that media coverage is crucial for collective actors to gain political resonance and influence. For this reason our framework includes the media's role for selecting, processing, and conveying the political information that subsequently appears as "news" in the public domain. In this view, whether and how events are chosen and covered by the media not only depends on a "political logic" in the communication process, but it is also importantly shaped by the requirements of a "media logic" (Mazzoleni 1987), a complex phenomenon shaped by the technical requirements of the media, the evolution of journalistic professionalism, and commercial imperatives (Hallin and Mancini 2004). For example, chances for achieving coverage may be enhanced by an event's "news value," its characteristics such as intensity, proximity, the status of the actor, or possibilities for dramatization and polarization, as well as its "fit" with substantive media agendas, story formats, presentational styles, and frames (e.g., Entman 2004; McCombs and Shaw 1972; Shoemaker and Reese 1996).

The degree to which EU policies and institutions conform to the "media logic" for selecting, processing, and conveying political information is not uniform. We may assume that important differences occur here across our three comparative dimensions: time, countries, and policy domains. Regarding developments over time, there is a growing commitment among European policy makers to improve the EU's public presence and transparency. Moreover, there seems to be a related tendency to be more open about conflicts of interest among EU institutions and among member states. Further, institutional reforms have limited the consensus principle and opened up the way to majoritarian forms of decision making that are better geared to capturing media attention. Among countries, differences in the perceived "newsworthiness" of EU policies and institutions may be expected to occur as a result of the degree to which EU integration is a controversial issue in national politics. Where this is the case, EU events will tend to draw more media attention, although that attention is likely to be focused on the implications of the event for national politics, rather than on the European dimension itself. Finally, we may expect differences in the degree and forms of media selection across policy fields. For instance, in such areas where the European Parliament has gained significant codecision powers vis-à-vis the European Commission, something

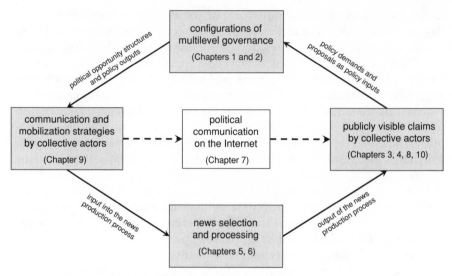

FIGURE 2.2. General outline of the theoretical model.

resembling a government–opposition binary polarity may develop and enhance media attention.

Figure 2.2 presents a simplified graphical overview of our theoretical framework. At the top of the figure, we find configurations of multilevel governance, which present the different types of policy outputs and political opportunity structures facing collective actors who seek to intervene with their demands and proposals into the policy process (discussed here and in Chapter 1). As indicated, such outputs and opportunity structures will vary from country to country, among policy domains, as well as over time. These opportunity structures shape collective actors' perceptions and purposeful actions in response to the emergent structures of European multilevel governance.

In modern democracies, much political mobilization and communication that seeks to affect policies has to pass through the filter of the mass media to reach policy makers as well as the wider public. This is especially true for less resourceful civil society actors who lack direct access to the decision-making process. However, in an era of "mediated politics," media attention has also become crucial to the strategies of actors from the core of the political system, such as governments and political parties, for legitimating their decision making. Through structured interviews with several hundred collective actors of different types, we have examined how Europeanization affects the strategic dilemmas they face and the tactical choices they make in their attempts to influence policy makers, and wider public opinion by means of the media. This part of our data is analyzed in Chapter 9.

Whether on the national or European level, there will always be many more attempts by collective actors to achieve public attention than can ever be accommodated by the limited carrying capacity of the mass media (Koopmans

2004a, Kriesi 2004). In addition, the news stories selected by the media can present and "frame" political information in different ways (Entman 2004). In this project, we study the media's "dual role" both as an institutionalized forum for carrying mediated politics resulting from collective actors' claim making and as a "political actor" who advances positions in the public sphere. We have investigated the considerations that mass media professionals employ in selecting, processing, and communicating European news by studying the views of more than 100 journalists (Chapter 5), as well as by a content analysis of editorials from four selected newspapers in each country, to examine the media's own "voice" over Europe expressed in its claim making, and opinion-leading efforts (Chapter 6).

The mediated "outputs" of the news production process in the form of collective actors' publicly visible claim making constitute our main dependent variable, since it is here that political communication and mobilization attempts become part of the public sphere in a real sense, and thereby have the potential to influence policy deliberation as well as public opinion. An important part of this book (Chapters 3, 4, 8, and 10) is devoted to an analysis of political claims by collective actors as they appear in the news. We seek to explain these claim-making acts as the consequence of the interplay of the other variables in our model: political opportunity structures, the strategic choices made by collective actors, and the media's selection, processing, and communication of political information as "news."

The main causal pathway in Figure 2.2 visualizes the process of public contestation and deliberation of policies based on the assumption that traditional mass media such as newspapers, radio, and television are the central arenas where public visibility, resonance, and legitimacy need to be gained. In the meantime, however, the Internet has become an important alternative route for collective actors to reach public attention. In the conceptual framework of Figure 2.2, we have visualized the role of the Internet as a horizontal arrow going through the middle of the figure, bypassing the media's news selection and communication processes. On the basis of an analysis of search engine results, as well as hyperlink networks among the Web sites of about 1,000 European collective actors, Chapter 7 explores whether and how the Internet restructures the chances of various types of collective actors to mobilize public attention. Beyond the general importance of this question for the future of democratic politics, this question is of special relevance to the EU, given the weakness of traditional mass media on the European level (Kevin 2003; Ward 2004), on one side, and the inherently transnational mode of communication that the Internet technically enables, on the other.

RESEARCH DESIGN: COUNTRIES, TIME PERIOD, AND ISSUE FIELDS

Our research design includes three comparative dimensions. Cross-nationally, the design includes seven national cases: Germany, France, the United Kingdom, Italy, Spain, the Netherlands, and Switzerland. This set of countries was chosen to include the most important EU member states, and to provide sufficient variation along potentially relevant dimensions such as the size of the country and the date of entry into the EU. Switzerland has been included as a nonmember state to investigate to what extent Europeanization processes are tied to EU membership.

Along the time dimension, our main focus is on the period in the early twenty-first century during which the European Union went through a number of crucial extensions, both in terms of the depth of integration – culminating in the introduction of the euro in 1999[6] – and in terms of its membership, expanding from fifteen to twenty-seven members. The precise period of study differs somewhat between the different data sets that we employ. Interviews with news media professionals, politicians, and representatives of various interest organizations were conducted in 2003. Our analysis of political communication on the Internet covers the period 2002–2003. Content data on political claims and editorials in print media were gathered for the years 1990, 1995, and 2000–2002. This allows us to place our findings in a longer time perspective, and to investigate how far important institutional changes, such as the Maastricht Treaty of 1992 or the introduction of the euro, have had an impact on levels and forms of Europeanization of public communication and mobilization.

Because we expect degrees and forms of Europeanization of public spheres to vary with different institutional settings, our study focuses on seven policy domains. The choice of these domains was made on the basis of the EU's institutional structure as laid down in the Maastricht and the Amsterdam Treaties. These treaties define different distributions of competences for decision making, policy development, and implementation between the supranational European institutions, intergovernmental decision-making arenas, and the governments and parliaments of member states. Within the so-called first pillar of common market policies, the European Commission, the European Court of Justice, and other EU institutions have important supranational decision-making powers that are binding for the member states. From this core of the EU we chose the two arguably most important issue fields of EU politics: monetary politics and agriculture.

The so-called second and third pillars of the EU consist of policy fields that are dominated by intergovernmental modes of decision making, in which the European Commission and other supranational EU institutions play a more limited role. The core actors that shape policies in these two pillars are the heads of government and ministers of the member states who meet in half-yearly European Councils (for the heads of government and foreign ministers) and specific Councils of Ministers for different policy fields. In the second pillar of foreign and defense policies we focus on debates around troop deployment, for both military and humanitarian purposes. The third pillar of EU decision

---

[6] The euro was introduced as an accounting currency on January 1, 1999. Euro coins and banknotes entered circulation only three years later.

making encompasses justice and internal policies, which are represented in our study by the field of immigration.[7]

We have further chosen two policy areas in which the treaties give EU institutions only a coordinating role and leave all formal decision-making power firmly on the level of the member states. We chose one example, pensions and retirement, of a socioeconomic redistributive issue, and one example, education, of an issue with a strong cultural and identity component. Finally, we also investigate the metafield of European integration itself, where the structure and membership of the European polity rather than specific policies are at stake. The field of European integration includes all debates, decisions, and mobilization around general questions of the EU's institutional structure, its collective identity, its normative foundations, and its finality, as well as the discussions around EU enlargement. Thus, we arrive at the following selection of policy domains:

- agriculture, more specifically the issues subsidies, livestock and dairy quotas, and animal disease control (e.g., bovine spongiform encephalopathy, EU quota regulations, General Agreement on Tariffs and Trade negotiations on agricultural subsidies);
- monetary politics (e.g., introduction of the euro, interest rate adjustments);
- troop deployment, for both military and humanitarian purposes (e.g., ex-Yugoslavia, Afghanistan, Iraq);
- immigration politics (e.g., Schengen cooperation, and asylum and refugee policies);
- retirement and pensions (e.g., retirement age, pension funds);
- education (all questions relating to primary, secondary, and tertiary education); and
- European integration (e.g., enlargement, institutional reform, constitutional discussions).

Beyond the three general dimensions of time, countries, and policy fields, there are various methodological and research design features that pertain to the specific parts of our research. These will be discussed in the respective chapters on interviews with media professionals (Chapter 5) and with collective actors (Chapter 9), on editorials (Chapter 6), and on political communication on the Internet (Chapter 7). In the present chapter we do, however, introduce the methodology and selection of data sources that we use to study our dependent

---

[7] The Treaty of Amsterdam 1999 incorporated policies on "visas, asylum, immigration and other policies related to free movement of persons" into the European Community, which moved them into the legal framework of the first pillar of the European Union. However, there was a five-year transition period after the Treaty of Amsterdam for this to enter into force, which means that for the period of our study this policy field effectively remains in the third pillar. In addition, it should be noted that "communitization" in immigration includes important and significant exceptions, for example, limiting the powers of the Court of Justice, meaning that the shift from the third to the first pillar has not resulted in the same depth of integration as that in other first-pillar policy fields.

variable, publicly visible claim making, because these data are used in several of the subsequent chapters, and the methodology that we use to analyze editorials and online political communication is to an important extent modeled on the political claim-making method.

MEDIA AS A DATA SOURCE: SELECTION OF NEWSPAPERS

A key decision in our research design is the selection of sources for retrieving data on political communication and mobilization. Whereas some study television in the search for Europeanized communication (e.g., de Vreese 2001), we select print media as the primary data source. Our considerations are substantive and practical. Historically, the advent of an independent press and mass circulation newspapers fulfilled an important step in the emergence of mediated politics in national public spheres (Hallin and Mancini 2004). Arguably, despite the onset of radio, television and Internet, the print media remains a crucial supply line for communication between political institutions and citizens. Television tends to have less impact than the press on the political agenda (see for example, Walgrave, Soroka, and Nuytemans 2008). Newspapers have a broader scope and more space than television, and Internet Web sites of newspapers make print media content more widely accessible and immediate than it was previously. In addition, newspapers allow a greater discursive elaboration and argumentation than television. This is an important consideration, given the quality and detail we need to capture on claims, especially with regard to tracing the communicative relationships that cross and link different political levels and countries (outlined in Figure 2.1). Its importance is heightened further when one considers that Europeanization is an incipient and emergent phenomenon and therefore requires a sensitive instrument for retrieval. Since television news coverage has less space and must be more selective, it is less likely to reflect incipient Europeanization tendencies. We have indeed been able to demonstrate this in a comparison of television and newspaper coverage for the German case (see Schlecht 2002). By choosing newspapers as our source, we maximize our chances of detecting less prominent and more partial forms of Europeanization. We realize, however, that this implies that our findings will overestimate rather than underestimate the degree of Europeanization of the mass media taken as a whole. Finally, a further consideration is that, as a format, television is even less comparable cross-nationally than the press, and it is certainly less available for retrieval, especially with regard to past historical years. For these reasons we chose print media, which has also been the main data source for other comparative projects addressing similar aims (e.g., Downey and König 2006; Peters et al. 2005; Trenz 2005, 2007; van der Steeg 2005).

Newspaper selection for retrieving data on claims is crucial to our comparative approach. It was not logistically feasible to cover all newspapers for seven countries. However, it was necessary that we draw a significantly large sample of claims from a range of newspaper sources, to provide evidence on the transformation of national public spheres. We selected four daily newspapers per country, which together were seen as best-fit functional equivalents for representing their national newspaper landscape. Our selection criteria also required variation by four newspaper types per country (left-broadsheet, right-broadsheet, tabloid or popular, and regional). We selected two broadsheets of public record with nationwide distribution, varied by political affiliation (center-left affiliation vs. center-right affiliation). We added a mass circulation popular or tabloid newspaper, to allow for variation regarding whether a newspaper addresses elite (broadsheet) or general (tabloid or popular) publics. Finally, we took a regional newspaper for examining subnational variations.

Finding cross-national functional equivalents is not straightforward. As Hallin and Mancini's (2004) research demonstrates, cross-national variations in newsprint landscapes are largely shaped by, and constitutive of, differences in countries' political systems. Specific media systems and press cultures are products of, derived from, and constitutive of specific types of liberal democracies, reflecting their important political cleavages. Subsequently, newspaper selection needed to take account of additional variations in specific countries, to accurately represent key political cleavages, which are reflected in their press landscapes.

Our selection in Table 2.1 was taken in consultation with national experts. Broadsheet selection was relatively straightforward. Although countries with federal and regional political systems, such as Germany and Italy, have newspapers originating from regions, such as *Süddeutsche Zeitung* (Munich) and *Corriere della Sera* (Milan), these largely address national readerships. Regional newspapers were also relatively unproblematic. Here we took a newspaper covering a sizeable region, with a distinct political, cultural, or linguistic heritage, such as *La Vanguardia* (Catalonia, Spain).

Popular or tabloid selection proved more difficult. In countries with mass circulation tabloids (Germany: *Bild*, Britain: *Sun*), these were taken. In countries without tabloids but with newspapers with a popular format and high circulation, we took these (*De Telegraaf*, for the Netherlands; *El Mundo* for Spain). France was somewhat problematic because there was no clear candidate for a national popular newspaper, although *Ouest-France*, which we chose as our regional newspaper, is also the largest national circulation newspaper and has a popular format. As a substitute, we added *L'Humanité* as a fourth paper, which is distinct from broadsheet newspapers and is politically close to the Communist Party.

A few country-specific issues remained. For Italy, where regional North–South divisions are a key political cleavage, and where there were also no clear candidates for popular newspapers, we decided that the press landscape would be better represented if we selected two regional papers (*La Nazione* for the North and *Il Mattino* for the South). More problematic still is Switzerland, where politics is strongly regionalized and language-based cleavages exist. For Switzerland, we therefore selected the two main official language communities,

TABLE 2.1. *Selected Newspapers*

Type	UK	France	Germany	Switzerland	Spain	Italy	The Netherlands
Left broadsheet	The Guardian	Le Monde	Süddeutsche Zeitung		El País	La Repubblica	Volkskrant
Right broadsheet	The Times	Le Figaro	Frankfurter Allgemeine Zeitung	Neue Zürcher Zeitung & Le Temps	Abc	Il Corriere della Sera	Algemeen Dagblad
Popular					El Mundo		Telegraaf
Tabloid	The Sun (The Mirror)		Bild-Zeitung	Blick & Le Matin			
Regional paper	The Scotsman	Ouest-France	Leipziger Volkszeitung		La Vanguardia	La Nazione & Il Mattino	Leeuwarder Courant
Other		L'Humanité					

Note: Our newspaper analysis used *The Sun*, but our journalists' interviews were from *The Mirror* (*The Sun* refused to cooperate; see Chapter 5).

French speaking and German speaking, and we took a center-right broadsheet and a popular newspaper for each.

Hardcopy, microfiche, or electronic (LexisNexis) copies of newspapers were collected for a sample of preselected days by trained human coders, who subsequently selected relevant articles from the main news sections of the newspaper and coded them into a database by using a highly detailed standardized coding scheme (Koopmans 2002) applying the claim-making method.[8] Extensive intercoder reliability tests were conducted for article selection, claim identification, and coding, and coders participated in regular discussions about difficult cases. Reliability easily satisfied conventional standards. For instance, the cumulative reliability coefficient for relevant article selection plus correct identification of claims within these articles amounted to 0.89. Reliability for individual variables was as high or higher.[9] We now outline the claim-making approach.

CLAIM-MAKING ANALYSIS: MEASURING EUROPEANIZATION FROM MEDIATED POLITICAL CLAIMS

In a world where mediated political communication is central to the politics and public life of democracies (Bennett and Entman 2001, p. 1; Mazzoleni and Schulz 1999), it is widely acknowledged that the political discourse carried by the mass media is a key location for public contestation

---

[8] Given the labor-intensive nature of the type of content coding we employ, we were not able to code all issues of all newspapers for all years. For 2000–2002 we coded one issue per week of each of the two quality papers; for 1990 and 1995 the sample was half as dense, with one issue per two weeks of each newspaper. The tabloid and regional newspapers were only coded for the year 2000 on the basis of a sample consisting of one issue per two weeks. Within the selected newspaper issues, all claims were coded, regardless of whether they had a European aspect, as long as they referred to one of our seven issue fields. However, to limit the coding effort, on half of the days for 1990, 1995, 2000, and 2002 only claims that had a European scope (in at least one of the basic aspects of the claim: actors, addressees, issue, or object actors) were coded. This restriction also pertains to the whole of the year 2001. We control for biases related to different samples for different years by excluding the claims that were coded from issues where the European reference restriction applies from all analyses where we are interested in levels and trends in Europeanization (including all claims in such analyses would lead to artificially inflated levels of claims with a European dimension). Where data were aggregated across countries, we weighted the data in such a way that each country contributes equally to the overall result. While differences among the other countries are smaller, Germany stands out with about 50% more claims than the other countries. This is a result of the dense information content of German newspaper reporting rather than an indication of a greater intensity of public debates on our seven issues in Germany. In earlier projects on entirely different topics, in which the same (Koopmans et al. 2005) or a similar methodology (Kriesi et al. 1995) was used, similarly high numbers of claims were found in the German press compared to other European countries.

[9] The only negative exception concerned the "object actor" variable, which indicates the actor in whose interests a claim is made. The reason for the unsatisfactory reliability of this variable is that object actors are often not stated explicitly in a claim and have to be inferred by the coder. This variable is not central to our analysis and we do not use it in the analyses reported in this book. A full report on the reliability tests can be found at our project Web site at http://europub. wzb.eu/.

(Gamson and Modigliani 1989) and "contentious politics" (Tarrow 1994). From a methodological perspective, news is a rich source for retrieving data on "mediated politics": it provides information on which actors successfully mobilize their concerns, what positions they take on issues, the ideological contents of their arguments, the interests they represent, who they address, support, and oppose, and whether this expands the debate, spatially, by communicating across national contexts and political levels. It is these political claims that we aim to capture from newspaper sources.

Political claim-making analysis (see Koopmans and Statham 1999; Koopmans et al. 2005) is a method for examining the publicly visible "mediated" dimension of politics. It is a content analysis method that developed initially as an extension to protest event analysis (e.g., Rucht, Koopmans, and Neidhardt 1999), by adding insights from public discourse approaches to social movements (e.g., Donati 1992; Franzosi 2004; Gamson and Modigliani 1989), as well as related approaches in communications research (e.g., Entman 2004; Neuman, Just, and Crigler 1992). The method is specifically designed to study political contention that is produced by actors' contributions to public debates in the media, such as by way of interviews, press conferences, or the publication of reports, and by other visible acts of political mobilization, such as protest demonstrations. Of course, many attempts to mobilize political claims fail to reach the public domain. As we already mentioned, the limited carrying capacity of the media means that it has to select which events, claimants, and opinions are newsworthy. For our research question, however, it is the publicly visible claims that count, since by definition only those that become public can contribute to a Europeanization of public spheres. A key difference from media content analyses in the communications research tradition is that the article is not the unit of analysis. In contrast to such studies, which often examine how journalists frame the news, the claim-making approach focuses on the role of political actors (which may include the media itself as an actor) and their "claims" – our unit of analysis – in shaping the public discourse and contestation. Traditional content analytic methods using article-level variables can tell us with which frequency certain actors and issues are mentioned, and to what extent they co-occur in news stories. However, they are able to tell us relatively little about the relations among actors, or the positions that they take with regard to which issues. It is precisely such information about who addresses who, on which issues, and in the name of whose interests that we need to answer questions about the Europeanization of public spheres and the different forms it may take.

Our perspective sees claim-making acts as a set of *communicative networks* that may link political actors across institutional levels of governance and across national borders. It extends beyond the traditional approaches in social movements and media research. First, by extending the scope of retrieval to include a full range of actors, it moves substantively away from the narrow focus in protest event analysis, on "protests," which at best represent the "tip of the iceberg" of public contestation. Second, by extending the type of communicative act that is included beyond protest events, claim-making analysis captures much more, qualitatively and quantitatively, of the discursive contents of political contention. Third, claim-making analysis moves beyond the media-centrism of traditional article-level content analyses, by retrieving information on the actor relationships that are reproduced and mediated in news. Finally, partly drawing inspiration from Franzosi's (2004) usage of "linguistic grammar" in public discourse, the claim-making approach attempts to reconstruct public contestation and debate by examining how actors establish communicative networks by making claims on other actors across political arenas and spatial boundaries.

Thus, claim-making analysis sees news as a record of public events and retrieves information on this aspect. A political claim-making act is a purposeful communicative action in the public sphere. *Claim-making acts consist of public speech acts (including protest events) that articulate political demands, calls to action, proposals, or criticisms, which, actually or potentially, affect the interests or integrity of the claimants or other collective actors.* Political decisions and policy implementation are included and seen as special forms of claim making, namely ones that have direct and binding effects. The unit of analysis is an instance of claim making (in short, a claim). Claims are broken down into seven elements, for each of which a number of variables are coded:

- location of the claim in time and space (when and where is the claim made?)
- claimant: the actor making the claim (who makes the claim?)
- form of the claim (how is the claim inserted in the public sphere?)
- the addressee of the claim (at whom is the claim directed?)
- the substantive issue of the claim (what is the claim about?)
- the object (beneficiary or maleficiary) of the claim: who would be affected by the claim if it is realized (for or against whom?)
- the justification for the claim (why should this action be undertaken?)

The ideal-typical claim has all these elements, as indicated in Table 2.2 (leaving out the when and where, which are self-evident).

Thus the grammar of claims consists of a "claimant – action – addressee – action – object – justification clause" sequence: an actor, the claimant, undertakes some sort of action in the public sphere to get another actor, the addressee, to do or leave something that affects the interests of a third actor, the object, and provides a justification for why this should be done. Many claims are not as differentiated as this type. Often several claim elements are missing, as indicated by the examples in Table 2.3.

The first row illustrates a very common form of "incompleteness" for mediated claims. Frequently, no justification is given for a claim. The example in the second row illustrates that claims often have no explicit addressees or objects (or at least the newspaper does not mention them). The third example illustrates a form of direct action, which contains no discursive elements but from which we can derive the issue at stake on the basis of the physical object of the action. In addition, the example illustrates that sometimes claimants are unknown or

TABLE 2.2. *The Structure of Political Claims: Part 1*

Who (Claimant)	How (Form)	At Whom (Addressee)	What (Issue)	For/Against (Ultimate Whom? Target)	Why (Frame)
A group of asylum seekers	engage in a hunger strike	demanding the government	not to deport to their country of origin	themselves (the group of asylum seekers)	because this would be in violation of the Geneva Convention.
The European Parliament	passes a resolution	criticizing the Turkish government and demanding	measures to improve the treatment of	political prisoners,	arguing that respect for human rights is a core value of the European Union.

TABLE 2.3. *The Structure of Political Claims: Part 2*

Who (Claimant)	How (Form)	At Whom (Addressee)	What (Issue)	For/Against (Ultimate Whom? Target)	Why (Frame)
The French agricultural minister	calls on	meat importers	to boycott the import of meat from other EU countries	to support French farmers.	
Joschka Fischer	holds a speech calling for		the drawing up of a European Constitution.		
	set fire to			an asylum seeker center.	
The Bavarian authorities	deport			a group of Kurdish refugees.	
A group of British economists	publish a report stating that				British non-participation in the common currency will lead to lower economic growth.

anonymous. The fourth example is common for state actors, who often do not have to make claims on others to do something but can directly make binding claims on object actors. As in the third example, the aim of the action may not be specified in a discursive statement but can be derived from the action itself. The final example is common for statements by experts who usually express no explicit aims, but present frames referring to the consequences of certain policy actions.

Importantly, claims are included in our data regardless of who makes them and where they are made. Actors appear in our sample, not because they have been preselected, but only to the extent, and in the way (e.g., for, or against, European integration), that they successfully make interventions in the mediated political discourse. This means our data include claims by state actors, economic actors, journalists, and news media, as well as representatives of civil society. Claims can be made by organizations and their spokespersons, as well as by diffuse collectives (e.g., a group of farmers). The claimants may be from the European, other supranational, as well as national, regional, and local levels, and they can be from the country where the newspaper is published, or from any other country of the world. Likewise, no restriction applies to the location where a claim is made. For example, claims on the situation of refugees in Australia or the deployment of African troops in Liberia are included in the same way as claims that are made in the countries of our study or on the level of the European Union. Thus, our data-gathering strategy is entirely neutral with regard to the geographical and political scope of claims. This allows us to make the question of the extent of Europeanization (or broader supranationalization) of public claim making a matter for empirical investigation. It also should be noted that we retrieve our cases from a sample determined by specific days selected in advance at regular time intervals within each year, which means that our findings are able to represent general trends.[10]

This "neutral" retrieval strategy is not as self-evident as it seems, but it is nonetheless essential. Most other studies on the Europeanization of public communication have employed data-gathering strategies that are biased toward finding Europeanized forms of public discourse in advance. Many focus on specific issues or events, or time periods, that have been preselected for their European-wide scope and relevance, such as the Haider debate (van der Steeg 2005), European election campaigns (de Vreese and Boomgaarden 2006), and the introduction of the euro (de Vreese, Peter, and Semetko 2001). Other studies focus on a wide range of issues but select only those media articles for analysis that contain keywords such as "Europe" or "EU" (Kantner 2004; Trenz 2005, 2007), thereby excluding those claims – which as we shall show still make up the majority of public discourse in most issue fields – that make no reference to European actors or policies whatsoever. It is worth noting that, in recognition of this, some recent studies have adopted our method over their own previous attempts in this regard (see Trenz, Menéndez, and Losada

---

[10] For further detail on the delimitation of claims and the coding of variables, we refer to our codebook (Koopmans 2002).

2008; Vetters, Jentges, and Trenz 2009). Another approach limits its sampling only to newspaper articles with "deliberative" opinion-leading contents and omits "mere news" (Peters et al. 2005, p. 142). This seems an unnecessarily restrictive and elite-biased retrieval strategy that detracts from the reliability of statements subsequently made about general Europeanization trends. Space limitations mean that not all claims are reproduced in news with their complete "deliberative" contents (see text herein), yet the actor relationships and communicative networks they produce are still visible and relevant. "Mere news" in our view is a central political substance of a mass public discourse.

Commonly aired objections in the political science community to using media sources for data on political action refer to the role of the media in processing this information: the media's selection bias (selection of which events and issues to report) and description bias (selection of the relevant information about events and issues to report). Against this, the established tradition for taking newspapers as a data source for collective action has produced a large number of studies assessing the impact of selection and description bias on the validity of newspaper data. Overall, such studies conclude that newspaper data does not deviate from accepted standards of reliability and validity, as long as one is interested in trends and differences rather than absolute numbers (see, e.g., Earl et al. 2004; Rucht et al. 1999). Limitations of selection and description biases may be reduced by drawing from more than one newspaper source, as we have done in this study. However, the most compelling argument in favor of using media sources is that our theoretical approach actually relies on the process of media selection to give meaning to our data and for interpreting our findings. From our perspective, political events and issues that go unreported are considered to be largely irrelevant, because if an actor's claims are not publicly visible then they can have little impact in shaping the opinions and responses of others, and in shaping or opening up a communicative space. It is an advantage of the claim-making method that it retrieves data for actors' claims from the interactive discursive context that is produced by their actual purposeful attempts to communicate their concerns to others, that is, claim making in the mass-mediated political discourse.

Although claim-making data are collected within the general theoretical perspective we have outlined, it is not prescriptive regarding the explanatory approaches that may be applied to interpret the data. It is the research question that determines whether, for example, the data are used to examine the media actors' own claim making within mediated political discourse, or the claim making mobilized by other political actors, whose activities and claims are reported in the news. Both are possibilities with this method; indeed, it has already been used to compare both for the German case (Koopmans and Pfetsch 2003).

As we hope to demonstrate in subsequent chapters, the claim-making approach produces analytic descriptive data sets that are highly flexible, allowing for a combination of cross-national, cross-issue, and cross-actor analyses, at different levels of aggregation, as well as diachronic studies. Moreover, it allows one to zoom in on selected actor types (see Chapter 10 on political parties in this book). It also facilitates situating studies of the qualitative detail of claims (arguments, frames) within a context in which one can establish their quantitative weight within the mediated political discourse. Chapters 8 on framing and 10 on parties' criticisms of European integration and the EU institutions are examples of such linking of quantitative and qualitative analyses. Claims data are also suited for combining with other sources, such as actor-level interviews that may elaborate publicly invisible aspects of collective action, as Chapter 9 on collective actors demonstrates.

Having clarified our understanding of Europeanization, the main elements of our theoretical framework, our three dimensions of comparison, the primary data source, and the measurement of our central dependent variable, we now turn to the empirical analysis. The next chapter, Chapter 3, follows on directly from this, by studying the general patterns of cross-national, cross-policy-field, and temporal variations that appear in claim making. Subsequently, Chapter 4 studies variations in degrees and types of Europeanization across collective actors and further investigates patterns of support and opposition to European integration.

PART II

EUROPEAN PUBLIC DEBATES

Visibility and Inclusiveness

3

The Europeanization of Public Spheres

Comparisons across Issues, Time, and Countries

Ruud Koopmans, Jessica Erbe, and Martin F. Meyer

In this chapter and Chapter 4, we present the main results of our media content analysis of the degrees and forms of Europeanization of public debates in twenty-eight European newspapers. We focus on differences across the seven issue fields included in our study, across the time period 1990–2002, across the seven countries of study, and across various categories of collective actors. This chapter focuses primarily on the visibility dimension, that is, the question to what extent and in which forms political debates in European mass media have become Europeanized. Chapter 4 will then focus on the participation dimension by zooming in on the role of particular categories of collective actors in Europeanized debates.

We begin by asking to what extent public debates have become Europeanized regarding the actors who appear in media debates. Are these primarily domestic actors from their own country, or do we find sizeable shares of statements by actors from the European supranational level, or from other European countries? In a second step, we look at the multilevel structure of claims. As we have seen in Chapter 2, theoretically there are many ways in which Europeanization of public debates can occur in a multilevel polity, depending not only on who makes the claims but also on who is addressed, criticized, or supported, and which polity levels actors relate to in framing and legitimizing their demands and proposals. The third and final step of the analysis in this chapter is to look at the way in which the European integration process and the role of European institutional actors are evaluated in the public debate in the mass media in different issue fields, and how this varies across time and across countries.

EUROPEAN VOICES: SPATIAL ORIGINS OF CLAIM MAKERS

Perhaps the most central aspect of Europeanization of public debates is the degree to which European actors appear in media debates. If newspaper readers only receive information on the opinions and proposals of actors from their own country, it is difficult to imagine Europeanization in a sense that would imply an exchange of opinions across national borders and across levels of the European polity. As argued in Chapter 2, claim making across the boundaries of polities can take two basic forms, either horizontal when actors from one country are present in the public debate in another country, or vertical when claims by actors from the European polity level enter the public debate in national mass media. We look at the extent of these forms of Europeanized claim making across three main dimensions of comparison: issues, time, and countries.

Issues

Which factors might determine the chances for actors from the European polity level and from other European countries to play a role in media debates in national newspapers? The political opportunity perspective sketched in the previous chapter leads us to expect that this depends on the way in which decision making in particular issue fields is structured. Simply put, we expect that the chances of actors to penetrate the media depend on their actual influence in the decision-making process in a particular issue field. We have selected our issue fields precisely because they vary in the distribution of power between the national and the European level, and in the extent to which decision-making power on the European level is dominated by supranational or intergovernmental forms of governance. In the fields of monetary politics and agriculture, the European Union has gained strong supranational prerogatives, and European institutions such as the European Commission and the European Central Bank can make decisions that are binding for the member states. On immigration and troop deployment there is a certain level of European-level common policy making, but mainly of the intergovernmental type in which decisions are made in negotiations between national heads of government and cabinet ministers during the European Councils and Councils of Ministers or in negotiations between member states outside of these forums. Education and pensions and retirement policies have largely remained the prerogative of individual national governments, and intergovernmental as well as supranational forms of decision making on the European level are still very limited. Finally, the meta-issue of European integration is characterized by a mixture of intergovernmental and supranational decision making, as changes in European polity structures and enlargement of EU membership require the consent and cooperation of both the individual member states and European-level institutions.

This leads us to the following two hypotheses about the effects of issue-specific opportunity structures on the presence of actors in public debates:

Claims by actors from the European polity level, such as the European Commission or the European Parliament, will be strongly represented in issue fields where decision making has important supranational components, such as European integration, monetary politics, and agriculture, and will be relatively marginal in other issue fields (H1).

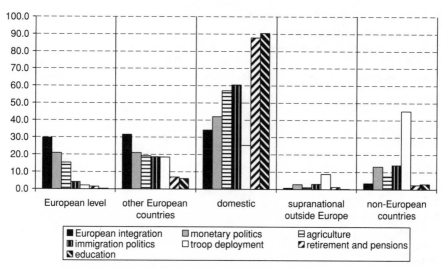

FIGURE 3.1. Spatial origins of claim makers by issue field.

Claims by actors from other European countries will be strongly represented in issue fields where decision making has important intergovernmental components, such as European integration, immigration, and troop deployment, and will be relatively marginal in other issue fields (H2).

Figure 3.1 divides the actors who made claims into five categories: those originating from the European polity level, other European countries, the particular country (i.e., the domestic country of the respective newspaper), extra-European supranational institutional arenas such as the UN or the North Atlantic Treaty Organization, and finally countries outside Europe. As indicated in the previous chapter, we define the European polity level to include not just the European Union and its component institutions but also non-EU supranational and intergovernmental institutions on the European level, such as the European Council or European Free Trade Association. However, the latter make up only a very small percentage (3%) of all claims by European-level actors, which indicates that to a very large extent Europeanization equals "EU-ization." Likewise, our definition of "European countries" is broader than the member states of the European Union at any given point in time, and it includes not only all twenty-seven current EU member states but also all applicants including Turkey, as well as other European countries such as Norway, Switzerland, Iceland, and the Balkan States. The vast majority of claims from European countries are, however, from actors from one of the EU member states (see Table 3.1).

A first thing to note in Figure 3.1 is that in six of the seven issue fields, domestic actors are the most important category, ranging from 34% of all claims on European integration to 90% of education claims. The only exception is the field of military troop deployment, where actors from non-European

TABLE 3.1. *Claims by Actors from Foreign European Countries Reported in the National Press by Nationality*

Country of Actor	Share of Claims (%)	Population (in Millions)	Share of European Population (%)
Germany	18.4	82	13.5
France	18.3	61	10.0
United Kingdom	13.9	61	10.0
Austria	8.9	8	1.3
Italy	4.2	60	9.9
Turkey	4.0	72	11.8
Spain	3.9	45	7.4
Poland	3.4	39	6.4
Belgium	3.0	10	1.6
Denmark	2.2	5	0.8
Czech Republic	2.0	10	1.6
Netherlands	1.8	16	2.6
Hungary	1.7	10	1.6
Greece	1.6	11	1.8
Switzerland	1.5	7	1.2
Sweden	1.5	9	1.5
Portugal	1.0	10	1.6
Former Yugoslavia (Serbia, Kosovo, Montenegro)	1.0	11	1.8
Other European countries	7.7	77	13.6
TOTAL	100.0	604	100.0

Note: Countries with 1.0% or more of claims are listed separately. All other European countries are grouped together in the residual category.

countries, first and foremost the United States, followed by countries such as Russia, Iraq, and Afghanistan, are the most frequent claim makers. Turning to European actors, we see that H1 receives full confirmation. Actors from the European polity level are responsible for 30% of all reported statements on European integration, 21% of claims on monetary politics, and 15% of claims on agriculture. As predicted by H1, in the other four issue fields the role of European-level actors is marginal, from 4% of claims on immigration to a mere 0.3% of education claims. Significant vertical Europeanization in the form of claims by European-level actors is thus indeed limited to supra-nationalized policy fields where actors such as the European Commission and the European Central Bank have gained direct and binding decision-making prerogatives.

The results regarding actors from other European countries are largely but not entirely in line with H2. Indeed, we find significant levels of claims by actors from other European countries in the European integration field (32%) as well as in the immigration (19%) and troop deployment (19%) fields, where European-level decision making is largely of the intergovernmental type. Also in line with H2, we find very few claims by actors from other European countries in the pensions (7%) and education (6%) fields. However, contrary to the predictions of H2, we find relatively high levels of claim making by actors from other European countries in the monetary politics (21%) and agriculture (20%) fields. Supranationalization of decision making therefore does not necessarily imply decreased attention for actors from other European countries, although as we will see there are indications that such a substitution process is occurring over time.

A further indication that the presence of actors in the public debate in the mass media to a large extent reflects their actual influence on decision making is that claims by actors from large and powerful European countries receive much more coverage in the media of other countries than actors from smaller European countries. Table 3.1 shows the shares of claims reported in national newspapers that were made by actors from various other European countries. Actors from Germany and France, true to these countries' reputation as the "motors" of European integration, turn out to be the most prominent foreign European actors (18% of foreign European claims each). The United Kingdom follows not far behind with 14%. Surprisingly, Austria comes fourth with 9%, but this is mostly due to the year 2000, in which 18% of all foreign European claims were made by Austrian actors. This was related to the affair around Jörg Haider and his radical right Freedom Party's participation in the Austrian government and the controversial boycott of Austria by the European Commission and several member states that followed.

The "big three," Germany, France, and the United Kingdom, account for half of all the foreign European claims, even though they are home to only one-third of the European population (compare the second and fourth columns of the table). This overrepresentation is strongest for France, indicating that France is the country that has been most efficient in putting its mark on European-level debates, a tradition that does not seem to have abated under the presidency of Nicolas Sarkozy. Compared to their population share, Italian and Spanish actors (4% each) play a very modest role in European debates outside their own borders. Claims by actors from Poland (3%) and Turkey (4%) mainly occurred in the context of enlargement discussions, but as in the case of Italy and Spain they are not equivalent to these countries' importance in terms of population. The smaller European countries draw shares of media coverage that are more or less equivalent to their population shares. Thus, European media debates are not biased toward large countries as such, but only toward the three core member states that act respectively as the most important motors (France and Germany) of, and the most important brake (the United Kingdom) on, European integration. The media attention for these three countries seems to go especially at the cost of the discursive influence of second-tier European powers such as Italy, Spain, and Poland. That smaller European countries have a more or less equitable share in claim making is likely due to the fact that in intergovernmental decision-making arenas, and especially in those where unanimity is required, their veto powers sometimes give them an influence far exceeding their numeric size. A recent example is the media attention that two smaller countries, the Netherlands and Ireland, were able to draw as a result of their rejection in national referenda of the European Constitution, respectively the Lisbon Treaty.

Time

Our second dimension of comparison considers temporal developments across the period 1990–2002. With the treaties of Maastricht, Amsterdam, and Nice during this period, the European integration process has deepened, and therefore the opportunity structure perspective leads us to expect an increase in both vertical and horizontal forms of Europeanization of claim making. Thus,

Over the course of the period 1990–2002, the shares of claims by European-level actors and by actors from foreign European countries will have increased (H3).

In one issue field, monetary politics, developments over the period of study have been particularly spectacular, as twelve member states gave up their national currencies, set up a common European Central Bank, and created a new currency, the euro. We therefore expect the following:

The increase in shares of claim making by European-level actors and by actors from foreign European countries will be particularly pronounced in the field of monetary politics (H4).

Figure 3.2 shows the geospatial origin of claim-making actors across the period 1990–2002. H3 is clearly confirmed where the share of actors from the European level is concerned, which rises from 9% in 1990 to 15% in 2002. However, the coverage of claims by actors from foreign European countries

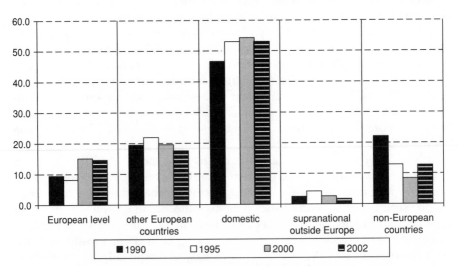

FIGURE 3.2. Development of the spatial origin of claim makers, 1990–2002.

shows a slight decrease from 19% in 1990 to 18% in 2002. Indeed, as H4 predicted, the increase in the share of European-level actors is very pronounced in the field of monetary politics, rising from 9% in 1990 to 29% in 2002 (not shown in the figure). Here too, however, there is no concomitant trend of increased horizontal claim making across European national borders. Initially, we can observe a rise from 21% claims by foreign European actors in 1990 to 31% in 1995, as in the process of the Economic and Monetary Union convergence toward the introduction of the euro, member states paid more attention than they did previously to one another's currency and interest rate politics. However, with the introduction of the euro and the establishment of the European Central Bank, rates of attention for other countries' monetary politics once again decreased to 19%, somewhat below the initial level of 1990. Similar trends are visible in the metafield of European integration, where the share of European-level actors rose substantially from 25 to 33%, but the share of claims from other European countries increased only slightly from 29 to 30% (not shown in the figure).

We can thus conclude that where the presence of actors in public debates in mass media is concerned, the deepening of the European integration process has led to a rise in vertical Europeanization, but not to increased horizontal flows of communication across national borders. As the changes in the monetary politics field suggest, there may even be a certain degree of trade-off between vertical and horizontal forms of Europeanization, as centralization of decision-making powers on the European level reduces the need to pay attention to the national policies of other countries, which in the case of monetary politics no longer determine their own exchange and interest rates. However, in other respects, increased interdependence created by common policies may make claims by actors from foreign European countries more relevant, for instance when budgetary deficits bring countries into conflict with other member states and with the European level in the context of the common currency stability pact. The net result of these countervailing tendencies may be precisely what we find in the data, namely that with increased Europeanization of policy making, the total attention given to actors from other European countries remains at a similar level, even while the nature of attention shifts. We will return to this issue, when we discuss the multilevel structure of claims.

Countries

As a final step in our analysis of claim makers in European public debates, we look at differences across countries. What can we hypothesize about the presence of actors from the European level and from other European countries in the national media of different countries? We consider two types of factors: first, the degree of autonomy of a country, as indicated by its population size and the dependence of its economy on trade with EU countries; second, the depth of formal European integration, as indicated by EU membership and opt-outs from certain aspects of European integration, such as monetary union and the Schengen area.[1]

Regarding the first set of factors, we hypothesize that attention given to actors from the European level and from other member states will be greater, the more a country is vulnerable to economic and political developments outside its borders. Countries with smaller populations have smaller economies, which are generally more sensitive to external shocks. Politically as well, small countries have less autonomy. They depend on external alliances to guarantee their security, and they have little potential to exert significant influence in international affairs on their own account. As can be seen in Table 3.1, Germany is, with more than 80 million inhabitants in terms of population size, the largest among our seven countries, followed by Britain, France, and Italy (about 60 million inhabitants each), and then Spain (40 million). The Netherlands (16 million) and Switzerland (7 million) are the two smallest countries in our sample. In terms of political power, Britain and France should be judged to be more autonomous than their population sizes suggest, and Germany less so. In contrast to Germany, which until reunification was aptly described as a "semi-sovereign state" (Katzenstein 1987), Britain and France are nuclear powers with permanent UN security council seats and remaining colonial vestiges in the form of military bases abroad and privileged relations with, and influence on, former colonies. Taking everything together, we can therefore distinguish three groups of countries: Germany, France, and the United Kingdom, the EU's "big three"; then two medium powers, Italy and Spain; and finally the two small countries, the Netherlands and Switzerland. We therefore make this hypothesis:

Shares of claims by actors from the European level and from other European countries will vary inversely to a country's power and autonomy in the international system and will therefore be lowest in Germany, France, and the United Kingdom, intermediate in Italy and Spain, and highest in the Netherlands and Switzerland (H5).

Independent of the size of an economy, it seems plausible that the dependence of an economy on foreign trade (imports and exports) in general and on intra-European trade in particular will affect degrees of Europeanization. If an economy depends strongly on trade with other European countries, it becomes more relevant to follow events in these countries, and take notice of the opinions of actors from these countries, as these may have repercussions on that particular economy. Table 3.2 presents the seven countries' total trade as a percentage of gross domestic product (GDP), the share of intra-EU imports and exports in total trade, and the resulting share of intra-EU trade as a percentage of GDP. As indicated by the trade-to-GDP ratio, the Netherlands has the most open economy (66%), followed by Switzerland (45%) and Germany (38%), which has the most open economy among the larger

---

[1] These hypotheses on country differences are partly drawn from Della Porta (2003).

TABLE 3.2. *Openness of the Economy*

Country	Trade-to-GDP Ratio (%)	Share of Intra-EU Trade (%)	Intra-EU Trade-to-GDP Ratio (%)
Netherlands	66	65	43
Switzerland	45	68	30
Germany	38	65	25
Spain	28	65	18
France	27	67	18
United Kingdom	28	56	16
Italy	26	58	15

Note: Openness of the economy refers to trade-to-GDP ratios, shares of intra-EU trade, and intra-EU trade-to-GDP ratios, 2005–2007.
Source: Eurostat (2007 share of intra-EU trade), Organisation for Economic Cooperation and Development (2005 trade-to-GDP ratio), and own calculation (intra-EU trade-to-GDP ratio).

countries. The other four countries have similar levels of trade openness, in the range of 26% to 28%. The share of intra-EU trade among total trade is about equally high in Switzerland, France, Germany, Spain, and the Netherlands (65% to 68%), but it is lower in Italy (58%) and the United Kingdom (56%). Combining these two indicators (final column of the table) shows us the importance of trade with other EU countries for the national economy. The Netherlands, where intra-EU trade amounts to the value of 43% of GDP, clearly shows the highest dependence on intra-EU trade, followed, perhaps surprisingly given the fact that it is not an EU member, by Switzerland (30%). Germany comes third with 25%, followed by Spain and France (18%), and finally the United Kingdom (16%) and Italy (15%). We therefore assume the following:

Shares of claims by actors from the European level and from other European countries will vary positively with the degree of dependence of a country's economy on trade with EU countries, and will therefore be highest in the Netherlands, Switzerland, and Germany, intermediate in Spain and France, and lowest in the United Kingdom and Italy (H6).

We now turn to the second set of factors that may explain cross-national differences in degrees of Europeanization, which is the depth of a country's European integration. The first and most obvious factor here is membership in the European Union. As a nonmember, Switzerland is not directly affected by EU decisions, and there are therefore fewer incentives for it to closely follow the actions and opinions of European-level actors than for the six member countries. Countries that are not EU members also have less need to pay close attention to events on the national level in other European countries, because they are not as strongly interdependent as countries that have agreed to a common market and common governance structures. Therefore, we make the following hypothesis:

Shares of claims by actors from the European level and from other European countries will be positively associated with EU membership, and they will therefore be lower in Switzerland than in the other six countries (H7).

Among the six EU member countries, differences in degrees of Europeanization may occur as a function of the extent of a country's involvement in common European regimes. The United Kingdom has not adopted the euro and has thus opted out from what arguably constitutes both materially and symbolically the most consequential advance in European integration during our period of study. The United Kingdom has also stayed outside another highly salient advance in European integration, the Schengen Agreement, by which most European Union members, including Germany, France, Italy, Spain, and the Netherlands, established common visa policies and abolished controls along their common borders as of 1995 (1997 in the case of Italy). Whereas the United Kingdom has not implemented the Schengen Agreement, three non-EU countries, namely Norway, Iceland, and Switzerland (the latter since 2008), have joined the Schengen area. Besides these two prominent examples, during the period 1992–1997 the United Kingdom also opted out from the Social Chapter included in the Maastricht Treaty of 1992, and more recently from the Charter of Fundamental Rights, which is part of the 2007 Treaty of Lisbon. As a result of these cumulative opt-outs, the extent of the United Kingdom's involvement in European integration is significantly smaller than is the case for the other five EU member countries. Therefore, we state the following:

Among EU member countries, rates of attention for actors from the European level and from other European countries decrease with the extent of a country's opt-outs from core aspects of European integration, and they will therefore be lower in the United Kingdom than in the other five member states (H8).

Figure 3.3 allows us to test the accuracy of the predictions of these four hypotheses (H5–H8) on cross-national differences. The figure displays the shares of actors from different geospatial origins in the public debate in the seven countries. The shares of actors from extra-European countries and supranational arenas are very similar in the seven countries. We therefore focus the comparison on actors from the European level and from other European countries, compared to domestic actors. The United Kingdom stands out with by far the lowest shares of claims by European-level actors (7%) and by actors from other European countries (12%) and the highest rate of claims by domestic actors (68%). Switzerland also displays a pattern that is clearly distinct. It has average levels of claim making by European-level actors (13%), but it has by far the highest share of claims by foreign European actors (29%) and the lowest rate for domestic actors (41%). In a comparison of the United Kingdom with Switzerland, it becomes clear that there is no support for H7 about the

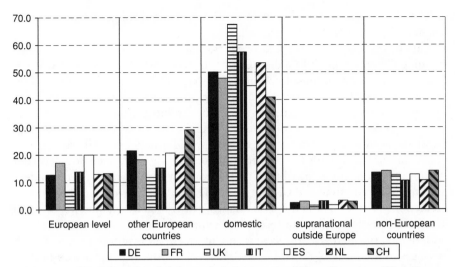

FIGURE 3.3. Spatial origin of claim makers by country (DE = Germany, FR = France, UK = United Kingdom, IT = Italy, ES = Spain, NL = the Netherlands, and CH = Switzerland).

effects of EU membership, as membership appears to be neither a sufficient nor a necessary precondition for Europeanized public debates. Although Switzerland is not an EU member, European-level actors appear twice as often and foreign European actors more than three times as often in Swiss newspapers than in the British press. However, as we will see in the next section, the fact that Switzerland is not an EU member is reflected in the type of claims that domestic Swiss actors make.

France and Germany show intermediary levels of Europeanization, which goes against H5, which stated that large, powerful countries would be more focused on domestic actors and would provide less discursive space for foreign and supranational European actors. A possible explanation for this deviation is that, unlike the United Kingdom, France and Germany have from the earliest stages made European integration an important vehicle for their national ambitions. For France, a strong role in the European Union has become a way to save some of the country's grandeur (with some success, as suggested by the overrepresentation of French actors in European media coverage as shown in Table 3.1); for Germany, it is a means to project its influence internationally while avoiding too much emphasis on its national interest and identity, which the Second World War has delegitimized both for internal and external usages. The United Kingdom, by contrast, has sought to retain some of its former imperial influence by cherishing a privileged relationship with the Anglophone superpower on the other side of the Atlantic. This implies, however, that size and power of a country as such need not be hindrances for a strong orientation on Europe. It is more a question of whether or not countries make the choice of using the European Union as a means to retain and maximize international influence, as France and Germany have, and the United Kingdom emphatically has not. H5 can therefore be rejected.

This leaves only H6 on trade openness and H8 on the effect of opt-outs standing. The extremely low degrees of Europeanization in the United Kingdom can, according to these hypotheses, be explained as a result of a combination of relatively limited economic dependence on trade with EU countries and formal opt-outs from core parts of the European integration process. Switzerland's high level of Europeanization, especially where attention for foreign European actors is concerned, can be interpreted as a result of its strong economic entwinement with EU countries, whereas Italy's relatively low levels of Europeanization can be attributed to an economy that is even less dependent on intra-EU trade than the UK economy. The only major deviation from the predictions of trade H6 is the Netherlands, which has by far the highest level of intra-EU trade but does not show the expected high levels of Europeanization. In fact, the Netherlands occupies an intermediary position, coming fourth among seven countries regarding the share of European-level actors (13%), third regarding actors from other European countries (20%), and again third where the share of domestic actors (53%) is concerned.

EUROPEAN TARGETS: THE SPATIAL SCOPE OF CLAIMS

Thus far, we have only looked at the claim makers in public debates. However, as argued in the previous chapter, this is just one element of the ways in which Europeanization of public debates can take place. In this section we will therefore broaden our view by including further elements of claim making, such as who is addressed and the scope of reference actors choose to back up their public statements. The hypotheses derived in the previous section were based on opportunity structure and political and economic interest arguments that can also be used to make predictions about the actors that are addressed and the spatial scope of a claim, that is, the polity level or levels on which the issue is situated by claimants. We refer to the combination of the addressee and scope as the "target" of a claim. Claims were classified firstly on the basis of their addressee (the actor that is explicitly targeted with criticism, support, or a call to action), and secondarily (if no explicit addressee was mentioned) on the basis of the spatial scope of the claim. In cases where reference was made to several polity levels simultaneously, the "highest" of these levels was decisive for the classification. For example, a claim referring both to the national constitution and to a European convention is classified as a claim with a European-level target. Our classification is therefore able to capture quite subtle forms of Europeanization, where most elements of a claim refer to the domestic level. Domestic claims are treated as a narrowly defined residual category, namely those that have domestic claimants and addressees, and make no reference whatsoever to nondomestic arenas. The hypotheses that we use to guide our analysis of claim targets parallel those derived in the preceding section, with the exception that we drop the hypothesis regarding power or autonomy, which received no support at all in the previous section. This results in the following hypotheses, which will guide the analysis in this section:

Claims targeted at actors and issues at the European polity level will be strongly represented in issue fields where decision making has important supranational components, that is, European integration, monetary politics, and agriculture, and will be relatively marginal in other issue fields (H1b).

Claims targeted at actors and issues in other European countries will be strongly represented in issue fields where decision making has important intergovernmental components, that is, European integration, immigration, and troop deployment, and will be relatively marginal in other issue fields (H2b).

Over the course of the period 1990–2002, the shares of claims targeted at actors and issues at the European level and in other European countries will have increased (H3b).

The increase in shares of claim making targeted at actors and issues at the European level and in other European countries will be particularly pronounced in the field of monetary politics (H4b).

Shares of claims targeted at actors and issues at the European level and in other European countries will vary positively with the degree of dependence of a country's economy on trade with EU countries, and they will therefore be highest in the Netherlands, Switzerland, and Germany, intermediate in Spain and France, and lowest in the United Kingdom and Italy (H6b).

Shares of claims targeted at actors and issues at the European level and in other European countries will be positively associated with EU membership, and they will therefore be lower in Switzerland than in the other six countries (H7b).

Among EU member countries, rates of attention for claims targeted at actors and issues at the European level and in other European countries decrease with the extent of a country's opt-outs from core aspects of European integration, and they will therefore be lower in the United Kingdom than in the other five member states (H8b).

In order not to complicate the presentation of the data unnecessarily, we omit claims made by non-European actors from further analysis and focus only on claims made by European-level actors, actors from foreign European countries, and domestic actors. According to the conceptualizations elaborated in the previous chapter, we can distinguish three types of Europeanization of claims made by European-level actors. If their claims are addressed at other European-level actors and related to Europe-wide issues, they are instances of *supranational claim making*. If they address actors or issues on the national level of one or more member states, they belong to the *top-down variant of vertical Europeanization*. Claims of the latter type can be subdivided into those directed at domestic actors and issues, and those targeted toward actors and issues in another European country.

Claims reported in the newspapers of one country that are made by actors from foreign European countries can also take three forms. If they are simply reports on the domestic or foreign politics of another European country, without any connection to either the European level or to the newspaper's country, they are examples of *weak horizontal Europeanization*. If they address domestic actors or issues in the country of the covering newspaper, they are examples of *strong horizontal Europeanization*. If they refer to actors or issues on the European level then they should be classified as a *mixture of (bottom-up) vertical and (weak) horizontal Europeanization*: vertical because a national actor directs claims at the European level, horizontal because a newspaper in one European country reports on the actions of actors in another European country.

Among claims by domestic actors, we make a somewhat finer distinction among four forms of claim making. If they are addressed at European actors or issues, they are examples of *bottom-up vertical Europeanization*. We subdivide this type of claims into two categories. First, if they have both an addressee at the European level and a European issue scope, we classify them as a *direct form of bottom-up vertical Europeanization*, because claims are directly addressed at European-level actors. Second, we distinguish an *indirect form of bottom-up vertical Europeanization*, in which domestic actors address other domestic actors, either to get something done on the European level (e.g., an agricultural subsidy) or to urge them to do something in the domestic arena but using European-level norms and rules as a legitimizing resource (e.g., to improve immigrant rights, referring to the European Convention on Human Rights, or to restrict asylum rights referring to the Dublin Convention), and in some cases also as a legitimizing reason *not* to do something (e.g., "we cannot act on our own and have to wait for a common European regulation" or "we cannot deviate from common European frameworks"). Third, if claims by domestic actors are directed at actors or issues in another European country, they are forms of *strong horizontal Europeanization*. Fourth, if domestic actors address actors and issues in the same country, they constitute classical examples of *domestic politics*. We will now look at how these ten forms of claim making vary across issues, time, and countries.

Issues

In Table 3.3 we first look at differences in patterns of claim making across issue fields. In all seven issue fields, claims by European-level actors are largely of the supranational type where they address other European-level actors on European issues. Such claims are (depending on the issue area) three to five times more numerous than claims by European-level actors directed at targets on the national level of member states (either domestic or in a foreign European country). Thus, there is little evidence for European "meddling" in the internal affairs of member states, at least not in the forum of the mass media. Apart from this finding, the issue differences across the three types of claims by European-level actors replicate the findings from the previous section, and strongly support H1b, which led us to expect all three types of claims to

TABLE 3.3. *Patterns of Multilevel Claim Making by Issue Field* (%)

Claimant	Target (Addressee and Issue Framing)	Type of Europeanization	EI	MON	AGR	IMM	TRP	PEN	EDU
European-level claimants	European-level target	Supranational	24.8	20.6	13.3	3.7	3.7	1.1	0.2
	Foreign European target	Mix vertical top-down and horizontal weak	4.3	3.0	1.4	0.8	0.6	0.0	0.0
	Domestic target	Vertical top-down	2.0	1.3	2.0	0.5	0.3	0.4	0.2
Claimants from other European countries	European-level target	Mix vertical bottom-up and horizontal weak	22.4	13.3	6.0	2.7	1.5	0.2	0.0
	Foreign European target	Horizontal weak	8.5	10.7	12.8	16.8	37.9	6.4	5.9
	Domestic target	Horizontal strong	2.1	1.1	2.2	2.7	0.8	0.6	0.3
Domestic claimants	European-level target	Vertical bottom-up direct	22.9	22.4	14.0	4.2	2.5	1.3	0.5
	Foreign European target	Horizontal strong	2.9	1.5	2.1	4.3	3.3	1.0	0.5
	Domestic target on European issue	Vertical bottom-up indirect	10.1	9.0	5.7	1.5	0.4	0.8	0.5
	Domestic target on domestic issue (including non-European foreign politics of own country)	Not Europeanized	—	17.1	40.6	62.7	49.1	88.4	91.9
TOTAL			100.0	100.0	100.0	100.0	100.0	100.0	100.0
N			2,837	1,940	916	1,312	791	894	1,937

Note: EI = European Integration, MON = Monetary Politics, AGR = Agriculture, IMM = Immigration, TRP = Troop Deployment, PEN = Pensions and Retirement, and EDU = Education.

be concentrated in the fields where supranational European policy making is relatively strongly developed, that is, European integration, monetary politics, and agriculture.

Whereas for claims by European-level actors we find a similar distribution across different targets in each of the issue fields, the results for claims by actors from foreign European countries show significant variation in the type of targets. In the fields of European integration (22%) and monetary politics (13%), the most important type of claim is that in which an actor from a foreign European country targets the European level. In the other five issue fields, by contrast, the predominant type of claims are those of the weak horizontal variant, which consist of coverage of the domestic politics of foreign European countries. In line with H2b, such attention for the domestic politics of other European countries is most prevalent in the two issue fields characterized by significant intergovernmental decision making, that is, immigration politics (17%) and troop deployment (38%; this latter percentage should be seen in the perspective of the earlier results, which showed that most claims on troop deployment are made by extra-European actors, which are not included in the present analysis).[2] The final type of claims by foreign European actors, those of the strong horizontal type with targets in the reporting newspaper's own country, turn out to be marginal in all issue fields, reaching a maximum of 3% in immigration politics.

Turning now to claims made by domestic actors, we find in line with H1b that both the direct and the indirect forms of bottom-up vertically Europeanized claim making are predominantly found in European integration (33% taking direct and indirect forms together), monetary politics (31%), and agricultural politics (22%). Comparing the direct and indirect forms, we find that the direct forms predominate in all issue fields (except education, where both types are equally unimportant); in other words, the majority of claims with European issue frames are not addressed at domestic actors, but either directly address European institutions and actors or do not explicitly mention an addressee. Strongly horizontally Europeanized claims again are relatively marginal, but, in line with H2b, they are mostly found in the three issue fields where intergovernmental European decision making promotes cross-national interdependence, namely immigration (4%), troop deployment (3%), and European integration (3%). Purely domestic claims, finally, are in line with the combined predictions of Hypotheses 1b and 2b most prevalent in the fields of pensions and retirement (88%) and education (92%). In immigration politics, purely domestic claims account for close to two-thirds of all claims (63%), whereas in troop deployment they amount to almost half of all claims (49%). As expected, the only issue

---

[2] The relatively low percentage of weak horizontal claims in the field of European integration is a bit of a methodological artefact, as any claims by actors from foreign European countries that have no explicitly stated addressee are automatically classified as belonging to the category of "mixed vertical bottom-up and horizontal weak" because the field of European integration by definition has a European-level issue scope.

fields where claims that are Europeanized in one way or another predominate are agriculture (59% Europeanized), monetary politics (83% Europeanized), and European integration (which is by definition always Europeanized).

Claims belonging to the two forms of strong, horizontal claim making (those with domestic claimants and those with foreign European claimants) together account for between 1% (education) and 7% (immigration) of all claims. These very modest shares indicate that European integration produces only very weak tendencies toward direct communicative interaction across national boundaries. If we add weakly horizontally Europeanized claims, the total flow of communication that crosses European borders becomes more sizeable, particularly as H2b predicted in the intergovernmental fields of troop deployment (42%) and immigration (28%). With the exception of the three fields where decision making has strong supranational components, horizontally Europeanized claims dominate strongly over vertically Europeanized claims.

Time

Next we turn in Table 3.4 to changes in patterns of claim making across the period 1990–2002. The results are in line with the trends found in the previous section regarding the actors who make claims, but they provide additional insight into how patterns of claim making have changed over time. In line with H3b we find a clear increase, from 10% in 1990 to 14% in 2002, in purely supranational claim making, whereby European-level claimants target European-level actors and issues. There is no trend, however, toward increased vertical claim making, both by European-level claimants (stable at around 3%) and foreign European claimants (stable at around 9%), and by domestic actors (stable at around 17%). The only weak trend in vertical claim making that is in line with H3b is that direct forms of vertical claim making (from 11% in 1990 to 12% in 2002) increase slightly in importance compared to indirect forms in which domestic actors are addressed on European issues (from 6% in 1990 to 5% in 2002). This indicates that European-level actors have become more important over time not only as claimants, but to a limited degree also as addressees by national-level claimants.

More clearly than when we looked only at claimants, Table 3.4 shows that the trend for horizontal forms of claim making goes in the opposite direction, particularly because of a marked decline in the share of weak horizontal claims. Coverage of domestic claim making in other European countries declined from 16% in 1990 to 10% in 2002. H3b is therefore confirmed with regard to the predicted increase in claims with European-level targets, but it is clearly refuted by the equally important decline in coverage of claims directed at foreign European targets. The overall result is that we cannot discern any general trend toward denationalization of claim making, as the share of purely domestic claims is stable at around 43%.

As expected on the basis of H4b, temporal trends are most pronounced in the domain of monetary politics (results not shown in table), in which

TABLE 3.4. *Patterns of Multilevel Claim Making by Year* (%)

Claimant	Target/Framing	Type of Europeanization	1990	1995	2000	2002
European-level claimants	European-level target	Supranational	9.8	7.3	13.7	13.9
	Foreign European target	Mix vertical top-down and horizontal weak	1.7	1.1	2.4	1.9
	Domestic target	Vertical top-down	0.9	1.4	0.9	1.2
Claimants from other European countries	European-level target	Mix vertical bottom-up and horizontal weak	8.6	8.5	10.0	9.4
	Foreign European target	Horizontal weak	16.0	15.9	10.3	10.4
	Domestic target	Horizontal strong	1.2	2.0	1.7	1.1
Domestic claimants	European-level target	Vertical bottom-up direct	11.3	10.6	13.4	12.1
	Foreign European target	Horizontal strong	1.9	2.3	2.2	2.2
	Domestic target on European issue	Vertical bottom-up indirect	5.7	5.4	5.5	4.5
	Domestic target on domestic issue	Not Europeanized	43.0	45.6	39.8	43.3
TOTAL			100.0	100.0	100.0	100.0
N			1,378	1,457	4,123	3,668

Note: In the Target/Framing column, domestic target on domestic issue includes non-European foreign politics of own country.

supranational forms of claim making increased strongly from 7% in 1990 to 27% in 2002. Bottom-up vertical forms of claim making targeted at European-level actors and issues also strongly increased over this period, both by actors from other countries (from 8% to 14%) and by domestic actors (from 14% to 24%). Coverage of the domestic monetary politics of other countries (the weak horizontal type), however, strongly declined, from 15% in 1990 to 7% in 2002 (results not shown in table). Strong forms of horizontal claim making also declined, from 4% in 1990 to 2% in 2002 (taking the two subforms with respectively foreign national and domestic claimants together). Like H3b, H4b is thus only confirmed where vertical forms of Europeanization are concerned, whereas horizontal Europeanization has actually declined strongly.

Monetary politics is the only one among the six substantive policy fields in which there is a clear decline in the importance of purely domestic claims, from 39% in 1990 to 10% in 2002, with the latter 10% belonging exclusively to the British and Swiss cases. This is due to the fact that with the full supranational-ization of this policy field in the Eurozone countries, monetary politics claims in these countries have by definition acquired a European dimension, and purely domestic claim making as we have defined it is no longer possible. With this strong decline of purely national claim making, monetary politics is, however, an exception. In the field of agriculture, purely domestic claims have become only slightly less frequent (from 36% in 1990 to 32% in 2002). By contrast, in the other four substantive issue fields we can either discern tendencies toward renationalization with rising shares of claims with purely domestic references (immigration from 44% to 68% purely domestic claims, troop deployment from 48% to 56%), or a stable pattern with very high levels (pensions and retirement and education with levels around 90%) of purely domestic claim making. In other words, across the seven issue fields, there is no general trend towards Europeanization of claim making. Instead, Europeanization is limited to the two fields where Europe has acquired supranational decision-making powers, that is, agriculture and especially monetary politics.

Countries

We now turn in Table 3.5 to differences in patterns of claim making across the seven countries. We find that supranational forms of claim making are most prevalent in Spain (20%), and least so in the United Kingdom (6%). Contrary to the expectation of H7b, the Swiss media cover claims on the European supranational level at an average level compared to the other countries. High levels of Swiss attention for what transpires in European Union politics are also indicated by the fact that Swiss newspapers have the highest rates of attention for claims by foreign-national actors targeted at European-level actors and issues (13%). Regarding this type of claim, the United Kingdom again displays the lowest level of attention (7%), but here Italy also scores poorly (8%). This pattern is repeated if we look at the coverage of the domestic politics of other countries, which is by far the highest in Switzerland (21%), lowest in the United Kingdom (6%), and also comparatively low in Italy (9%).

TABLE 3.5. *Patterns of Multilevel Claim Making by Country (%)*

Claimant	Target/Framing	Type of Europeanization	Germany	France	United Kingdom	Italy	Spain	The Netherlands	Switzerland
European-level claimants	European-level target	Supranational	12.1	16.0	5.9	13.4	19.8	11.1	12.8
	Foreign European target	Mix vertical top-down and horizontal weak	2.0	3.3	0.6	1.6	2.4	2.4	2.2
	Domestic target	Vertical top-down	1.0	1.2	1.2	0.9	1.2	1.4	0.9
Claimants from other European countries	European-level target	Mix vertical bottom-up and horizontal weak	9.1	10.3	6.5	7.5	12.0	9.4	13.4
	Foreign European target	Horizontal weak	13.7	10.2	5.8	9.1	10.5	12.9	21.2
	Domestic target	Horizontal strong	2.7	1.4	1.5	1.0	1.5	0.8	0.4
Domestic claimants	European-level target	Vertical bottom-up direct	13.8	16.0	13.4	8.0	16.3	12.5	7.8
	Foreign European target	Horizontal strong	3.0	1.9	1.8	1.3	2.4	3.1	1.7
	Domestic target on European issue	Vertical bottom-up indirect	3.7	4.7	9.1	3.8	3.3	4.9	6.3
	Domestic target on domestic issue	Not Europeanized	39.0	35.0	54.2	53.3	30.7	41.4	33.3
TOTAL			100.0	100.0	100.0	100.0	100.0	100.0	100.0
N			2,377	1,182	1,786	1,743	972	1,175	1,392

Note: In the Target/Framing column, domestic target on domestic issue includes non-European foreign politics of own country.

Regarding claims by domestic actors, we find that the Swiss pattern reflects that the country is not an EU member: Direct bottom-up claims by domestic actors targeting the European level have the lowest prevalence in Switzerland (8%), although the Italian level of this type of claims is also very low (8%). The results in Table 3.5 also somewhat relativize the low levels of Europeanization that we found thus far for the United Kingdom. As it turns out, a sizeable share of claims by domestic British actors are targeted at the European level. The share of direct vertical claims is close to the average for the seven countries (13%). The United Kingdom, moreover, leaves all other countries behind where indirect forms of vertical claim making by domestic actors are concerned, that is, claims addressing other domestic actors on European issues (9%). The share of indirect and direct forms of vertical claim making by domestic actors taken together is also highest in the United Kingdom (23%). This reflects the fact that European integration is a highly contentious issue in British domestic politics. Even though the United Kingdom still comes out as the country with the overall lowest level of Europeanized claims (46%), we can now see that this is entirely due to low levels of attention for claims by European-level and foreign national actors, and not to low levels of claim making on European issues by domestic actors, which are actually more frequent than in the other countries. British public debate is Europeanized, but in a very parochial way, being focused mainly on what British actors do and say with regard to Europe. The Swiss pattern is diametrically opposed. Domestic Swiss actors do not address European issues very frequently (14%), especially not in a direct way. However, Swiss media debates show the highest level of attention for claims by nondomestic actors.

All in all, these results, like those in the previous section, conform to the expectations drawn from the trade openness (H6b) and opt-out (H8b) hypotheses. In addition, however, the role of EU membership (H7b) now comes clearer to the fore, explaining the relatively low salience of European issues among Swiss domestic actors, and their high salience for British domestic actors. The Netherlands continues to deviate somewhat from our expectations because they show average levels of all types of Europeanized claim making, whereas their full participation in European integration and very high level of intra-EU trade had led us to expect Dutch public debates to be the most Europeanized among the seven countries.

The results for the two countries that stand out most can, however, be well understood by using a combination of the trade openness, EU membership, and opt-out hypotheses. In the Swiss case, non-EU membership in combination with a high level of trade with EU countries leads to a pattern of high levels of horizontal Europeanization, but low levels of vertically Europeanized claim making by domestic actors. In the British case, low levels of intra-EU trade combined with a series of opt-outs from European integration and a high level of contestation among domestic actors on European issues leads to the opposite pattern of low levels of horizontal Europeanization, but high levels of vertically Europeanized claim making by domestic actors.

EVALUATIONS OF EUROPEAN INTEGRATION
AND EUROPEAN INSTITUTIONS

Our next step is to ask whether Europeanized claims take a positive or a negative position toward European integration. We distinguish two aspects of actors' stances toward European integration. First, for all claims with a European-level target we coded whether they were favorable or unfavorable toward further European integration. Each claim that argued for an extension or against restrictions of the European Union's competences or membership received a score of +1 on this position variable. Claims that argued for restrictions or against extensions in the European Union's competencies and membership received a score of −1. Claims that did not take a position with regard to the direction of European integration or that were ambivalent in this regard received a score of 0. Second, in those cases in which claims directly addressed European-level actors or institutions (i.e., those of the supranational and direct bottom-up Europeanization types), we looked at how actors evaluated these European-level addressees. A score of −1 was given when the claim implied a critical evaluation of the addressee; +1 indicated support, and 0 indicated an ambivalent or neutral stance with regard to the addressee.

Issues

Again, we start by discussing differences across issue fields. As we have seen, the more decision-making competencies European-level institutions have, and the more these competencies have a supranational rather than intergovernmental nature, the greater is the amount of Europeanized claim making in the public debate in the mass media. Here we hypothesize that the rising salience of decision making on the European level goes along with rising controversy over these competencies and increased challenges of the concrete decisions that European institutions take. As long as in a particular issue field European decision-making powers are limited and only mildly consequential for most European citizens, a permissive consensus can prevail, characterized by low levels of attention, and a relatively supportive or at least indifferent attitude with regard to European integration and the role of European institutions. Once Europe gains consequential decision-making powers in an issue field, both levels of attention and levels of criticism will rise, implying what one might call a *normalization* of Europeanized contention toward what is customary in national politics, namely intense and controversial debate. Thus we make the following hypothesis:

Negative attitudes toward further European integration and criticism of European institutional actors will be greatest in those issue fields where European-level decision-making powers are the most extensive; in other words, they will be most prevalent in monetary and agricultural politics, less so in the fields of immigration and troop deployment, and least widespread in the fields of pensions and retirement and education (H9).

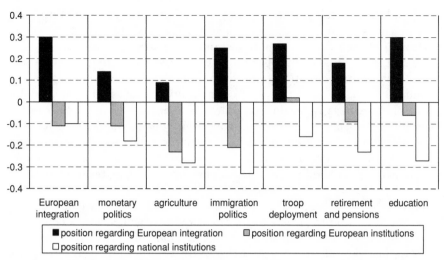

FIGURE 3.4. Evaluation of European integration and European institutions by issue field.

To test this hypothesis, Figure 3.4 shows the average position toward European integration across issue fields, as well as the balance of criticism and support for the actions of European institutions regarding these issues. To have a standard of comparison for the normalization thesis, we compare the evaluation of European institutions to that of national institutions in non-Europeanized claim making on the same issue. Several important conclusions can be drawn. First, in all seven issue fields, claim making is on average supportive of further European integration, indicating broad support for the general direction of the European project. At the same time, claim makers are in six of the seven issue fields critical of the concrete actions and positions taken by European institutions. However, this cannot be straightforwardly interpreted as a sign of Euroscepticism, as the role of European institutions is generally evaluated less negatively than that of national institutions. Rather, one may describe the overall pattern as one of "critical Europeanism" (Della Porta and Caiani 2007a), combining support in principle for further European integration with critical stances toward the concrete policy positions and actions of European institutions and actors.

If we compare the results across issue fields, we find that they are broadly in line with H9. Positions with regard to further integration are least positive in monetary politics and agriculture, where European integration has already proceeded quite far, and where fewer actors are in favor of further extensions of European competencies and critical of the current state of affairs. By contrast, in immigration politics, troop deployment, pensions and retirement, and education politics, there is quite strong support for further European integration. In line with H9, positions regarding European institutions are least critical in three fields where European competencies are relatively weakly developed: troop deployment, pensions and retirement, and education. Troop deployment is the only issue field where we find a slightly positive average evaluation of the role of European institutional actors. The strongly negative evaluation of the role of European institutions in immigration politics seems at first sight to be a deviation from this pattern, but here we should take into account that this is generally a very controversial field, as indicated by the yet much more negative evaluation score for national institutional actors. As in troop deployment, pensions, and education politics, the distance between the evaluation of European and national institutional actors is relatively large in immigration politics, indicating that the actions of European institutions in this field are generally seen as less controversial than those of national actors.

In line with the expectations, the fields of European integration, monetary politics, and agriculture, where European actors have gained strong competencies, show signs of a normalization of the evaluation of European institutions. Here we find the smallest deviations from the evaluation of national actors. European integration is the only issue field in which the role of European actors is judged slightly more negatively than that of national actors. All in all, these results provide strong support for H9, with the qualification that the boundary between issues with weak and strong support for European integration and weaker and stronger criticism of the role of European institutions runs especially between the fields with strong supranational European governance (monetary politics and agriculture) and the other issue fields.

Time

The normalization thesis not only predicts issue differences in support for European integration but also leads us to expect that, as European-level competencies have increased over time, support for further steps in the European integration process will have declined, and the role of European institutional actors will be regarded more critically. Thus we make the following hypothesis:

With increasing transfers of competencies toward the European level over the period 1990–2002, support for further European integration will have eroded and the role of European institutional actors will have come to be viewed more critically (H10).

The results displayed in Figure 3.5 fully confirm H10 where support for the European integration process is concerned. Even though in 2002 the average evaluation of the integration process was still positive (+0.19), the level of support had strongly declined compared to 1990 (+0.39). Starting out from different levels, this erosion of support for further European integration is visible in all seven countries, providing strong support for the normalization thesis. From 1990 to 2000, we see a similar development of increasing criticism of European institutional actors, with average evaluations declining from −0.04 to −0.20 in 2000. After that, however, evaluations of European institutions

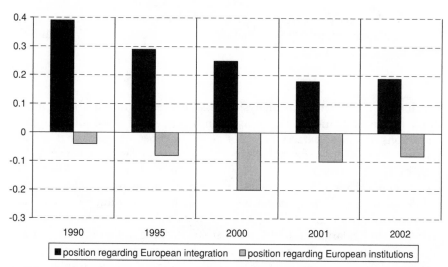

FIGURE 3.5. Development of the evaluation of European integration and European institutions, 1990–2002.

become less negative again, rising to an average evaluation of −0.08 in 2002, the same level of criticism as in 1995.

A closer qualitative inspection of the data shows that the peak in criticism in 2000 is due to various issues in the fields of monetary politics and European integration. In monetary politics the introduction of the euro stirred controversy, leading to a decline in evaluations of European institutions in that field from −0.02 in 1990 to −0.21 in 2000. After its introduction, however, the common currency gained legitimacy, reflected in rising evaluations of the role of European institutions up to a score of −0.08 in 2002. In the field of European integration, increased criticism was related to three controversial issues. First, the provisions in the Nice Treaty introducing qualified majority voting were seen by various actors as an infringement on national sovereignty and an overextension of the EU's power. In the case of Britain, the European Charter on Human Rights, from which the United Kingdom decided to opt out, was another focus of criticism. Second, there were controversial discussions on the European Union's course toward Turkey's membership candidacy, which many actors objected against. Third, the European Union's decision to sanction Austria for the participation of Jörg Haider's right-populist FPÖ (Freiheitliche Partei Österreichs, or the Freedom Party of Austria) in the government drew a wave of criticism, not only from Austria but also from actors in other countries across Europe. Generally, the critical debates that peaked in 2000 can be seen as revolving around the issue of overextension of the European Union, both geographically and in the sense of infringing on the sovereignty of individual member states. While these debates lost some of their intensity in the two subsequent years, it was precisely these issues that returned with full force to the agenda in the later controversies around the European Constitution and the Treaty of Lisbon, which were rejected in the 2005 referenda in France and the Netherlands, and in 2008 in Ireland.

Countries

As a final step in the empirical analysis of this chapter, we turn to cross-national differences in evaluations of the European integration process and European institutions. Because Switzerland is not an EU member, claims in that country mostly refer to a different set of issues than those in the six member states. In Switzerland, the main issue is whether to join the European Union or not, which implies that the evaluative dimension refers to the perceived advantages and disadvantages of *becoming* a member. In the other countries, the advantages and disadvantages of *being* a member, as well as evaluations of further deepening and enlarging the EU, are at stake. Because of these fundamentally different points of reference, it does not make much sense to compare evaluations of European integration in the Swiss media directly with those in the other countries. Therefore, our hypotheses will refer only to expected differences among the six member countries. At the end of this section, we will briefly discuss the results for Switzerland.

As a general point of departure, we hypothesize that a member country's position toward European integration and European institutions will be more positive, the higher are the material benefits received from European integration. In this light, one of the hypotheses that we developed to explain levels of Europeanization of claim making also seems useful to explain the evaluative direction of Europeanized claims. The stronger a country's economy is oriented toward intra-EU trade, the greater will be the country's material interest in the maintenance and extension of the institutions and regulations governing the common market:

The greater the dependence on intra-EU trade, the more positive will be the evaluation of the European integration process and of European institutions. Therefore, we expect support to be highest in the Netherlands and Germany, intermediary in Spain and France, and lowest in Italy and the United Kingdom (H11).

We propose two further hypotheses. Apart from dependence on intra-EU trade, the material benefits that a country draws from European integration depend on whether it is a net beneficiary of, or a net contributor to, the European Union. Table 3.6 (computed on the basis of Della Porta 2003, p. 11) shows the average yearly budgetary balance (using the European Commission's United Kingdom rebate definition) for the period 1994–2000. Among our six member states, Spain is the only country that had a strongly positive balance of benefits during the period of study, amounting to no less than 4% of the Spanish GDP each year. The other five countries were all net contributors, but the Netherlands (−0.39%) and Germany (−0.57%) more so than France,

TABLE 3.6. *Budgetary Balance of Payments to, and Received from, the EU as a Percentage of GDP*

Country	Percentage
Germany	−0.57
France	−0.14
United Kingdom	−0.21
Italy	−0.13
Spain	+3.99
Netherlands	−0.39

Note: The budgetary balance reflects yearly averages, 1994–2000.
Source: The allocation of 2000 EU operating expenditure is by member state. Brussels: European Commission (2001).

the United Kingdom, and Italy (−0.14%, −0.21%, and −0.13%, respectively). Therefore we make the following hypothesis:

The more positive the balance of payment transfers to and from the European Union, the greater will be support for European integration and European institutions. Therefore, we expect support to be by far the highest in Spain, intermediary in France, the United Kingdom, and the Italy, and lowest in Germany and the Netherlands (H12).

Finally, we hypothesize that countries develop an interest in maintaining and furthering European integration, the more they are able to influence debates on the direction it takes. Countries with a disproportionately large share in Europeanized debates will thus be more supportive of further integration and of the role of European institutions than actors who are underrepresented in these debates. Table 3.1 has shown that Germany, France, and the United Kingdom have a disproportionately large voice in debates on European integration, with France standing out with a particularly strong overrepresentation compared to its share of the European population. By contrast, we found that the two medium European powers, Italy and Spain, are strongly underrepresented in European debates. The smaller countries of the European Union, including the Netherlands, were represented in European debates roughly in proportion to their population share. This leads us to the following hypothesis:

The more a country is overrepresented in Europeanized debates compared to its share in the European population, the more will it be supportive of European integration and European institutions. Therefore, we expect support to be strongest in France, also comparatively strong in Germany and the United Kingdom, intermediary in the Netherlands, and weakest in Italy and Spain (H13).

Figure 3.6 shows the average position toward European integration and European institutions in the media debate in the seven countries. To better judge the significance of evaluations of European institutional actors, we have

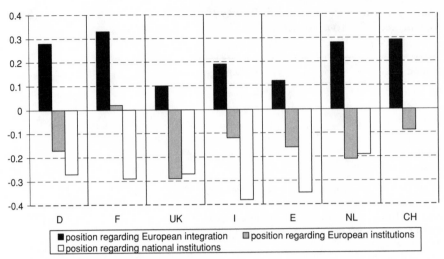

FIGURE 3.6. Evaluation of European integration and European institutions by country (D = Germany, F = France, UK = United Kingdom, I = Italy; E = Spain, NL = the Netherlands, and CH = Switzerland).

added the average evaluation of national institutional actors in debates with a purely national frame of reference. The figure shows that support for the European integration process is strongest in the French media debate (average evaluation of +0.33). In Germany and the Netherlands (both at +0.28) we also find relatively high levels of support, whereas Spain (+0.12) and the United Kingdom (+0.10) show the lowest levels of support for the European integration process. Italy (+0.19) takes an intermediary position.

Regarding the evaluation of European institutions, France again tops the bill as the only country where the evaluation of European institutions is on average slightly positive (+0.02). Here, too, the United Kingdom is situated at the other end of the spectrum (−0.29). Here, however, we find that the German (−0.17) and Dutch (−0.21) public debates are comparatively critical of European institutions, whereas Spain (−0.12) and Italy (−0.16) show somewhat lower levels of criticism of European institutions. These findings develop further meaning when we compare them to the evaluation of national institutional actors. In France and Italy, European institutions are evaluated much less negatively (or, in the French case, even positively) compared to national institutional actors. In Spain and Germany, European institutions are also viewed less negatively than national ones, but the difference is smaller. In the United Kingdom and the Netherlands, however, national institutions are viewed slightly more positively than European ones.

To look at the combinations of evaluations of the European integration process and of European institutions more directly, we conducted an additional analysis of the subset of claims that entailed both an evaluation of the integration process, and of European institutions, excluding from the analysis those

TABLE 3.7. *Distribution of Europhile, Eurosceptic, and Critically Europeanist Claims by Country*

Country	Europhile (%)	Eurosceptic (%)	Critically Europeanist (%)	Total (%)	N
Germany	45.3	42.2	12.5	100.0	991
France	54.6	35.1	10.3	100.0	909
United Kingdom	35.1	61.2	3.8	100.0	348
Italy	51.0	40.4	8.6	100.0	502
Spain	40.4	50.2	9.4	100.0	223
Netherlands	43.5	38.5	17.9	100.0	496
Switzerland	52.2	39.3	8.4	100.0	542

cases in which both evaluations were neutral or ambivalent. We distinguish three types of positions. First, *Europhile* positions are characterized by positive evaluations of both the integration process and of European institutions Second, *Eurosceptic* claims are characterized by negative evaluations of both. Third, we distinguish claims combining positive evaluations of the European integration process with critique of European institutions, which we describe as *critical Europeanism* (Della Porta and Caiani 2007a).[3] Among the critically Europeanist claims we also include the rare reverse combination in which European institutions were supported for being prudent or reluctant regarding further extensions of the integration process, most importantly in the context of the enlargement process. An example was when Amnesty International urged the European Commission to stick firmly to its human rights criteria in negotiations on Turkish membership. Table 3.7 shows how claims were distributed across the three types of stances toward European integration in the seven countries.

The table shows that most claims fall into one of the two nonambiguous categories of Europhile and Eurosceptic claims. Europhile positions are most frequent in France, where they account for 55% of all claims. Also in Italy, a comparatively large percentage of claims is Europhile (51%). On the other side, the United Kingdom has by far the lowest percentage of Europhile claims (35%). Euroscepticism is with 61% of claims most widespread in the United Kingdom, and also quite widespread in Spain (50%). The French public debate contains the least Eurosceptic claim making (35%), which is also not so widespread in the Netherlands (39%). Critically Europeanist claims, which are characterized by a positive attitude toward European integration per se but a critique of current shortcomings, such as a lack of accountability, transparency,

---

[3] In terms of technical operationalization, the Europhile position is defined as having at least one of the two evaluations positive and none negative; Euroscepticism is defined by at least one of the two evaluations negative and none positive; and critical Europeanism is defined by a positive evaluation of the European integration process and a negative evaluation of the role of current European institutions.

or efficiency, are a comparatively small minority everywhere. They are, however, most prevalent in the Netherlands (18%) and to a lesser extent Germany (13%). By contrast, criticism of the European Union in the United Kingdom is seldom of a constructive nature. Against 61% fully negative Eurosceptic claims stand only 4% claims that combine criticism of European institutions with a positive stance toward the integration process.

How does this pattern fit the three hypotheses (H11–H13) on cross-national differences in support for European integration? The pattern cannot easily be reconciled with any single one of these hypotheses. The balance of payments hypothesis, H12, receives the least support because Spain, which is by far the strongest beneficiary of transfers, is the country with the second-lowest level of support for European integration. France's strong advocacy for European integration is best understood in the light of the discursive influence hypothesis (H13). Our data provide suggestive evidence that France is the country that has best succeeded in boosting its influence through European integration, creating a symbiosis between European integration and the French national interest. This hypothesis may also help us understand why enthusiasm about European integration is tempered in the Spanish and Italian media, because these countries have not been able to put a strong mark on European debates during the period of study. The United Kingdom's strongly Eurosceptic position can best be understood in the light of the country's comparatively limited dependence on intra-EU trade (H11).

To understand the comparatively strong prevalence of critical Europeanism in the Netherlands and Germany, the balance of payments hypothesis offers the best explanation. The two other hypotheses predict high levels of support in these countries, which have high levels of intra-EU trade and a reasonably proportionate influence in European debates. This should make them loyal EU members, were it not for the fact that they are strong net contributors who sometimes feel that they pay too much and are not always convinced of the efficiency of EU institutions. Being a strong net contributor over prolonged periods of time creates legitimacy problems for the EU, even among the most loyal members. Thus, all three hypotheses make some contribution to the clarification of the cross-national differences found, even though, standing alone, none of them offers a sufficient explanation of patterns of support and opposition toward European integration.

Finally, we briefly look at the results for Switzerland. Overall (see Figure 3.6), public debates in this country are relatively positive toward European integration (+0.29) and not very critical of the role of European institutions (−0.09). The stumbling block on the road to Swiss membership that our data reveal is that claim makers in the Swiss media give by far the highest grades to their national institutions (an average score of 0.00). Therefore, the comparison between the evaluation of European and national institutions ends up more negative in Switzerland than in any of the other countries. Indeed, worries over the loss of typically Swiss institutional features such as communal and cantonal autonomy, strong direct-democratic institutions, and the country's well-guarded international neutrality are known to play an important role in Swiss hesitations about joining the European Union (Christin and Trechsel 2002).

CONCLUSIONS

In political and scholarly debates about Europeanization, it is often assumed that public debates in mass media pay only scant reference to European actors and issues, and that if reference to them is made then such claims refer to European integration and European institutions primarily in a negative light. Too little and too negative attention for European actors and issues in public debates in the mass media are seen as important reasons behind a lack of knowledge and scepticism about European integration among the general public. The data presented in this chapter show that there is no empirical basis for these assumptions.

We found strong support for our hypotheses drawn from a political opportunity structure perspective, which state that the roles of various actors and references to different polity levels in public debates depend first and foremost on the formal distribution of power among polity levels, and on whether European decision making takes a primarily supranational or intergovernmental form. Contrary to the claim of lacking attention for European actors and issues, we found that actors from the European polity level were highly visible participants in public debates in those issue fields where the European Union has gained strong supranational competencies – monetary politics, agriculture, and European integration. These were also the policy fields where European actors and policy contexts were mentioned most often as targets of claims. Immigration and troop deployment, the two policy fields where European policy making is more limited and primarily intergovernmental, displayed lower levels of Europeanization of claim making (see Meyer 2010), which moreover was more often of the horizontally Europeanized variant in which reference was made to actors and issues in other European countries rather than to actors and issues on the European polity level. Only in the fields of education and pensions and retirement policies did we find that public debates paid hardly any attention to European-level and foreign actors and issues. In the light of our comparative findings, however, this cannot be ascribed to a lack of media attention for European dimensions – which is flatly contradicted by high levels of attention in those issue fields where Europe does matter a lot – but to the simple fact that in these issue fields the European Union has thus far gained only limited prerogatives and the national political arena remains strongly predominant as a relevant frame of reference for collective actors.

Looking at developments over time, we found that across the period 1990–2002, levels of Europeanization have increased as the political opportunity structure perspective led us to hypothesize, and particularly where we would expect this to be most pronounced, namely in monetary politics. However, these increases pertained exclusively to vertical Europeanization in which

European-level actors and policy contexts figure either as claim makers or as targets of claims. By contrast, horizontal forms of Europeanization stagnated or sometimes even declined. This, too, is most clearly visible in the field of monetary politics, suggesting that there is a certain degree of trade-off between vertical and horizontal Europeanization, in which increased supranationalization of policy making erodes direct transnational communicative linkages. This transforms the communicative structure from a horizontal, transnational network structure into a hierarchical, vertical structure, in which actors in national polities are linked indirectly through common references to European actors and policy contexts (Chapter 7 on political communication on the Internet reveals a similar pattern).

The upshot of this is that, during the period of study, we do not so much observe a general shift toward Europeanized claim making but rather primarily a shift within the category of Europeanized claims, in the direction of claims involving European-level claimants and addressees, and away from coverage of domestic claim making of other European countries. Arguably, this is a shift from weaker toward stronger forms of Europeanization, but it is important to note that this takes the form of a shift from foreign-political toward European coverage, rather than a shift from domestic to Europeanized claim making. This result therefore better fits the intergovernmentalist perspective (e.g., Moravcsik 1993, 1998), which sees European integration as a state-centered process of "foreign politics by other means," rather than the Europeanization perspective (e.g., Hix and Goetz 2000), which tends to see European integration as leading to a transformation of domestic politics.

We also did not find support for the thesis that public debates in mass media are characterized by a particularly negative evaluative bias toward European actors and the European integration process. Our data document the end of the permissive consensus in the sense that evaluations of the European integration process have over time become less positive and those of European actors and institutions more negative. However, there is no basis for reading an anti-European bias into this. To begin with, even though support is no longer as unequivocal as it was at the beginning of the 1990s, on average the evaluations of the European integration process remained positive throughout the period of study. Moreover, the negative evaluations of European actors and institutions are strongly relativized by the fact that evaluations of domestic actors and institutions were even more negative.

European actors may yet have to become accustomed to the fact that public debates are generally focused on political contestation rather than on highlighting areas of consensus, for the simple reason that public actors generally have few incentives to make public statements in support of others with whom they compete for influence, resources, and votes. Some critics of the allegedly deficient European public sphere seem to want to have it both ways: high levels of attention and high levels of public support for European institutions, but this is simply not a realistic scenario given how public debates function in democracies. Instead of anti-European biases, our data document a gradual normalization of public debates over European integration characterized by both higher levels of attention and higher levels of controversy, bringing public debates on European issues ever closer to the usual pattern found in domestic public debates. Rather than deplore this trend, supporters of European integration would do well to embrace it, as precisely these rising levels of criticism and controversy – which not coincidentally are most pronounced in those issue fields where Europe's influence is greatest – are evidence of the European Union's coming of age.

Although these issue differences and temporal trends apply to all seven countries of our study, we found some important cross-national variation. Theoretically, these differences were best explained by a number of political opportunity structure and economic and political interest variables. Countries with high levels of dependence on intra-EU trade (the Netherlands, Germany, and Switzerland) tended to display higher levels of Europeanization and more favorable evaluations of European integration. Disproportionate influence in Europeanized public debates (France) also seemed to contribute to favorable evaluations of European integration. By contrast, countries with lower dependence on intra-EU trade (the United Kingdom and Italy), comparatively marginal influence in transnational European debates (Spain and Italy), and particularly countries that have opted out from important aspects of European integration (the United Kingdom) showed lower degrees of Europeanization and more negative evaluations of the integration process and European institutions.

Membership of the European Union turned out to be neither associated with high levels of Europeanization nor with support for European integration and European institutions (which were both lower in the United Kingdom than in non-EU-member Switzerland). However, EU membership did affect types of Europeanization. In the Swiss case, Europeanization of public debates took the form of high rates of claims by foreign actors on European issues, whereas Swiss domestic actors made fewer EU-related claims than did their counterparts in the other six countries. In the United Kingdom, we found the opposite pattern, with few claims by actors from the European level and from other European countries, but high levels of domestic contestation over Europe.

The degree to which a country profits from monetary transfers within the European Union did not provide an explanation for levels of support for European integration and European institutions, as Spain, which is by far the strongest net recipient among our countries of study, displayed the second-lowest (after the United Kingdom) level of support for European integration and European institutions. However, patterns of support and criticism in Germany and the Netherlands may be influenced by the fact that these countries have consistently been strong net contributors. Actors in these countries comparatively frequently display a pattern of critical Europeanism in which support for the integration process is coupled with criticism of concrete European policies and institutions.

Overall, France comes out as the clearest supporter of European integration, Germany and the Netherlands as critical supporters, and the United Kingdom as the uncontested champion of Euroscepticism. The Spanish and Italian positions are less outspoken, but Spain tends more toward the Eurosceptic pole, and Italy is more a lukewarm supporter. In the latter two countries, criticism of European institutions is somewhat relativized by the fact that national institutional actors are viewed strongly negatively, which may make Europe appear as the lesser evil. The reverse is true in the Netherlands and the United Kingdom, the only two member countries in which national institutions are viewed more positively than European ones. This also applies to Switzerland, in which the main barrier toward membership does not seem to be a particularly critical attitude toward European institutions, but the fact that national institutions are regarded even more positively.

4

Winners and Losers, Supporters and Opponents in Europeanized Public Debates

Ruud Koopmans

INTRODUCTION AND THEORETICAL FRAMEWORK

In the previous chapter, we focused on degrees, types, and evaluations of Europeanization of public debates across issue fields, countries, and time. Although most studies of Europe and the media stop at this level of analysis, the public debate is ultimately carried by the strategic and often conflictive discursive actions of concrete collective actors. Europeanization is therefore not just a phenomenon that we can read from aggregate measures of media content, but also a particular type of discursive strategy that some actors are able and willing to choose, whereas other actors may employ – either by choice or by lack of other options – discursive strategies that remain national in focus and content. Moreover, when actors make Europeanized claims, they may do so both to support and to oppose the European integration process and European institutions.[1]

The advantage of our claim-making approach is that we are able to make this shift to the actor level of analysis and to investigate which actors are more likely than others to make Europeanized claims, and which are more likely to support the integration process and European institutions. Moving to the actor level is also important to assess whether the European integration process is affected by a democratic deficit and an attendant communication deficit. The results presented in Chapter 3 show that if there is a public sphere aspect to the European democratic deficit, the problem is not that European actors and issues are not sufficiently present in public debates or that they are portrayed in an excessively negative light. However, this leaves open the possibility that there are qualitative aspects related to the kind of collective actors that are represented in Europeanized political communication that contribute to the democratic deficit.

---

[1] The first part of this chapter is largely based on Koopmans (2007).

To analyze how the Europeanization of public debates affects the opportunities for public claim making of different collective actors, we again follow the lead of theories of social movements and collective action, which have emphasized the role of political opportunity structures for explaining patterns of political mobilization (e.g., Kriesi et al. 1995; Tarrow 1994). Hix and Goetz have related this theoretical tradition to the study of Europeanization: "a new institutional arena at the European level impacts on domestic political systems by providing a new 'structure of opportunities' for domestic actors" (2000, p. 12). The transfer of competencies from the national to the intergovernmental and supranational European arenas opens up opportunities and makes resources available for some actors, but not – or not to the same extent – for others. Similarly, the erosion of undivided national sovereignty may improve the opportunities of some actors, but it may also negatively affect those of actors who had obtained institutionalized access to national resources and opportunity structures. European integration inevitably implies a redistribution of power, not just institutionally but also regarding public debates and political mobilization (see also, e.g., Marks and McAdam 1999; Moravcsik 1994; Rucht 2000).

Next to shifting political opportunity structures, the chances of actors to intervene in Europeanized public debates may be influenced by differences in the news selection process between national coverage and international or European news coverage. National news reporting is subject to less strict selection pressures than is international or supranational coverage. In nondomestic news coverage, international press agencies play a more important role, and among foreign correspondents there is a stronger tendency to rely on institutional sources and news routines (e.g., Meyer 1999; Schulz 1997). This implies greater difficulties for less resourceful actors to get access to European and foreign news coverage, and a greater reliance in such news on institutional actors, especially executive and governmental actors such as the European Commission, or national foreign ministers and heads of state.

While there is consensus that European integration affects the relative opportunities for different actors, it is less clear in which direction such changes go. On the one hand, the weakness of democratic access on the European level and the bureaucratic and arcane nature of the European decision-making process may lead one to expect a European public sphere that is inhabited primarily by bureaucrats, statesmen, and perhaps a few other resourceful actors. On the other hand, the European Union and other European-level institutions are also often seen as counterweights against entrenched national powers, which offer opportunities for a variety of interest groups, nongovernmental organizations (NGOs), social movements, and other civil society actors (e.g., Eder, Hellmann, and Trenz 1998; Soysal 1994; Wiener 1998). Hix and Goetz discuss various reasons why European integration may benefit either resourceful elite actors or actors that are relatively weak in the domestic arena, but they ultimately arrive at the optimistic conclusion that "the openness of the EU policy process and the pursuit of neo-pluralist strategies by the Commission (such as subsidizing under-represented groups) ensure that both diffuse and concentrated interests tend to be able to pursue exit and veto opportunities and have access to key information" (2000, p. 14).

In this chapter, we investigate the empirical merits of these different views on the consequences of Europeanization for the participation chances of various types of collective actors. We address the question of participation in Europeanized public debates from two angles. First, we ask who participates in Europeanized public debates of the three basic types distinguished in Chapter 2 (supranational, vertical, and horizontal), and we compare this to debates that remain fully within a national frame of reference. From the point of view of the democratic deficit, we are especially interested in contrasting the accessibility of Europeanized political debates across three categories of actors: government and executive actors, legislative and party actors, and civil society actors. By analyzing which actors are overrepresented and which are underrepresented in Europeanized claim making, we get an indication of who benefits most from the Europeanization of public debates. Second, we turn to actors' subjective evaluations and ask what positions with regard to European institutions and the European integration process they take in the public debate. This gives us an indication of the extent to which actors consider European institutions as their allies and see the European integration process as congruent with their interests.

We hypothesize that actors who have limited access to Europeanized public debates will be more critical of European integration and institutions, whereas the actors whose voices are most prominent in debates on European issues will be more favorably inclined toward the European project.

This hypothesis, too, can be derived from the literature on political opportunity structures, which has shown that closed political institutions tend to provoke confrontational challenges, whereas open opportunity structures invite more consensual and cooperative strategies from collective actors (e.g., Kriesi et al. 1995, pp. 44–51).

THE NATURE OF NATIONALLY CONFINED PUBLIC DEBATES

To judge whether certain types of actors are underrepresented or overrepresented in Europeanized claim making, we first need to establish a standard of comparison. This standard consists of claims that are not Europeanized in any sense: in other words, these are claims that are made by actors from the same country as the newspaper that reports them, and that make no reference whatsoever to other European countries or to European-level actors, issues, legal frameworks, or norms. To keep the reference category as pure as possible, we moreover exclude claims that refer to supranational or intergovernmental levels beyond Europe, such as to the United Nations.

Table 4.1 shows the shares of different actors in such ideal-typical "nationalized" claim making in six issue fields (this table excludes the issue of European

TABLE 4.1. *Claims by Own National Actors with No European References by Actor Type and Issue Field* (%)

Actor Type	Total	Monetary Politics	Agriculture	Immigration	Troop Deployment	Pensions and Retirement	Education
Government/executive	36.5	40.0	45.4	43.9	42.7	30.0	32.2
Judiciary	2.4	0.3	0.7	5.6	—	2.5	1.9
Legislative and parties	19.6	7.6	8.3	27.1	25.6	28.9	15.8
Subtotal state and party actors	58.5	47.9	54.4	76.6	68.3	61.4	50.0
Media	6.2	12.6	2.7	5.3	22.4	5.0	4.5
Economic interest groups	15.7	34.9	31.6	5.1	2.8	25.2	11.0
Other civil society groups and organizations	19.6	3.5	11.2	13.0	9.3	8.4	34.6
Subtotal nonmedia civil society actors	35.3	39.5	42.9	18.1	9.3	33.6	45.5
TOTAL	100.0	100.0	100.0	100.0	100.0	100.0	100.0
N	4,446	340	408	862	246	798	1,792

integration, because it has by definition a European dimension).[2] We distinguish six categories of actors: government and executive actors, the judiciary, legislative and political party actors, news media, economic interest groups, and other civil society actors.[3] When relevant, information on specific actors within these categories is given in the text. Legislative actors and political party representatives have been taken together because in our sources it was difficult to distinguish them. The same persons could alternatively be identified as parliamentarians or as party spokespersons, and it was difficult to decide which to code. The category of media actors consists of explicit claims made by journalists of the coded newspaper, as well as quotations of comments and editorials from other newspapers. Economic interest groups include firms and employers' associations, economists and financial experts, and labor unions, as well as various professional groups such as farmers. The other civil society category consists mainly of social movement organizations specializing in issues such as women's emancipation, retirement, peace, human rights, aid to immigrants, health, and the environment.

The picture of national public debates that emerges from Table 4.1 is one of a strong dominance of institutional and resourceful actors. In all issue fields, government and executive actors are the most important voices in public debates. In monetary politics, agriculture, immigration, and troop deployment, they are responsible for between 40% and 45% of all claims. In pensions and retirement (30%) and education politics (32%) their predominance is less outspoken. The judiciary only plays a noteworthy role in the field of immigration, where it contributes to discussions on residence and asylum rights. The contribution of legislative and party actors is in all fields inferior to that of government and executive actors, but the extent of the difference varies importantly. In monetary politics and agriculture the executive's share of claims is more than five times as high as that of legislative and party actors. In the other issue fields, legislative and party actors are more important claim makers, with shares between 16% (education) and 29% (pensions and retirement). In five out of the six fields, state and party actors taken together are responsible for 50% or more of all claims, with a maximum of 77% (immigration). Only in monetary politics does their share fall slightly below half of all claims (48%). However, this does not make monetary politics an exception to the general rule that resourceful actors dominate the public debate, since the majority of civil society claims in this field are made by employers and business firms (16%) and economic and financial experts (17%). The influence of these actors contrasts sharply with that of other groups that arguably have a stake in monetary

[2] In the countries that are part of the Eurozone, there can likewise be no monetary politics claims that are purely national for the period since the introduction of the euro. The monetary politics claims in Table 4.1 therefore refer either to the years 1990 and 1995 or to Switzerland and the United Kingdom for 2000–2002.

[3] More detailed tables including data on specific civil society actors can be found in Koopmans (2007).

politics: labor unions (2%) and consumer groups (no claims at all) are virtually absent from public debates on monetary politics.

In other issue fields, too, less well-organized and less powerful groups have only a very limited voice in the public debate. Consumer groups (2%, included among economic interest groups) and environmental groups (1.5%, included among other civil society groups) are quite insignificant in debates on agriculture, even though the period of our data includes controversies over consumer safety and environment-related issues such as bovine spongiform encephalopathy and foot-and-mouth disease. Likewise, immigrants (4%) are marginal in public controversies over their rights, the peace movement is marginal in debates on troop deployment (1%), and pensioners and elderly people (2.5%) hardly have a voice in debates over pensions and retirement. There are only a few examples of civil society groups that do command considerable public attention: farmers in the field of agriculture (22%), labor unions in debates on pensions and retirement (14%), and school-related actors (teachers, parents, and students) in the field of education (29%). The media, finally, are especially relevant as speakers on monetary (13%) and troop deployment (22%) issues.

WHO PARTICIPATES IN EUROPEANIZED PUBLIC DEBATES?

These results suggest that nationally confined public debates are strongly biased toward actors who command strong institutional power. The question is to what extent Europeanization of public debates alleviates or exacerbates these power differentials. We begin this investigation by looking in Table 4.2 at the strongest form of Europeanization, namely the participation of supranational and intergovernmental actors from the European level in public debates. To analyze this type of supranationally Europeanized claim making, we distinguish the same actors as in Table 4.1. "Government/executive" now refers to European institutions such as the European Commission, the various EU Councils of Ministers, the European Central Bank, or the Council of Europe. Likewise, the other categories refer to the European-level equivalent of national organizations and institutions, such as the European Parliament, and European-level parties, interest groups, and NGOs. In addition to formal organizations on the European level, we also coded a claim as having a European-level actor if it was supported by a coalition of actors from a range of European countries, such as a demonstration in Brussels of farmers from various countries.

Table 4.2 leaves no doubt about which actors from the European level are most effective in putting their mark on public debates. In all six substantive issue fields, the share of executive actors is two to three times as large as it is in Table 4.1 for the reference category of national actors making purely national claims. In spite of what is sometimes said about its deficient communication strategies (e.g., Meyer 1999), the European Commission is by far the most often cited European-level organization, and it is responsible for more than half of all executive claims, followed at a distance by the various European Councils. Commission President Romano Prodi alone is cited 333 times in our sample,

TABLE 4.2. *Claims by European-Level Actors by Actor Type and Issue Field* (%)

Actor Type	Total	Monetary Politics	Agriculture	Immigration	Troop Deployment	Pensions and Retirement	Education	European Integration
Government/executive	80.3	92.6	86.2	74.4	88.1	81.7	68.5	72.0
Judiciary	0.7	—	0.4	1.8	—	2.0	—	1.2
Legislative and parties	15.6	4.0	8.8	18.3	11.0	4.1	15.8	24.3
Subtotal state and party actors	96.7	96.6	95.4	94.5	99.2	87.8	84.2	97.5
Media	0.2	0.2	—	—	—	—	—	0.3
Economic interest groups	1.7	2.7	2.1	0.6	0.8	10.2	0.0	0.9
Other civil society groups and organizations	1.3	0.6	2.5	4.8	—	2.0	15.8	1.2
Subtotal nonmedia civil society actors	3.1	3.2	4.6	5.5	0.8	12.2	15.8	2.2
TOTAL	100.0	100.0	100.0	100.0	100.0	100.0	100.0	100.0
N	4,233	1,232	522	164	118	49	19	2,129

more than any national politician, and 2.5 times as often as all European-level civil society actors taken together (131 claims). As on the national level, the European executive dominates over the legislative. However, the relationship is much more skewed than it is on the national level. The European Parliament's role is largest in discussions on European integration, but even there its share (24%) is only one-third of that of the various branches of the European executive (71%). That European-level media do not play a significant role is not surprising, but that European-level civil society actors command a share of only 3% of all claims stemming from European-level actors is suggestive evidence of a severe democratic deficit. It is difficult to see how the absence of any form of public visibility could not negatively affect the bargaining power of civil society groups within the European decision-making process.

However, we should not jump to conclusions on the basis of this one form of Europeanization of public debates alone. What about horizontal Europeanization of public debates, such as transnational claims by actors from other European countries? Table 4.3 shows us which actors benefit from such transnational flows of political communication. We find many tendencies that also characterize claim making by European-level actors, only less outspoken. Government and executive actors play an important role in horizontally Europeanized claim making, ranging from 43% in education politics to 78% in debates on troop deployment. Legislative and party actors fare much worse (between 4% in agriculture and 15% in European integration) and command in every issue field a smaller share than among the claims with a national frame of reference in Table 4.1. Most civil society actors are likewise underrepresented among horizontally Europeanized claims when compared to the claims with a purely national frame of reference. For the media the story is different. In most issue fields, claims made by foreign European news media are represented to a similar extent as are national media in Table 4.1. Often this takes the form of overviews of voices from foreign media, either on important national controversies that have aroused attention abroad or on common European issues. The main conclusion remains, however, that the actors that manage to cross the boundaries of national public spheres are overwhelmingly core executive actors such as heads of government and cabinet ministers. Like supranational Europeanization, the transnational flow of public communication offers additional opportunities for those actors that are already dominant on the national level, and it exacerbates rather than compensates for the weak position of civil society actors.

We now turn to the final, vertical variant of Europeanization, in which national actors directly address European institutions or frame issues with reference to European identities, interests, norms, and legal frameworks. National actors operating in their own national public arena face the strategic choice whether or not to refer in their claims to European dimensions or to remain fully within a national frame of reference. As any other form of resource deployment, discursive framing is a matter of choice under conditions of limited resources and opportunities. Actors frame issues in a certain way because they hope

TABLE 4.3. *Claims by National Actors from Other European Countries by Actor Type and Issue Field (%)*

Actor Type	Total	Monetary Politics	Agriculture	Immigration	Troop Deployment	Pensions and Retirement	Education	European Integration
Government/executive	67.6	66.9	71.2	65.1	78.0	43.8	43.4	68.0
Judiciary	0.6	—	1.5	3.3	0.3	2.7	3.9	0.3
Legislative and parties	11.6	7.5	4.1	12.3	7.8	12.3	10.1	15.0
Subtotal state and party actors	79.9	74.3	76.8	80.1	86.1	58.9	57.4	83.5
Media	7.9	7.9	5.3	6.6	10.6	2.7	3.9	8.4
Economic interest groups	5.8	13.6	11.8	1.5	0.8	28.7	5.5	2.5
Other civil society groups and organizations	6.4	4.1	6.2	11.9	2.6	9.6	33.3	5.5
Subtotal nonmedia civil society actors	12.2	17.9	18.0	13.3	3.3	38.4	38.7	8.1
TOTAL	100.0	100.0	100.0	100.0	100.0	100.0	100.0	100.0
N	4,722	1,028	340	396	396	73	129	2,360

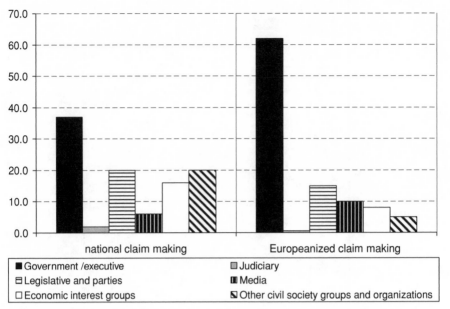

FIGURE 4.1. National and Europeanized claim making by actor types (in percent).

(or have learned from past experience) that such framing increases their chances of having an impact on public debates and policy decisions.

The results in Table 4.4 show, in line with our earlier results, that government and executive actors are more likely to use Europeanized frames than legislative and party actors. Except in the education field, the share of government and executive actors is larger among the claims with a Europeanized frame in Table 4.4 than it is among the purely national claims in Table 4.1. Legislative and party actors command similar shares in both tables in most issue fields, but in immigration politics and pensions and retirement they are clearly underrepresented among Europeanized claims. The share of civil society actors is again lower than among purely national claims. The only exception is pensions and retirement politics, but a closer inspection of the kind of civil society actors that account for this result confirms the general trend that Europeanized claim making correlates with institutional power. Civil society actors that have a higher share in pensions and retirement claims with a Europeanized frame are employers and financial experts, while the share of labor unions declines and pensioners' organizations are completely absent among the Europeanized claims (not shown in the table).

Combining the three types of Europeanization, we see that the results are clear. As Figure 4.1 shows, the only actors that are systematically overrepresented in supranationally, horizontally, and vertically Europeanized claim making are government and executive actors. Across all issue fields, they are responsible for 37% of all purely national claims (see the Total column in Table 4.1), but across the three forms of Europeanized claim making their

TABLE 4.4. *Claims by Own National Actors with a European Frame of Reference by Actor Type and Issue Field* (%)

Actor Type	Total	Monetary Politics	Agriculture	Immigration	Troop Deployment	Pensions and Retirement	Education	European Integration
Government/executive	41.6	36.5	48.0	46.4	48.5	40.7	32.1	42.6
Judiciary	0.6	0.2	1.4	3.2	3.1	3.4	1.9	0.4
Legislative and parties	17.4	10.1	9.8	19.6	22.7	5.1	15.1	23.5
Subtotal state and party actors	59.7	46.9	59.3	69.3	74.2	49.2	49.1	66.4
Media	19.1	20.2	10.2	17.4	21.6	5.1	7.5	20.9
Economic interest groups	14.4	26.9	25.9	3.9	0.0	35.7	11.4	5.0
Other civil society groups and organizations	7.2	7.0	5.6	9.2	4.2	10.2	32.1	7.7
Subtotal nonmedia civil society actors	21.2	32.9	30.5	13.3	4.2	45.7	43.4	12.7
TOTAL	100.0	100.0	100.0	100.0	100.0	100.0	100.0	100.0
N	5,316	1,610	589	280	97	59	53	2,628

share rises to 62% (average computed across Tables 4.2–4.4). Media actors are, somewhat surprisingly perhaps, the only other actor type that is more prominently represented in Europeanized claim making (6% of purely national claims against a share of 10% of Europeanized claims). Europeanization of claim making does not strengthen the hand of legislative and party actors, whose share is 20% in purely national claim making against 15% across all forms of Europeanized claim making. That may not seem a large difference, but to appreciate its importance one must look at the relative influence of legislative versus executive actors. Among purely national claims, the executive outnumbers legislative and party actors less than two to one, but among Europeanized claims the proportion is almost four to one. Civil society actors, finally, are clearly the least able to profit from the opening up of Europeanized discursive spaces. Among purely national claims, they command a reasonable share of 35% of all claims (Table 4.1), but among Europeanized claims they are responsible for only 13% of claims (Tables 4.2–4.4 combined).

Specific civil society actors are better considered in the context of the specific issue fields in which they are most active. In almost all cases such an issue-specific perspective reveals a considerable decline in discursive influence for these actors among Europeanized claims (percentages not shown in the tables). For instance, farmers make 22% of the purely national claims on agriculture (Table 4.1), but only 11% of Europeanized claims (Tables 4.2–4.4 combined). In monetary politics, employers command 16% of national claims, but only 5% of Europeanized claims. Labor unions likewise have less influence in Europeanized debates in the issue fields where they are strong (14% against 8% in pensions and retirement and 9% against 5% in education). Pensioners' groups, already very weak among national claims in pensions and retirement politics (2.5%), are even weaker (0.6%) among Europeanized claims. The same holds for consumer groups on agricultural issues (2% versus 0.8%), and to a lesser extent for immigrants in their field (4% against 3%). The only example of a civil society actor that does better among Europeanized claims concerns employers' organizations in the pensions and retirement field, whose share among Europeanized claims (9%) is slightly higher than among purely national claims (8%).

A MULTIVARIATE ANALYSIS OF THE DETERMINANTS OF EUROPEANIZED CLAIM MAKING

Thus far, we have focused in detail on differences across actors and issue fields, but we have at the same time ignored cross-national and temporal differences in degrees and forms of Europeanized claim making, which are as we saw in the previous chapter also important. In addition, there may be significant differences across media in different countries, as well as across media of different types (left versus right, tabloids versus quality, and national versus regional newspapers; for further analyses of differences across newspapers, see Chapter 5). A full analysis of the determinants of Europeanization of claim making must therefore take into account differences across actors, issue fields, countries, time, and newspapers simultaneously. This also allows us to test the robustness of the findings of Chapter 3 in a multivariate context. We therefore conducted a series of multivariate logistic regressions with the likelihood that a claim will be Europeanized in the supranational, horizontal, or vertical senses as the dependent variables. As independent variables we include the following.

1. Actor type: We use legislative–party, socioeconomic interest groups, media and journalists, other civil society, and government and executive actors as the excluded reference category.
2. We use the country of the claim-making actor, with actors from non-EU member Switzerland as the excluded reference category. Because the number of cases for other countries was too low, we have included only claims made by actors from our seven selected countries in the analysis.
3. We use whether an actor from one of the seven countries is from the subnational – that is, regional or local – level, with national-level actors as the reference category.
4. Newspaper type: We use regional, tabloid, and left-wing quality papers, with right-wing quality papers as the excluded reference category.
5. We use newspaper country, with Swiss newspapers as the excluded reference category. Because of multicollinearity problems caused by the fact that claims by actors from a particular country are overwhelmingly concentrated in newspaper sources from that country, we unfortunately cannot include newspaper country and country of the claim-making actor in one and the same regression.[4]
6. We use issue field, with education as the excluded reference category.
7. Time: We use 1995 and 2000–2002, with 1990 as the excluded reference category.

In Table 4.5, we first look at what determines the likelihood that a particular claim will be made by an actor from the European level or by an actor from another EU member state. For obvious reasons, the country and level (European, national, or subnational) of the claim-making actor is not included as an independent variable in these regressions since the level or country of the actor is what we want to explain. The coefficients in the table are odds ratios. Odds ratios lower than 1 indicate that a claim maker from a particular category is less likely to be a European-level actor or an actor from an EU member state; a ratio higher than 1 indicates a positive association.

The findings in the preceding section about differences across types of actors are confirmed in a multivariate context. Civil society organizations – be they socioeconomic interests groups, news media, or other civil society groups – are extremely unlikely to be publicly visible claim makers on the European level. In line with the previous findings, European-level legislative and party actors

---

[4] Most correlations between claimant country and newspaper country were above 0.70, and some were above 0.80.

TABLE 4.5. *Determinants of the Likelihood That a Claim Will Be Made by a European-Level Actor or an Actor from an EU Member State (Odds Ratios)*

Variable	European-Level Actor	Actor from an EU Member State
Actor type (ref. cat. government and executive)		
Legislative and parties	0.744***	0.589***
Judiciary	0.806	0.679
Socioeconomic interest groups	0.085***	0.595***
Media and journalists	0.010***	0.824**
Other civil society actors	0.135***	0.721***
Newspaper type (ref. cat. right-wing quality papers)		
Left-wing quality[a]	1.080	1.071
Regional	0.851	0.799*
Tabloid[b]	1.068	0.703*
Country of newspaper (ref. cat. Swiss newspapers)		
Germany	1.119	0.603***
France	1.356***	0.679***
United Kingdom	0.751***	0.516***
Italy	1.514***	0.616***
Spain	1.485***	0.672***
Netherlands	1.387***	0.779***
Issue field (ref. cat. education)		
European integration	29.019***	4.548***
Monetary politics	32.144***	3.795***
Agriculture	28.938***	2.633***
Immigration	6.413***	2.680***
Troop deployment	4.673***	2.310***
Pensions	4.793***	1.175
Time (ref. cat. 1990)		
1995	1.073	1.275**
2000–2002	1.580***	1.019
N (weighted)[c]	20,206	20,206
Nagelkerke R^2	0.275	0.067

[a] Including *L'Humanité* for France.
[b] Including *De Telegraaf* for the Netherlands.
[c] As a result of our sampling strategy (see Chapter 2), claims coded for the years 1990 and 1995 had a somewhat higher chance of being non-Europeanized (in the sense of having no European reference in any of the actor, addressee, issue, or object actor variables) than those coded for the period 2000–2002. For the analyses reported in Tables 4.5 and 4.6, we therefore weighted non-Europeanized claims in the years 1990 and 1995 by a factor of two-thirds (0.67).
* $p < .05$, ** $p < .01$, *** $p < .001$.

are also less prominently visible than European-level executive actors, but the difference is smaller than for civil society actors. The findings on claim makers from other member states are similar but less stark.

Next, we look at the influence of media sources on patterns of Europeanization. The distinction among left-wing and right-wing quality papers, tabloids, and regional papers has little impact on the likelihood that claims by European actors or actors from other member states are covered. The only significant finding is that regional and tabloid papers are slightly less likely to contain claims by actors from other member states. In line with Chapter 3, differences across countries are important, though. The findings highlight once more the exceptionally parochial orientation of the press in the United Kingdom, which provides the least space both to European-level actors and to actors from other member states. Next to the United Kingdom case, a main line of difference runs between non-EU member Switzerland, on the one hand, and the member states, on the other. Swiss newspapers are significantly less likely to report claims by European-level actors but more often report claims by actors from other countries. As we argued in the previous chapter, this suggests a substitutive relation between vertical and horizontal Europeanization. In the media of EU member states, much attention is given to European actors and institutions (except in the United Kingdom), but less to actors from other member states. In Switzerland, which is at a more incipient stage of Europeanization, we find high levels of attention for the surrounding European countries, but less attention for actors from the European level proper.

This reading fits the findings for developments over time. We find evidence for an increase in rates of claim making by European-level actors in the most recent period, 2000–2002. Claim makers from other member states were, however, more prominent in 1995. The reason seems to be – as we suggested in Chapter 3 – that increased Europeanization in an issue field often first leads to more attention for claims made in other member states, but once strong European-level prerogatives are institutionalized then attention turns to European-level actors and institutions.

In line with the descriptive findings of Chapter 3, we further see that the issue field is by far the most important determinant of the likelihood that a claim will be made by a European-level actor. Claims in the fields of European integration, monetary politics, and agriculture are much more likely to be made by a European-level actor than claims on the reference issue of education. Claims on immigration, troop deployment, and pensions are also more frequently made by European-level actors. We thus once more find strong confirmation for the political opportunity structure perspective, which predicts that levels of Europeanization are first and foremost determined by the formal distribution of power between the European and national levels in different issue fields. The findings for claim makers from other member states are similar, but the differences across issues are less strong.

In a second step of our analysis, we now leave claims by European-level actors aside and focus in Table 4.6 only on national actors from one of the seven countries. We investigate three forms of Europeanization of their claim making: whether they make claims on the issue of European integration (which is by definition a form of vertical Europeanization); whether in making claims on one of the other six issues they refer to European institutions, regulations, or norms (also a form of vertical Europeanization); and finally whether they

TABLE 4.6. *Determinants of the Likelihood that a Claim by an Actor from One of the Seven Countries Will Have a European Scope (Odds Ratios)*

Variable	Claim on European Integration Issue	Claim on Other Issue with Vertical European Scope	Claim with Horizontal European Scope
Actor type (ref. cat. government and executive)			
Legislative and parties	1.112	0.789*	0.354***
Judiciary	0.188***	0.786	0.442*
Socioeconomic interest groups	0.226***	0.734***	0.467***
Media and journalists	1.628***	1.657***	1.397***
Other civil society actors	0.454***	0.746*	0.468***
Country of claimant (ref. cat. Swiss actors)			
Germany	0.550***	1.656***	2.568***
France	0.801**	1.512**	2.937***
United Kingdom	0.342***	0.991	1.527**
Italy	0.357***	1.198	1.732***
Spain	0.636***	1.903***	1.478**
Netherlands	0.411***	1.465*	2.426***
Subnational actor (ref. cat. national-level actors)	0.632***	0.493***	0.430***
Newspaper type (ref. cat. right-wing quality papers)			
Left-wing quality	0.787***	0.913	0.946
Regional	0.800*	0.622***	0.907
Tabloid	0.910	0.681	0.708
Issue field (ref. cat. education)			
European integration	—	—	21.185***
Monetary politics	—	164.844***	7.911***
Agriculture	—	39.351***	12.743***
Immigration	—	8.394***	6.280***
Troop deployment	—	5.865***	4.524***
Pensions	—	2.155***	1.599
Time (ref. cat. 1990)			
1995	0.898***	1.118	1.267*
2000–2002	0.944	1.733***	1.206*
N (weighted)	12,205	8,447	12,205
Nagelkerke R^2	0.126	0.585	0.210

* $p < .05$, ** $p < .01$, *** $p < .001$.

refer to actors or policies in another member state (a form of horizontal Europeanization). In contrast to the preceding analysis, we now include the country of the claiming actor as a predictor of Europeanization instead of the newspaper country, and we also include whether an actor is from the subnational level within one of our countries. The choice to focus on claimant country rather than newspaper country is made not only because of the theoretical focus of this chapter on differences across actor types, but also because it is warranted on empirical grounds. We separately performed all analyses reported in Table 4.6 with newspaper country rather than actor country. The results were very similar, but the amount of variance explained was in all three cases lower, suggesting that the country of claimants is a more important determinant of the degree of Europeanization of claims than is the country of the reporting newspaper.

Again we find multivariate confirmation for the previous findings. Claims by governmental and executive actors are more likely to be vertically or horizontally Europeanized than those by legislative and party actors, as well as civil society actors. The exception among civil society actors are the news media, which contrary to the common criticism that they would be dominated by a national frame of reference actually refer more often to European-level actors and regulations, as well as to actors and policies in other member states, than any other category of actors. We also find that subnational actors from the regional and local levels of the polity are systematically less likely to make Europeanized claims, be it claims on the issue of European integration or claims on other issues that refer to the EU level or to other member states. We thus see little evidence that actors from the subnational level turn to the EU or to allies in other countries to increase their leverage against national authorities. Such a "boomerang effect" (Keck and Sikkink 1998) is often seen as a core characteristic of multilevel polities such as the EU, but neither our results for civil society actors nor those for subnational actors provide any evidence for such an alliance between supranational institutions and actors that are relatively weakly placed within national polities. To the contrary, what we find is the precise opposite: National level actors, and within that category especially executive actors, are much more likely to revert to the European level than are subnational actors and civil society actors.

Regarding the country of the claimant, we find that the most prominent cleavage is between non-EU member Switzerland and the six member states. Swiss actors are more likely to make claims on European integration than actors in the other countries. The reason is that in Switzerland the question of whether or not the country should join the EU, or should harmonize its policies with those of the EU, is high on the agenda. By contrast, Swiss claimants are less likely to refer directly to European institutions and regulations, although with Italian and British claimants the difference is not statistically significant. Swiss claimants are also less likely to refer to actors and policies in other member states than are claimants in the other countries.

The newspaper type again turns out to be of limited importance. Left-wing quality and regional newspapers are somewhat less likely than right-wing quality papers to report claims on European integration. Regional newspapers are also less likely to report vertically Europeanized claims on other issues. Perhaps surprisingly, Tables 4.5 and 4.6 show that tabloid newspapers do not differ significantly from national quality newspapers regarding the degree of Europeanization of the claims they report.

The findings for issue fields provide further strong evidence for the political opportunity explanation. The more competencies Europe has in a field, the more often will claimants refer to the European level or to other member states in their claim making. Regarding vertically Europeanized claims, this is most clearly the case for monetary politics, while agriculture comes as a good second. The second and third pillar issues of immigration and troop deployment come next, whereas pensions and retirement claims are only somewhat more likely to be vertically Europeanized than claims on education. The findings are similar for horizontal Europeanization, although pensions and retirement claims do not differ significantly in this regard from education claims.

Finally, regarding trends over time, the first column of Table 4.6 shows that the issue of European integration has not become more prominent over time. However, the table does provide evidence for a modest trend of increased Europeanization in other issue fields. Compared to the reference year 1990, claims in the period 2000–2002 were significantly more likely to refer to European-level dimensions of an issue, and both in 1995 and in 2000–2002, they were more likely to refer to actors and issues in other member states.

WHO SUPPORTS AND WHO OPPOSES EUROPEAN INSTITUTIONS AND EUROPEAN INTEGRATION?

Having established which actors populate the Europeanized public sphere, we now ask what positions they take with regard to European institutions and European integration. Our guiding hypothesis on the basis of the political opportunity structure perspective is that collective actors' subjective attitude toward Europe reflects the degree to which they profit from the Europeanization of public debates in the sense of increased voice and visibility.

We expect, therefore, that government and executive actors will be more favorable toward European integration and European institutions than legislative and party actors, and we expect both to be more supportive of European integration than civil society actors. The media, finally, are expected to fall somewhere in between, but more on the supportive side.

To validate these expectations, we limit our analysis to claims that have a European dimension (i.e., we exclude the purely national claims reported in Table 4.1, as well as those from Table 4.3 that only refer to the national policies of foreign European countries) and look at how actors evaluate European institutions and the European integration process. We begin by looking at claims that directly address European actors and institutions, either by appealing to them to fulfill certain demands, or by expressing criticism or support. The scores between $+1$ and -1 indicate to what extent European institutions are evaluated positively or negatively by a particular category of actors (see the previous chapter for a more detailed explanation of the coding of these variables). To allow us to place the evaluations given to European institutions

TABLE 4.7. *Evaluation of European Institutions by Actor Category*

Actor Category	Evaluation of European Institutions	Evaluation of National Institutions	Difference in Evaluation of European and National Institutions
Immigrants	(+.20)	−.57	+.77
Judiciary	+.14	−.35	+.49
Central banks	+.04	−.02	+.06
Government/executive	−.02	−.09	+.07
All state and party actors	−.06	−.17	+.11
Science, research, and other professionals	−.09	−.27	+.18
Employers and firms	−.15	−.22	+.07
Legislative and parties	−.25	−.31	+.06
All nonmedia civil society actors	−.30	−.34	+.04
Media	−.30	−.18	−.12
Unions and employees	−.31	−.39	+.08
Students and educational professionals	−.33	−.47	+.14
Economists and financial experts	−.34	−.15	−.19
Other civil society groups and organizations	−.38	−.29	−.09
Farmers	−.50	−.42	−.08
Consumers	(−.75)	−.29	−.46
Average	−.12	−.21	+.09
N	4,681	8,481	12,182

Note: Scores in parentheses are based on fewer than ten cases. The N in the final column is less than the sum of the other columns because in some cases European and national institutions were both addressed in one claim.

into perspective, Table 4.7 also gives the average scores for the evaluation of national addressees. Thus, the table shows if a particular category of actors views European institutions more or less positively than national institutions.

As we expected, state and party actors (−.06) evaluate European institutions much more positively (or better: less negatively) than civil society actors (−.30). However, within both categories, there is large variation. Government and executive actors (−.02) as well as central banks (+.04) and the judiciary (+.14) are relatively positive about European institutions, whereas legislative and party actors are much more critical (−.25). There is also important variation among civil society actors. Consumers groups, farmers, the residual category of other civil society organizations, financial experts, students and educational professionals, labor unions, and employers all conform to our

expectations and display below average levels of support for European institutions. That employer organizations and business firms are the least negative
also fits our hypotheses, because they were better represented in Europeanized
public debates than most other civil society actors. Two other categories of
civil society actors deviate from this pattern. Science, research, and other professionals are slightly less negative about European institutions ($-.09$) than the
overall average, and immigrants even top the list with a positive score of $+.20$,
which is, however, based on few cases. We can speculate that what these actors
have in common and may explain their supportive stance is that they both
have a transnational habitus, and they profit in an above average manner from
the internal freedom of movement within the European Union in the form of
cross-national scientific exchange and research funding, and simplified travel
and visa regulations for immigrants.

The media are a further deviation from our expectations. Because news
media are overrepresented among Europeanized claims, we had expected them
to be favorably inclined toward European institutions. However, media actors
turn out to take a negative position, close to the average for nonmedia civil
society actors. To make sense of this result, we must realize that the media have
a special position in the public discourse. All other actors must struggle to get
media attention. The media, however, can decide for themselves whether or
not to speak out publicly, without having to pass any selection hurdles. Thus
underrepresentation or overrepresentation of the media in Europeanized public
debates is not a function of opportunities and constraints; it is just a matter of
editorial choice.

In Table 4.8, we investigate whether these patterns hold if we look at general
support for or opposition to the European integration process (see Chapter 3
for operationalization). The first important thing to note is that evaluations of
the integration process are much more positive than evaluations of concrete
European actors and institutions. Whereas almost all actors were on average
critical of European institutions, with the single (and only slight) exception of
farmers no category of actors is, on average, opposed to European integration.
Regarding differences among actors, the results confirm the earlier findings.
State and party actors are more supportive of European integration than are
civil society actors, and, within the former category, Euroenthusiasm is clearly
more limited among legislative and party actors than it is among government
and executive actors. Most civil society actors display below average levels of
support for European integration, and again employers and business organizations are comparatively positive about European integration. The difference
with the position of labor unions is, however, much smaller than shown in
Table 4.7, suggesting the plausible interpretation that both groups are more
or less equally supportive of European integration, but that employers are less
dissatisfied with how European integration has been concretely implemented
by European institutions than labor unions are. In contrast to Table 4.7, immigrants no longer deviate from other civil society actors, but science, research,
and other professionals again display a high level of support for European

TABLE 4.8. *Evaluation of the European Integration Process by Actor Category*

Actor Category	Evaluation of the Integration Process
Government/executive	+.32
Science, research, and other professionals	+.30
All state and party actors	+.27
Judiciary	+.20
Employers and firms	+.18
Central banks	+.16
Unions and employees	+.15
All nonmedia civil society actors	+.14
Immigrants	+.14
Media	+.13
Legislative and parties	+.13
Economists and financial experts	+.12
Students and educational professionals	+.09
Consumers	+.08
Other civil society groups and organizations	+.02
Farmers	−.02
Average	+.24
N	13,437

integration. The news media are again close to the average for nonmedia civil society actors.

We may conclude, then, that the hypothesis that the degree to which actors profit or stand to lose from the Europeanization of public debates is mirrored in their support for European integration receives considerable but not complete support. We are aware that there is a caveat here. Could it be that it is not discursive influence that determines actors' attitude toward Europe, but that the causal direction is the other way around, namely that the critical attitude of some actors toward the European Union is the reason why they do not mobilize on the European level and do not frame issues in a European context? This alternative reading of our results does not strike us as convincing because there is no reason why actors who are opposed to European policies and institutions would refrain from mobilizing on the European level, from addressing European policies and institutions, or from asking their national governments to do something about them. When we speak of Europeanized public debates, we do not mean a unisono chorus of Europhiles, but a contested discourse in which – just as in national public debates – opponents have as much reason to make their voices heard as supporters. Moreover, the myriad of civil society groups and NGOs that have organized and committed their scarce resources to setting up European representations and federations speak against a lack of attempts to gain a foothold on the European level. However, the voices of these

TABLE 4.9. *Determinants of the Likelihood of Eurocritical Claim Making by Actors from the Seven Countries (Odds Ratios; Only Evaluative Claims with a European Scope)*

Variable	Negative Evaluation of European Integration or European Institutions
Actor type (ref. cat. government and executive)	
Legislative and parties	2.623***
Judiciary	0.567
Socioeconomic interest groups	2.263***
Media and journalists	2.230***
Other civil society actors	1.757***
Subnational actor (ref. cat. national-level actors)	1.949*
Country of claimant (ref. cat. Swiss actors)	
Germany	1.082
France	1.287
United Kingdom	2.630***
Italy	1.177
Spain	1.675**
Netherlands	1.741***
Newspaper type (ref. cat. right-wing quality papers)	
Left-wing quality	0.947
Regional	0.541***
Tabloid	1.755*
Issue field (ref. cat. pensions and retirement and education)	
European integration	0.820
Monetary politics	1.072
Agriculture	2.678**
Immigration	0.852
Troop deployment	0.728
Time (ref. cat. 1990)	
1995	1.460**
2000–2002	1.588***
N	4,078
Nagelkerke R^2	0.134

* $p < .05$, ** $p < .01$, *** $p < .001$.

many European-level civil society organizations are hardly ever heard among the voices that come to us from Brussels.

A MULTIVARIATE ANALYSIS OF EUROCRITICISM

Again, we ask to what extent the findings in this and the previous chapter on support for and opposition against European institutions and the European integration process hold in a multivariate analysis. Table 4.9 presents the results of a logistic regression with the likelihood that a claim made by a national-level actor is Eurocritical as the dependent variable. "Eurocriticism" encompasses both Eurosceptic claims (which are critical of both the integration process and of the actions of European institutions) and critically Europeanist claims (which support the integration process while criticizing current European policies and institutions) as defined in the previous chapter. A claim is thus operationalized as Eurocritical when it either takes a negative stance toward a deepening or widening of European integration, or when it is critical of European institutions and actors. The reference category consists of claims that positively evaluate the integration process and European policies or institutions.

We find multivariate confirmation for our descriptive results on actor differences in degrees of opposition and support regarding the European Union. With the exception of the judiciary, all actor types display higher degrees of criticism of the European integration process and European institutions than government and executive actors. Once we control for other variables, legislative and party actors turn out to be even somewhat more Eurocritical than news media, socioeconomic interest groups, and other civil society actors. Of course, the category of legislative and party actors is a very broad one, which includes parties and politicians from across the political spectrum, including both Europhile and Eurocritical voices. For this reason, we will further on in the book (Chapter 10) devote an entire chapter to differences in degrees of support for and opposition to European integration across political parties. Here it suffices to conclude that on the whole there is quite a high degree of polarization on European issues within the core of the political system, between generally highly Europhile governments and executive agencies, and fairly Eurocritical parliaments and parties. The explanation for this cleavage that we advance is that government and executive actors have won a lot and have more to win by increased Europeanization of decision-making power, because they are by far the most powerful actors on the European level. Parliaments and parties, by contrast, have a lot to lose by increased Europeanization, because it erodes their national control power over the executive branch without much compensation on the European level, given the structural weakness and public invisibility of the European Parliament. The fact that subnational actors are significantly more likely to make Eurocritical claims points in a similar direction. Contrary to what is often supposed, we do not see much evidence that regional and local actors are engaging in alliance making with European actors to increase their political leverage.

In addition to differences across types of actors, some differences across actors from different countries are important. In line with the results in Chapter 3, the United Kingdom stands out as the country with the highest levels of Eurocritical claim making, and the Netherlands and Spain also show significantly higher levels of Eurocriticism.[5] We also find some significant

---

[5] If we include the newspaper country instead of the claimant country in the analysis, the results are exactly the same with significantly more Eurocritical claims in British and to a lesser extent also in Dutch and Spanish newspapers.

differences across newspaper types in the frequency of coverage of Eurocritical claims. Whereas earlier we found no significant differences between tabloid and quality papers regarding the degrees of coverage of European actors and issues, we now see that in the tabloid press Europeanized claims are significantly more likely to be Eurocritical than claims in the quality press. However, between left-wing and right-wing quality papers there are no significant differences. Regional papers, finally, are less likely to cover European actors and issues (see Tables 4.5 and 4.6), but if they do, such coverage is less likely to contain Eurocritical claims. On the whole these cross-media differences are rather modest, certainly when compared to the strength of the coefficients for claimant types.

CONCLUSIONS

The mass-media public sphere, on which European political communication relies even more than national political communication, is a highly competitive environment in which actors compete for limited public visibility, resonance, and legitimacy (Koopmans 2004). In this chapter, we have argued that European integration shifts the distribution of discursive opportunities to influence public debates, improving the voice and visibility of some actors, and weakening those of others. Our results clearly demonstrate that thus far European integration has remained a project by political elites, and as far as discursive influence is concerned, also to the benefit of political elites. Core executive actors such as heads of state and government, cabinet ministers, and central banks are by far the most important beneficiaries of the Europeanization of public debates, in whichever form it occurs. Legislative and party actors – those actors from the core of the political system who are directly accountable to the electorate – are much less well represented in Europeanized public debates, both in an absolute sense and even more so relative to government and executive actors. Such an erosion of the contribution of parliaments and political parties to public debates on Europeanized issues seems problematic from the normative point of view of democratic legitimacy and accountability. The same is true for the extremely weak representation of civil society actors in Europeanized public debates. Less resourceful civil society interests such as consumers' organizations, environmental groups, or pensioners are even more strongly underrepresented in Europeanized public debates than more powerful groups such as labor unions and business interests.

The differences among the three forms of Europeanization are also problematic from the point of view of the democratic quality of public debates. The strongest form of Europeanization, namely the participation of European-level actors in public debates, is also by far the most exclusive. Civil society actors are almost completely absent among the voices coming down from the European level. Transnational flows of political communication across member-state boundaries are less exclusive, but still this horizontal form of Europeanized political communication is mainly a playground for statesmen and a few other powerful interests. The only form of Europeanized political communication in which the role of civil society actors approaches that in purely national debates is the vertical variant, in which national actors make claims within a European frame of reference, either directly addressed at European institutions or addressed at national authorities but referring to European identities, norms, and legal frameworks. But even there the position of most civil society actors is weaker than in public debates of the "traditional" type, which remain confined to a purely national frame of reference.

These differences across actor types are confirmed by multivariate analyses, which in addition show that actors from the regional and local levels are less likely to make Europeanized claims than those from the national level – a further indication that the opportunity structures opened up by Europeanization benefit especially those actors that already occupy central positions of power within the national polity. We thus see little evidence for the "boomerang effect" hypothesis (Keck and Sikkink 1998), which states that actors that are weakly placed within national polities, such as subnational and civil society actors, refer to institutions, legal frameworks, and norms on the supranational level to increase their bargaining power vis-à-vis national authorities.

We have further shown in this chapter that the discursive influence of actors in Europeanized and non-Europeanized arenas is closely related to patterns of support for and opposition to European institutions and the European integration process. As a general rule, actors who are less influential in Europeanized public debates tend also to be more critical of European institutions and less supportive of the integration process than actors whose voices are more prominent in Europeanized public debates. The only consistent exception to this rule consists of science, research, and other professionals, who are supportive more than the average amount concerning European integration, even though they are underrepresented in Europeanized public debates.

These findings, too, receive further support in a multivariate analysis, which additionally shows that the relation between more limited access to Europeanized debates and a more critical stance toward the integration process and toward European institutions also applies to subnational compared with national actors. In spite of all the rhetoric of Europe as the ally of the weak that one encounters both in the public debate and in the scientific literature, subnational actors and civil society actors are significantly more likely to take a Eurocritical stance than national-level governmental actors. We interpret this finding as a reflection of the shift in the balance of power that occurs as a result of Europeanization, which benefits the national executive that has privileged access to the European decision-making process, at the expense of other categories of national-level actors, as well as regional and local actors.

PART III

MASS MEDIA

Performance, Claim Making, and Framing

5

Making Europe News

Journalism and Media Performance

Paul Statham

Media performance is often held responsible for the European Union's perceived democratic deficit and its lack of visibility, resonance, and legitimacy in the hearts and minds of citizens.[1] Politicians are never slow to blame the media when their EU integrationist attempts stall. Likewise, some academics claim that a supposedly Eurosceptic press is influential when EU projects fail to gain public support, but they seldom mention the media as a causal factor in cases when integration advances (for an example, see Taylor 2008). For their part, EU elites consider that better quality coverage in national media would be the best way to improve their own public legitimacy (Michailidou 2007). Thus, a link is often made between the European Union's perceived "deficit" and mass media performance. In this chapter, we address an important aspect of media performance, that is, the role of journalists, the actors who supply the information about Europe to the public domain. The first aim is to provide a general picture of how journalism has responded to the transformation of politics resulting from advancing European integration. The second is to examine whether, based on journalists' own assessments, this has involved a transformation of political journalism, and, if so, in what ways.

Journalists are defined as those who take decisions directly affecting news contents (Donsbach and Patterson 2004). This definition covers editors and reporters, who participate in daily decisions that influence information gathering and selection processes, as well as actually writing the news. The advent of European multilevel governance presents important challenges for journalism compared to national politics. From one perspective, it presents fewer opportunities; journalists may find news space for European stories very limited, run up against nationally focused structures of news production, and be provided with few resources by news organizations to cover a level of politics for which there is little readership interest. From another, it presents new opportunities for journalists; it opens up career possibilities in a new field about an important

---

[1] The chapter draws partly on Statham (2008).

form of politics away from the established routines of the national news beat. In this view, journalists may have greater chances to educate and inform readers about important political developments that are relatively remote or obscure, and that national governments sometimes like to keep that way. Europe may even allow journalists greater scope for shaping the political message and acting as opinion leaders. Important questions are these: How has European journalism evolved? What factors external and internal to news production account for these developments? Has this required changes in journalistic norms, values, and practices? Finally, what type of advocacy is prevalent over Europe?

In the next section we discuss journalism over Europe and critically review the existing research field. Then we outline a conceptual approach for several factors that potentially shape journalists' news decisions. This structures the empirical study. In the subsequent section we provide information on the interview sample and research design. We then provide the detailed study of journalism based on 110 interviews across seven countries. This is followed by a concluding discussion on journalism and media performance.

IN SEARCH OF EUROPEAN JOURNALISM

The relationship between media and political institutions within liberal democratic nation states has been much discussed (for a critical review, see Blumler and Kavanagh 1999; for a historical thesis, see Hallin and Mancini 2004). A key development has been the emergence of independent professional journalism. Whereas in the nineteenth century the press and political parties were closely linked, partisan news organizations have largely declined (McQuail 1994). Nonetheless, most newspapers are still associated with a particular party or ideology. This means that although journalists view themselves as professionals committed to the norm of objectivity (Tuchman 1978), they still have an advocacy role in shaping political information. Advocacy means taking up a coherent and consistent position on political issues through the news. Indeed, this advocacy is to a large extent the *raison d'être* for the press, because it is the shared political values that they express through news that binds them to their readerships. Patterson and Donsbach (1996, pp. 455–456) describe the characteristics of European newspapers in the following terms: "[The] news is professionally produced and aims more to inform than to persuade. Nevertheless, the vitality of these newspapers flows in considerable measure from their role as political advocates and from the staunch loyalty of their partisan readers."

There are many important contributions on political journalism, but it is possible to identify some common ground (among many others, see, e.g., Gans 1979; Lippmann 1922[2007]; Patterson 1997, 1998; Schudson 1995; Seymore-Ure 1974). Journalists are professionals. They work within news organizations that operate within constraints and opportunities shaped by commercial and institutional factors, including ownership, market share, and a nationally specific relationship between the media and political system (Hallin and

Mancini 2004). Thus news organizations usually have a clear relationship to institutional politics, identifying to a greater or lesser extent with left or right political parties and addressing readerships with identifiable political leanings (Blumler and Gurevitch 1995). Such factors attribute newspapers with a specific organizational culture that finds expression in its "editorial line," a set of values with which most journalists consciously identify. Taking such contextual factors largely as given, we focus on news organizations as environments that provide specific constraints and incentives for journalists to operate and take news decisions.

Journalists aim to provide the information for citizens to make decisions about governance, especially who to vote for, and which policies to support. According to Denis McQuail (1994, p. 145), their institutional product, news, is "characterised by a high degree of objectivity, key marks of which are obsessive facticity and neutrality of attitude." However, journalists are committed to more than the neutral transmission of political facts. First, they may try to make news interesting to inform and educate the public, drawing them into politics instead of assuming that their readers' political views are fixed or complete. Second, they may take on a "watchdog" role by investigating politicians' and public officials' performances with the goal of safeguarding public trust. Further, investigative journalism aims to reveal aspects of politics to citizens that the powerful may have deliberately concealed. Hence the journalist is not only a fair-minded analyst of political events, but sometimes also a political actor (Page 1996; Patterson 1998). When this role takes on a strong interpretive form, the journalist becomes what Michael Schudson (2007, p. 140) calls a "professional truth-teller," following a mission to expose what are perceived as deceitful self-interested political powers. There is much debate about the most preferable type and what constitutes good and bad journalism. Here we largely sidestep these issues. However, it is important to recognize that these norms are also relevant, empirically, as the reference points that journalists use to monitor and evaluate their own performances.

Regarding the research field on Europe, the review by Semetko, de Vreese, and Peter from 2001 indicates a lack of systematic evidence (p. 121): "We know of no studies to date that have looked specifically at the role and impact of European integration on domestic news coverage... We know little about political communication and news organisations from a comparative perspective and even less about how news differs cross-nationally in terms of the reporting of domestic and European political affairs." There are a few early studies evaluating EU correspondents on British newspapers (Morgan 1995) and the EU's communication performance (Meyer 1999; Tumber 1995). More recently, there has been an increase in research on journalism and Europe (e.g., AIM Research Consortium 2007; Baisnée 2002; Gleissner and de Vreese 2005; Huber 2007). However, understandably, given resource limitations, these have often been small "*n*" (small-number) case studies located in one or two countries and focused on one type of journalism, which places limits on the possibility of generalizing from their findings. Alternatively, the few attempts at large-scale coverage (e.g., Raeymaeckers, Cosjin, and Deprez 2007) provide descriptive information about the numbers, geographical scope, and infrastructure of journalism, but they tell us relatively little about journalists' understandings that inform their practices. Still others make abstract speculations about possible changes in journalism, though it is difficult to see on what empirical basis these are made (e.g., Heikkilä and Kunelius 2006). Finally, theorization of the relationship between media and politics beyond the nation-state remains somewhat thin on the ground (though see Meyer 2009). Overall, despite recent advances, there is relatively little in the way of joined up approaches, addressing different aspects of journalism, systematically, and inclusively of cross-national experiences.

APPROACH

From the literature, it is possible to see that journalistic styles range from the *descriptive* to the *interpretive*. Descriptive reporting is driven by "facts," whereas the more interpretive approach is driven by the theme around which a story is built and gives the journalist more control over the news message (Patterson 1997). In the descriptive mode, journalists are primarily mediators of political information – claims, events – from external sources. Their news decisions shape the information flows that are of crucial importance to polities. By contrast, when they are in the interpretive mode, journalists are political actors who intervene in debates with their own voice. Their news decisions seek to shape public opinion and policy responses. Although this is an analytic distinction, it is clear that news reporting is based more on the descriptive approach, whereas commentaries and editorials are based on the interpretive approach.

In Figure 5.1 we present a simple general model for seven factors that influence journalists' news decisions, which is drawn from the communications literature. The model distinguishes between the actors external to news production (public; political actors) and journalists working within news organizations, and it analytically separates the two styles of journalism, *descriptive* and *interpretive*. It identifies seven factors that may influence journalists' news decisions.

Starting with external factors to news production, we first look at journalists' perceptions of their *readerships' demand* (Label 1 in the figure) for information, and second at the extent to which they think political actors attempt to influence coverage through communication strategies, that is *source strategies* (2). We then give special attention to journalists' views of the quality of information supplied by the European institutions, the *EU's performance as a source* (3). Turning to factors internal to news production, we examine journalists' experiences of news gathering, selection, and writing news reports, that is, their *reporting decisions* (4); and then, their *commentating decisions* (5) when writing commentaries and editorials. Another important set of decisions are journalists' efforts to influence other actors' opinions through their writing,

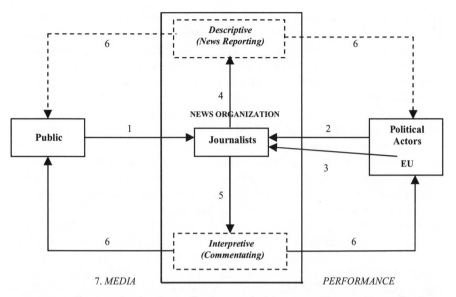

FIGURE 5.1. Factors shaping journalists' news decisions over Europe: Journalists' perceptions of 1, readerships' demand; 2, political actors' source strategies; 3, EU institutions' performance as a source; 4, news reporting decisions; 5, commentating decisions; 6, targeting strategies; and 7, norms for media performance.

their *targeting strategies* (6), which are more directly evident when they commentate than report politics (this is why the line from news reporting is dotted in the figure). Finally, another factor that can shape journalists' news decisions is their own evaluations and norms for *media performance* (7). We use these seven factors to structure our inquiry and build up a general picture of news decision making over Europe. Each of these factors may vary across countries, journalists, or newspaper types. In the next section, we provide detail on the sample and design of the study.

SAMPLE AND INTERVIEW METHOD

Professional journalists are a social group sharing a common orientation and ethos that affects how they see their work (Tumber and Prentoulis 2005). Hence their views are a potentially rich data source. Of key importance are journalists' understandings of factors that influence their news decisions.[2] Analyzing how journalists "see their world" provides factual information on their practices, but it also allows us to gain insight into the understandings, norms, and values

---

[2] This methodological approach has similarities to one of the few other large cross-national studies of political journalism that is based on journalists' survey responses (see Donsbach and Patterson 2004; Patterson and Donsbach 1996).

that shape their actions. To understand journalists' responses to the multileveling of governance, it is necessary to draw from a broad sample of national experiences. It is also important to account for variations within journalism, both between different types of journalist and those working on different types of newspaper. This implies the need for a design that allows comparison across these contexts.

The study draws on 110 interviews with journalists selected from our sample of twenty-eight national and regional newspapers – see Chapter 2 – to which four transnational ones were added. However, one modification was necessary. The British tabloid newspaper *The Sun*, after discussions at the editorial level, refused to allow any of its journalists to participate. The reason given was because it is a newspaper that campaigns in a partisan way over Europe. Indeed our claim-making data confirms that *The Sun* is the most Eurosceptic newspaper in our sample. It produces the most negative mean position scores over European integration of all newspapers, both in its reporting of other actors' claims – descriptive bias – and in its own claim making through editorials – interpretive bias (findings available on request). *The Sun* was replaced with its tabloid rival *The Mirror*, though it should be noted that *The Mirror* takes the opposite stance to *The Sun* over Europe.

We selected four journalist types (editor/leader writer, EU correspondent, journalist covering agriculture, and journalist covering immigration) for each of the four newspapers selected per country. Our sample of journalists thus varies across different professional roles, distinguishing between reporters and commentators and between EU specialists and reporters on normal news beats. For the transnational sample, we added four English-language newspapers targeted at elite–business readerships: *Financial Times (Europe)*, *International Herald Tribune (Europe)*, *Wall Street Journal Europe*, and finally, the *European Voice*, which is a weekly with limited circulation but with a Brussels elite readership. Here we interviewed only editors/leader writers and EU correspondents. The interview schedule for the transnational press was modified when necessary.[3]

Recruitment efforts were effective, achieving 110 interviews from a possible 120. The shortfall occurred because some correspondents covered more than one role, or some roles did not exist on some newspapers. Each interview was conducted in 2003–2004, took at least an hour, and was undertaken in the journalist's own language. To render this large amount of information manageable, we used an interview schedule containing closed survey-like questions but requiring interviewees to elaborate openly on their answers. The questions are structured around topics on news infrastructure; readerships' demand; source strategies; reporting practices; commentating; political role and advocacy (Statham, Firmstone, and Gray 2003). All responses, closed and open (which were translated into English), were coded into an SPSS database. This allows qualitative comments to be used in a way that is linked to closed responses to specific questions. Thus interpretation is based on linked

---

[3] For a detailed study of journalists from the transnational press from this project, see Firmstone (2008b).

quantitative and qualitative responses. Not all questions were relevant for all journalist types, which accounts for the varying "*n*" (or number) in presented tables. Furthermore, more questions were asked than those presented here, and this additional information was used for interpretive purposes.

FACTORS EXTERNAL TO NEWS PRODUCTION

Here we examine journalists' perceptions of factors that are external to news production but that may influence their news decisions and evaluations over Europe. These are the first three factors represented in Figure 5.1. First, we look at journalists' perceptions of their readerships' demand for political information; second, we look at the extent to which journalists think that political actors attempt to influence coverage through communication strategies that supply information. Third, we give special attention to journalists' perceptions of the quality of information supplied by the European institutions.

Perceptions of Readerships' Demand

Newspapers are commercial enterprises. They need to advance their market share and establish loyalty among a readership that identifies with the newspaper and buys it regularly. This means that journalists have incentives to appeal to the political tastes and understandings of their targeted audience. Hence journalists' perceptions of their readers' demand for political information over Europe is likely to shape their evaluations of its newsworthiness. For example, if public interest in European affairs is low, as evidenced by opinion polls, there are fewer incentives for journalists to report them. Additionally, if readers' knowledge of European politics is low, then journalists may consider the European level not worth covering in a story.

To assess how perceptions of readerships' demand may shape their thinking, we asked journalists to assess their readerships' interest and understanding of European politics compared with politics in general. We asked, "How interested do you think your readership is in politics?"; "How interested do you think your readership is in European politics?"; and "To what extent do you think your readership understands how European politics works?" Possible responses were as follows: not at all = 0, a little = 0.33, moderately = 0.67, greatly = 1.00. After responding, interviewees gave open comments to explain their choices.

For journalists on national and regional newspapers, the findings are clear-cut: They consider their readerships to be less interested in European politics (0.50) than politics in general (0.73), and that readers have a low understanding of the workings of European politics (0.37).[4] From this evidence, perceived readership interest is likely to be a factor that leads to less rather than more European coverage. Interestingly, however, this does not hold for the journalists on transnational newspapers, who felt their readerships had a greater

---

[4] Figures are means based on 97 responses (weighted by country).

interest in politics (0.93), a relatively much greater interest in European politics (0.93), and a better understanding of how EU politics works (0.63). Transnational journalists perceive a greater readership-thirst for European news, which provides incentives for coverage.

This difference was underlined by their comments. Journalists from the national and regional press highlighted the barriers to their readers' comprehension. Their remarks identified low readership interest in Europe resulting from its complex and remote nature, the resilience of readers' national-focused interpretative frameworks, and a history of information deficits over Europe. Here are some typical comments: "They (readers) are still more interested in national politics: there the frontiers are stronger clear-cut, the conflicts more controversial, the actors better-known and the impact on their own life is bigger" (Home Affairs correspondent, *FAZ*). [Are the readers interested in European politics?] "Not very much. Not as much as they should be, but that's [be]cause they're not told much about it" (Chief Leader Writer, *The Guardian*). "[European politics is] too complex to become popular. It is a complex process of institutionalisation that escapes most people's understanding" (Director, *ABC*). By contrast, journalists from transnational newspapers emphasized their readerships' international outlooks and specialist knowledge requirements, needing to keep abreast of global political affairs. For example, the *Financial Times (Europe)*'s editor thought, "The FT's big strength... is the emphasis we put on the relationship between business and politics. That is something that our readers (mainly business people) prize very highly."

Journalists writing for national and regional audiences felt that their readerships lag behind in their understanding of the importance of European politics. For them, readerships' demand produces few incentives for covering Europe. In contrast, the transnational press is more driven by its elite readerships' demand for transnational and global coverage, delivered with international interpretive frameworks, especially on political and business topics.

Political Actors' Source Strategies

The media system depends on inputs of information from the political system. This is supplied by political actors from institutions, social and economic interest groups, NGOs, and social movements, who make demands in relation to events. Journalists are confronted by a barrage of competing claims, from which only a small number appear in print as a result of limited carrying capacity. Thus the political discourse carried by the media is a competitive field where collective actors engage in acts of "strategic political communication" (Kriesi 2004) to gain influence. Political actors' mobilization attempts constitute their agenda-building or agenda-setting activities (Everett and Dearing 1988; Hilgartner and Bosk 1988). Often these are purposeful and strategic attempts to symbolically package and frame information for journalists (Gamson and Modigliani 1989). Such efforts are discussed in journalism studies as "source strategies" (Schlesinger and Tumber 1994).

Hence another external factor that may influence journalists' new decisions over Europe concerns the amount and type of information that political actors target at them. Their available information resources will depend partly on which political actors mobilize claims and how they frame them. For example, if actors representing national political institutions make more efforts than European actors, then their specific nation-focused agendas are likely to shape the information resource pool of journalists. If European institutions make fewer publicity efforts for their political aims than other actors, then these will be less visible to journalists and less likely to reach copy. It also should be noted that actors have vested interests. For example, in cases of unpopular legislation, national governments may have their interests served by promoting a view of European governance that depicts themselves as relatively powerless in the face of supranational EU decisions. It is therefore important to know "who" the most frequent source strategists are.

To build up a picture of who makes the most effort to supply information, we asked journalists to describe the frequency with which they were contacted by a list of political actors, varied by actor type (institutional or civil society) and political level (non-EU above nation-state, European, national, regional). The question appears in the tabular footnote to Table 5.1.[5]

Table 5.1 shows the list and ranks actors according to the frequency which journalists from national and regional newspapers considered them as source strategists. The striking finding is the predominance of national source strategists. Four national actors are ranked in the top five. National governments are the only actors who "regularly" (0.66) target journalists, whereas national interest groups (0.61), political parties (0.57), and campaign and protest groups (0.44) come second, third, and fifth, respectively. This underlines the importance of mobilization efforts by national actors compared with regional, European, and (non-European) supranational, transnational, and international ones, in shaping the information available to journalists. Overall we see a hierarchy of national actors, followed by regional and only then European and international ones.

It is well established that powerful institutional actors have more routine access to journalists than do civil society actors and social movements (Schlesinger and Tumber 1994). One would generally expect to find a hierarchy of source strategists that reflected this actor-type difference, with institutional actors prominent. Within political levels our findings confirm this. However, what is interesting is that Table 5.1 shows how little, comparatively, European and other actors above the nation-state try to make themselves heard to journalists on national and regional papers. The institutions of the European Union (0.46) constitute the only actor above the nation-state who makes noteworthy communication efforts. However, even this makes the EU a source strategist only on a par with national campaign and protest groups (0.44), and regional

---

[5] Editors were not asked this question, as they are not recipients of "source strategies" to the same extent as beat journalists; thus $N = 73$.

TABLE 5.1. *Journalists' Perceptions of the Frequency of Political Actors' Source Strategies (National and Regional Newspapers)*

Actor	Rank	Score
National government	1	0.66
National interest groups (e.g., trade unions, employers associations)	2	0.61
Political parties (national)	3	0.57
EU institutions or Commission	4	0.46
National campaign and protest groups	5	0.44
Regional or local government	6	0.40
Regional or local interest groups (e.g., trade unions, employers associations)	7	0.40
Scientific experts or policy think tanks working in this field	8	0.37
Supranational or transnational institutions (e.g., WTO, World Bank, UNHCR)	9	0.31
Regional or local campaign and protest groups	10	0.30
European interest groups (e.g., trade unions, employers associations)	11	0.28
International or transnational campaign and protest groups	12	0.23
International or transnational interest groups (e.g., trade unions, employers associations)	13	0.22
European campaign and protest groups	14	0.21
All		0.39
N		73

Notes: The question asked for this table was as follows: "Some public actors and organizations take 'active' initiatives to get their message across by supplying news stories, for example, through organizing press statements, publicity stunts, or other campaign activities. How often do the following types of organization target you with such publicity activities?" The answer was scored as follows: 0 = never, 0.33 = from time to time, 0.67 = regularly, and 1 = always or very often. In the "Score" column, the figures are aggregated mean scores ranging from 0 to 1, weighted by country. WTO = World Trade Organisation; UNHCR = United Nations High Commissioner for Refugees.

and local governments (0.40) and interest groups (0.40). In contrast, European interest groups (0.28) and protest groups (0.21) make very few efforts indeed.

As a political actor, Europe seems to make relatively little effort to penetrate the information resource pool of journalists and, to the limited extent that it does, institutional not civil society voices are the ones heard. On this evidence, the impact of source strategies would be to present journalists with sources of political information that prioritize the interpretative frameworks of national political actors overall, and those of institutions from the European actors.

Another general point is that we found greater variation across types of journalist than across countries or newspaper type.[6] Notable differences include

[6] Using one-way analysis of variance (ANOVA) tests for each variable for source strategies, there were significant differences (< 0.05) for eight of the fourteen variables for journalist type (groups: EU correspondents, editors, and journalists on policy fields), compared to four for country, and two for newspaper type (groups: left broadsheet, right broadsheet, tabloid or popular, and regional). For full results, contact the author.

that European institutions target EU correspondents considerably more often (0.76) than they do other journalists (0.28). This shows that the EU directs its communication at the topical specialists. By contrast, national governments target EU correspondents (0.64) and other journalists (0.67) at similar levels. It seems the EU makes little effort to compete with national actors to influence normal beat journalists, but it competes with them for the attention of EU correspondents.

Our enquiries with journalists from the transnational press again reveal interesting differences from the national and regional press.[7] Transnational journalists receive significantly more information mobilized by European institutions, political parties, interest groups, and even campaign and protest groups than they do from national and regional actors, including governments. Especially prominent as source strategists are the two main party groups from the European Parliament, the right European People's Party–European Democrats (PPE-ED) and left Party of European Socialists (PES). This perhaps gives an indication of at least some nascent European-level party competition mediated through the transnational press. Overall, information flows from the EU-level political system are strongly directed at transnational newspapers, and to a limited extent at specialist European correspondents for national and regional newspapers.

The EU's Performance as a 'Source'

It is also important to examine the quality of the EU institutions' information provision, not least because their communication strategies have been identified as a factor limiting the effectiveness of their media visibility (Meyer 1999; Tumber 1995), though they have more recently made efforts to improve this (Raeymaeckers et al. 2007).

To examine the EU's quality as a source, we asked journalists to assess aspects of the *information-provision* and *political-communicative* qualities of the information provided by the EU institutions' communications, judged by their suitability for news. By information-provision qualities we refer to the "objective" information contents of their communications, such as providing "material that is usable news copy," "material that is accurate," or "specialist knowledge or expertise." By political-communicative qualities, we mean the political contents of the EU's communications, such as "having a clear political line," "being transparent," and "being open to discussion." We asked journalists to compare these six aspects of the EU's communication with that of national actors, and about differences in "overall professional standards." The question we asked for each of the seven aspects of the EU's communication appears in the tabular footnote to Table 5.2, which shows journalists' rankings,

---

[7] The actor list for transnational journalists was modified to allow for specification between different types of EU-level actors and governments of different countries.

TABLE 5.2. *Journalists' Evaluations of European Institutions'
Communication, Compared to National Political Actors
(National and Regional Newspapers)*

EU Communication	Rank	Score
Providing specialist knowledge or expertise	1	0.12
Providing material that is accurate	2	0.05
Providing material that is usable news copy	3	−0.05
Overall professional standards	4	−0.17
Being open to discussion[a]	5	−0.18
Being transparent	6	−0.23
Having a clear political line[a]	7	−0.37
All		−0.12
N		54

Notes: The question asked for this table was as follows: "In comparison to the national political actors that you deal with, please rate whether the following aspects of European institutions' communication are better, no different, or worse." The answer was scored as follows: +1 = better, 0 = no different, −1 = worse. In the "Score" column, the figures are aggregated mean scores ranging from −1 to +1, weighted by country.
[a] Figures are missing for the Netherlands case.

and scores, weighted by country.[8] After giving their response, journalists elaborated openly on the EU's communicative performance.

The ranking of journalists' perceptions clearly shows that the EU's information provision is seen as better than its political-communicative performance. The three information-provision aspects providing specialist knowledge (0.1), accurate material (0.0), and material that is usable news copy (−0.1) were rated higher than its three political-communicative ones, namely, openness to discussion (−0.2), transparency (−0.3), and having a clear political line (−0.4). Turning to the comparison with national actors' communication, we see that, generally, journalists consider the EU's overall professional standards for communicating (−0.2) to be slightly worse than that of national actors.

Journalists' comments clarify *how* they view the EU's communication. Regarding being informative, many highlighted limitations that were due to the EU's technocratic style, its complexity, which was due to the number of countries and issues involved, and the remoteness of EU institutions and their press office. A typical remark was this: "[It is] worse because there is a huddle of competences in Brussels, where different nations follow their different interests. Additionally the way of life in Brussels is not very conducive: It seems many have lunch between 11 a.m. and 4 p.m. and then go home" (Bonn Correspondent, *Bild*). Some criticized the suitability of information received: "The most stupid are the service of spokesmen and Eurostat that fax 30 pages of numbers

[8] Here N = 54 because we asked only journalists who indicated they had experience of EU communications.

as if we have time to figure it out" (EU Correspondent, *Ouest-France*). "They [European institutions] say 'take the whole thing and look for the focus,' the national ones say 'take 2 sheets, it's our focus, and if you like I'll then give you the whole thing'" (Editor, *El Mundo*). However, the EU received praise from others for the objectivity of its information. Some appreciated the expertise of the information and that it is less likely to be delivered with political spin: "They try to give a lot of info and they try less than national governments to dodge issues by using 'stiff talk' (langue de bois)" (Socio-Economic Editor, *L'Humanité*) and "Less spinning here" (Brussels Correspondent, *Times*).

However, journalists mostly consider the political aspects of the EU's communication to be problematic. Typically, one journalist remarks, "There is less openness, less transparency and I cannot see a clear political line" (Editor, *Leipziger Volkszeitung*). However, this overall negative view holds more for the Commission than the European Parliament, where the existence of political cleavages and party politicians helps journalists to report political messages: "The people who are motivated and understand how to sell politics, who are operating through the [European] Parliament are very good. The [EU] institutions are bad" (Brussels Correspondent, *Mirror*).

Interestingly, regarding EU communication, the opinions of transnational journalists did not differ from their colleagues. Overall, they considered this to be worse than national governments, with the exception of the *International Herald Tribune*'s Brussels correspondent, who compared it to the "equally bad" U.S. government. Transnational journalists also hold strong reservations over the EU's political communication performance. For example, one (*Wall Street Journal Europe*) criticized the Commission's media savvy: "The main thing is that the Commission tends to . . . hire experts, who are very good at their subjects, but have zero idea how the press works, and which strings to pull to get a good quote or a good spin on a story in a newspaper." Overall, this shows that the EU's media performance will not be improved simply by increasing the quantity of information flows and their supply lines, but that journalists of all types hold concerns about the suitability of its communications for making news copy.

FACTORS INTERNAL TO NEWS PRODUCTION

We now turn to the factors in Figure 5.1 that are internal to news production and that may shape journalists' news decisions over Europe. First, we assess journalists' experiences of news reporting and their views on their *descriptive* role of covering political events and occurrences. Second, we look at their *interpretive* role, when they commentate over Europe, and inquire whether their advocacy is more educational, partisan, or ideological. Another part of this story of the media as a political actor is provided by examining "who" journalists attempt to influence when commentating. Last, we examine journalists' own views on media performance over Europe to assess the norms through which they regulate their behavior.

News Reporting Decisions

Obviously, there is not space here to give an in-depth study of news reporting. To provide an overall view of developments, we first report general findings on the response of news organizations to the advent of European multilevel governance, to give an idea of the resources available and context for journalism. Second, we zoom in on journalists' experiences by asking them about several considerations that shape their reporting decisions.

The resources that news organizations decide to commit are clearly important in shaping the opportunities for European journalism. In general our study found relatively little evidence for organizational efforts to transform news production processes and journalist practices specifically to enhance European coverage. Newspapers have responded to the challenge of reporting European affairs in an ad hoc way. They try to incorporate Europe as a "topic" into preexisting news-gathering and reporting practices. New posts for European correspondents tend to occur as a branch of foreign affairs. Changes within the organization to cover Europe are usually at the initiative of a few key individuals and not a systematic response to an institutional concern. Overall the limited innovations have been responsive rather than proactive and have brought only limited transformations of journalists' practices.

Turning to the factors that might shape journalists' reporting decisions, we find that most studies on journalism emphasize the barriers to effective coverage of European governance (Baisnée 2002; Huber 2007; Meyer 1999; Morgan 1995; Raeymaeckers et al. 2007). These include resource limitations for news gathering and research; journalists' poor linkages to EU institutions; the obscure nature of European politics and its lack of "news values"; editors' low prioritization of European stories; journalists' poor language skills and knowledge deficits; their overuse of nationalized interpretative frameworks; and news organizations following their proprietor's alleged political line over Europe.

If news organizations do not prioritize European coverage, journalists may have limited possibilities for gathering information and building up topical knowledge, for example as a result of a lack of funding for investigations and research or simply by not being present in Brussels. In addition, the status of European news within a news organization, and its editorial line, will impact on a journalist's ability to successfully place a European story or angle within the limited news space available. Alternatively, journalists' perceived difficulties in reporting on Europe could be due to the weakness of their contacts and sources within European political institutions, which would affect their access to official documents, or experts, or quotable public figures and politicians. Another problem may arise from the difficulty of fitting European stories within existing news values[9] and formats. For example, news values may demand exciting

---

[9] Galtung and Ruge's classic research (1965) on news values demonstrated that, for journalists, newsworthiness is based on a complex set of criteria in which an event's characteristics – e.g., prominence, human interest, conflict, "the unusual," timeliness, and cultural proximity (Shoemaker and Reese 1996) – influence its chances of being reported.

TABLE 5.3. *Journalists' Concerns, Considerations, and Difficulties When Reporting on European Affairs (National and Regional Newspapers)*

Concern	Rank	Score
Availability of news space	1	0.84
Necessity to capture audience attention	2	0.68
Access to important public figures	3	0.55
Availability of resources for research or investigation	4	0.50
Pressure of deadlines	5	0.47
Lack of expert knowledge on topic	6	0.40
Access to official documents	7	0.39
Lack of clear cues and positions from politicians	8	0.37
Own lack of understanding of topic	9	0.35
Pressure from senior editors or journalists	10	0.23
Pressure from management or organizational pressure	11	0.14
All		0.44
N		87

Notes: The question asked for this table was as follows: "News reporting is a pressurized and sometimes difficult task. Please mention whether any of the following is a concern, consideration, or difficulty for you when reporting a story relating to Europe." The answer was scored as follows: 1 = yes, 0 = no. In the "Score" column, the figures are aggregated mean scores ranging from 0 to 1, weighted by country.

conflicts between personalities, whereas Europe may deliver technocratic debates between faceless bureaucrats. In addition, journalists may face pressures from their news organizations, either its management or editors, to follow a specific political line on Europe, which may influence their selection and writing decisions. For example, Anderson and Weymouth (1999) claim that Rupert Murdoch's British newspapers promote Euroscepticism to serve their proprietor's interests.

To investigate these factors, we constructed a list of eleven possible *concerns* or *considerations* or *difficulties* for journalists, relating to their resources, journalistic practices, Europe's news values, and organizational pressures from the newspaper (political and work oriented). Table 5.3 shows journalists' ranking for these perceived problems relative to one another (weighted by country).

In general, we found that the experiences of journalists from different countries, working on different types of newspapers, and between different types of journalists did not vary significantly.[10] This suggests that there is a common experience for European news reporting that largely transcends differences pertaining to national media cultures, within journalism, and across newspapers.

From the list of possible concerns, a key finding is that the most prominent are difficulties that journalists experience in communicating European

[10] Using one-way ANOVA tests for all eleven variables testing by country, newspaper type, and journalist type, we found significant differences (<0.05) only for the availability of resources variable between types of newspaper and between countries, and significant differences between types of newspaper for space as a concern. Further details are available from the author on request.

stories within limited space requirements and using existing news values. The availability of news space (0.84) and the necessity to capture audience attention (0.68) were ranked by far the highest. Journalists' open comments added substance to this picture. They see problems arising from the complex nature of European politics and the obscure type of political information available from Brussels, which lacks the news values that would increase communicability to readerships. News space limitations are not just a general concern but also a specific intrinsic problem for European news, as one interviewee identified, "The main problem regarding stories of the EU is the complexity of the EU issues. A journalist has to explain much more. This results in problems of space" (Agricultural/Brussels Correspondent, *FAZ*). Most underlined this view: "When writing stories about Europe it is even more difficult and complicated to break down the issue into an understandable form" (Chief Editor, *Blick*); "It's difficult to get anything in about the Common Agricultural Policy. CAP is mainly figures, if you could make it into personalities or have an element of conflict then that would help. All the newsdesk are interested in is 'are they having a fight or not'?" (Rural Affairs Editor, *The Scotsman*); "In general it is difficult to get an item on Europe in the paper, as it is regarded as boring, and there is too little debate about it" (European Correspondent, *Leeuwarder Courant*); "The space is not sufficient for EU issues. Because of that we don't deal on a daily basis with EU issues. It is necessary to be able to explain things well to the reader. Extreme synthesis cannot be made on very technical and complex things" (EU Correspondent, *La Nazione*).

Within this common viewpoint, journalists from popular (1.00), tabloid (0.90), and regional (1.00) newspapers find limited news space especially problematic. Tabloid journalists (0.80) also find it hardest to capture the audience's attention for Europe. On this *Bild*'s political editor elaborates: "It is difficult to access the relevant actors and it is difficult to convert European issues into the language of BILD. There are no photos of Europe because the actors are unknown."

The other clear-cut finding from Table 5.3 comes from the especially low ranking of pressures from the management and the organization (0.14), and pressure from senior editors and journalists (0.23). Journalists do not to seem to experience overt institutional pressures, either regarding their work performance or to pursue a specific political line when covering Europe. Their comments illustrate concerns with the practice of European journalism, not from their organizational environment.

Regarding investigative resources (0.50) and access to expert knowledge (0.40), official documents (0.39), and public figures (0.55), findings were mixed, with some journalists experiencing problems, and others not. Problems regarding investigative resources tended to depend on a newspaper's resource allocation to European affairs, for example, "we cannot do investigations, we do not have enough resources to have someone working for a week on an issue" (Socio-Economic News Editor, *L'Humanité*). In contrast, problems with access tended to refer to difficulties with the EU institutions' approach to political communication: "Access: I can't cover the Justice and Home Affairs council of the EU because it is closed to the media. I can't even get hold of the papers until several months after they've been discussed" (Home Affairs Editor, *The Guardian*).

Interestingly, journalists on transnational newspapers broadly shared these views. They also identified important concerns with making EU stories interesting to readers and a lack of space for EU news. The complexity and incommunicability of EU politics is a concern for those writing for transnational elite publics too: "I think it's the language and understanding issue. Europe is constructed in such a way that ... is too complex for the average European. It doesn't resemble anything on the national level, and the decision making is opaque" (*International Herald Tribune*).

Overall, it seems that the primary concern for all types of journalist is how to fit the European level into news formats, given that it has to compete for news space. European-level politics appears to be inherently unsuited for making news and the information received difficult to make relevant to readers. Conversely, journalists seem to face little unwanted pressure of an interfering or political type from their news organizations.

Commentating Decisions

Pressures from within news organizations may shape the context for commentating, for example, the need to follow public opinion and attract readers, or to stay close to the line of an affiliated political party, or to follow a proprietor's stance. Such pressures may influence a newspaper's "editorial line" over Europe. Against this, journalists may see their autonomy in shaping the editorial line as an important expression of their professional independence. Indeed, journalists may experience more freedom to express themselves over Europe, because the issue often cross-cuts the party lines that strongly define politics at the national level. In addition, the relative newness of European multilevel governance may provide greater opportunities for journalists to take up stances, because patterns of understanding are less established than for national politics.

Editorials and commentary sections of newspapers allow journalists a special status within mediated public debates as "opinion leaders" (Eilders, Neidhardt, and Pfetsch 2004; Statham 2007b; Firmstone 2007). When commentating, they have greater scope for giving interpretive political messages. This potentially allows journalists to open up debates on topics, focus readers' attention, and provide cues for how to interpret them. It is here that journalists have opportunities to be a "political actor" (Page 1996; Patterson 1998). In this opinion-leading role, they have more scope to be an "advocate journalist," who takes sides and does so in a consistent, substantial, and assertive way to promote a particular ideology or group, which may, or may not, follow party political lines (Donsbach and Patterson 2004, p. 265).

To build a picture of journalists' advocacy, it is important to know the type of aims that shape their news decisions and commentating. First, journalists' aims may be *informative*. Here they attempt to raise awareness and open up understanding for a political issue among readerships. Second, journalists may be motivated by *political* aims. In these cases, their goal in covering a political issue is to attribute it with a specific interpretive slant, so that their readers' view of the issue is partial and politically biased. By distinguishing whether journalists' *informative* and *political* aims are strong or weak, we arrive at four types of advocacy: business as usual; educational; partisan; and ideological.

Starting with *business as usual* advocacy, journalists' aims are weakly informative and weakly political over European topics. Here journalists see no special need to take a stance over Europe, either to educate their readers or to promote a partisan stance. Turning to *educational* advocacy, journalists are more strongly motivated by informative aims, deciding that Europe is a topic that merits coverage. They provide more and better information for readers so that they have the tools to understand issues. For example, educational advocacy may unpack the complexities of multilevel governance, or explain where power lies in the EU, thereby opening up and making Europe familiar to readers but without promoting a political stance that is either for or against the European project. By contrast, the opposite of this is *partisan* advocacy. Here journalists' motivations are political. They cover European stories to promote a specific political interpretation of the European Union by attributing a systematic political bias. This partisan advocacy tries to push the debate for or against Europe, but in a way that largely fails to inform readers about the topic, just saying which position they should take. Finally, in the case of *ideological* advocacy, journalists' aims are strongly informative and political. Here journalists systematically take up and promote a clear stance for or against Europe, but their political slant is packaged in a way that raises awareness and informs substantively about the issue. Journalists attempt to lead, influence, and open up an informed political debate over Europe. Such media campaigns may be consistent with the position of a political party to which a newspaper is affiliated, or alternatively the paper's editorial line over Europe may be independent from party positions. Overall, an important question is this: Do journalists act as educators, partisans, or ideologues, or is European integration simply business as usual for them? What factors shape journalists' commentating over Europe, and how do they define their aims?

To examine journalists' commentating decisions, we asked them to contrast their experiences in writing opinion articles over Europe with those for national politics for several factors. Some factors related to the news organization, about whether the newspaper was more likely to follow a party's line, the proprietor's stance, or national public opinion polls, or alternatively express an independent stance. Others dealt with journalists' aims when commentating, whether they were more likely to be nationalist, or whether their opinion leading was more informative, seeking to improve public knowledge, or political, trying to shape the stances of political elites. Table 5.4 gives the precise question and ranks journalists' perceived differences. We also asked interviewees to elaborate on the most important difference.

TABLE 5.4. *Journalists' Perceived Differences When Commentating on European Compared to National Affairs (National and Regional Newspapers)*

Difference	Rank	Score
Newspaper is more likely to defend what it sees as the national interest	1	0.55
Newspaper has more of a duty to improve public knowledge	2	0.53
Newspaper is more likely to express its own position, independently from other actors	3	0.46
Newspaper is more likely to try to influence the positions of political elites	4	0.42
Newspaper is more likely to follow the perceived position of the proprietor	5	0.16
Newspaper is more likely to follow the line of the political party with which it is most closely associated	6	0.14
Newspaper is more likely to follow the line indicated by national public opinion polls	7	0.12
All		0.34
N		87

Notes: The question asked for this table was as follows: "When commentating on political affairs relating to Europe, such as the Convention on the Future of Europe, is the newspaper's role in any way different than when giving an opinion on national affairs, with respect to the following statements?" (interviewer reads out left-hand column). The answer was scored as follows: 1 = yes, 0 = no. In the "Score" column, the figures are aggregate mean scores ranging from 0 to 1, weighted by country.

Generally we found that journalists' experiences did not significantly vary much across countries, newspaper types, and journalist types.[11] Again, this points toward a common experience for European journalism.

A first clear finding is that journalists consider their newspaper an independent opinion leader, able to express its opinions over Europe (0.46), whereas there is very little perceived pressure to follow the views of associated political parties (0.14) or proprietors (0.16), or to chase national public opinion (0.12). Journalists' own perceived flow of opinion leading is from themselves to external actors, that is, from the media system to the political system. They are not "passive" journalists acting "as the instrument of actors outside the news system" (Donsbach and Patterson 2004, p. 265); rather, they consider themselves sufficiently independent to have a say over Europe. Second, regarding how they commentate, it seems that defending national interest (0.55) ranks relatively high as a consideration. This may be taken as evidence for the persistence of journalists' nationalist interpretative frameworks over Europe. Third, journalists emphasize they have an educational duty to improve public knowledge

---

[11] Using the one-way ANOVA tests for each variable, the only significant differences (<0.05) were among countries for the two variables of newspaper more likely to try to influence political elites and newspaper more likely to follow line of political party it is associated with. We found no significant differences across journalist types and newspaper types.

(0.53), which is stressed more than their efforts to influence political elites (0.42). This points more toward *informative* than *political* aims for advocacy.

Such an impression was strongly reinforced by journalists' open comments. They emphasize difficulties over unpacking and raising awareness about Europe. By far the overwhelming difference for journalists when commentating on Europe compared to national politics is the need to explain and express matters more clearly, which is due to their readership's lack of knowledge: "There's an attempt to explain things better when the EU level is spoken of, it's a task of giving more clarity, knowing that the reader isn't as familiarized with the EU's functioning compared to national politics" (Editor, *El Pais*); "On European issues (we) have to be a lot more informative since more explanations are needed for the reader to understand the opinion piece" (Correspondent, *El Mundo*); "The public does not know much about the subject so the paper has the duty to inform" (Editor, *Leeuwarder Courant*); and "The newspaper sees itself as pro-European, internationalist, it feels it has duty to inform and explain because of levels of ignorance of the subject and the failings of government over the EU" (European Editor, *The Guardian*). These examples, selected from many, underline that journalists see the key difference to be the need to inform and educate their readerships. It indicates that they seem to be motivated by *informative* much more than *political* goals.

In addition, their comments show that the relative underdevelopment of European politics, and lack of established party divisions compared to the national level, allows greater freedom to shape the message: "[There is] bigger freedom to express opinion because there is less conditioning from national political actors or political groups" (Agriculture Correspondent, *La Nazione*); "At the national level, there is more interest in the standpoints of the political parties, which can be overcome at the European level, [so we are] less partisan concerning Europe" (Correspondent, *El Mundo*); And "European affairs are commented on with more freedom as party politics is not important. On a national level, trenches of party politics dominate. There are a lot of prejudices" (EU Correspondent, *FAZ*). However, it is also evident from these comments that this additional freedom is not taken as an opportunity for attributing a political bias, but for filling an information gap that is left open by national party politics.

One exception in this respect is the Swiss tabloid *Blick*. The *Blick* aims to be informative and to attribute a political bias. In the words of its chief editor, "The most important thing is that the *Blick* writes against its public when it comes to European politics; it does it consciously, rather than writing as its public thinks." It has adopted a political opinion-leading role over Europe, and it constitutes a relatively rare case of ideological advocacy.[12] We should perhaps also recall here that *The Sun*'s refusal to participate in our study was due to its

---

[12] This is confirmed by examining news contents. *Blick*'s own claim making through editorials – interpretive bias – produces one of the highest pro-European mean position scores over European integration from the sample of twenty-eight newspapers. However, its reporting of other actors' claim making – descriptive bias – produces one of the lowest mean position scores over European integration (that is, one of the least favorable). Findings are available from the author on request.

Eurosceptic partisanship. For the most part, however, press advocacy appears to be educational, aiming to raise awareness for Europe within the politics of a newspaper's editorial line, rather than being partisan.

The findings for transnational journalists go in the same direction as their colleagues on national and regional papers. Again their commentating was informative and aimed at building up awareness and understanding more than attributing a political slant. However, the transnationals see more of a watch-dog role for themselves at the EU level. As a *European Voice* correspondent put it, "Number one, we have to explain how the EU works in clear and simple terms. Second, we have to try and make up for the fact that EU institutions, generally speaking, aren't exactly models of transparency, by trying to put as much information that the people in important positions want to keep secret, in the public domain."

Generally, the findings indicate that the press sees its advocacy role as an educator over Europe, much more than as a partisan or ideologue.

Targeting Strategies

Our findings indicate that journalists follow more educational than partisan goals over Europe; however, it is still important to know who they try to influence, and how often. Journalists' own mobilization efforts, that is, their *targeting strategies*, may be directed at elites, or specific interest or target publics, or at general audiences. To address this, we examine where European institutions fit among the perceived targets of journalists' political commentaries.

To address who journalists target, we focused on their commentating practices, and we asked them to describe the frequency with which they attempted to influence a list of political actors, varied by actor type (institutional or civil society) and level (non-EU above nation-state, European, national, or regional). Table 5.4 shows an overall ranking and score for the frequency with which journalists from the national and regional press try to influence specific actors through commentating.[13]

It is worth noting that we found stronger evidence for cross-national differences, compared to variations between types of newspaper and journalist.[14] The main difference was between the British journalists who especially targeted national governments and national political parties, even more so than their readerships, whereas all the other countries targeted their readerships more than their national political system. It seems that the influence of national press cultures are prominent in shaping who journalists try to influence, and that the British press tries harder to influence national political elites over Europe.

---

[13] Only journalists who make decisions about or write commentaries responded; hence, $N = 86$.

[14] Applying one-way ANOVA tests for each variable, we found significant differences (<0.05) by country for two-thirds of the variables. Differences were significant only for three variables for newspaper type, and for none by journalist type. Full results are available from the author on request.

TABLE 5.5. *Journalists' Targeting Strategies (National and Regional Newspapers)*

Target	Rank	Score
Public	**I**	**0.47**
Your readership	1	0.76
National public opinion	2	0.57
Informed political opinion – "the chattering classes"	3	0.56
Scientific experts or policy think tanks working in this field	4	0.25
Journalists from other newspapers	5	0.20
Governments and political parties	**II**	**0.38**
National government	1	0.53
Political parties (national)	2	0.43
Regional or local government	3	0.41
EU institutions or Commission	4	0.30
Supranational or transnational institutions (e.g., WTO, World Bank, UNHCR)	5	0.23
Interest groups	**III**	**0.28**
National interest groups (e.g., trade unions, employers associations)	1	0.42
Regional or local interest groups (e.g., trade unions, employers associations)	2	0.30
European interest groups (e.g., trade unions, employers associations)	3	0.22
International and transnational interest groups (e.g., trade unions, employers associations)	4	0.17
Campaign and protest groups	**IV**	**0.21**
National campaign and protest groups	1	0.28
Regional and local campaign and protest groups	2	0.23
European campaign and protest groups	3	0.18
International or transnational campaign and protest groups	4	0.15
N		86

Notes: The question asked for this table was as follows: "When you are writing an article that gives you the scope to express an opinion on behalf of the newspaper and comment on political events, how often do you try to get your message across to the following actors?" The answer was scored as follows: 0 = never, 0.33 = from time to time, 0.67 = regularly, and 1 = always or very often. In the "Score" column, the figures are aggregated mean scores ranging from 0 to 1, weighted by country.
WTO = World Trade Organisation; UNHCR = United Nations High Commissioner for Refugees.

Generally, Table 5.5 shows that the press' efforts are more oriented to public constituency building than influencing political elites. Journalists target their political information at public constituencies (0.47) more than actors from institutional politics (0.38) and interest (0.28) and campaign/protest groups (0.21). Their own readerships (0.76) are the only constant target, followed by national public opinion (0.57) and informed public opinion, "the chattering classes" (0.56). After this, political actors begin to register, but really only national ones: governments (0.53), political parties (0.43), and interest groups (0.42). It is striking that journalists on the national and regional press attempt to influence EU institutions only from time to time (0.30), to the same limited extent as regional and local interest groups (0.30), and even less than regional governments (0.41). It is perhaps worth noting that even the newspapers' specialists on Europe, the EU correspondents, attempt to address national governments (0.42) and political parties (0.42) more than EU institutions (0.35). In sum, we find little evidence for journalists trying to influence European institutional politics through their writing, which is much more targeted at public readerships, and to a lesser extent national institutional politics.

Turning to the transnational press,[15] we find that journalists also direct most efforts at their own readership (1.00) and at shaping the "chattering classes" of informed opinion among transnational (0.87) and national (0.87) elites. In addition, they attempt to influence the Commission (0.80), Council of Ministers (0.80), and European Council (0.80), and the national governments of Britain (0.73), France (0.73), Germany (0.73), and Italy (0.73). Although the European Parliament (0.67) and its main party groups, on the right, the European People's Party–European Democrats (0.47) and on the left, the Party of European Socialists (0.47), are prominent source strategists, journalists target them less than they do other EU institutions. In other words, journalists target more where power lies at the supranational level. Overall, the transnational press' efforts are more prominent and channeled at national and transnational elite publics, as well as the powerful EU institutions and national government actors. This gives some support to the view of transnational journalism as an emerging actor within European politics at the supranational level.

Journalists' Evaluations of Media Performance

As journalists' news decisions are likely to be shaped by their normative views of their role, we inquired into journalists' evaluations of media performance over Europe. Here we asked journalists this question: "Much is made of the 'democratic deficit' of the EU; what role do you see the press having in reducing this 'deficit' by informing and educating the public?" Their open comments unpack *how* they see their role.

Some criticize the media's performance: "(The) Media can do it a lot but the problem is how they do it. They are a little behind, they don't give much importance to the EU and they are not clear about EU" (Co-Director, *Repubblica*). However, most comments indicate that journalists perceive the "democratic deficit" to be a problem within institutional politics, that is, the political system and not the media system. They think the media should expose such perceived deficits, but they are clear that this is an informative and not a political role. Journalists tend not to see the "democratic deficit" as their responsibility,

---

[15] The actor list for transnational journalists was modified to allow for specification between different types of EU-level actors, and governments of different countries.

nor do they adopt pioneering normative stances: "The media are no substitute for Parliamentary control" (EU Political Journalist, *FAZ*); "To discuss, explain, verify, (journalists) can help people to understand the importance of the EU. Nevertheless, EU decision making lacks transparency. EU Commissioners are perceived as not politically responsible because they are not elected" (Co-Director, *Repubblica*); [on own perceived role regarding the "democratic deficit"] "We're a commercial organisation so it's not our job. I do believe there is a 'democratic deficit', and it's an interesting topic and we try and cover it" (Associate Editor, *The Scotsman*); and "There's generally a low understanding of the functioning of EU institutions; only the newspapers can fill this gap" (Correspondent, *El Pais*). Overall, the perceived "democratic deficit" is seen as an important topic but not as a justification for transforming existing journalistic practices and norms, nor as an opportunity for an enhanced political role.

Interestingly, journalists on the transnational press shared this understanding. They viewed their primary role to be information provision and located the responsibility for the so-called democratic deficit in the EU institutions' poor efforts at bridging the gap to their citizens. Generally, it seems that journalists evaluate their role by standards of professional performance. This is how they view their potential contribution to improving Europeanized political communication flows, whereas they see the responsibility for the current perceived democratic deficit to be beyond the scope of their actions, and firmly located within the political system, specifically the European institutions.

DISCUSSION: A EUROPEAN JOURNALISM?

Generally, this study demonstrated that journalists' decisions about writing news reports and commentating vary relatively little across countries. This suggests that there is something approaching a common experience for European journalism. Journalists certainly highlighted many of the same problems and shared a common understanding of their professional role and aims.

Many problems that journalists mentioned were constraints that are external to news production and over which they have virtually no influence: the restricted market that results from low public readerships' demand for European news; the limited and national-focused sources of information that journalists receive from the political system; the relatively feeble efforts of EU institutions to be "sources"; and the low communicative qualities of EU politics, which is high on technical information but extraordinarily lacking in the contents, such as personality conflicts, that people recognize as politics. On this evidence, it seems overly simplistic to lay the responsibility for Europe's supposed communication deficits at the door of journalistic performance. After all, journalists can only mediate the political world that they are given. Better quality information flows from the political system, and especially the EU, would be a prerequisite for transforming these current restraints.

Regarding factors internal to news production, journalists felt able to ply their trade free from interference by their news organizations, proprietors, and affiliated political parties. However, they find Europe a difficult topic to write about and frame within established news values and norms. Limited news space is a universal problem. As commentators, journalists certainly do not shy from offering opinions about Europe, and they see few constraints from within their news organizations. They also witness more openness in possibilities for commentating over European-level debates compared with national ones, because political battle lines are less clear and readerships' understandings less formed. Crucially, however, journalists see their professional goals very much as raising awareness and opening up debates over Europe. For the vast majority, their advocacy is strongly educational, shaped by informative aims. A rare exception was the Swiss *Blick* tabloid, which had consciously transformed its editorial line to be a pro-European campaigner, even running against its readers' views.

Generally, the press is not reticent in pushing opinions over Europe, at present its aims are strongly informative much more than partisan. These educational norms and values largely shape journalists' practices and how they define their own role. It is mainly public knowledge deficits that motivate journalists to elaborate on European governance, not that they see themselves as advocates with a political ax to grind. Journalists view the "democratic deficit" as an interesting story, but they show little inclination for using it as a justification for taking up a role as a partisan actor. Their conduct over Europe seems to support Thomas E. Patterson's claim (1997, p. 447) that "journalists are driven by news opportunities, not by political values." They consciously distinguish between the media and political systems, but responsibility for any perceived communication shortfalls is left squarely on the shoulders of elected politicians. In this sense, the media follows the political system over Europe more than it tries to ideologically lead political debate, and this is how the journalists perceive their role.

Misguided expectations for journalism partly arise because media performance is often judged in academic debate by unrealistic normative standards. A more useful starting point for assessing media performance is to identify the ways in which professional journalism, operating within its current market and institutional context, has adapted to the challenge of covering a politics that has transformed as a result of European integration. From this realist view, there is relatively little to criticize journalists for regarding their media performance over Europe, other than, sometimes, a lack of innovation and imagination in the way they ply their trade. We found nothing to suggest that news organizations and journalists – even operating with existing norms and practices – would be unable to adapt if politicians made Europe more salient, politicized, and relevant for citizens. If the political system led the way in making Europe directly relevant to the public, then incentives would be provided for the media system to follow. However, in the current market and institutional context, it is unrealistic to expect journalists to take this step as some individual transformative leap of consciousness. Nor, from a normative viewpoint, would it be especially desirable for them to do so.

Finally, another set of findings related to differences for journalists on transnational papers. The small transnational press has adopted a specialist role for mediating European news. Transnational journalists receive greater flows of information from EU political institutions, and they make more efforts to influence EU actors through opinion leading than do their national and regional colleagues, who remain largely locked within circuits of information flows with national political actors. Mostly, transnational journalists' views on reporting difficulties and on advocacy concur with national and regional ones. However, the transnational press has greater incentives for supplying European news by operating in a market gap between national media systems and catering for political and business transnational elites. We found some evidence to support the idea that the transnational press is starting to fill a role for mediating news between European institutions and small transnational elite publics.

6

The Media's Voice over Europe

*Issue Salience, Openness, and Conflict
Lines in Editorials*

Barbara Pfetsch, Silke Adam, and Barbara Eschner

The previous chapter has highlighted the role of the media as conveyors of news about Europe. We have seen that journalists understand their advocacy over Europe to be more information driven and educational than ideological. In this chapter[1] we seek to understand how the press contributes as political actor to the Europeanization of national public spheres. Therefore, in this part of the overall study we treat the media as distinctive claimants (Page 1996; Pfetsch and Adam 2008), who, like other collective actors – such as governments, parties, or civil society – make their own contribution to public debate. According to professional standards, the format in which the media legitimately raise their own voice is the editorial.[2]

In contrast to the news section of the press, the purpose of editorials is related to the deliberative aspects of media performance. In the opinion section the press establishes a particular political profile that sets it apart from its competitors and reaches out to a specific audience segment (Eilders et al. 2004; Pfetsch 2008a). Here the newspaper seeks to express its distinctive normative view on issues of public concern. The objective is to advise, evaluate, comment, rebuke, and imagine the world as the newspaper wishes it to be. In public debate, the significance of editorials is twofold: First, editorials serve as a figurehead that defines the political identity of a press title. Through their claims in editorials the media make use of their right to present themselves as autonomous actors in public and political debate (Neidhardt, Eilders, and Pfetsch 2004, pp. 16–17). Second, by speaking up openly in opinion articles the press intends to exert influence on political debates. Editorials – and particularly the editorials of a nation's agenda-setting quality press – are paid close attention by opinion leaders such as politicians, activists, and journalists. There is also

---

[1] The chapter draws partly on Pfetsch, Adam, and Eschner (2008).
[2] When we speak of the editorial, we also include other forms of distinct opinion pieces that are set apart from the news formats of the press. For a detailed discussion see Eilders et al. (2004) and Pfetsch (2008a).

empirical evidence that news commentators have a significant impact on public opinion and its change over time (Page, Shapiro, and Dempsey 1987).

Regarding Europeanization, Bruter (2005) argues that the disposition of "good news" about Europe (as opposed to negative aspects) stimulates European identity. The political implication of this finding is that media provide important linkages for a European community of communication. Hence, we may also conclude that in studies on Europeanization the national media must not be dismissed as a significant actor for the emergence of a European public sphere. In the framework of our study, then, the press is treated as a potentially powerful claimant that may act as a facilitator of or obstacle to Europeanization.

To scrutinize the role of the media as actors in Europeanization, in addition to examining journalistic practices, norms, and professional conduct that we discussed in Chapter 5, it is also necessary to study the outputs of the media system. In this chapter, we examine the concrete manifestation of journalists' claim making in editorials of the national press. We focus on the visibility of EU issues and actors in media claims and the congruence of the debate on European integration. Our analysis will demonstrate that the media's voice on Europe is highly constrained, first by the national political context and second by the logic and the specific appeal of the media type. By applying the claim-making approach of the overall project and the selection of newspapers and countries, we are able to show that Europeanization systematically varies according to these conditions.

THEORETICAL CONSIDERATIONS AND EXPECTATIONS

To assess the media's role in the transnational communication across Europe, we draw on two core ideas in the research on Europeanization and the public sphere. First, our study joins up with scholars who claim that opening up national public debates for issues and actors from the EU and other member states may contribute to the connecting of Europe by means of communicative interactions (Habermas 2001, p. 120; Koopmans and Erbe 2004). This theoretical position was outlined in Chapter 2. A necessary precondition for this process to work is the *visibility* of the debate about issues of transnational concern and issues that are at stake between European countries on the elite and citizen levels. Only if citizens have the chance to become aware of the relevance of European topics and actors can we speak of an interconnected European debate (Adam 2007a; Koopmans and Erbe 2004; van der Steeg 2005).

The visibility of EU issues in public debates requires the media to attribute salience to topics of EU integration on their agenda. In their opinion and commentary section, media may enhance Europeanization by highlighting the issue of EU integration prior to other issues. Thus our analysis of editorials allows us to gauge the media's willingness to discuss EU issues. We also assess the media's potential for opening up public debate to European actors and their perspectives. By providing editorial space for the European and

EU member-state actors, the media prevent the closure of the debate and contribute to overcoming purely national perspectives. This places cross-border flows of communication at the focus of attention. In fact, we may treat the media as a facilitator of Europeanization, if they overcome their parochial nationally confined angles and reach beyond the territorial state. It is the specific potential of national media to follow "the extension of social spaces which are constituted by dense transactions, beyond national borders" (Zürn 2000, p. 187) with their commentating that may qualify the media as engines for European debates. The strength to which national media direct responsibility, support, or criticism to actors outside the national realm defines whether debates can be described as national, transnational, or European.

Another theoretical idea regarding Europeanization in national mass media refers to the *congruence* of debates across countries. Here we draw on the argument by Eder and Kantner (2000) that Europeanization requires issues to be debated at the same time under similar points of reference in different European countries. In this case a shared system of meaning is expected to emerge that would give European citizens a common basis for decisions. Regarding the congruence of European debates, the question is not only whether media mention common issues, but also whether they discuss them with respect to similar political interpretations. One way to capture the framing of EU issues is to relate them to the cleavages and policy options that structure the general political debate of a given country (Voltmer 1998–1999).

In our study, we use two indicators to determine whether the topic of EU integration is discussed with similar points of reference across EU countries: First, we examine whether national media agree on the relevant conflict lines that need to be addressed regarding EU integration (see Pfetsch 2008b); second, we analyze whether the media advocate the same positions on these conflict lines.

As we study the role of the media in Europeanization, we must take into account that processes of political communication are highly context sensitive (Esser and Pfetsch 2004, pp. 393–399). Gamson and Lasch (1983, p. 397) point out that every political discourse exists within a certain "issue culture," in which a catalogue of specific idea elements and symbolic devices is used to express ideas. National media are neither independent of these issue cultures nor separate from the political culture that prevails within their country. Instead, the involvement of the media with national issue cultures and political cultures is essential with respect to the interpretation of European integration issues. Indeed Juan Díez Medrano's study (2003) demonstrates well that the media's frames of Europe represent the long-term expectations of the impact of European integration on national collectives.[3]

---

[3] The significance of the national political culture for processes of Europeanization is also highlighted by studies that demonstrate the impact of the opinion of the national elite, national satisfaction with democracy, national policy traditions, and conflict constellations on the representation of Europe (Adam 2007a, 2007b; Peter and de Vreese 2004; Peter, Lauf, and Semetko 2004).

If we take into account the national issue cultures in European politics, then we should expect differences across countries in claim making by the press. Perhaps the most crucial factor that shapes national political cultures with regard to EU politics is depth of integration.

We assume that the media in countries that are fully involved in European integration – including the Monetary Union and the Schengen Agreement – attribute more salience to the issue, show European and EU-member state actors more strongly, and expose different conflict lines compared to media in countries that are rather hesitant members or that have not (yet) joined the EU (H1).

Our hypothesis rests on the assumption that common political institutions and decision-making structures, even if they are not fully legitimized by a European electorate, stimulate the Europeanization of public communication. We propose that a country's involvement in these common structures will affect how media shape European debates.

We investigate H1 by comparing national media. In particular, we expect to find differences in media claim making between three types of countries.[4] First, there is the category of fully integrated EU countries: Germany, France, Italy, the Netherlands, and Spain are – with the exception of Spain – founding members of the European Union; all have joined the Monetary Union and the Schengen Agreement. A second country category is constituted by the United Kingdom. By staying outside central projects such as the common currency and the Schengen Agreement, the United Kingdom has decided to limit the depth of its integration within the EU. The third country category consists of Switzerland, which has not yet joined the EU.

The second aspect that may constrain the role of the media in Europeanization is inherent in the segmentation of the media system (Hallin and Mancini 2004). There is evidence that the division between the press and television as well as the division between the quality press and the tabloid press or between public and private broadcasting does play a role in the public representation of European issues. For instance, public television has been shown to contribute more strongly to Europeanization than private television, and quality more than tabloid newspapers (de Vreese 2007; Kevin 2003; Peter and de Vreese 2004; Peter et al. 2004). Accordingly, we expect to observe variation in media claim making about European issues and politics across different types of newspapers.

We hypothesize that the regional press and the tabloid press tend to be more parochial and more Eurosceptic than the national quality press (H2).

---

[4] The uneven distribution of countries in the specified groups shows the limitations of our data. We are aware of the fact that, to fully test for our thesis on the depth of integration, more countries need to be included in those categories that have limited depth of integration as EU members (e.g., the new accession states) or non-EU members (e.g., Norway). Nevertheless, our study might be a first step in testing this depth-of-integration hypothesis. In addition, it may guide us to new hypotheses if, for example, we find clear-cut divisions within the big group of fully integrated member states.

Our hypothesis stems from the insight that the various media types cater to specific audience segments. The national quality press appeals to the political elites and also reaches them to a quite substantial degree. As European integration has always been a project of the political elites, we expect the national quality press to make European issues and actors more visible and be more open and supportive toward them. By contrast, the regional press and local press target a readership that is more interested in local and parochial politics. Readers of these newspapers tend to have a lower level of education and, as educational status correlates positively with EU support (Hix 2005, pp. 163–164), they are likely to be less Europhile than the average reader of the quality press. This difference in the readership is even more pronounced between quality and tabloid newspapers. The latter is therefore most likely to hook up on the rather Eurosceptic sentiments of its readership. Regarding regional newspapers, it is difficult to formulate clear-cut expectations. On the one hand, one may expect readers' interest to be mainly on local issues. On the other hand, one could also argue that the strong focus of EU integration on some regions (e.g., structural funds), and the possibility for regions to sometimes circumvent strong national regulations with the help of EU integration, may foster issue salience and openness toward Europe in regional newspapers.

DATA AND METHODOLOGY

For the empirical analysis we draw on the claim-making approach of the overall study. The voice of the media is treated as an aggregate of all claims made in editorials or commentaries of the newspapers under study. The procedures for identifying and coding claims described in Chapter 2 were fully applied. Each editorial was recorded as *one* claim of a journalist in which he or she makes demands. Thus, we consider the authors of editorials as individual claimants who attribute responsibility, support, and criticism to specific addressees. As editorials sometimes connect different topics, we allowed for coding of the three main topics within each claim. If at least one of them referred to EU integration, we included the claim in the category "EU integration." It turned out that most of the analyzed editorials in the category "EU integration" mentioned the issue as the most important topic.

The selection of newspapers includes all the press titles of the overall study except for the French paper *L'Humanité*. *L'Humanité*, the paper of the Communist Party, was excluded since it neither fits the category of a tabloid paper nor can it be treated as a regional paper. The reasons for choosing each specific outlet were described in Chapter 2 (see Table 2.1 in that chapter). However, while we have plausible criteria for the selection of the center-left and a center-right quality newspaper and the tabloid newspapers (in countries where they exist),[5] the choice of the regional newspaper was somehow problematic.

---

[5] To test this hypothesis, we collapsed the categories "popular" and "tabloid" of Table 2.1 into one category, "tabloid."

Analyzing only one regional newspaper per country – two for Italy and Switzerland – does not allow us to draw far-reaching conclusions about the role of this press type in Europeanization. Thus, our analysis can only be a starting point for testing how press formats differ or converge regarding Europeanization. Nevertheless, if our assumption about the media's catering to specific audience expectations is correct, we may find a clear-cut difference between the quality newspapers on the one hand and the regional and tabloid press on the other hand in all countries (H2). This difference might be especially strong in those countries that have a fully fledged tabloid press (Germany, Switzerland, and the United Kingdom).

Choosing editorials for our study was straightforward because we set up strict rules about how to identify them. Editorials and commentaries were defined as opinion articles written by a journalist or editor of the newspaper. They appear every day, often in a specific layout that sets them apart from news articles. For the selection of coding material, we had to cope with the problem that the output of editorials in the national press varied considerably. To reach a sufficient number of commentaries in all countries for coding and still be able to manage the workload of coding in those countries with a high number of commentaries, we had to think about a strategy that yields about the same number of editorials in each country.

We decided to customize the samples for each country's setting, and we applied the following strategy: In countries with a low number of commentaries (France, the Netherlands, and Switzerland), we selected all commentaries that fit our seven issue fields (EU integration, agriculture, monetary politics, immigration, troop deployment, pensions, and education) in all four national newspapers on every day of the year. In the United Kingdom, Italy, and Spain – countries that yield a medium number of commentaries – we selected and recorded the commentaries of three days per week. Germany turned out to be the country with the most commentaries. Here we decided to analyze commentaries of three days in every other week. On the days of the sample we looked through all four newspapers per country and selected all commentaries related to the seven issue fields.

The samples of editorials of the twenty-seven newspapers under study were analyzed for the three-year period between 2000 and 2002. Our selection procedure resulted in 5,063 commentaries for the broader editorial agenda of these newspapers constituted by the seven issue fields under study (EU integration, monetary politics, agriculture, immigration, troop deployment, retirement or pension politics, and education); 1,409 of these commentaries deal with the issue of EU integration. The editorials were coded by native speakers who were carefully trained before coding and supervised throughout the whole coding period. The supervisors of the country teams were constantly in contact to solve coding problems. For the reliability test, coders in each country team coded a random sample of seven editorials from the *Scotsman*, *The Times*, and the *Guardian* for 2002. The intercoder reliability scores were measured as the average match between the coders. The overall reliability calculated on the core variables of the analysis turned out to be satisfactory with an average match of 75%, with deviations mostly occurring among adjacent categories. The reliability for specific variables is indicated at the bottom of the respective tables or figures.

FINDINGS

The Visibility of Europe: Issue Salience of European Integration on the Commentary Agenda

For analyzing the visibility of EU integration in media claim making, we used the indicator of issue salience. To assess their relative salience, claims on EU integration were compared to claims on the six other issue fields of our study (agriculture, monetary politics, immigration, troop deployment, pensions, and education). As each issue field has been defined differently in breadth, we do not compare the results for issue salience within a country. Nevertheless, the seven-issue sample can highlight the differences in the attribution of relative salience between the countries of the study.

Our findings in Table 6.1 indicate that in Germany, Spain, France, Italy and, to a lesser degree, the Netherlands, the issue of European integration is highly visible on the editorial agenda, since between 27% and 42% of analyzed claims refer to it. The British press devotes a lesser amount of commentating to EU integration than the newspapers of the continental European countries. Contrary to our hypothesis (H1), the press in the non EU-member state Switzerland attributes high salience to EU integration. With more than 40% of all coded editorials, the issue of EU integration is highly visible in the Swiss press. This rather unexpected finding cannot be resolved completely in our study. However, we interpret the high attention to EU integration as a reaction to the fact that the relationship between Switzerland and the EU has become the key division in Swiss politics (Kriesi et al. 2006a). Moreover, EU politics has been at stake in several referendums, so that the press has reason to monitor the issue closely.

Our assumption that the quality press will bring EU integration more into prominence than the regional or tabloid press (H2) is confirmed for all EU member countries on the continent, except for France. Generally, the quality newspapers attribute a higher share of claims to European integration than do regional or tabloid newspapers. The biggest gap can be seen in Italy: Here regional newspapers devote 25% of all editorials to the topic of European integration, whereas the quality newspapers' share amounts to more than 37%.

In the United Kingdom and Switzerland we must reject the hypothesis, because the quality press does not attribute more attention to EU integration than the tabloid or regional press. Interestingly, the tabloid press in these countries puts as much – in the United Kingdom even more – emphasis on the

TABLE 6.1. *Share of EU Integration on the Commentary Agenda of the National Press (%)*

	Germany	Spain	France	Italy	The Netherlands	United Kingdom	Switzerland	Average
Share of EU integration of all editorials	28.4	31.3	42.3	32.3	26.5	19.6	40.8	31.6
Quality press	30.2	34.5	39.0	37.6	30.7	18.0	41.5	33.6
Regional press	22.4	30.1	51.2	25.0	29.5	13.9	—	29.3
Tabloid press	14.3	23.5	—	—	18.0	29.4	38.1	25.6

Notes: The basis is all coded issue fields (EU integration, monetary politics, agriculture, immigration, troops deployment, retirement or pension, and politics or education). Numbers are as follows: Germany, 1,004 commentaries (821 quality, 134 regional, and 49 tabloid); Spain, 595 commentaries (307 quality, 186 regional, and 102 tabloid); France, 447 commentaries (326 quality and 121 regional); Italy, 694 commentaries (402 quality and 292 regional); the Netherlands, 732 commentaries (355 quality, 149 regional, and 228 tabloid); the United Kingdom, 910 commentaries (511 quality, 202 regional, and 197 tabloid); Switzerland, 681 commentaries (547 quality and 134 tabloid). Also note that the Average column has been weighted by the number of commentaries in each country so that each country contributes with the same share. Reliability is as follows: Issue Field 1 = 98%; Issue Field 2 = 74%; Issue Field 3 = 92%.

issue as the quality newspapers. It seems that in countries where the depth of integration is a contentious issue, the tabloid press is a front runner in taking up this issue for a general readership.

The Prominence of and Openness for European Actor Constellations

The performance of the press in making European and other EU member state actors visible is analyzed only with respect to editorials on EU integration. By investigating how the media portray the actor constellations in these editorials, we see whether they open up the communicative space for transnational actors or whether they keep the debate within national circles.

In the empirical analysis we proceeded in several steps. First, we computed a summary variable that measures to what degree the press attributes responsibility (addressee) and concern (affected actor) to actors beyond the nation-state. To identify the scopes of actor constellations, we divided the editorials on European integration into four categories. First, we identify commentaries that only mention actors from the EU, other EU member states, or upcoming EU member states. These editorials are regarded as "fully Europeanized." The second category refers to commentaries that name only a European actor but do so alongside a national domestic actor or an actor from a country outside Europe. These are referred to as "partly Europeanized." Fully Europeanized and partly Europeanized commentaries are contrasted with editorials that have neither European actors nor actors from other European countries. These editorials are either "fully nationalized" and refer only to national domestic actors, or, alternatively, refer to a combination of national domestic and non-European foreign actors ("other non-European and domestic/other non-European").

Regarding their openness for European actors, the media of Germany, Spain, France, Italy, and the Netherlands are prone to overcome national views (see Figure 6.1). Between one-half and two-thirds of the claims on European integration display a fully transnational set of actors. We also see that the press in Germany, France, and Italy seldom restricts the picture by focusing only on national perspectives. Their share of fully national editorials is less than 10%. In Spain and the Netherlands the actor cast is more contained, since about 20% of claims are fully national. If we rank the countries within this group according to their openness toward European actors, we see that the press in France and Italy is leading. The German press, which is similar to France and Italy in the (rather low) level of featuring only national claims, shows a stronger tendency to involve actors from non-EU countries, particularly from Turkey. The Dutch and the Spanish press, which also belong to the group of countries with rather Europeanized actor constellations, show the highest mention of national claims.

Compared with the press of the continental EU members, the British newspapers must be classified as a contrasting case. In the United Kingdom, fully Europeanized claims make up only 25%, whereas 45% of claims are completely

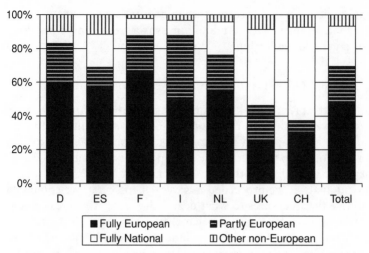

FIGURE 6.1. Openness toward European actors by country in the field of EU integration. The basis is as follows: All claims of journalists in which an addressee or affected actor is identified in the issue field of EU integration only. Numbers for each country are as follows: Germany (D), 253; Spain (ES), 157; France (F), 178; Italy (I), 221; the Netherlands (NL), 191; United Kingdom (UK), 175; Switzerland (CH), 234; total, 1409. (Note that the Total column has been weighted by the number of EU commentaries in each country so that each country contributes the same share. Reliability is as follows: addressee, 83%; affected actor, 88%.)

confined to national actors. The British press does not discuss the topic of EU integration less frequently, but it seems to close its communicative space to the views on EU issues from other European countries. Sifft et al. (2007, p. 145) confirm these findings when showing that the British newspaper *The Times* has the least discursive references to other European countries and the most to its own national realm. On this point the United Kingdom is similar to Switzerland. The Swiss debate on EU integration is strongly bound to the representation of nation-state actors. Nearly 55% of the press' claims in Switzerland must be categorized as fully national.

The described patterns of actor constellations across countries also hold up if we include the newspaper type in the picture (Table 6.2). Comparing the mean score of openness within countries between the tabloids and regional press on the one hand and quality newspapers on the other hand, we hardly find any differences in the continental EU member states. In contrast, while the United Kingdom and Switzerland already engage in a rather parochial pattern of actor constellations, a major gap between the tabloid press and the broadsheets becomes apparent here. While there is a generally low attention to European actors, the tabloid press is particularly keen on focusing on national actors and thereby keeping the debate within the national boundaries.

To test the significance and the strength of variation in the degree of Europeanization across countries and newspaper types, we conducted an analysis

TABLE 6.2. *Degree of Europeanization by Media Types and Country – Means and Multiple Classification Analysis*

Mean	Germany	Spain	France	Italy	The Netherlands	United Kingdom	Switzerland	Average
Quality	.71	.54	.75	.67	.70	.46	.40	.61
Regional	.70	.78	.80	.73	.56	.39		.68
Tabloid+	.90	.65			.65	.18	.11	.36
All media	.72	.62	.76	.69	.66	.35	.34	.59
N	253	157	178	221	191	175	234	1,418

Dependent variable (M)	Independent variable		Strength of model
	Country (β)	Newspaper type (β)	R^2
Europeanization	.34***	.11***	.15

Notes: The basis is all claims of journalists in which an addressee or affected actor is identified in the issue field of EU integration only. The Average column has been weighted by the number of EU commentaries in each country so that each country contributes with the same share. The range is from 0 (not Europeanized at all) to 1 (fully Europeanized). The reliability is addressee = 83%; affected actor = 88%.

* $p < 0.1$, ** $p < 0.05$, *** $p < 0.01$.

161

of variance (multiple classification analysis). The beta values – which are the standardized measures for the strength of effects of single variables – indicate that the differences between countries are more important than those between newspapers. The level of Europeanization varies significantly across countries with a beta coefficient of $\beta = .34$, while a significant but much lower effect is detected for newspaper type with a beta coefficient of $\beta = .11$. These findings show that the national political contexts are a more decisive factor for media performance in Europeanization than the logic and the audience appeal that are embodied in particular types of media outlets.

Congruence of Debates Across Countries: Conflict Lines in Commentaries on European Integration

To explore whether the voice of the press converges in their framing of EU integration, we draw on the analysis of conflict lines (CLs). The idea of this variable, introduced by Voltmer (1998–1999, pp. 78–79), is to describe the dimensionality of a political issue by linking it to a general political value or principle. It is further assumed that these values or principles are closely related to ongoing social conflicts of a political culture. We applied the tool for analysis because we wanted to grasp the underlying structure of contention about EU integration from the media's point of view. Since the measure proposed by Voltmer was not suitable for European politics, we adapted it with respect to conflicts on EU integration.[6] Drawing on a wide body of research, we identified the dimensions of arguments[7] over Europe. The resulting catalogue of nine conflict lines captures the disputes on EU integration at a detailed level. For the current analysis, we categorized the nine conflict lines into five general types of conflict, which are shown in Table 6.3.

The first conflict line (CL1) deals with the membership question in a rather fundamental way. The argument refers to the question of whether a country should become or remain a member of the EU or reject or withdraw from the integration process in general. Another type of conflict is related to institutional power questions. Here the relation between member states (CL2) and the relation between the EU level and the national level (CL3) are discussed.

---

[6] Voltmer (1998–1999, pp. 78 ff.) developed the idea of measuring the political positioning of the media with respect to conflict lines. She argues that conflict lines of policies resonate with ideological left versus right positions in the political space. However, according to Voltmer and Eilders (2003) and scholars of European policy (e.g., Mittag and Wessels 2003, p. 419), European integration is a political issue that cannot be easily subsumed under a left–right divide. Thus, the measurement of conflict lines by Voltmer cannot be adapted to the frames and positions that the media imply with respect to European integration. Since we find the idea of conflict lines as mechanisms to structure political debates convincing, we started out with the original research tool by Voltmer and revised it for our purposes. The conflict lines that we see emerging in the issue of European integration are introduced in the empirical part of this chapter.

[7] This first draft of conflict dimensions was complemented by a prestudy on the editorials of our sample in seven European countries.

TABLE 6.3. *Conflict Lines in the Debate about EU Integration*

Type of Conflict	Dimension	Line	Questions Raised and Positions Taken
Fundamental	Membership	CL1	Should a country become/remain EU member or withdraw?
Institutional	Relation between member states	CL2	Should all EU member countries have an equal say or should some EU countries move faster toward integration?
	Relation between member states and EU	CL3	Should integration strengthen the problem-solving power of the supranational level or the national level?
Conflict on role of citizens	Relation between EU and citizens	CL4	Should citizen rights be extended or should they remain as they are?
	Citizens' identity	CL5	Does EU integration need a European identity or is EU integration also possible if citizens remain with a purely national identity?
Conflict on goals of EU integration	Widening–deepening	CL6	Should EU reforms stress the depth of integration or should they stress enlargement and slowing down political reform?
Conflict on role of EU	Foreign policy	CL7	Should EU security rest on national arrangements or on common arrangements?
	Monetary policy	CL8	Should monetary policy strengthen the common EU responsibility or should the national economies have more autonomy?
	Social policy	CL9	Should the EU stress its liberal market approach to social policy or should it strengthen its role as provider of welfare?

For instance, should all EU member states have equal decision-making power at all times, or should it be possible for some member states to proceed while others remain behind (CL2)? Another example is the dispute over strengthening the supranational or intergovernmental (i.e., by nation-states) levels of decision making (CL3).

Another type of conflict refers to the role of citizens in EU integration. Conflict Line 4 (CL4) highlights the often mentioned argument about granting more participatory rights to the individual citizen. Conflict Line 5 (CL5) refers to the question of political identity. It talks about the type of identity that is necessary in a European community. The next type of conflict refers to the general goals of EU integration (CL6). Here the options are whether EU reforms should stress the depth of political integration or push for enlargement at the cost of slowing down political reform. Finally, the last type of conflict connects EU integration to arguments in substantial policy fields such as monetary and foreign policy. The arguments in this category refer to whether the EU or national governments should be the deciding actor on these issues (CL7 and CL8). Regarding social policy, the EU can be seen as a provider of welfare or as a liberal market-driven union (CL9).

Table 6.4 shows the conflict lines that dominate the debate on EU integration in the press of the seven countries under study. The newspapers of the continental European member states discuss EU integration primarily in terms of two conflict lines. First, the debate focuses on the relation between the member states and the European Union. Second, the editorials stress the goals of political integration, meaning the question of enlargement versus deepening. Between 65% and 80% of all conflict lines in EU integration that are detected in the press editorials of Germany, Spain, France, Italy, and the Netherlands refer to these two dimensions. Thus, in the majority of their editorials, journalists were engaged in discussing institutional and political questions that are at the core of future political development of the EU. Moreover, the newspapers in these five countries emphasize remarkably similar preferences on EU integration conflict lines.

Whereas the continental European press agrees on the two central questions that further EU integration must answer, the British press takes a different turn. The United Kingdom's newspapers discuss the role of European integration in the light of foreign and monetary policy. Particularly, the British debates are about joining the euro or not – the most important aspect of integration in the period of our study. This debate was not "long finished" as in the continental EU countries, so the framing of the issue is different. Obviously the press in the United Kingdom participates vividly in the national political debates over Europe and focuses on the most contentious issue of European integration for the country at the time.

Finally, the press of the non-EU member state Switzerland – not surprisingly – is the only one that does not take an interest in the characteristics of EU integration. It sticks to the basic conflict of whether Switzerland should become more strongly involved in the integration project or remain outside. Nearly 70% of all conflict lines coded in Switzerland refer to the fundamental membership conflict.

With the exception of Italy and the Netherlands, regional and tabloid newspapers in the continental EU countries present a less elaborated picture of conflict lines related to EU integration than do papers of the quality press.[8] If

---

[8] The data that show how each single newspaper employs conflict lines are not included as otherwise the tables would have been hardly readable. These data can, however, be directly obtained from the authors.

TABLE 6.4. *Conflict Lines in the National Press* (%)

Type of Conflict	Dimension	Line	Germany	Spain	France	Italy	The Netherlands	United Kingdom	Switzerland	Average
Fundamental	Membership (yes – no)	CL1		1.1	6.1	2.9	0.8	4.8	67.6	10.6
Institutional	Relation between member states	CL2	9.6	6.7	8.1	7.2	5.9	0.8	5.0	6.1
	Relation between member states and EU	CL3	33.8	30.3	43.9	41.3	39.8	20.0	9.4	31.9
Conflict on role of citizens	Relation between EU and citizens	CL4	3.7	4.5	4.1	0.7	5.1	4.0	2.2	3.5
	Citizens (identity)	CL5	1.5			3.6				0.8
Conflict on goals of EU integration	Widening–deepening	CL6	39.7	36.0	26.4	28.3	39.8	18.4	10.8	28.0
Conflict on role of EU	Foreign policy	CL7	9.6	10.1	5.4	15.2	4.2	17.6	4.3	9.7
	Monetary policy	CL8	0.7	4.5	4.1	0.7	2.5	32.0	0.7	7.3
	Social policy	CL9	1.5	6.7	2.0	0.0	1.7	2.4	0.0	2.0
TOTAL %			100.0	100.0	100.0	100.0	100.0	100.0	100.0	100.0
N			136	89	148	138	118	125	139	926

Notes: The basis is the most important conflict line employed by journalists in the issue field of EU integration only. The Average column has been weighted by the number of EU commentaries in each country so that each country contributes with the same share. The reliability is Conflict Line 1 = 82%.

the German, French, and Spanish regional press or tabloid newspapers employ conflict lines on the topic at all, they attribute around twice as much attention to the enlargement-widening conflict than does the quality press. In the United Kingdom the controversy about the euro is the most central frame for the tabloid and regional press. More than 43% of all coded conflict lines here deal with this basic conflict; in the quality press the share lies around 20%. Thus, the tabloid press hooks up on the most controversial aspect of the EU in national debate. The same pattern can be observed for Switzerland, where the nation is arguing about joining the EU or whether to withdraw in general. This fundamental conflict dominates all newspapers, but even more the regional ones and the tabloid press.

If we sum up our findings on conflict lines, we conclude that the framing of arguments over Europe raised by the media reflects the nationally politically contested ones: the Swiss struggle over entry, the United Kingdom controversy over the euro, and the contestation of Germany, France, Spain, the Netherlands, and Italy over advancing the institutional design of the EU. Interestingly, at least from this level of coding, it seems that questions of European integration are hardly debated in any country in the specific terms of the often-referred-to "democratic deficit" of the EU, which directly addresses the role of citizens. This question of citizens' roles lies at the core of any concerns dealing with political support and input legitimacy of the EU. We were also surprised that we found very little debate on the relation between the member states. However, this finding fits with that throughout the overall study regarding the relatively low emergence of horizontal linkages.

The analysis of conflict lines has provided evidence about the interpretation context of the EU integration issue in the national press. In our next step we wish to investigate what positions the newspapers take on these conflict lines and whether their positions converge across countries. We find that the press of the continental EU group strongly advocates a supranational model of integration against an intergovernmental one. An interesting case with respect to the voice of the media is France, where the political elite is deeply divided on which role the "grand nation" should have in further integrating Europe (e.g., Goulard 2002). The press, in contrast, strongly pleads for a supranational model of EU integration, thus breaking with the French tradition that places the nation-state in the center of political thought.

Regarding the question of enlargement versus deepening, Table 6.5 also reveals that the press of the continental European countries stresses its preference for a deepening of political integration prior to enlargement.

The British press deviates from the position of its continental counterparts, since in the United Kingdom the debate supports an intergovernmental Europe. In their editorials, British journalists argue that the nation-state should prevail over any common regulations. The emphasis on sovereignty thus makes up 63% of all coded conflict positions. In addition, the British press places some emphasis on the enlargement of the EU (17%), while claims in favor of deepened integration are the rare exception (2%).

TABLE 6.5. *Press's Position on Dominant Conflict Lines* (%)

Dimension	Position	Germany	Spain	France	Italy	The Netherlands	United Kingdom	Switzerland	Average
Membership	Withdrawal			0.9	2.2	1.1	0.9		0.3
	Full involvement	7.1	3.4	5.2	7.6	6.7	1.9	67.5	8.0
Relation between member states and EU	Intergovernmental			1.7			20.4		7.6
	Supranational	21.2	22.0	33.0	30.4	30.0	0.9	3.9	20.4
Widening vs. deepening	Focus: deepening	25.3	18.6	21.7	21.7	23.3	1.9	3.9	16.5
	Focus: widening	17.2	13.6	7.8	9.8	16.7	16.7	6.5	12.7
Foreign policy	Traditional	1.0	1.7		2.2	2.2	11.1		3.2
	Common	8.1	15.3	8.7	14.1	2.2	5.6	5.2	8.2
Monetary policy	Traditional	1.0	5.1	5.2	1.1	2.2	31.5		6.4
	Common						1.9		2.6
	Other positions	19.1	20.3	15.8	10.9	15.6	7.2	13.0	14.1
TOTAL %		100.0	100.0	100.0	100.0	100.0	100.0	100.0	100.0
N		99	59	115	92	90	108	77	661

Notes: The basis is the position taken by journalists on the most important conflict lines employed in the issue field of EU integration only. The Average column has been weighted by the number of EU commentaries in each country so that each country contributes with the same share. Also note that only the dominant conflict lines are presented here. Additionally, the case numbers are lower than they are in Table 6.2 because only explicit positions have been analyzed. The reliability is Conflict Line 1 = 82%.

Our findings clearly indicate that the media's point of view reflects national political cultures toward the EU. The French case, however, demonstrates that a deeper analysis of substantial arguments reveals differences between national political cultures and the positioning of the press. This is also the case for Switzerland. The Swiss press supports in unison a stronger involvement in the European Union. Nearly 68% of all coded conflict positions in Switzerland regarding the topic of EU integration argue in favor of involvement. This attitude of the press does not reflect the opinion of either the political elite or the public.

When comparing the quality newspapers with the regional press and tabloid press within a country, we find a strong consensus about positioning on the conflict lines. Quality newspapers and regional or tabloid newspapers do not support opposing extremes of specific conflict lines. All newspapers in Germany, Spain, France, Italy, and the Netherlands aim for a supranational integration model and for deepened integration processes. Newspapers in Switzerland agree on their support for the involvement within the European integration project. Those in the United Kingdom concur regarding the preference for enlargement and an intergovernmental Europe in general and in monetary issues. There is only one difference between the quality and tabloid or regional newspapers in the United Kingdom: When issues of EU integration are discussed in connection with foreign policy matters, the quality press asks for common policy arrangements whereas the tabloid press and regional press demand more national autonomy.

DISCUSSION

The analysis of the voice of the media indicates that the press contributes – in differing levels and degrees – to the Europeanization of national public spheres: The issue of EU integration is widely covered on the editorial agenda; it is discussed with some form of openness for European perspectives; and, at least within our continental EU countries' press, there is consensus not only on the roadmap of EU integration but also on the positions to be advocated. Regarding the variation in the national media's degree of Europeanization, a country's depth of integration (H1) has turned out to be more relevant than different types of media (H2). It seems that the press attributes higher salience to Europe in those countries that are involved in all major integration projects and that have actively driven the political process of integration for many years. The newspapers in France, Germany, Italy, the Netherlands, and Spain are more open to comment on European actors and they are more prone to discuss the goals and the political future of the integration project than is the press in those countries that are hesitant members or still stay outside. Moreover, in the more strongly integrated countries the press attributes responsibility more strongly to European actors than to national ones.

The national political culture becomes most salient when we study conflict lines and positions. In the continental EU countries, the press not only agrees on the most urgent questions of the further process of integration but also puts forward similar answers to these questions. The press in the five continental EU countries calls for a supranational model of integration in which the deepening of integration is more important than enlargement.

In the press of the United Kingdom, a different debate takes place. Here the contentious issue is whether the country should join the Monetary Union. As a consequence, the arguments relate to the importance of national sovereignty and the question whether the euro threatens national economic policy. Finally, the Swiss press raises the membership question and calls in unison for stronger Swiss involvement in the EU.

However, the depth of integration cannot be the only factor that explains variation between countries in the attitude of the press. We find, for example, an unexpectedly high level of attention to EU integration in Switzerland, and we also find some variation within the continental European member states.

Interestingly, we do not find clear-cut differences across newspaper types within our countries. Quality newspapers are not as distinct from regional and tabloids as we expected. Only in the continental European countries does the quality press give more relative weight to Europe than the regional and tabloid outlets. Regarding the actor constellation, we mainly find differences between newspapers in those countries that are less involved in the integration project. Here, the tabloid newspapers' commentaries have a remarkably parochial scope. In regard to positioning, we find that the quality press, like the regional and tabloid outlets in a country, argues more or less within the same conflict lines. There is but one – small, but interesting – difference: Regional and tabloid newspapers tend to stress those conflict lines that are of greater concern to a broad population (e.g., the question of enlargement in France, Germany, and Spain). This evidently indicates that in this press sector the audience preferences are more emphasized.

Our findings on the voice of the press nicely complement the results of the claim making of other actors in the national public sphere that were outlined in Chapter 4. Our analysis, however, stresses the importance of the role of the press as an essential protagonist to enhance transnational communication across Europe. Thus the editorial analysis corroborates that the press belongs to the crucial actors that carry the debate on the future of the EU. Moreover, journalists emphasize transnational European scopes and raise their voices in favor of the EU in their editorials.

If we discuss our findings with respect to the larger picture of the media's performance in building up a European public sphere, we may be optimistic about the willingness of the print media to function as agents of transnational political communication within the EU. Our study shows that in countries that belong to the long-standing inner circle of the EU, the press appears to form a European voice that makes Europe visible and argues with similar vigor and in a similar direction. It makes European issues and actors visible and converges regarding the conflict lines discussed and positions advocated. The British and the Swiss cases, however, show that this potential to form a common space of communication depends largely on the political context of the debate. The further a country is integrated within the European community, the stronger the press takes part in a common European debate. This shows that the full democratization of the EU is not a necessary precondition for European debates (Gerhards 2000, p. 292). Instead, we find that common political structures and institutions already trigger the national press' attention toward European issues and openness toward transnational European scopes.

7

Transnational Political Communication on the Internet

Search Engine Results and Hyperlink Networks

Ruud Koopmans and Ann Zimmermann

INTRODUCTION

Whereas the visibility of political messages in the traditional media depends in a relatively centralized fashion on the selection decisions of journalists and editors, visibility on the Internet is an emergent property that arises from millions of small, decentralized decisions by Internet users. When using a search engine we click on certain results and not on others; when surfing the Web we follow one offered hyperlink or another; and if we have a Web presence of our own we may establish links to a few other Web sites, but not to many others. As a result of many such small actions by millions of users, visibility will become distributed unequally on the Internet, because some sites appear prominently among search engine results and others not, and some sites are on the receiving side of many hyperlinks while others receive none. The question that we address in this chapter is how the structure of political communication on the Internet compares with what we find in the traditional media.

From the perspective of its technical features, the Internet offers the possibility to circumvent the selection biases of traditional media, which, as we have seen in earlier chapters, favor elite actors and offer limited possibilities for transnational communication. The Internet, by contrast, allows everybody to present and retrieve information without being dependent on the selection and description biases of traditional mass media. With limited resources and skills, one can set up a Web page and thereby make one's opinions accessible to a worldwide public. However, in practice, the Internet is bound to be less egalitarian and transnational than what it technically allows for. The ease with which Web sites can be set up has produced an enormous oversupply of Web offerings. The amount of available Web sites is so vast that, even for a relatively limited topic, it would be impossible for a user to look at more than a very small proportion of all the Web sites that offer information or opinions on that issue. Without the assistance of some kind of map that guides the user through the endless Web space, the Internet would be a labyrinth in which nobody would be able to find their way. Online information is therefore in practice often accessed with the assistance of navigation tools, the most important of which are search engines and hyperlinks. Both act as selection mechanisms that make some Web sites more visible and more easily accessible than others. In this chapter, we investigate the nature of these online biases by contrasting them with our data on conventional print media.

PREVIOUS RESEARCH REGARDING ONLINE POLITICAL
COMMUNICATION

The Internet's impact on the democratic inclusiveness of public political communication is often discussed in terms of binary oppositions: optimists and pessimists, utopias and dystopias (Fisher and Wright 2001), technical determinists and social determinists (Dahlberg 2004), or mobilization theorists and reinforcement theorists (Norris 2000b). Some predict positive effects of the Internet on the democratic quality of public debates; others predict negative effects; and yet others foresee no relevant effect at all, such as, for example, Resnick's normalization of cyberspace thesis (Resnick 1997). The central issue of contention in these discussions is the Internet's role in overcoming or exacerbating biases that limit the equality of access to and the inclusiveness of participation in the offline public sphere, which in modern democracies is largely dominated by mass media such as newspapers, radio, and television. Today, the euphoria of the beginnings has mostly vanished and there are hardly any serious authors who still expect the Internet to be the cure for the problems of modern democracies. However, the empirical exploration of the Internet's actual effects on patterns of political communication remains limited.

Regarding how the Internet may affect political communication, one of the most common approaches is to analyze the Internet's potential of enhancing a deliberative, Habermasian public sphere characterized by openly accessible, egalitarian, and transparent debates (e.g., Dahlberg 2001; Gimmler 2001). Others focus on the formation of alternative online (counter) public spheres that might challenge the existing power structures (Downey and Fenton 2003; Plake, Jansen, and Schuhmacher 2001). Empirical investigations of these questions have been largely limited to the analysis of online forums, chats, and Usenets (e.g., Poor 2005; Schneider 1997; Tsaliki 2002). In this way, online public spheres are reduced to something that takes place on single Web sites. Consistently, the Internet is explored as a mere collection of unconnected Web sites. However, as Agre (2002, p. 311) points out correctly, "The problem in either case is that the public sphere is, and always will be, a much larger phenomenon than an Internet discussion forum." Therefore, our analysis of online communication will focus on the World Wide Web. Among the numerous Internet features that are available, only the World Wide Web fulfils the basic requirement of a public sphere, namely that it is a forum of communication that can in principle be joined and observed by every citizen.

SELECTION PROCESSES AND VISIBILITY ON THE INTERNET

Orientation within the Internet is no great problem if the user already knows exactly which actor's views he or she is interested in. In this case, all one needs to do is to find out the Web address of this person or organization. Some actors pay substantial sums for a Web address that is easy to identify and to memorize. However, if this would be the only way to find information online, the Internet would be just a new way of accessing information on actors that are already known to the user. Such prior knowledge and interest will be strongly influenced by the degree of visibility that collective actors have been able to achieve in the offline mass media. Internet communication would under this scenario do little more than reproduce the existing offline patterns of visibility in public debates.

It is therefore more interesting to look at the process of information retrieval by users who do not yet have a preexisting interest in one particular Web site, but who want to get a broad overview of information and opinions about a certain topic. The two most often used means of access to Web information are search engines and links that are recommended or offered on Web sites. According to several studies, the proportion of people who use search engines varies between 70% and 90%. A similar share of users, between 60% and 90%, relies (alternatively or additionally) on surfing links among Web sites (Alexander, Powell and Tate 2001; Fittkau and Maass 2000; Graphics, Visualisation & Usability Center 1998).

We can thus distinguish two forms of selection that structure access to political communication on the Internet:

- *vertical selection by way of search engines*, which presents a hierarchical sample of relevant Web sites on a search issue defined by the Internet user, and
- *horizontal selection by way of hyperlinks*, which helps the user to find new information by following links between Web sites.

Vertical Selection by Search Engines

The selection by way of search engines can be denoted as vertical since it is based on the allocation of varying degrees of visibility to Web sites by a few centrally placed online actors. The selection of information by journalists in the offline media may be characterized as a vertical selection process in a similar way. The selection criteria that are used for listing Web sites differ from one search engine to another. Some offer the possibility of buying high visibility on their result lists. Like the commercial trade in easy Web addresses, this selection mechanism tends to reproduce offline differences in power: The offline rich can buy themselves a prominent Web presence. However, most of the commonly used search engines use more "democratic" criteria. Generally, engines do not search the World Wide Web directly but rather extract results from the contents of their databases. There are two basic kinds of database building and indexing – manual and automatic. So-called directories depend on humans for building their databases. Short descriptions of Web sites are submitted to the search engine's directory by the Web site owners, or editors write descriptions for sites they review. A search looks for matches only in the submitted descriptions. Search engines that create their database automatically are so-called true search engines. They search the Web by using software called "spiders," "robots," or "crawlers." When such Web crawlers find pages, they pass them on to another computer program for "indexing." This program identifies the texts, hyperlinks, and other content in the page and stores it in the search engine's database so that it can be searched by keyword.

Different types of database building and indexing obviously lead to different results; for example, some search engines index more Web pages than others, or they focus on different kinds of pages. No two search engines therefore cover the exact same collection of Web pages. In addition, search engines employ different forms of results ranking. The general aim is to return the most relevant pages at the top of their lists. To determine this relevance, crawler-based search engines follow a set of rules (algorithm). Exactly how a particular search engine's algorithm works is a closely kept trade secret. However, all major search engines follow some general criteria. One important criterion is the location and frequency of the keyword on a Web page. Pages with search terms appearing in the HTML title tag are often assumed to be more relevant to the topic than other pages. Search engines also check if the search keywords appear near the top of a Web page, the assumption being that the pages most relevant to the topic will mention those words right from the beginning. This location–frequency method is very susceptible to attempts of Web site owners to influence their position within the result list. By repeating a word hundreds of times on a page (spamming), they try to get their page higher in the listing.

Search engines watch for common spamming methods in a variety of ways and have developed so called offpage ranking criteria that cannot be easily influenced by Web masters. The most popular of these is hyperlink analysis. By analyzing how pages link to each other, a search engine can determine both what a page is about and whether that page is deemed to be "important" and thus deserves a high ranking within the result list. Sophisticated techniques are used to screen out attempts by Web masters to build artificial hyperlinks designed to boost their rankings. Another offpage factor is click-through measurement. This entails that a search engine monitors the results that a user selects for a particular search, and it uses this information to eventually drop pages that are not attracting clicks while promoting pages that pull in many visitors. Since past popularity of a Web site determines the prominence in the search listing, the theoretical effect of such ranking criteria is a path-dependent process that reinforces the visibility of Web sites that are already popular and prominent. This will over time inevitably introduce structural inequalities in the Internet space, by making some Web sites more visible and more easily accessible and others less so.

Horizontal Selection by Hyperlinks

Hyperlinking is a technology that either enables the internal navigation within a Web site or establishes links between different Web sites. Wilkinson, Thelwall, and Li (2003) define internal hyperlinks as those that have a source page and target within the same site. External hyperlinks provide direct access from a source Web site to a target Web site with a different URL, which is usually run by a different actor. Such external hyperlinks are not to be conceived of "simply as a technological tool but as a newly emerging social and communicational channel" (Park 2003). Or, as Garrido and Halavais state, "Since establishing a hyperlink is a conscious social act executed by the author of a Web site, we may assume that some form of cognitive, social, or structural relation exists between the sites" (2003, p. 10). Hyperlink affiliation networks have also been explained in terms of credibility, prestige, and trust (Brin and Page 1998; Kleinberg 1999). A Web site that is perceived as highly credible, prestigious, and trustworthy will receive more hyperlinks than other Web sites. The inevitable result of such selection processes is that some Web sites will be on the receiving side of many hyperlinks from other actors, whereas other actors will receive few hyperlinks or none at all (Egloff 2002).

When we understand hyperlinks as a type of relationship, the tools of social network analysis can be put to use to describe observed patterns of connections and disconnections within a network of Web sites (Jackson 1997; Park 2003; Park and Thelwall 2003). Centrality measures can indicate the degree of concentration of hyperlinks on certain target Web sites. Such analyses can also reveal intermediary brokerage positions in the form of Web sites that provide crucial connections among clusters of Web sites. Search engines such as Google use such measures of structural positions of Web sites as one of their criteria to determine the most influential Web site within a group, by looking at the hyperlink structure that surrounds individual Web sites (Henzinger 2001).

We denote the way of selection by hyperlinks as horizontal since it is not determined by a few centrally located actors. Instead, communicative structures emerge from numerous discrete acts of actors who decide independently to which other actors they want to provide hyperlinks and to which not. As Pennock et al. (2002, p. 5207) put it, "The World Wide Web is a reflection of human culture – a massive social network encoding associative links among almost 10^9 documents... authored by millions of people and organisations around the globe. The Web's structure has emerged without central planning, the result of a bottom-up distributed process."

It is important to note that since the selection criteria of search engines are – among other criteria – also based on the number and kind of hyperlinks a Web site receives from other Web sites, the two forms of selection are correlated. Thus, the distinction between vertical selection (search engines) and horizontal selection (hyperlinks) should be seen as relative rather than absolute.

SELECTION BY SEARCH ENGINES

Having clarified how search engines and hyperlink networks act as online selection mechanisms, we now turn to our empirical analyses, beginning with search engine results. In each of the seven countries of our study the two most often-used search engines were chosen.[1] Two search strings, one more general and one more specific, were defined for each of our seven issue fields and translated in each country's language (for Switzerland, translations were both in German and in French).[2] Given our interest in the Internet as a transnational space, it was of course a consideration whether to search in the national languages of the seven countries, or, alternatively, only in English. We decided against the latter option because outside a rather small business and scientific elite, most people search the Internet in their own language.

For each search string, the first ten relevant results were included in the first round of coding, and the first five relevant results in the second round of coding. The two rounds of coding were conducted in July and November 2002. Since the results of searches can vary from day to day, it was exactly scheduled on which day the country teams should search with which search string. Altogether, we collected a sample of 2,640 Web sites that contained relevant textual information on the search issues.[3] In a next step, we searched for the most important claim maker – an actor who expresses an opinion about the issue in question – within each selected text and thus arrived at a sample of

[1] Google.de, Fireball.de; Google.es, Altavista.es; Google.fr, Voila.fr; Arianna.libero.it, Search .alice.it (Virgilio); Google.nl, Vindex.nl; Google.uk, MSN.uk; Search.ch.

[2] The English search strings were *monetary politics* and *interest rate decision*; *agriculture subsidies* and *BSE cows*; *immigration politics* and *deportation*; *troops deployment* and *troops peacekeeping*; *pension politics* and *pensions demographic*; *education politics* and *education equal opportunities politics*; and finally *EU reforms* and *EU enlargement*. All search strings also included 2002 to get as much actuality as possible.

[3] We excluded Web sites that were located outside Europe, unless they belonged to supranational institutions (e.g., the UN) or transnational organizations (e.g., Amnesty International). This restriction was necessary because particularly for the searches in English (Web sites based in the United States), Spanish (sites from Latin America), and to a lesser extent in French (especially sites from Quebec), we obtained many results from other countries where the same language is spoken. A user who would want to exclude U.S. sites from searches in English would probably add *UK* or *Britain* to her search string or use the option to search only in sites from the United Kingdom. However, using this option would have strongly biased our results toward home country Web sites. We therefore chose the compromise of excluding non-European Web sites to avoid a built-in transnational bias for countries whose national languages happen to be world languages, while retaining the possibility to investigate cross-national communicative linkages within Europe or with supranational institutions and transnational organizations. We are aware that this decision remains to some extent contestable, because there is a real sense in which users from countries where a global language is spoken are more likely to be confronted with information from other countries that speak the same language. For our analysis, we have chosen to exclude transnational communication within global language communities and to focus on the question to what extent the Internet facilitates communication across national and linguistic boundaries within Europe, or between the national level and supranational and transnational organizations.

TABLE 7.1. *Share of Different Types of Actors among Owners of Web Sites, Claim Makers on Web Sites, and Claim Makers in Print Media in Seven Countries on Seven Issues, 2002*

Actor Type	Owners of Web Sites (%)	Online Claim Makers (in %)	Claim Makers in Offline Print Media (%)
Media	46	7	9
State actors and parties	26	64	71
Socioeconomic interest groups	9	20	17
NGOs, social movements, and other civil society organizations	16	8	3
Other actors	2	3	1
TOTAL	100	100	100
N	2,171	2,171	2,171

Notes: All data were weighted by country and by issue in such a way that all seven countries and all seven issues contribute equally to the overall results. NGO = nongovernmental organization. Strength of the correlation between the medium (online–offline) variable and the actor category variable: Cramér's $V(N = 4,342) = 0.154, p < .001$.

2,172 claims.[4] We will compare the claim makers that we found in our online searches to those that appeared in newspaper coverage on the same seven issue fields in the year 2002.

Types of Online and Offline Actors Compared

To investigate whether the Internet can help less prominent and powerful actors to overcome the selection biases of the offline media, we first look at which actors own the Web sites that our searches delivered. As the first column of Table 7.1 shows, almost half (46%) of the Web sites that were listed by search engines were run by news media organizations. In the large majority of cases these were not specialized online media, but the online versions of newspapers and radio and television networks. Through their online versions, traditional news media have thus gained a substantial amount of control over the political information and opinions that circulate on the Internet. A person who uses a search engine to look for information on political issues has a chance of almost one in two of landing on the Web site of the same news media that also dominate the offline public sphere.[5]

---

[4] The number of claims is lower than the number of texts because some texts only offered information but no opinion on the issues in question, often in the form of tables and figures on interest rates, numbers of bovine spongiform encephalopathy (BSE) cases, inflow of immigrants, and so on.

[5] The predominance of news media Web sites was most pronounced in the United Kingdom (75%) and least in France (26%). This contrast is linked to the fact that these are also the countries where state and party actors are least (United Kingdom, 8%) and most prominent (F, 42%)

Yet, the other 54% of Web sites that we found in our searches were run by various political and societal collective actors. This, one might argue, is an improvement in accessibility of the online public sphere compared to the centrality of news media in the dissemination of politically relevant information in the offline world. However, there is a clear hierarchy in the degree to which various actors can profit from the opportunities that the Internet offers to reach audiences without the intervention of the news media. Actors from the core of the political system (government, administrative agencies, political parties, etc.) are more successful (26% of the Web sites found) in reaching the online audience than are socioeconomic interest groups such as employers, labor unions, or professional organizations (9%), and NGOs, social movements, and other civil society organizations (16%).

The owners of Web sites need not be the same actors as the claim makers whose opinions are represented on these sites. This is especially true for the media Web sites, which may contain claims by media actors themselves (e.g., editorials), but mostly report claims that were made by other political and societal actors. The Web sites of nonmedia actors must not necessarily contain claims by the Web site owners themselves, either, but may also include texts that represent the claims of other actors, sometimes even those of political adversaries. The second column of Table 7.1 shows that the actors that profit most from indirect visibility of their claims on the Web sites of other (especially media) Web site owners are state and political party actors, who are responsible for 64% of the online claims, although their share among the websites listed in the search engine results was, with 26%, much lower. Socioeconomic interest groups profit from indirect visibility to a lesser degree, and they account for 20% of online claims against 9% of Web sites. NGOs, social movements, and other civil society organizations, by contrast, do not get much from indirect visibility: Their share of online claims is only 8% and the large majority of these claims occur on their own Web sites.[6]

Clearly, many of the features that characterize the offline public sphere are reproduced on the Internet. News media are the predominant gatekeepers, and among the claim makers institutional actors are strongly predominant. Still, the Internet might in a relative sense be a more conducive environment for civil society actors than the offline media. We can assess this by comparing the second to the third column of Table 7.1, which shows the distribution of

---

among the Web site owners that we found in our searches. Cross-country differences for the remaining two actor types were less important.

[6] This hierarchy of visibility is similar in all seven countries, as well as across the seven issue fields. State actors and political parties are the predominant online claim makers in all issue fields (between 77% in troop deployment and 47% in pensions and retirement). Socioeconomic interest groups are less important in immigration, troop deployment, and European integration (less than 10% in each of these fields), and most prominent in pensions and retirement (25%). NGOs, social movements, and other civil society organizations achieve a substantial level of visibility only in the immigration and education fields, where they are responsible for 27% and 26%, respectively, of all claims.

claim makers in the print media on the same issues in the year 2002. The two distributions turn out to be quite similar, with state and party actors dominating both online and offline, followed at a distance by socioeconomic interest groups. However, the differences between the online and offline shares of actors do point in the direction that the Internet is a slightly less selective environment for civil society actors and especially for NGOs and social movements than the offline media. NGOs and social movements command a share of only 8% of the online claims, but this is still significantly more than the 3% that they achieve in print media. Socioeconomic interest groups are also slightly better represented online than offline (20% vs. 17%), whereas state actors and political parties are slightly less prominent online (64% vs. 71% in the offline print media). As indicated by the Cramér's V at the bottom of the table, the difference between the distributions of actors online and in the print media is statistically significant.

This result persists in a multivariate context, using multinomial regression with actor category as the dependent variable and policy field, country, and Internet versus print media as the predictor variables. Including the Internet variable in this model significantly improves the model as indicated by a χ^2 statistic comparing models with and without this variable of χ^2 (3, $N = 4,328$) $= 82.856$, $p < .001$. However, inclusion of the Internet variable increases the explained variance (as indicated by Nagelkerke's pseudo R^2) only slightly from 18% to 20%, when compared to a model that includes only the policy field and the country. We thus find some modest support for the hypothesis that the Internet is a less selective environment for civil society actors. The magnitude of the difference between the online and offline arenas is, however, quite small.

The Geopolitical Scope of Online and Offline Claim Makers

We now turn to our second research question, namely whether the Internet facilitates the transnational exchange of politically relevant information and opinions. We distinguish two types of supranational actors, that is, extra-European ones, such as NATO, the UN, or Amnesty International, and European ones, such as the EU, the Council of Europe, or the European Trade Union Federation. Further, we distinguish three categories of national actors, that is, those from the same country where we conducted our searches ("domestic"), those from other European countries, and those from outside Europe. If the hypothesis is correct that the Internet offers better opportunities for the transnational flow of political information and ideas than traditional news media, then we should find greater shares of foreign national and supranational actors in our online search results compared to print media content.

We again begin by looking at the owners of the Web sites that we found in our searches. The first column of Table 7.2 shows that 75% of the Web sites were from the country where the search was conducted, 13% were based in foreign countries, and 12% belonged to various supranational organizations,

TABLE 7.2. *Share of Actors of Different Geopolitical Scope among Owners of Web Sites, Claim Makers on Web Sites, and Claim Makers in Print Media in Seven Countries on Seven Issues, 2002*

Actor Scope	Owners of Web Sites (%)	Online Claim Makers (%)	Claim Makers in Offline Print Media (%)
Extra-European supranational	6	7	3
European supranational	6	15	13
Domestic	75	56	58
Foreign European countries	12	8	13
Foreign non-European countries	1	12	13
Unknown	1	3	0
TOTAL	100	100	100
N	2,171	2,171	2,171

Note: All data were weighted by country and by issue in such a way that all seven countries and all seven issues contribute equally to the overall results. NGO = nongovernmental organization. Strength of the correlation between the medium (online–offline) variable and the actor scope variable: Cramér's $V(N = 4,342) = 0.147$, $p < .001$.

agencies, and institutions.[7] One reason why searches led to Web sites outside the home country was that some of the search languages were also spoken in other European countries, such as English in Ireland, Dutch in Belgium, French in Belgium and Switzerland, and German in Austria and Switzerland. A second reason is that some organizations offered their entire Web sites or specific information on them in several languages.

Overall, 14% of the Web sites offered at least some information in a language other than the search language. If several languages were offered, English was not surprisingly the most frequent additional language (65% of the multilingual Web sites), followed by German (35%), French (33%), Italian (21%), Spanish (19%), and Dutch (12%). These Web sites were not necessarily multilingual throughout, as is indicated by the fact that only 9% of the coded texts that referred to the search topic were offered in more than one language. The largest group of Web sites that offered information in more than one language was that of supranational actors, which offered 30% of their texts in more than one language. By contrast, only 4% of the national Web sites in our seven countries offered texts in more than one language.

The second column of Table 7.2 shows that when we look at claim makers rather than Web site owners, the proportions of foreign and supranational actors increase. Supranational actors are responsible for 22% of the online claims, and foreign national actors command another 20%, whereas compared

[7] These results are similar across countries. The share of home country Web sites is, however, a bit lower in France (59%) and the United Kingdom (69%) than in the other countries. This is because more foreign or supranational Web sites offer information in English and French than in the other languages.

to the distribution of Web site owners, the share of national actors declines from 75% to 56%. In other words, when national Web sites offer a platform to the claims of other actors, they regularly provide a place for claim makers from other countries or from the supranational level.

The final step in our analysis is again to compare the distribution of online claim makers to the distribution of claim makers in the offline print media in the same period and on the same issues. Again the two distributions are very similar, although, as the Cramér's *V* statistic at the bottom of the table shows, there are statistically significant differences between them. The share of claim makers from the home country is almost identical online and offline (56% and 58%, respectively). Search engines are somewhat more likely to pick up supranational claims than newspapers are (22% against 16%), whereas newspapers contain more claims from foreign countries (26% against 20%). The results do not suggest that search engine results are any less nationally focused than the content of newspapers.[8]

Again, we tested the robustness of these findings in a multivariate context by using multinomial regression analysis, with the geopolitical scope of actors as the dependent variable, and policy field, country, and Internet versus print media as the predictor variables (detailed results available from the authors on request). Including the Internet variable in this model significantly improves the model, as indicated by a χ^2 statistic comparing models with and without this variable of χ^2 (4, $N = 4,328$) = 72.543, $p < .001$. However, inclusion of the Internet variable only marginally increases the explained variance (as indicated by Nagelkerke's pseudo R^2) from 32% to 34%, when compared to a model that includes only the policy field and the country. The policy field in particular turns out to be a much more powerful predictor of the geopolitical scope of claims than whether a claim was found in the newspaper or on the Internet.

Although offline and online mechanisms of selection diverge strongly, their outcomes are very similar, both when we look at the distribution among actors of varying institutional power and when we look at the visibility of actors of different geopolitical scopes. How can this similarity be explained? Part of the explanation is certainly that media Web sites (mostly online versions of offline media) make up an important part of the search engine results. Online journalists will base their decisions on the same news values as their offline colleagues – that is, if there is any separate decision-making process at all, because often there are only minor differences between the online and offline editions of the same medium. It is worth noting, however, that the prominence of online media in the search results itself needs to be explained as an emergent result of the unconscious, decentralized selection process that

---

[8] While online and offline results are similar in all countries, there is some variation. Germany, Spain, and Italy display the same pattern as the overall results. In Switzerland and the Netherlands, national actors are more predominant online than offline. In the United Kingdom and in France it is the other way around.

generates online visibility. Online media can only be so prominent in the search results because other Web sites provide links to them, and because users often click on search results that are offered by online media. This same decentralized process governs the selection that produces visibility for nonmedia Web sites. That state actors and parties appear prominently in search engine results and that NGOs and social movements do not is the emergent result of the fact that more Web sites provide links to state and party actors than to NGO and social movement actors, and that Web users click more often on state and party Web sites than on NGO and social movement Web sites. In the next section, we will provide evidence on hyperlink networks that supports this reading of the online selection process.

SELECTION IN HYPERLINK NETWORKS

Selection by way of search engines shares an important feature with the offline media. In both cases, citizens must rely on what a gatekeeping institution – a newspaper, a television station, or a search engine – offers according to criteria over which they have no control. In both the online and offline sphere, there are possibilities for citizens to seek politically relevant information independent of gatekeepers. In the offline public sphere this is a rather time-consuming and costly process, which involves writing or calling institutions, politicians, and organizations and requesting material from them. The Internet, however, allows citizens high-speed access to a world of information at virtually no cost. Citizens may use search engines to make a selection from the available information, but they can also choose to navigate the Web independently, surfing from one Web site to another by following hyperlinks. Often, users will combine these two strategies. For instance, they may start by entering keywords in a search engine, but once they have found an interesting starting Web site for their quest, they may continue by surfing from that Web site to another and so on. In this section, we want to investigate whose Web sites a user who relies on surfing hyperlinks is likely to encounter.

While the metaphor of "surfing" suggests the user's freedom from constraints, in reality the user must surf on "waves" (hyperlinks) that are supplied by others (the owners of Web sites) and that lead him to destinations that he has not selected himself. In that sense, hyperlink surfing also relies on gatekeepers, namely the owners of Web sites, who decide to provide links to some other Web sites but not to many others. Web sites to which few other Web sites provide links will remain as inaccessible to the user as are Web sites that are not listed prominently in search engine results. Therefore, we need to investigate which types of actors are more likely to be on the receiving end of hyperlinks. The more often a Web site is targeted by hyperlinks, the more likely it is that Internet users will encounter the information and opinions that it offers. We will ask the same questions as those we already discussed for search engines. First, is hyperlink surfing more likely to lead to Web sites of less prominent and powerful actors, or will it lead the user to the same actors that also predominate in search engine results and in the offline media? Second, is hyperlink surfing more likely to provide access to foreign and supranational Web sites, or is it as likely to lead to actors from the user's home country as are search engines and offline media?

We conducted an analysis of hyperlinks for the seven countries and added Web sites from the European and non-European supranational levels. Because of the technical complexity and time-consuming character of hyperlink analysis, we limited the issues that we investigated to three: agriculture, immigration, and European integration. Given the large number of actors that are active in these fields, we focused on a predefined structured sample of Web sites that included the most important actors in the three fields within each of the categories that we also used for the search engine analysis: state and party actors, socioeconomic interest groups, NGOs and social movements, and media. For reasons of cross-national comparability, the criteria for selecting Web sites were exactly the same in each country. Here are some examples of actors that were selected in each country: the main agency responsible for border protection; the local government of the capital city; the five most important farmers' organizations; the most important labor union representing workers in the state sector; the most important animal protection organization; the most important antiracist organization; the four most important national TV channels; the most important regional newspaper in the region with the strongest regional identity; and so on. We included the Web sites of 134 organizations and institutions in each country.[9] We did the same for the European and extra-European supranational levels, but because many of the predefined categories did not have an equivalent on the supranational level, we ended up with smaller numbers (70 organizations for each supranational level) than we did on the national level. All in all, we investigated the hyperlinks on 1,078 Web sites.

Data on hyperlink networks can be obtained by human observation or by using specialized computer programs. For a small sample of Web sites, human coding is the best way to generate valid data. However, for our aim to investigate hyperlink connections among more than 1,000 often very large Web sites, this method was not feasible. Therefore, we used a computer-assisted tool, a so-called Web crawler, which automatically collects the required data from Web sites.[10] After testing several programs, we chose Xenu's Link Sleuth, which meets our needs most adequately and provides the most reliable data compared

---

[9] A full list of criteria and selected organizations can be found on our project Web site at http://europub.wz-berlin.de.

[10] We encountered two minor problems. First, there are slight differences in the operating procedures of Web crawlers, which implies that their results will not be exactly identical (Park and Thelwall 2003). Further, Web crawlers are not able to identify hyperlinks that are programmed in certain formats, such as JavaScript. We checked whether there was any association between the use of such formats and the type or nationality of the actor, and we found no such connection.

TABLE 7.3. *Receivers and Senders of Hyperlinks by Actor Type in Seven Countries and on the Supranational Level in Three Issue Fields, 2003*

Actor Type	Total Number of Hyperlinks		Number of Web Sites in Sample	Average Number of Hyperlinks per Web Site	
	Received	Sent		Received	Sent
State and party actors	10,110	7.987	423	23.9	18.9
Socioeconomic interest groups	1,602	2,386	153	10.5	15.6
NGOs, social movements, and other civil society actors	3,052	4,042	311	9.8	13.0
Media	3,187	3,536	191	16.7	18.5
TOTAL	17,951	17,951	1,078	16.7	16.7

with other programs.[11] Altogether, we identified more than 16 million hyperlinks on the 1,078 selected Web sites. Only the external hyperlinks – those connecting the Web sites of different actors – were relevant for our analysis. These still amounted to 384,532 hyperlinks. We narrowed the range of observation further by focusing only on those hyperlinks that connected sites within our sample of Web sites. This left us with 17,951 hyperlinks for analysis. On average, then, our selected Web sites contained links to about seventeen other Web sites in our sample.[12]

Table 7.3 shows the frequency at which Web sites of different actor types were the targets and senders of hyperlinks. The results indicate that even the selection process by way of hyperlinks, in which the gatekeeping function is maximally decentralized, tends to reproduce the kind of inequalities that we already found in the search engine results and in the offline media. State and party actors (twenty-four received hyperlinks on average) are about 2.5 times more likely to be the target of hyperlinks than are socioeconomic interest groups or NGOs and social movements (on average, eleven and ten received hyperlinks, respectively). Mass media fall in between with an average of seventeen received hyperlinks. The differences in the propensity of actors to send hyperlinks to other actors are less pronounced.

State and party actors are the only net receivers of hyperlinks: They receive more links from other actors than they send. This is related to the fact that the linking behavior of state and party actors is relatively self-centered: 70% of the links they send are directed at other state and party actors. By contrast, only

---

[11] Xenu's Link Sleuth can be downloaded for free at http://snafu.de/tilman/xenulink.html. The program is designed to allow Web masters to check for broken hyperlinks. To find broken hyperlinks, Xenu searches the whole Web site and compiles a list of all hyperlinks, internal as well as external.

[12] Several hyperlinks from one Web site to the same other Web site were counted only once.

TABLE 7.4. *Receivers of Hyperlinks by Geopolitical Scope of Actor in Seven Countries and on the Supranational Level in Three Issue Fields, 2003*

Actor Type	Total Number of Hyperlinks		Number of Web Sites in Sample	Average Number of Hyperlinks per Actor	
	Received	Sent		Received	Sent
Extra-European supranational	3,034	1,372	69	44.0	19.9
European supranational	2,479	1,689	75	33.1	22.5
Total links to national level	12,438	14,890	933	13.3	16.0
TOTAL	17,951	17,951	1,077	16.7	16.7

23% of the links of socioeconomic interest groups, 36% of the links of other civil society groups, and 30% of the links of media are directed at the same actor type, and each of these categories sends more links to state and party actors than to actors of their own type (51%, 43%, and 46% respectively). The results indicate that hyperlink surfing gravitates toward the Web sites of state and party actors, and away from those of socioeconomic interest groups and other civil society actors. Once a hyperlink surfer has reached a state and party actor Web site, there is, moreover, a strong tendency for her to remain there because the large majority of links from these Web sites point to other state and party actors.

We now turn to the question whether hyperlink surfing is more likely to transcend national boundaries. Table 7.4 shows how often Web sites on the European and extra-European supranational levels and on the national level were the targets and senders of hyperlinks. Extra-European (forty-four received links on average) as well as European supranational Web sites (thirty-three received links) turn out to be 2.5 to 3.5 times more likely to receive hyperlinks than are Web sites of national actors (thirteen received links). They are also somewhat more likely to be senders of hyperlinks, but the difference with national actors is much smaller here. As a result, supranational Web sites are net receivers of hyperlinks, especially the Web sites of extra-European supranational actors who receive more than two times as many links as they send (on average forty-four links received and twenty sent). National Web sites, by contrast, are net losers in the hyperlink exchange process. Compared to the search engine analysis, these results suggest a much stronger position of supranational actors in hyperlink networks. National Web sites were very strongly predominant in search engine results (88% of all Web sites), and supranational Web sites were relatively marginal (6% each for extra-European and European supranational Web sites). By contrast, in hyperlink networks there are strong gravitational tendencies toward the Web sites of supranational actors.

It is, however, too early to conclude that hyperlink networks are less nationally bound than are search engines or offline media. The results in Table 7.4 group all national Web sites together, regardless of whether they are from a user's home country or from one of the other six countries. Our search engine analysis suggests that access to online information is strongly focused on sources from the home country. Of the national-level Web sites in the search engine results, 75% were domestic. This result may have been partly caused by the fact that we conducted our searches in national languages. Our study of hyperlink networks allows us to circumvent the issue of the choice of search language, because we did not select Web sites according to their language or languages; our design also does not impose any restrictions regarding the language of the target Web sites of hyperlinks.

To investigate the degree of transnationality of hyperlink networks, we computed network density measures within and across countries and supranational political levels. Density measures summarize the distribution of connections in a network by comparing the number of realized connections between a set of actors to the maximum possible number of connections (Scott 1991). A network density of 100% means that all possible links between actors have been established; a density of 0% means that no connection at all has been realized.[13] Our network includes 1,078 actors. With 17,951 realized connections on 1,162,084 logically possible connections, the density of the whole network is 1.6%.

Table 7.5 shows the network densities within countries, between countries, and between countries and the European and extra-European supranational levels. It shows these densities in two directions (except within countries, where this distinction does not make sense): from the row country to the column unit (numbers before the slash) and to the row country from the column unit (numbers after the slash).

The results indicate that network links are strongest within countries, ranging from a density of 5.0% realized links in Italy to 10.3% in Germany. The second most developed links are those from countries to extra-European supranational Web sites, ranging from a density of 2.7% for the Netherlands to 3.9% for Germany. The next most important links are those from countries to the European supranational level, ranging from 1.7% for non-EU member Switzerland to 4.0% for Germany. Links in the reverse direction, from the European level to national Web sites, are only half as dense and strongly focused on Germany (a density of 2.2%), the United Kingdom (1.7%), and France (1.7%). Web sites in Switzerland are the least likely to receive links from the European level (0.5% density), which is, of course, apart from the

---

[13] The density of networks depends on their size, which makes the comparison of density across networks of different sizes problematic. In general, density tends to decrease with an increasing network size, since the number of logically possible relationships in a square network grows exponentially as the number of actors increases linearly. Our analysis is not affected by this problem, because the numbers of cases in each country are equal by design.

TABLE 7.5. *Density of Network Links among Actors of Different Geopolitical Scope in Seven Countries and on the Supranational Level in Three Issue Fields, 2003*

Country of Actor	Within Same Country	From/To Other Country (averages)	From/To European Supranational	From/To Extra-European Supranational
Germany	10.3	0.3/0.4	4.0/2.2	3.9/1.1
United Kingdom	8.6	0.1/0.4	2.7/1.7	3.3/2.1
France	6.7	0.2/0.4	2.7/1.7	3.5/1.4
Italy	5.0	0.3/0.2	2.5/0.9	3.4/0.8
Spain	5.8	0.2/0.2	2.3/0.9	3.3/0.8
Netherlands	7.8	0.2/0.1	2.3/1.0	2.7/0.7
Switzerland	6.8	0.3/0.2	1.7/0.5	3.5/0.5
Average	7.3	0.2/0.2	2.6/1.3	3.4/1.1

Notes: The density of network links has been calculated as the number of realized links as a percentage of all possible links. Reading example: Links from Germany to other countries have a density of 0.3% averaged across the six other countries; links to Germany from other countries have a density of 0.4% averaged across the six other countries. See text for further examples.

country's small size also a result of the fact that it is not an EU member. While European Web sites are most likely to link to Germany, extra-European supranational Web sites link most frequently to the United Kingdom (2.1%), followed by France (1.4%) and Germany (1.1%).

The most striking result of Table 7.5 is the very weak development of cross-national network links, which have an average density of only 0.2%, that is, more than thirty times lower than the density of within-country networks, but also much lower than the density of links to the European and extra-European supranational levels. Regarding the sources of cross-national linkages, the United Kingdom stands out with a particularly low density of links going to other countries (0.1%). Regarding the targets of cross-national links, we find the same hierarchy of nations as we did earlier. Germany, France, and the United Kingdom are (relatively speaking) frequent targets of links from other countries (0.4% density each), whereas the other four countries are only half as likely to be targets of cross-national links. Concomitantly, Germany, France, and the United Kingdom are net receivers of links from other countries, while Italy, the Netherlands, and Switzerland receive fewer links than they send to other countries. For Spain, transnational links received and sent are of the same magnitude.

There is thus no straightforward answer to the question of whether hyperlink surfing is more likely to lead the user beyond national boundaries than the use of search engines. National communication predominates quite strongly in both. Users of search engines have a high probability of landing on a search result from their home country, and likewise users who follow hyperlinks are more likely than anything else to jump from one Web site to another Web site in the same country. However, compared to the search engine results where domestic outnumber supranational Web sites by more than seven to one, the difference in the densities of within-country networks and links from the national to the supranational level are much smaller (about three to one). Whereas supranational Web sites are more likely to be found by surfing hyperlinks than by using search engines, the opposite is true for Web sites from other countries. Web sites in other European countries commanded only a very modest share in our search engine results (12% compared to 75% home country Web sites), but the difference between the densities of within-country and between-country networks revealed by our hyperlink analysis is of an even larger magnitude. This finding indicates that the low prominence of foreign Web sites in our search engine results is not an artefact of our decision to search in national languages, but a more general feature of the structure of political communication on the World Wide Web.

We verified these findings in a multivariate context by way of regression analyses with the number of links sent and received by Web sites as the dependent variable, distinguishing between links sent and received within the same country or supranational political level, and links across countries or political levels. Because our dependent variables are counts with overdispersion, we used negative binomial regression analysis. As predictor variables we included dummies for the actor type (with state and party actors as the reference category), the country or political level (with Switzerland as the reference category), and whether an organization specializes in one of the three issue fields of agriculture, immigration, and European integration (with generalist, non-issue-specific organizations as the reference category). Regarding the latter, we expect generalist organizations to receive and send more links than issue-specific organizations because they are active in a wider field that contains more potential sources and targets of hyperlinks. The exception may be actors active in the field of European integration, which is not a circumscribed policy field in the same way as agriculture or immigration.

Additionally, we took into account the fact that hyperlinking frequently involves reciprocity: I will link to your Web site, if you link to mine. Such reciprocity will, all other things being equal, imply that Web sites that send many hyperlinks will also receive more hyperlinks. An additional reason to expect such a correlation between the number of links sent and received is the varying size of Web sites. Large Web sites with many pages on different topics and subtopics are likely to contain more hyperlinks. Because these Web sites contain more information on a wider variety of topics, they are also more likely to be chosen by other Web sites as the target of hyperlinks. For these reasons, we included as a predictor variable in each regression the corresponding flow of hyperlinks in the opposite direction. For example, among the predictors of the number of links sent by a particular Web site *to* other Web sites in the same country, we include the number of links that this Web site receives *from* other Web sites in the same country.

These expectations are confirmed by the results in Table 7.6, which show that there is indeed a strong relation between the number of hyperlinks sent

TABLE 7.6. *Negative Binomial Regression of Hyperlinks Sent and Received on Actor Type, Country or Level, and Issue Field*

Variable	Links Sent to Other Countries/Levels	Links Sent to the Same Country/Level	Links Received from the Same Country/Level	Links Received from Other Countries/Levels
Actor type				
Media[a]	−0.054 (0.32)	0.103 (0.76)	−0.173 (1.92)	0.077 (0.56)
Socioeconomic interest groups	0.120 (0.91)	0.315 (2.58)**	−0.545 (6.38)***	−0.621 (5.10)***
NGOs, social movements, other civil society	−0.028 (0.25)	−0.080 (0.79)	−0.612 (7.44)***	−0.507 (4.94)***
Country/Level				
Germany[b]	0.127 (0.72)	0.125 (0.72)	0.213 (1.89)	1.021 (6.58)***
France	−0.158 (0.89)	0.011 (0.06)	−0.143 (1.27)	0.995 (5.80)***
United Kingdom	−0.408 (2.28)*	0.049 (0.30)	−0.068 (0.66)	1.157 (7.01)***
Italy	−0.018 (0.10)	−0.205 (1.05)	−0.308 (2.49)*	0.170 (0.97)
Spain	−0.125 (0.68)	−0.208 (1.09)	−0.300 (2.45)*	0.190 (1.11)
Netherlands	−0.224 (0.93)	0.059 (0.33)	−0.010 (0.09)	0.296 (1.70)
Extra-European supranational	−0.415 (1.64)	0.015 (0.07)	−0.228 (1.56)	2.656 (13.57)***
European supranational	0.346 (1.64)	−0.133 (0.72)	−0.327 (2.36)*	2.044 (10.76)***
Issue field				
Agriculture[c]	−0.433 (2.82)**	−0.420 (3.28)***	0.056 (0.53)	−0.071 (0.55)
Immigration	−0.455 (2.61)**	−0.156 (1.02)	−0.248 (1.96)	−0.163 (1.14)
European integration	0.626 (3.10)**	0.225 (1.14)	−0.231 (1.31)	0.093 (0.40)
Links received				
Same country/level	—	0.055 (14.07)***	—	—
Other countries/levels	0.037 (4.34)***	—	—	—
Links sent				
Same country/level	—	—	0.037 (12.07)***	—
Other countries/levels	—	—	—	0.056 (11.57)***
Constant	1.704 (11.41)***	1.563 (9.56)***	2.132 (23.15)***	0.281 (1.98)*
Observations	1,078	1,078	1,078	1,078
Wald $\chi^2(15)$	73.88***	297.29***	380.68***	582.19***

Notes: Robust z statistics are given in parentheses.

[a] Reference category: state and party actors.

[b] Reference category: Switzerland.

[c] Reference category: generalist (non-issue-specific) organizations.

* $p < .05$; ** $p < .01$; *** $p < .001$.

and received, independent of actor type, country or level, and the issue field in which an actor is active. Moreover, we find such a relationship between hyperlinks sent and received both within the same country or political level and across countries or political levels.

When we control for such reciprocity and size effects, several significant effects of the type and location of Web sites remain. If we first consider the determinants of the number of links sent to Web sites in the same country or on the same supranational level, we find two such effects. Socioeconomic interest groups are more likely to send links to other Web sites in the same country, and groups active in the field of agriculture are less likely to establish such hyperlinks. We do not have a compelling explanation why socioeconomic interest groups are more likely to send hyperlinks. The agriculture effect, however, supports our expectation that the Web sites of actors who are specialized in circumscribed issue fields will establish fewer hyperlinks. Indeed, the coefficient for Web sites in the immigration field is also negative, although it is not significant.

In the next regression, in which the number of hyperlinks sent across the boundaries of national or supranational polities is the dependent variable, both the agriculture and the immigration effects are significant in the expected negative direction. By contrast, actors who are active in the field of European integration are significantly more likely to establish transnational hyperlinks, which is of course linked to the transnational nature of this issue field. Further, this regression shows that Web sites based in the United Kingdom are less likely to send hyperlinks to other countries or to supranational organizations. In a multivariate context, this corroborates the observation we drew from Table 7.5, and it is also in line with the findings of Chapter 3 regarding public debates in the British print media, which also showed very low levels of attention for claims made by nondomestic actors.

In the third and fourth columns of the table we turn to the determinants of the number of hyperlinks that Web sites receive. Here we find confirmation for our earlier descriptive finding that civil society actors (both socioeconomic interest groups and NGOs, social movements, and other civil society groups) are less likely to be on the receiving end of hyperlinks than are state and party actors. This turns out to be the case both for links within the same country or political level and for transnational links. Media Web sites do not differ significantly from state and party Web sites in their tendency to either send or receive hyperlinks. We further find (see the third regression) that Italian and Spanish, as well as European, supranational Web sites are less likely to receive links from the same country or political level, but these effects are quite modest.

We find a broader range of significant effects on the likelihood of Web sites to receive transnational links. As already noted, civil society actors are less likely to be targets of such hyperlinks, but contrary to our expectations we do not find significant negative effects for Web sites of actors who operate in the circumscribed issue fields of agriculture and immigration. Regarding the effects of country or political level, we find confirmation for our earlier descriptive

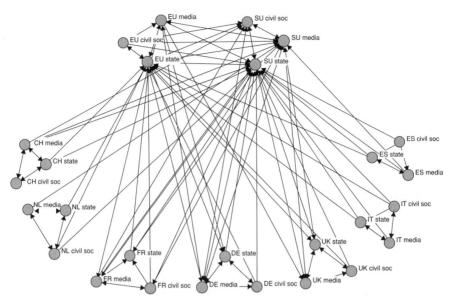

FIGURE 7.1. High-density linkages among actors on different geopolitical levels. The threshold to delimit high-density links is twice the density of the whole network, which is equal to 3.2% (CH = Switzerland, NL = the Netherlands, FR = France, DE = Germany, UK = United Kingdom, IT = Italy, ES = Spain, EU = European supranational, SU = other supranational).

finding that supranational Web sites (both European and extra-European), as well as Web sites in the three largest and most powerful countries in our sample – Germany, France, and the United Kingdom – are more likely to be the target of transnational hyperlinks. The effects for Germany, France, and the United Kingdom do not differ significantly from each other. More surprisingly, perhaps, given the substantial differences in the population size of these countries, there are no significant differences either in the likelihood of receiving transnational hyperlinks among Italian, Spanish, Dutch, and Swiss Web sites. This is in line with the findings reported in Chapter 3 for the print media, which also showed an overrepresentation of actors from the EU's "big three" in transnational coverage and very modest shares of Italian and Spanish actors in transnational public debates.

We conclude our analysis of hyperlinks by presenting in Figure 7.1 a graphical overview of the main findings. Apart from the seven countries and the two supranational levels, the figure also distinguishes between state and party actors, civil society actors (including socioeconomic interest groups), and media within each of the geopolitical units. Arrows have been drawn if the density of links of one group to the other is at least twice as strong as the density of the whole network. The general picture that emerges is that of national public spheres that are highly segmented from one another, but that are linked in what resembles a federative structure to the European and extra-European supranational levels, which are themselves also strongly interlinked. This federation has a strong bottom-up component (national actors linking to the supranational level) but the reverse linkages are much less developed. None of the Spanish, Italian, Dutch, and Swiss actors are recipients of strong links from the supranational level. The same is true for civil society actors in Germany and the United Kingdom.

In the case of the European supranational level, the isolation of European-level civil society groups is noteworthy, and it confirms our finding regarding their marginality in public debates in print media in Chapter 4. They neither link strongly to the national level nor receive many links from the national level. More generally, the federated structure is somewhat less developed in relation to the European supranational level, as is visible in the figure by the lower numbers of arrows sent and received by European supranational actors compared with extra-European supranational actors. This is remarkable given the fact that we selected our actors for their relevance in the issue fields of agriculture, immigration, and European integration, which would seem to favor linkages to European-level actors rather than to global supranational actors. European supranational governance, particularly in these fields, is more developed than global forms of governance, but our results suggest that the progress of European integration is not matched entirely by the development of a Europeanized online public sphere. The lack of strong horizontal connections among the seven European countries does not suggest strong horizontal Europeanization tendencies, either. None of the cross-national links comes close to the threshold criterion of twice the overall network density.

CONCLUSIONS AND DISCUSSION

Our aim has been to analyze the structure of online political communication with regard to two leading questions. First, does the Internet, compared with traditional offline media, offer better chances for less powerful actors to gain visibility? Second, is the Internet a more transnational and especially Europeanized communicative space? In contrast to most existing studies, we did not focus on the contents and format of single Web sites or small samples of Web sites; instead we strove to gain an overview of the overall structure of political communication on the World Wide Web. Also in contrast to many earlier studies, we investigated political communication on the Internet in direct comparison with offline media, thus allowing us to directly engage the question regarding the extent to which the information that is offered to a newspaper audience differs from what an Internet user is likely to encounter when she ventures into the Web space in search of political content.

The centrality of media professionals in the offline news selection process is often seen as introducing a bias in favor of powerful, institutional, and national actors, while excluding the views of civil society actors and of supranational and foreign actors. Selection on the Internet, by contrast, does not depend on the conscious selection of a few gatekeepers, but on the aggregation of the online behaviors of millions of individual users and online organizations. Despite these divergent selection mechanisms, our findings reveal highly similar outcomes. Both regarding the type of actors that achieve the highest levels of visibility, and regarding the prominence of national actors compared with foreign and supranational actors, it does not make much difference whether we analyze the content of newspapers, inspect the Web sites that are prominently listed by search engines, or follow the hyperlinks that are offered on Web sites. In all three cases, the types of actors whose views we are most likely to encounter are those of state and party actors from the home country.

There are some minor differences that suggest that the Internet is somewhat less biased in favor of powerful, institutional actors. In the search engine results, civil society actors were slightly more visible than they were in newspapers. Regarding the transnationality of Internet political communication, our results are ambivalent. On the one hand, both the search engine analysis and (more outspokenly) the hyperlink analysis showed a higher level of visibility for supranational actors than in the newspapers. On the other hand, the Internet is much less transnational than offline newspapers when it comes to directing attention to the views of actors in other countries than one's own. This finding was particularly pronounced in the hyperlink analysis, which revealed that there are very few cross-national linkages among Web sites, even among actors of the same type.

The reason that offline media are better equipped to convey the views of actors from other countries may be that journalists, and particularly foreign correspondents, act as translators, who transfer foreign-language information and opinions to an audience in their home country. Such translation is relatively limited on the Internet, where only 9% of the search engine results contained multilingual information. It seems therefore that, far from being obstacles to transnational discourses, media professionals are crucial intermediaries in the cross-national exchange of information and opinions. Our comparison between offline media and the Internet shows that, without this mediating effort, we would actually have less rather than more cross-national communication.

These differences between the Internet and offline media notwithstanding, our main finding is that the hierarchies of visibility that emerge in these two communicative arenas are very similar. In the offline media, journalists try to gauge what political actors and the public at large find important and relevant, and they select the news accordingly. On the Internet, the aggregation of millions of linking and clicking behaviors allows a direct measurement of what the public and political actors find relevant and leads to much the same outcome. This result suggests that journalists and editors, by way of their professional routines, trained observation skills, and intuition, essentially do what search engine algorithms do mechanically on the basis of their vast memory and calculation capacities: They observe what readers or viewers find interesting, and what the sources of their information find relevant, and accordingly decide to cover certain things prominently and to ignore many other possible news stories. To some extent, the similarity of offline and online distributions of visibility is due to the fact that, as our search engine analysis revealed, the online versions of offline media play an important role as providers of online political communication. However, our hyperlink analysis, in which media Web sites were much less prominently represented, shows that very similar patterns of visibility are also produced by the linking behavior of nonmedia actors, who also focus strongly on the home country and on the Web sites of state and party actors or news media.

All in all, our results show that Europeanized communication on the Internet faces similar limitations, and it is characterized by strong elite biases comparable to those found in offline media. The deficits of Europeanized political communication, most importantly the strong dominance of governmental and executive actors and the marginalization of civil society, are therefore unlikely to be solved by the advance of the Internet as a means for political communication.

8

Framing the European Union in National Public Spheres

Juan Díez Medrano and Emily Gray

INTRODUCTION

Do Europeans share a common representation of Europe, as most research on attitudes toward European integration assumes, or do these representations vary across functional and national lines? Recent research on the topic in Spain, Germany, and the United Kingdom provides a mixed answer, by showing that some representations are shared and others are not (Díez Medrano 2003). In particular, Díez Medrano demonstrates that British frames diverge from those existing in Germany and Spain in ways that help explain British Euroscepticism. Given the rocky ratification process of recent EU reform treaties and the impact that frames have on attitudes and behavior, the task of discovering what these frames are in the largest number of European states possible has become all the more pressing. Empirical research on the topic of frames is, in fact, at the center of contemporary work in the social sciences. This interest reflects an emerging consensus about the centrality of mental representations of reality in the explanation of behavior (see the pioneering work of Tversky and Kahneman 1981). The study of European integration has not been spared from this cognitive turn in the social sciences, and scholars in this field have begun to integrate frames into their descriptions and explanations (de Vreese 2003; Menéndez-Alarcón 2004; Robyn 2005). Publicized frames occupy center stage in these discussions. Television and newspaper frames in particular are conceived both as unconscious expressions of commonly shared understandings in the population and as instrumental presentations of reality by interested media and nonmedia agents.

Researchers are just beginning to systematically examine these publicized frames from a comparative perspective. The recent focus on media frames in studies of the European public sphere, in particular (de Vreese 2003; Díez Medrano 2003), coincides with the claim by some scholars that the existence of similar meaning structures across public spheres is a fundamental defining feature of a Europeanized public sphere (e.g., Díez Medrano 2003;

Eder et al. 2000; Risse 2002). We still know little, however, about prevalent frames about European integration in most of the EU member states. Díez Medrano studies Germany, the United Kingdom, and Spain. De Vreese concentrates on the Netherlands, the United Kingdom, and Denmark. Recently, Duchesne and von Ingelgom (2008) have expanded the list of countries to include Belgium and France. In turn, Bücker (2008) has done similar work for Poland. This research has been carried out with different methodologies, however, which somewhat limits the comparability of results. Furthermore, except for the work by Díez Medrano and by de Vreese, it has focused on ordinary citizens only, leaving out the public sphere, where many of these frames are generated. In this chapter, we move beyond the pioneering efforts just discussed by focusing on a larger number of countries, by examining a wider array of newspapers, and by analyzing the frames used by all actors with access to the public sphere rather than just the media's own voice expressed through editorials.

Our analytical approach takes inspiration from the emergent literature on the contextual factors that affect a given frame's chances of diffusion in the media, what specialists describe as the "discursive opportunity structure" (see Ferree et al. 2002b; Koopmans and Olzak 2004; Koopmans and Statham 1999). The empirical findings show that public actors in different countries represent the European Union in very similar ways. For all the talk of Europe's cultural diversity, Europeans are generally thinking about the same beast when they reflect on the European Union. Nonetheless, the empirical results reported here also confirm previous findings by revealing significant contrasts between the United Kingdom and the rest of the countries. This does not mean that the rest of the countries form a homogeneous whole: far from that. Rather, it means that the United Kingdom is more consistently different from other countries, and on frames that are relevant to patterns of support for European integration. At a more theoretical level, the empirical findings presented in this chapter demonstrate that an actor-driven logic is at work in the framing of claims, and they speak to the validity of approaches to the European public sphere that have tended to privilege the role of national over that of social sources of frames.

THE CONCEPT OF FRAME AND ITS ANALYTICAL RELEVANCE

Frames are images of reality. As such, they bear only a loose relationship to the reality to which they refer, but it is they, and not reality itself, which ultimately shape behavior. To disregard frames in the study of behavior mistakenly assumes that all actors represent reality in the same way. A now thriving literature on frames challenges this common assumption. This literature has mainly focused on contrasting national frames and has demonstrated that national frames intersect, with some shared and some unique elements (Lamont and Thévénot 2000). This comparative approach has been successfully used to explain policy contrasts between countries (e.g., Bleich 2003; Saguy 2003) as well as attitudes toward European integration among the population (e.g., Díez Medrano 2003; Hooghe and Marks 2004).

State actors and institutions, political parties, interest groups, social movements, public intellectuals, and the media play a major role in the diffusion of political frames across the population. This is because many political issues lie beyond the population's direct experience. In today's world, the media play the roles of both agent and primary vehicle for the transmission of frames to the population (Gamson and Wolfsfeld 1993; Koopmans and Olzak 2004). This recognition justifies a focus on the media when one is examining the production and diffusion of frames.

This chapter is primarily descriptive. It seeks to characterize the way public actors in this seven-country study represent European integration and the European Union in their claims. We are guided, however, by an analytical framework drawn from the literature of frames and by common sense and empirically grounded expectations about the contrasts that we may find. Actors featured in the media formulate their frames primarily guided by the following: (1) strategic considerations, which lead them, for instance, to emphasize more resonant frames in the population; (2) a dialogic context with specific opponents and sympathizers (see Steinberg 1999); (3) a thematic logic that establishes appropriate or standard ways of discussing certain topics; and (4) an actor-driven logic that reflects the actors' different identities and their embeddedness in institutional contexts. We will pay particular attention to the impact of the *actor-driven* logic outlined here. What this actor logic means is that actors generally use frames that correspond to role expectations and practices linked to the actor's status identity. It also means that, within this constraint, the actor's frames resonate with other frames that conform to his or her understanding of the world. We are aware, however, that this actor logic cannot always be disentangled from the strategic logic just highlighted, especially when we deal with political actors. We focus on two differentiating factors: the actors' professions and their national origins. Political partisanship is another variable within the actor logic, but we do not consider it in this chapter because party positions regarding European integration will be dealt with in Chapter 10. By focusing on a set of functional distinctions, our chapter makes what we think is an original contribution to the literature on frames about European integration, which until now has focused exclusively on national contrasts. This focus on functionally related discourses is relevant for substantive and methodological reasons.

Substantively, it allows us to determine whether different sets of actors construct different meanings for the objects that surround them, based on the identities that are conferred on them by their activities and institutional locations. Methodologically, the actor-driven logic operates not only at the level of nationality but also at the level of professions, and therefore research on national contrasts in frames about European integration ought to control for those effects when one is selecting materials for the description of national frames and the analysis of these contrasts.

We expect the media to portray the European Union in more negative ways than do other actors in the public sphere because the media have been assigned and play a key role in auditing government action in democratic societies (H1).

We also expect that political elite actors use political frames more often than do actors speaking as members of interest groups or of civil society groups (H2).

This is because their role as politicians constrains them into focusing their attention on the political aspects of the world that surrounds them. Furthermore, we state the following:

We expect national actors to conceive or describe the European Union from the perspective of sovereignty more frequently that do European Union actors (H3).

We expect this mainly because the state's main function in the international arena is to protect its sovereignty. Finally, we expect contrasts in the ways actors with different nationalities frame the European Union. More specifically and similar to the power–autonomy hypothesis scrutinized in Chapter 3, we state the following:

We expect that actors from powerful countries (e.g., the United Kingdom and France), because of such things as the possession of a nuclear deterrent, a permanent seat at the UN, or membership in the G-8, are less dependent politically on the European Union and, consequently, more sensitive to issues of sovereignty than are actors from other European countries (H4).

RESEARCH DESIGN

Our examination of frames relies on content analysis. While traditional content analysis has privileged the media as actor, our focus is on the frames that both the media and other actors portrayed in newspapers use when discussing the European Union or European integration. We analyze these frames quantitatively, as when we examine the proportion of claims that contain a particular frame, and qualitatively, as when we retrieve the original language used by political and media actors in framing the EU. We coded up to three frames, classified into four types: identity frames, instrumental frames, historical frames, and frames internal to the European integration process.[1]

1. Identity frames answer this question: What is the EU and what does it stand for? For example, the EU is "too centralized" or "overregulated," the EU stands for "subsidiarity," for "Christian values," for "peace," or for "equality," or the EU represents a "loss of sovereignty."

---

[1] We did this for claims centered on the general topic of European integration or centered on any other policy area but that included a European integration frame.

2. Instrumental frames answer this question: What is the EU good (or bad) for? For example, the EU helps "fight unemployment," the EU leads to "high taxes," the EU provides its members with a "greater weight in international relations" or with "security."[2]

3. Historical frames make links to historical periods or experiences perceived as positive (e.g., "enlightenment" or "classical antiquity") or negative (e.g., "past national isolation," "the Cold War").

4. Frames internal to the European integration process causally link two aspects of the European integration process. For example, "enlargement makes institutional reforms necessary." These are the typical kinds of "spillover" arguments that have been central to the functionalist view on European integration (Haas 1958).

For analytical purposes, we then grouped the long list of coded frames into a manageable series of sixteen clusters. For example, we constructed the democracy and rights frame cluster by aggregating five specific frames: rule of law, democracy, pluralism, human rights, and (preventing or overcoming) dictatorship or totalitarianism.[3] Regarding actors, we distinguish between the frames used by media actors and by nonmedia political actors in the public sphere. Media actors are those that speak in the name of the newspaper and nonmedia political actors include individuals or organizations representing state institutions and political parties, interest groups, or civil society.

THE FRAMING OF THE EU IN NATIONAL PUBLIC SPHERES

General Observations

We begin our analysis with a description of the most prevalent frames in the seven countries. Table 8.1 presents the frequency of different types of frames for the seven countries and distinguishes between nonmedia and media actors. In each of the countries, the denominator for each percentage is the number of claims with at least one frame. Thus, the first percentage in the table, 19.8%, means that 19.8% of the claims with at least one frame and made by nonmedia actors use an economy, trade, and price frame. In general, the frame categories comprise statements with varying valence (positive, neutral, or negative). The only exceptions are the frame categories of economy, trade, and price and democracy and rights, for which Table 8.1 distinguishes between positive and negative statements. The table makes clear that the European Union is primarily conceived as an association of democratic countries for the accomplishment of economic goals.

---

[2] If the claim established a connection between EU integration and values and norms (identity frame) or aims outside EU integration (instrumental frame), then this link was coded.

[3] Where we have aggregated data for frames across countries, the data have been weighted so that each country makes an equal contribution to the overall result.

TABLE 8.1. *Most Mentioned Frames by Nonmedia and Media Actors*

	Total	
Frame	Nonmedia	Media
Economy, trade, and prices (total)	19.8	19.4
Of which: positive economy, trade, and prices	7.2	3.5
Of which: negative economy, trade, and prices	3.3	6.2
Democracy and rights (total)	12.9	16.1
Of which: positive democracy and rights	6.0	4.1
Of which: negative democracy and rights	1.8	4.2
Sovereignty complex	10.9	11.2
Security and peace	8.8	7.0
Historical frames	8.2	10.8
Strong bloc	7.3	10.1
Equality	8.2	8.3
Efficiency	6.2	7.4
Citizen	6.9	11.4
Community of values	6.1	5.3
Exclusion	4.0	3.8
National interest	3.4	2.9
Globalization complex	2.6	3.6
National identity	2.5	2.0
N	3,654	1,227

Notes: Columns percentages add up to more than 100 percent because claims could contain more than one frame. The "economy, trade, and price," (total) and the "democracy and rights" (total) categories include positive, neutral, and negative frames.

The most frequent way of framing the EU is as an economic union, with about 19% of all frames concerning economic and trade issues,[4] and with the euro, European Central Bank policies, and EU enlargement at the center of these debates. There are subtle differences across countries in the way these topics are discussed. In Germany, and to a lesser extent in the Netherlands and Switzerland, the euro and European Central Bank policies are framed predominantly in terms of their contribution to stabilize prices. In France, Italy, and, to a lesser extent, Spain, the trade-offs between budgetary discipline, a strong euro, and price stability on the one hand, and economic growth and unemployment on the other, are more often debated. In Britain, together with more debate on the economic trade-offs of pursuing a monetary policy basically inspired by that of the Bundesbank, hesitation about membership leads public actors to frame the Economic and Monetary Union (EMU) in a broader range of economic topics such as investment, export opportunities, and convergence between the British and the EU's economic cycles. Subtle contrasts also distinguish countries in

---

[4] This category includes frames such as economic stability, strength in global competition, economic growth, economy of scale (internal market), own (national) economy, national exports, competition in Europe, costs, taxes, unemployment, inflation, prices, and foreign investment.

their discussions of European Union enlargement. Although the enlargement is predominantly framed as an opportunity for economic growth for both old and new members, concern over a decline in social standards ("wage dumping") through outsourcing and labor immigration is greater in Germany and in the Netherlands than in the rest of the countries. Public actors in the United Kingdom are the ones who frame enlargement most positively, as in the following quote by British Prime Minister Tony Blair: "Enlargement is about the stability provided by national working together rather than fighting together and the prosperity that comes from the single biggest market in the world" (*The Times*, December 8, 2000).

The second-most frequent representation of the European Union is as being grounded in and upholding democratic values. Almost 13% of the claims by nonmedia actors and 16% of the claims by media actors refer in one way or another to the European Union's democratic credentials. This framing of the European Union emerges in discussions over EU enlargement to Central and Eastern Europe and to Turkey, and very frequently also during the debate over sanctions against Austria because of Jörg Haider's Freedom Party's participation in government. In all countries but the United Kingdom, the European Union is also framed in terms of a democratic deficit (see the subsequent discussion). Finally, other frequent political frames about the European Union refer to the EU's impact on sovereignty (11%),[5] and its actual and potential contribution to peace and security (7% among nonmedia actors and 8% among media actors).[6]

The civic, republican conception of the European Union that emerges from these frames is not matched by an equally powerful "ethnocultural" representation. Cultural understandings, shared values, and collective identities are seldom drawn on by public actors in their constructions of the EU. The conceptualization of the EU as a community of values (community of values, Western values) and the EU's impact on national identity (national identity) are the two most frequent ethnocultural frames. About 6% of nonmedia actors and 5% of media actors use the former whereas about 2% of both nonmedia and media actors use the latter. Other, less frequently mentioned, ethnocultural frames are religious beliefs such as Christianity or Islam, ideologies such as neoliberalism or cosmopolitanism, and general principles such as diversity, unity, or civilization.

A similar lack of an anchoring point as with ethnoculture can be observed with respect to public actors' emphasis on historical events or periods. Although about 8% of the frames refer to historical events or periods, these historical events or periods cover a wide range of themes, from references to antiquity to the September 11 attacks. The most mentioned ones refer to antiquity, WWII, the Nazis or fascists, communism, the Cold War, divided Germany, French–German cooperation, and Europe's history of warfare in general. The

---

[5] These are frames such as sovereignty, centralization, subsidiarity, and federalism.
[6] These are frames such as peace, unity, security, and political stability.

main anchoring points of the European historical memory thus seem to be the classic Greek–Roman heritage, war, French–German rivalry, communism, and fascism. The numbers in each of these categories are small, however.

Functional Actor Categories and Representations of Europe

Media and Nonmedia Actors. When we compare the frames used by media and nonmedia actors, the most significant finding is that they are remarkably similar. For example, comparable proportions of nonmedia and media actors use the three most mentioned frames, economy, democracy, and sovereignty, in their claims (for economy and trade, 19.8% of all nonmedia actors' frames and 19.4% of all media actors' frames; for democracy and rights, 12.9% and 16.1%, respectively; for sovereignty, 10.9% and 11.2%, respectively). These findings suggest that media by and large comment and follow what nonmedia actors say when discussing European integration. Notwithstanding these similarities, one also detects some contrasts. The media, for instance, use negative economic and democracy frames more often than do nonmedia actors. Media actors are also more likely to focus on issues of the EU's relationship to its citizens than are nonmedia actors. Whereas 11.4% of media frames are citizen frames (civil society, active citizenship, public sphere or space, credibility, participation, opportunity space for citizens, acceptance of the EU by citizens), 6.9% of nonmedia actors' are. As we expected (H1), this finding points to a generally greater concern among media than among nonmedia actors to fulfill the so-called watchdog function and hold the EU institutions accountable on democratic grounds.

State–Political versus Interest Group–Civil Society. The actors' logic outlined at the beginning of this chapter also leads us to expect contrasts between state or party and interest group or civil society actors and between EU and national actors. This section examines the former. We expect state and party actors to use political frames more often and economic frames less often than do interest group and civil society actors, mainly because their world of experience is that of politics (H2). The comparison between state–party and interest group–civil society frames reveals a great deal of overall similarity. Table 8.2 reports statistically significant correlation coefficients, conveying either a more frequent or a less frequent use of certain frames by the two sets of actors (see Table 8.2; empty cells mean that the measured correlations are not statistically significant). A positive coefficient indicates that interest groups and civil society groups use a particular frame significantly more often; a negative coefficient indicates that state and party actors use a frame significantly more often. Our statistical results support our hypothesis: Interest groups and civil society actors display a greater propensity to use economic frames than do state and party actors. About 37% of interest group–civil society actors' frames fall in the economic category compared to 19% of state–party actors' (percentages not shown in the table). The contrast between the two types of actors is particularly marked in Britain,

TABLE 8.2. *Correlations between State–Party and Interest Group–Civil Society Frames by Country*

Frame	Germany	France	United Kingdom	Italy	Spain	The Netherlands	Switzerland	Total
Economy, trade, and prices	+0.18**	+0.12**	+0.26**			+0.11**	+0.20**	+0.15**
Democracy and rights			−0.11*					−0.03*
Sovereignty		−0.09*		−0.08*				−0.04*
Security and peace	−0.08*							
Historical frames	−0.06*			+0.11**				−0.05**
Strong bloc			−0.11*					
Equality	−0.09**					+0.12**		
Efficiency					+0.18*			
Citizen								
N	934	664	395	603	189	533	336	3,654

Note: Only statistically significant coefficients are reported in the table; complete results are available from the authors. Positive values (e.g., +0.12) indicate that a higher proportion of interest group–civil society actors than state–party actors used this frame. Negative values (e.g., −0.09) indicate that a higher proportion of state–party actors than interest group–civil society actors used this frame.

* *p* < .05, ** *p* < .01.

the Netherlands, and Germany, where 54%, 41%, and 40% respectively of the frames expressed by interest group–civil society actors fall in this category, compared with 24%, 27%, and 19% of those expressed by state or political actors. Italy and Spain are the only countries where we do not find this contrast.

If we focus more closely on the economic frames used by interest group–civil society actors in the United Kingdom, the Netherlands, and Germany, then we find that in the Netherlands and Germany they concern the effects of the introduction of the euro, the economic impact of the upcoming enlargement of the EU to 25 member states, and, in Germany in particular, Eurozone interest rates and the European Central Bank's monetary policies. In the Dutch public sphere, the groups who use economic frames most often are economists, financial experts, research institutes, and think tanks, while in the German public sphere businesses, employers' organizations, economists, and financial experts are the main interest group–civil society claim makers. In Britain, the principal focus of interest group–civil society actors' claims is the issue of whether or not Britain should join the single currency.

European versus National Actors. We now examine the contrast between European Union and national actors. We ask three questions: The first is whether they use the same frames. The second is whether there are significant differences in the degree of similarity between EU and national frames across countries. The third question is whether reported EU actor frames are identical across countries. This last question allows us to determine the media's role in shaping the image projected by EU actors. Table 8.3 shows the correlation coefficients for the association between type of actor (EU vs. national) and types of frames. A positive coefficient indicates that EU-level actors use a particular frame significantly more often; a negative coefficient indicates that national actors use a frame significantly more often. The main finding is that, as we predicted (H3), national actors use sovereignty frames more often than do EU actors.[7]

Further analysis of the within-country percentages underlying the correlations in Table 8.3 reveals that the frames used by EU actors differ by country. In fact, this finding holds even when one controls for the EU actor's country of origin and for the type of EU institution.[8] This is strong evidence for the significant role that the media in each country play in shaping the public debate by choosing what topics or actors to report on and how to transcribe what actors say.[9] The Spanish press, for instance, hardly includes EU actor claims

---

[7] National actors also seem to use economic frames more often than do EU actors, but this is mainly due to compositional effects, as we were able to confirm through multivariate logit analysis.

[8] These results are available from the authors upon request.

[9] In some exceptional cases (since most of the claims are nonspecific statements addressed to international audiences), it also reflects the fact that EU actors sometimes tailor their claims to the countries to which they are addressed, and that they do this by adopting the framing style of their addressees. For example, Romano Prodi was once quoted in *The Times* as saying that the United Kingdom has little control over its economy because it is surrounded by the euro and

TABLE 8.3. *Correlations between EU and National Actors' Frames by Country*

Frame	Germany	France	United Kingdom	Italy	Spain	The Netherlands	Switzerland	Total
Economy, trade, and prices		−0.13**	+0.27**				+0.19**	+0.09**
Democracy and rights			−0.13*					−0.05**
Sovereignty		+0.10*				+0.11*		+0.12**
Security and peace								
Historical frames	+0.08*	+0.12**						+0.05*
Strong bloc			−0.14*					
Equality		−0.12*	−0.15*	−0.15**		+0.14**		
Efficiency	−0.08*							
Citizen								
N	660	467	284	425	119	332	186	2473

Notes: Only statistically significant coefficients are reported in the table; complete results are available from the authors. Positive values (e.g., +0.12) indicate that a higher proportion of national actors than EU actors used this frame. Negative values (e.g., −0.08) indicate that a higher proportion of EU actors than national actors used this frame.

* $p < .05$, ** $p < 0.01$.

with an economic frame: only 1%, compared with a weighted average of 21% for the entire sample (percentages not shown in the table). Since only 4% of national actors use economic frames in their claims, compared with a weighted average of 25%, it seems that the Spanish press or the Spanish public simply do not pay much attention to topics with economic content. The United Kingdom and Switzerland are two other countries in which the percentage of EU actor frames with economic content lies well under the average for all seven countries considered, except that in this case the finding does not seem to betray a lesser interest by either press or public in economic aspects in general. In the United Kingdom, 13% of the frames used by EU actors contain an economic frame compared with 42% of those used by national actors; meanwhile, in Switzerland, 11% of the frames used by EU actors contain an economic frame, compared with 27% among national actors.

An examination of national and EU frames with a sovereignty content affords us another opportunity to see the role that national political debate and the press play in shaping how claims made by EU actors are presented in national public spheres. Here the average percentage of EU frames about sovereignty is equal to 7%. In the United Kingdom, however, this percentage climbs to 20%! In sum, one can say that, on average, national actors use sovereignty frames more often than do EU actors, but that both the nature of national political debates and the national newspapers' filtering strategies lead to reported EU actors' frames that reinforce the images of the EU created by national actors.

National Categories and Representations of Europe

Contrary to the image of cultural diversity that many opponents of European integration and the European Union institutions themselves frequently convey, portrayals of the European Union and the European integration process show more similarities than differences. Contrasts that do occur generally do not follow clearly interpretable patterns and do not allow for the distinction of clusters of countries. As in virtually all of the analyses reported in this book, the most significant and consistent national contrast we find is that between the United Kingdom and the rest of the countries.

To sort out the complex distributions of frames across countries and detect commonalities and contrasts, we estimated multinomial logit models, one for media actors and another for nonmedia actors. This complex technique allows us to determine how well our list of sixteen frame categories discriminates among the countries. The results of this analysis revealed that, taken together, the seven countries do not greatly distinguish themselves from one another by the use of a particular combination of frames and that contrasts are greater

---

affected by the decisions taken by the European Central Bank's decisions but has no influence on it. This, according to Prodi, constituted the "biggest loss of sovereignty" (*The Times*, February 16, 2001).

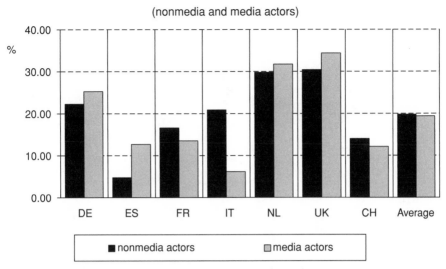

FIGURE 8.1. Percentage of claims with an economic frame by country (DE = Germany, ES = Spain, FR = France, IT = Italy, NL = the Netherlands, UK = United Kingdom, and CH = Switzerland).

when one examines media actors than when one examines nonmedia actors.[10] There exist, nonetheless, contrasts between countries with regard to the use of specific frames. Although they cannot be easily interpreted because they do not generally follow consistent patterns and because they rarely apply consistently to both nonmedia and media actors, they bear witness to some cultural diversity in Europe in the way people conceive the European Union.

Spanish media and nonmedia actors, for instance, characterize the European Union in economic terms less often than do actors from other countries. Figure 8.1 shows that 5% of the examined claims by nonmedia Spanish actors contain an economic frame compared to a seven-country average of 20%. In Figure 8.2, we also see that nonmedia actors in Italy tend to use a disproportionately large percentage of positive economic frames in their claims compared with actors in other countries, whereas British media actors use a disproportionately large percentage of negative economic frames. No less than 14% of the examined claims by British media actors depict the European Union's economic impact in negative terms, compared with a seven-country average of 6%.

National contrasts also emerge when one examines how actors from different countries evaluate the democratic credentials and values that underpin the European integration project. The United Kingdom appears again as an outlier in a landscape of relative homogeneity. Figure 8.3 shows that whereas

[10] The Cox–Snell pseudo-R^2 coefficients we obtained for these models are 30.0% for media actors and 18.8% for nonmedia actors.

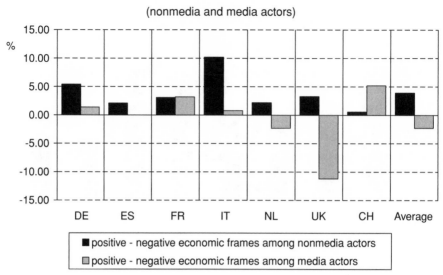

FIGURE 8.2. Balance of positive and negative economic representations of the European Union by country: percentage of claims with positive economic frames minus the percentage of claims with negative economic frames (DE = Germany, ES = Spain, FR = France, IT = Italy, NL = the Netherlands, UK = United Kingdom, and CH = Switzerland).

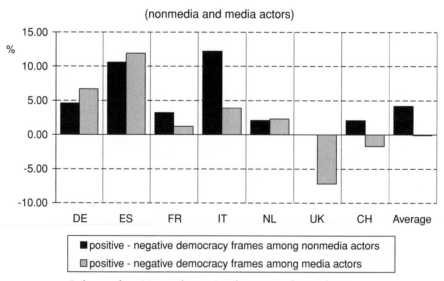

FIGURE 8.3. Balance of positive and negative democracy frames by country: percentage of claims with positive democracy frames minus the percentage of claims with negative democracy frames (DE = Germany, ES = Spain, FR = France, IT = Italy, NL = the Netherlands, UK = United Kingdom, and CH = Switzerland).

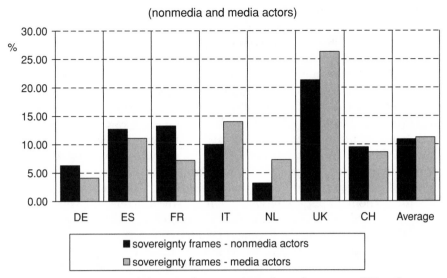

FIGURE 8.4. Percentage of claims with a sovereignty frame by country (DE = Germany, ES = Spain, FR = France, IT = Italy, NL = the Netherlands, UK = United Kingdom, and CH = Switzerland).

German, Spanish, and Italian actors, especially nonmedia ones, stress the European Union's democratic credentials and values, the British media show a comparably strong tendency to bemoan the European Union's democratic deficit. This striking contrast, which is obvious when one simply subtracts negative from positive democracy frames, as in Figure 8.3, becomes even more apparent when we compute ratios between positive and negative uses of the democracy frame in these countries. Among German nonmedia actors, *positive* dominate over *negative* democracy frames at a ratio of 24 to 1, whereas in the United Kingdom the relationship is the exact opposite and *negative* dominate over *positive* democracy frames at a ratio of 19 to 1.

When we move to less frequently used frames, such as sovereignty, one still detects significant country contrasts. Figure 8.4 shows that German actors and Dutch nonmedia actors less frequently link the European Union to sovereignty concerns, whereas British actors do so most often. Only 3% of the examined claims by Dutch nonmedia actors include the sovereignty frame, compared with 21% of those made by British nonmedia actors.

Beyond these frame-by-frame country comparisons, we want to investigate more systematically across the whole spectrum of frames whether countries significantly differ in the way they conceptualize the European Union and which frames are responsible for these contrasts. For this, we rely on multinomial logit and discriminant analysis. These two related statistical techniques allow us to determine whether countries or sets of countries stand out for their characterization of the European Union in terms of one or several frames. We summarize the results of these analyses performed with both the nonmedia and media actor samples. The statistical results confirm both the similarity of national frames about European integration in most of the countries, and the singularity of British representations of the European Union.

Nonmedia Actors. A simple multinomial logit model, with the frames as independent variables and the seven countries as categories of the dependent variable, results in a Cox–Snell pseudo R^2 of 19%. This statistic, whose values span the range from 0 to 100, with higher values meaning a greater correlation, tells us that our countries differ only moderately in the way they conceptualize the European Union. We are thus entitled to speak of the existence of a commonly shared frame about the European Union. Europeans from these seven countries think and represent the European Union in very similar ways.

With this homogeneity between the frames in the different countries in mind, we now proceed to focus on the small, but significant, contrasts suggested by the multinomial analysis. To highlight country contrasts and determine what variables or groups of variables are most responsible for these differences, we estimated a discriminant analysis with the framing data. The two clusters of frames that contribute most to discriminate between countries account for 63% of the variation we observe between the countries. We focus on these two clusters of frames and on the specific frames that contribute most to discriminate between countries.[11] The first cluster of frames accounts for 35% of the variance. It distinguishes countries based on how often nonmedia actors emphasize the European Union's community of values, its democratic credentials and aspirations (positive evaluations of the EU as representing or leading to democracy and human rights), and its opposition to diverse forms of exclusion (exclusion complex – e.g., frames that describe the EU as instrumental to countering nationalism, racism, xenophobia, ethnocentrism, and fascism–nazism). These frames can be conceived as politicocultural or value representations of the European Union, which, in more concrete terms, portray the European Union as a cultural community embodying enlightenment values such as democracy and tolerance tradition and resting on a Christian (or Judeo-Christian) heritage. Furthermore, this cultural conception of the European Union appears to be antagonistic to another conception of the European Union, which depicts it as a space where countries follow or are admonished to follow their national interest.

The statistical results just described mean that countries where conceptions of the European Union as a community of values are prevalent are also countries where instrumental representations of the European Union tend to be absent, and vice versa. The singularity of the United Kingdom compared to the rest of the countries is apparent in Figure 8.5, which displays the percentage distributions for the use of the relevant frames across countries. One can see Italy at one pole, with high percentages of claims speaking to the EU's democratic credentials and values, commonly shared values, and the EU's struggle against exclusion, and a small percentage of claims portraying the EU as an

---

[11] Full results are available from the authors upon request.

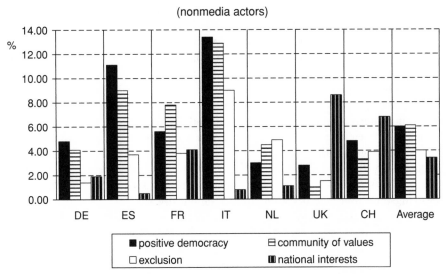

FIGURE 8.5. Percentage of claims with positive democracy, community of values, exclusion, and national interest frames by country (DE = Germany, ES = Spain, FR = France, IT = Italy, NL = the Netherlands, UK = United Kingdom, and CH = Switzerland).

arena for the defense of national interest, and the United Kingdom at the other pole, with just the opposite prevalence of these different claims.

The second cluster of frames corroborates the United Kingdom's outlier status. This combination of frames explains about 28% of the variance. It is therefore almost as relevant as the first one. The frame that is by far the most highly correlated with this discriminant function is the sovereignty frame. We saw earlier that the United Kingdom stands out for the relatively high frequency of such claims (see Figure 8.4).

Nonmedia and Media Actors' Frames Compared. The overall similarity between nonmedia and media actors' frames leads us to expect a similar picture of cross-national framing contrasts when we focus on media actors. The existence of some major within-country contrasts, however, suggests that the statistical analysis of these framing contrasts will not be identical. In this subsection, we simply outline the main contrasts between the results of the statistical analysis with nonmedia actors' frames and that with media actors' frames.

A first contrast is that frames differ more across countries when we focus on media actors than when we focus on nonmedia actors. The pseudo R^2 for the multinomial analysis that uses media frames as the independent variables and country as the dependent variable is equal to almost 30%, which is substantially higher than the 19% obtained for nonmedia actors.[12] A second contrast

---

[12] To be able to estimate the multinomial and discriminant models, we have had to randomly assign a value of 1 to four Swiss cases (the national identity, exclusion, globalization complex,

emerges when we estimate a discriminant analysis to determine what combinations of frames best explain cross-national differences. The fact that media frames differ more across countries than do nonmedia actor frames results in a more parsimonious statistical solution than the one described for political actors. Indeed, the first two discriminant functions explain 71% of the variance, with the first one alone accounting for 53%. Given the disproportionate relevance of the first discrimination function, we focus only on this one when analyzing international contrasts among media actors.

The most relevant frames in the first discriminant function are sovereignty and negative economic. The country scoring highest on these variables is the United Kingdom, at great distance from the rest of the countries. We find that this becomes clearer by going back to Figures 8.2 and 8.4, with the former showing the difference between the percentages of positive and negative economic frames, and the latter showing the percentage of claims by media actors that use the sovereignty frame. The finding that sovereignty and negative economic frames appear as leading indicators of this first discriminating function, while they did not appear together in the analysis for nonmedia actors, reflects the fact that British media actors hold much more negative images of the economic impact of the European Union than do nonmedia actors.

In conclusion, this analysis has shown that frames among nonmedia and media actors differ little across countries and that they differ more among media than among nonmedia actors. The main cleavage between the nonmedia actors' frames across countries is that between those countries that think of the European Union in cultural terms while disregarding national interest and those that think of the European Union in terms of national interest while disregarding cultural commonalities. Meanwhile, the main cleavage between media frames across countries is that between those countries where the European Union is conceived as a threat to sovereignty and as not fulfilling its economic promise, and those where this view is not as prevalent. Subtleties aside, what both analyses point out is that the main cleavage in this sample of countries is that between the United Kingdom and the rest of the countries. The United Kingdom's nonmedia actors stand out for their representation of the European Union in terms of national interest and for their lack of perception of a common European culture, whereas the United Kingdom's media actors stand out for their representation of the European Union in terms of sovereignty and negative economic images. At least with respect to the United Kingdom, these findings strongly support the international power hypothesis presented earlier (H4). But do frames in France match the expectations of the international power

and negative economic effects variables) and one Italian case (negative economic effects). This is because zero frequencies for these countries and variables led to singularity in some of the estimation matrices. The cases were chosen at random, with the provision that the cases selected for the negative economic effects frame had to contain a neutral economic frame. Since the sample is relatively large, these value attributions should not have changed the final results of the analysis.

hypothesis? As was also our conclusion in Chapter 3, we say, not really. The key test for this hypothesis is the extent to which claims include a sovereignty frame (second discriminant function for nonmedia actors and first discriminant function for media actors). Even though nonmedia actors emphasize the frame somewhat more in France than do nonmedia actors in other countries, the contrast with the United Kingdom is significant.

Beyond Numbers: Discourse and the Singularity of the United Kingdom's Representation of Europe. The finding that the United Kingdom stands out compared to the other six countries, because of its conceptualization of the European Union in sovereignty terms, stress on the national interest, questioning of the European Union's democratic credentials, and the absence of a complementary cultural representation, can be substantiated through examples that illustrate when, why, and by whom the frame is invoked. A qualitative analysis of the frame data reveals that the sovereignty frame was used in connection to general discussions about the reform of the European Union's architecture (i.e., the Maastricht Treaty and Constitutional Treaty), as well as European Monetary Union, foreign and defense policy, and adherence to the Social Chapter. Alan Sked's remarks in an article in *The Times* in 1990 exemplify general critiques in the early 1990s against the Treaty of the European Union. Sked was at the time a member of the Faculty at the London School of Economics and a vocal critic of the European Community. On the occasion of the Helsinki Conservative Leaders' summit, Sked invited Margaret Thatcher, then Prime Minister of the United Kingdom, to resist short-term moves to create a European government, central bank, or a common foreign and defense policy, and to protect British national sovereignty "at all costs":

Europe's response to war, terrorism, aggression, and blackmail is likely to be so inadequate that British national sovereignty must be protected at all costs ... The Prime Minister's task in Europe is crystal clear ... to support the creation of the single market, while resolutely resisting federalism. Yet what chance does she have of defeating the federalists?　　　(*The Times*, August 28, 1990)

Ten years later, a similarly negative reaction was triggered in some Eurosceptic circles by President of the European Commission Romano Prodi's EU Mission statement, in which he called for a deepening of integration to confront the twin challenges of globalization and EU enlargement. In an article by Edward McMillan-Scott, UK Conservative MP, one reads that Prodi's EU Mission statement will add to the worries of those concerned about the direction of the EU and that Prodi's statement is a "centralising document of little practical value" (*The Times*, February 10, 2000).

Prompting the reference to "sovereignty" in the British media criticizing the European Commission's reform proposals were ambitious initiatives, primarily monetary union and the creation and then reinforcement of the second pillar of the EU. The former, in particular, motivated a controversial remark by the United Kingdom's Trade and Industry Secretary, Nicholas Ridley, in an interview for *The Spectator* that stirred public outcry in the rest of Europe. On this occasion, Ridley said that handing over sovereignty to the European Commission is "tantamount to giving it to Adolf Hitler," and that moves toward European Monetary Union were a "racket designed to take over the whole of Europe" (*The Spectator*, July 14, 1990). Ridley's remarks were reproduced the same day in Dutch, German, Italian, and Spanish papers. The Dutch paper *Het Algemeen Dagblad*, in particular, reported that the British House of Commons itself had deplored the incident and expressed that as long as Ridley would be Minister, the credibility of the United Kingdom within the European Commission would be harmed.

The "sovereignty" frame is used in multiple contexts and by multiple actors. It is not always actors who oppose steps to European integration who contribute to its diffusion. Very often, it is public actors, generally foreign, who involuntarily strengthen its presence in the public sphere by using it to counter those who claim that the EU contributes to erode the United Kingdom's sovereignty. As Marc Steinberg shows in his dialogical discourse analysis of nineteenth-century class conflict in England, the weak (in the United Kingdom, those in favor of European integration) usually find themselves using their opponents' frames, even though they try to turn them against these opponents (Steinberg 1999). This puts them at a rhetorical disadvantage, and at any rate ends up reinforcing the dominant frames. Thus, we read Douglas Hurd, Foreign Affairs Secretary and a moderate in the Thatcher and Major governments, saying during the debate on the Treaty of the European Union "We are going to keep our separate governments, our legal systems, our constitutions, our traditions. At the same time we will hold more and more practical policies in common. This is not eroding sovereignty, it is using it" (June 11, 1990). Similarly, we also read Jacques Santer, President of the European Commission between 1995 and 1999, saying in an interview to the BBC that was reported in *The Guardian*, that despite the extension of qualified majority voting and EMU, Britain would keep its identity. His own country had not lost its identity and there was no reason why Britain should lose its own: London would keep its artistic traditions, cabbies' banter, smell of fresh mown lawn, and so on (*The Guardian*, May 5, 1995).

In the end, what one observes is frequent debate between those who decry the potential loss of sovereignty and those who try to either inactivate the argument or give it a positive twist, as when Kenneth Clarke, Chancellor during Major's Premiership, caused an uproar among Eurosceptic Conservative MPs, or when Secretary of Education Michael Portillo contradicted Major's policy on monetary union. In an address to the European Movement, Clarke claimed that it was a mistake to believe that monetary union need be a huge step on the path to a federal Europe. For Clarke, joining the common currency would not necessarily mean the end of British sovereignty (*The Guardian*, November 2, 1995).

Although a plurality of actors use the sovereignty discourse, the exchanges just described leave the distinctive impression that it is used primarily by British conservative political actors. This impression is correct. Although conservative party members in all countries of our study are generally those most prone to use the sovereignty frame, the sovereignty frame is infrequent in most of them, and the left–right contrasts pale in comparison with those in Britain. The percentage of claims by Conservative Party members that use the sovereignty frame is 18%, compared with 5% of the claims by Labour Party members. When we analyze the media's voice, we discover a similar left–right cleavage. Whereas 25% of *The Times*' claims and 32% of *The Sun*'s claims use the sovereignty frame, only 8% of *The Guardian*'s do. What is more striking, however, is that *The Scotsman* uses the sovereignty frame in 47% of the claims, most clearly when arguing against joining the euro.

If one makes an exception for *The Scotsman*, which does not easily fit in the left–right cleavage, one would be tempted to say that the British singularity with respect to the other countries in the sample, in terms of its framing of the European Union, is mainly due to the obsession with this topic among conservative politicians and newspapers. This would be an oversimplification, however, for the sovereignty frame that distinguishes Britain emerged already in the late 1940s and was heavily used by the Labour Party before its pro-European conversion in the late 1980s (see Díez Medrano 2003). The emphasis that left and right have historically placed on sovereignty when discussing European integration explains its hegemonic role as a representation of the European Union in Britain and the fact that not only opponents but also supporters of European integration inevitably invoke it in their arguments.

Emphasis on the national interest is another distinguishing feature of the way British actors frame the European Union. The two frames are certainly related in the British actors' cognitive landscape, as illustrated by the following quote: "Where, case by case, we believe we can promote the national interest by majority voting, we will agree to it" (Robin Cook, Foreign Secretary, in *The Scotsman*, November 18, 2000).

This stance fits within neorealist and liberal intergovernmental perspectives, but it could also be made to fit in constructivist accounts. That is, one could see a concern with national interest as common to all countries, which is expressed more often when large groups in society perceive international arrangements as counter to this interest, or one could see the use of the national interest frame as contingent on legitimate ways of approaching international politics, as understood from the following quote: "Officials both in Brussels and Berlin say that Germany has now become more confident about asserting its own interests in the EU, in a way that France, Britain and Spain have always done" (*The Guardian*, April 30, 2002). Whereas the first approach would draw a unidirectional causal connection between how actors perceive the national interest implications of a policy and the use of the sovereignty frame (e.g., this runs against the national interest; therefore, we oppose a surrender of sovereignty), the second approach would be compatible with an interpretation where a principled rejection of a surrender of sovereignty causally precedes the use of a national interest justification in places where this type of argument is constructed as legitimate.

Different theoretical approaches would thus point toward different lines of inquiry into the factors underlying framing contrasts between the United Kingdom and other European countries. Are British national interests more negatively affected than other national interests by an integrated Europe? Are Britons more sensitive to surrenders of sovereignty? If so, why? Is the language of interest more legitimate in Britain than elsewhere? If so, why? At this stage, we can only point to this distinguishing feature of British discourse on European integration. The national interest frame, like the sovereignty frame, is used by both British supporters and opponents of steps to European integration, with Labour among the supporters and the Tories among the opponents, and with Labourites using it slightly more often than do Tories. Thus, on the one hand one hears Margaret Thatcher saying, "If anyone is suggesting that I would go to Parliament and suggest the abolition of the pound sterling, no! We shall block things that are not in Britain's interests" (*The Times*, October 29, 1990). Then, on the other hand a month later, we hear John Smith's equally combative stance: "It would be against the national interest if Britain allowed itself to be excluded from full monetary union and establishment of a single currency; there can be no question of accepting 'division two' status for our country in the community of the future" (*The Times*, November 29, 1990). Prime Minister John Major moved away from these extreme positions in the mid-nineties. From then on, governmental positions on EMU in Britain have oscillated between "yes, but" and "wait and see," while the yes–no discourse has been relegated to the opposition parties' MP's and the rank and file. The defense of the national interest remained, however, at the core of discourse on European integration, as in the following quote from John Major: "Our ability to influence the debate on the single currency now, when it matters, would be destroyed if we exercised our 'opt-out' now . . . that would not be in our interests" (*The Times*, June 29, 1995). More positively inclined toward the euro, Tony Blair said this seven years later: "If the economics are in the right place, if the tests are met, then it is overwhelmingly in our interest to join . . . it is in our interests for us to be a key and major player in Europe" (*The Guardian*, May 22, 2002).

The third frame that most distinguishes Britain from other countries is the questioning of the European Union's democratic credentials or what is referred to as the "democratic deficit." "Democracy" is, after the conception of the European Union as a market, the most important frame about the European Union, and one that is shared across countries. There is something about which everybody agrees and this is that the European Union is founded on and promotes democratic values, although British actors, as we have seen, do not stress this point as do public actors in other countries. The Haider case, to which many claims refer, offered in fact an opportunity for the ritualistic assertion of this shared value. Many of the uses of the "commonality of values" frame in France were actually used in connection with the Haider affair, as when Thierry de Montrial, writing for *Le Figaro*, argued for European countries to interfere with Jorg Haider's entry in the Austrian government by saying that "The only way to prevent the return of the old demons in Europe is to give new life to the political debates, within the context of rigorously formulated democratic values" (*Le Figaro*, February 10, 2000; our translation from the French).

Democracy is invoked for all sorts of reasons, going from support for to opposition against further integration. The British, however, stand out for criticizing the European Union's democratic credentials to oppose transfers of sovereignty. Illustrative of this tendency is a comment by Neil Herron, leader of an anti-European organization, "metric martyrs," that opposes the European Union's directives requiring goods to be sold in metric units, upon hearing that his organization had lost a High Court case: "This shows that an Act of Parliament passed in the UK can be overruled by a mere directive from a gathering of unelected bureaucrats over which we have no democratic control; this decision brings about the 'death of democracy'" (*The Times*, February 19, 2002). British actors, more than other countries' actors, position themselves against European integration on grounds that it is not democratic. This is just the opposite of what Germans actors do, which is to push for more integration to make the European Union more democratic. Thus, we read in *The Guardian* that Angela Merkel, leader of the Christian Democratic Union at the time, reacts positively to proposals by the Social Democratic Party of Germany to further EU integration, in particular by strengthening the European Parliament, with the argument that "We have a democratic deficit in the EU and that must change" (May 1, 2001). The British actors' perception of a democratic deficit in the EU is grounded on things such as the unelected character of the Commission, the centralized character of EU governance, the lack of accountability to the British electorate of non-British Commissioners and European Parliament members, and the lack of European political parties. What remains puzzling is why the British public has not warmed to the EU, despite the gradual strengthening of the European Parliament in the past eighteen years and why, on the contrary, public actors systematically oppose efforts to strengthen the European Parliament's powers, as does former United Kingdom Chancellor Norman Lamont in the quote that follows: "Europe does not need an elected parliament, for it will inevitably push for more powers for itself, and for a centralised Europe" (*The Times*, April 13, 1995). It seems plausible that implicit in the British use of the democratic deficit frame is a sense among opponents of European integration that Britain and Europe are two different communities, as public opinion surveys reveal when they show that Britons identify as Europeans less often than do populations from other countries. It is beyond this chapter's scope, however, to further explore this hypothesis (on this issue, see Díez Medrano 2003).

One might get some leverage in the search for an explanation of the United Kingdom's frame distinctiveness from comparing the United Kingdom with

France. Indeed, the United Kingdom's opposition to transfers of sovereignty agrees to some extent with the "world power status" expectation outlined at the beginning of the chapter. France, however, appears to contradict the hypothesis. Where does this contrast with the United Kingdom come from? Is it a reflection of France's being less of a great power or is it a reflection of the French population's having stronger European feelings than has the British population? Further comparative and empirical research between these two cases may allow us to solve this puzzle.

CONCLUSIONS

This chapter goes beyond previous cross-national studies by examining the public spheres of a larger number of countries and differentiating between framing by several actor types. Our approach is original in exploring the actor logic at work in the process of framing the European Union. The actor-driven logic manifests itself in framing contrasts between countries and, secondarily, in framing contrasts between political actors, media actors, and civil society actors, and between European Union actors and national actors. Actors in the public sphere of these seven countries represent the European Union as a mainly economic institution formed by democratic countries. The European Union is also described as limiting the states' sovereignty and, to a slightly lesser degree, as contributing to peace and security in Europe. One of this chapter's major conclusions is indeed that collective actors in the European Union largely share a common frame on European integration issues. This conclusion points to the existence of a shared political culture within Europe. The main contrast observed in this analysis is that between the United Kingdom and the rest of the countries included in this study. British political actors emphasize sovereignty and national interest in their approach to the European Union and fail to see the European Union as a group of countries sharing the same values.

The actor-driven logic also expresses itself in framing contrasts between political, civil society, and media actors. We certainly uncovered striking similarities between the ways in which political and media actors framed the EU, but (a) media actors were more likely to focus on issues of the EU's relationship to the citizen than nonmedia actors were; (b) civil society actors tended to frame the European Union in more economic terms than did political actors and media actors; and (c) media actors tended to be more critical of the European Union than were nonmedia actors. The actor-driven logic would indeed predict that those removed from power be more critical of the European Union than those in power, and that the media, as transmission belt between the state and society, echo both the concerns of political elites and those of civil society. From the latter perspective, the British media take this position most often. Although more research is needed, one cannot rule out the implication that the British media are closer to their citizens and less focused on the opinions of political elites than are other countries' media. The actor-driven logic also seems to operate in the explanation of the disproportionate number of economic frames among civil society actors. Indeed, an in-depth analysis of the claims that included economic frames has revealed that civil society frames disproportionately represent the views of groups from which one would expect such economic frames: business interests and economic experts, rather than NGOs, citizens' organizations, or social movements.

The literature on modernization predicts that, as polities modernize, cultural cleavages are replaced by functional or class cleavages. In the past, this prediction has been refuted by empirical work that shows that this has often not been the case. Strong territorial cleavages often persist in highly modern states such as Spain or the United Kingdom, which make these states vulnerable to fragmentation in times of crisis and demand tremendous investments in state boundary maintenance. One can further test modernization theory's prediction with respect to European integration, using frame analysis. The question to be answered is whether functional or ethnonational cleavages prevail in conceptualizations of the European Union. This chapter shows that there are few national or functional contrasts when it comes to imagining the European Union. This similarity in the frames about the European Union in the seven countries examined here, with Britain's partial exception, hints at socioeconomic, political, and cultural similarities that, if reflecting slow-moving convergence processes, may eventually lead to the predominance of functional and class contrasts over national ones. Were this to happen, the European Union would have certainly become something akin to traditional nation-states on a broader scale. Although some scholars argue that the European Union does not need to become a nation-state writ large to be a stable and legitimate polity, periodic monitoring of frames on European integration across states is a useful tool toward assessing progress in the direction of cultural homogeneity.

Our main goal in this chapter has been to describe patterns of variation in the frames used to debate the European Union across countries and actor types, and to point to some factors that may explain these trends. Future research would benefit from an examination of the consequences of such framing on the general population's attitudes and behavior and from an examination of the factors that lead to certain frames' successful diffusion in the public sphere while others fail. Research in this area has already begun to develop under the label of "discursive opportunity structures," that is, aspects of public discourse that determine a given message's chances of diffusion in the media (Koopmans and Olzak 2004; Koopmans and Statham 1999), but much more remains to be done. Future research must also further explore the mechanisms at work in how media report public actors' claims. This chapter has shown, for instance, that the frames reported for claims made by European Union actors vary by country in ways that make them consistent with the frames used by national actors. It would seem that the media filter European Union actors' frames in ways that are familiar to their readership. Further research is needed to examine the factors at work in this filtering process more closely.

PART IV

POLITICAL ACTORS

Collective Action and Party Competition

9

Going Public in the European Union

Action Repertoires of Collective Political Actors

Hanspeter Kriesi, Anke Tresch, and Margit Jochum

INTRODUCTION

It is our contention that, today, all relevant political actors – state actors, political parties, interest associations, and social movement organizations – face a double strategic challenge as a result of two crucial transformations of their political opportunity structure – the Europeanization of politics and the increasing public orientation of politics. Both of these processes have already been discussed (see Chapters 1 and 2). For this chapter,[1] it is crucially important to understand that the process of European integration has led to the creation of a polity of an unprecedented kind – a system of multilevel governance that encompasses a variety of authoritative institutions at supranational, national, and subnational levels of decision making. Following the work of some influential political scientists (Green Cowles, Caporaso, and Risse 2001; Hooghe and Marks 2001; Jachtenfuchs and Kohler-Koch 2003), we view the EU as a distinct structure of governance with characteristics of its own. The development of this EU polity has gone hand-in-hand with the widening scope of decision making and its public politicization at the supranational level. The precise nature of the very complex political structuring of the decision-making processes within this new polity is rather unclear and leaves much room for interpretation. We do not want to enter the debate on the architecture of this structuring, but we would like to consider its implications for the strategic orientation of collective political actors' action repertoires. For these actors, the emergence of the new supranational layer of decision making at the EU level implies a transformation of their political opportunity structure, which represents a new resource or constraint and complicates their matrix of strategic choices (see also Chapter 4).

A further important premise for this Chapter is that Western European countries have experienced the rise of a new form of representative democracy,

---

[1] The chapter draws partly on Kriesi, Tresch, and Jochum (2007).

which Manin (1995) characterizes as "audience democracy." In audience democracies, the citizen public no longer manifests itself only during elections, but it also has a say every day between elections, in the form of opinion surveys, focus groups, or all sorts of protest events. Elected representatives, in turn, face an ever-growing pressure to respond to public opinion, and to bring the political debate from the smoke-filled back rooms out onto the public stage where it takes place in front of the media audience. This model of the audience democracy, which has succeeded classic parliamentarism and party democracy, builds on developments that have long been noticed by specialists of political parties and political communication. The former have observed the decline of mass parties based on strong ideologies and embedded in closely monitored social contexts. They have pointed to the corresponding rise of a new type of party that, less dependent on traditional party bureaucracies and activists, establishes a direct link between the party leaders and their electorate. Against the background of these developments and the related loss of partisan functions, Mair (2000a, 2002) foresees the possible coming of a democracy without parties or, in other words, of a "populist" democracy. Specialists of political communication, in turn, have observed that, in Western Europe, the originally party-centered political communication is increasingly becoming a media-centered one (Hallin and Mancini 2004; Swanson and Mancini 1996). The growing role of the public and of media-centered political communication constitutes yet another modification of the political actors' opportunity structure and a challenge for their political strategies.

In this chapter, we analyze how political actors in Western Europe deal with this double strategic challenge. Our analysis builds on comparative data that have been collected by the national research teams in a work package dedicated in particular to the actors' strategies. These data include supranational actors at the EU level and national actors from the seven countries of our study. In the first section of this chapter we discuss the emergence of an EU polity and its consequences for the choice of the *target level* of political intervention in the context of the increasing Europeanization of politics. In the second section, we discuss the implications of the growing public orientation of politics for the choice of specific *action repertoires* to influence European policies. In line with the general theoretical perspective developed in Chapter 2, we theorize in both sections primarily about differences between the strategic choices of various types of political actors, who are not all equally affected by the emergence of new opportunity structures. In the third section, we present the data that have been used in this chapter; finally, in the fourth section, we turn to the presentation of our results.

THE STRATEGIC CHALLENGE OF THE EMERGENCE OF AN EU POLITY

With the emergence of a new EU polity and the expansion of its functional scope, a growing number of national actors have become involved in EU decision making and are now part of a multilevel governance process (Kohler-Koch 2003, p. 13). Maurer, Mittag, and Wessels (2003) give an account of the remarkable and persistent shift of attention of individual and institutional resources from the national to the EU level. Given this development, we expect domestic political actors to act at both the national and the EU level to influence European policy making. While the action repertoire of all kinds of political actors is likely to be Europeanized to a certain extent, we have reasons to believe that the national level remains the dominant focus for strategic interventions for all four types of actors considered here.

First, as far as *state actors* are concerned, in the system of joint decision making of different levels, national administrations are responsible for the coordination of EU policy making at both the European and the domestic level (Hix 2005, pp. 38 ff.): They play a central role in the prelegislative and postlegislative stages of EU policy making, but they remain primarily national actors because they are accountable to national governments, are taking their cues above all from domestic politics, and are at the front line of the implementation of EU policies at the national level. Second, while *political parties* have developed Eurobranches as another organizational layer in addition to the national, regional, and local ones, the electoral competition for EU elections has remained segmented along territorial boundaries of the nation-states. Moreover, EU elections are second-order elections, given that no actual executive power is at stake (van der Eijk and Franklin 1996, p. 12). For the parties, this simple fact implies that they privilege the national level, even if they are also concerned with policy making at the EU level. If there is one party family that can be expected to be more EU oriented than the others, it is the left, given its traditional internationalism and its comparatively coherent organization at the EU level. Third, for *interest groups* and *social movement organizations* (SMOs), influence attempts are most effective when they involve multiple tactics (Baumgartner and Leech 1998, p. 155). In the EU, a system of multilevel governance with an uncertain nature of influence (e.g., shifting alliances, multiple points of access), and a combination of influence tactics at different levels, is the most promising strategy to influence European politics (Beyers 2004, p. 215). *Interest groups* might indeed use a mixture of indirect activities at the EU level and direct interventions at the national level. In fact, interest groups are commonly regarded as the most Europeanized type of political actors. They have created specific associations to represent their collective interests at the EU level. Their membership in these new European associations provides the powerful national interest groups with a channel to influence policy making at the EU level indirectly.

Nevertheless, even the main national interest groups have incentives to target the national level in the first place. Given that the national governments act as key intermediaries who incorporate the views of national interest groups before coming to the EU bargaining table, the main interest groups are expected to remain primarily linked to national arenas, as the states' veto power ensures them a continued monopoly of pressure group activities (Hix 2005; Kohler-Koch 1994; Streeck 1995). Regarding SMOs, finally, protest politics at the EU level is a small albeit growing phenomenon. Imig and Tarrow (2001b), however, rather suggest that the Europeanization of SMOs only rarely takes the form of full-fledged European-wide campaigns and mostly corresponds to a "domesticated" variant in which national movements protest at home against policies of the EU. Marks and McAdam (1999) also point to the fact that protest politics is relatively poorly suited to the EU. It is expensive in terms of time and money to transport activists to Brussels, and the structure of political opportunities in the EU is decidedly more open to conventional inside-oriented activities than to unconventional public-oriented activities.

Within these general constraints, the relevance of the EU level for the actors' strategies depends both on its salience and its accessibility. As far as salience is concerned, it is obvious that interventions at the EU level are most important for supranational actors, such as the EU bureaucracies or the European interest associations. Next, it is equally plausible to assume that the EU level is more important for collective actors in EU member states than for their colleagues in nonmember states, whom we expect to target the EU level less frequently. For the sake of brevity, we make no further distinctions between EU member states in this chapter, despite the considerable variation in the degree of compatibility between the EU policy process and domestic processes (Hix 2005, p. 40; Kohler-Koch 2003, p. 16), which may have important implications for the actors' strategies both at the domestic and the EU level. Third, the salience of EU decision making is expected to vary by policy domain. It is the policies of the so-called first pillar – the four freedoms of movement (goods, capital, services, persons), agriculture, competition, trade, monetary and exchange policy, and, recently, also visa and asylum policies – and constitutional issues concerning the construction of the EU polity, where decision making at the EU level has become most salient. Although all three policy domains of our study – EU integration, agricultural policy, and immigration policy – belong to the high-salience category, we expect actors involved in immigration policy to target the EU level less frequently than actors involved in agricultural issues or questions regarding the institutional design of the EU. While the Treaty of Amsterdam has progressively integrated immigration policy into the first pillar,[2] the shift of decision-making competences to the supranational level is still less pronounced (Lavenex 2001, p. 854), and policy making in this area takes the form of "intensive transgovernmentalism," characterized by the involvement of national actors below the level of head of governments (e.g., ministerial offices, law-enforcement agencies; see Wallace 2000, p. 33).

Considering accessibility, it is well known that the new level of the multilevel polity has altered the distribution of political power between different types of actors, reinforcing some actors to the detriment of others. Executive actors at the national and the EU level are the main beneficiaries of this redistribution of power. Through their representation in the EU Council, member state governments possess key executive functions in the EU (Hix 2005, p. 40). The growing interaction of national administrations in the day-to-day running

---

[2] The Treaty of Amsterdam aims at the development of a common policy on asylum and migration within a period of five years after its entry into force.

of the EU government led to what Wessels (1997) has called the "fusion" of the administrations at the different levels. As a result, the administrative arena has been strengthened compared with the parliamentary arena. As prime interlocutors of the executive in the administrative arena, interest groups have also benefited from this shift of power. As far as non-state actors are concerned, the question is, however, whether the new level is above all accessible to those actors who already have access at the national level, or whether it serves a compensating function for the nationally peripheral actors. Beyers (2002) formulates two competing hypotheses in this respect: a "persistence hypothesis," according to which European access builds on the strength of domestic networks, and a "compensation hypothesis," according to which European access compensates for the lack of domestic access. He mainly found support for the persistence hypothesis. Similarly, the "Matthew Effect" discussed by Merton (1973, pp. 439–59) with respect to the system of science, stipulates that there is a principle of cumulative advantage that operates in different systems to produce the same results: The rich get richer at a rate that makes the poor become relatively poorer, and, similarly, power gets ever more concentrated in the hands of the privileged few

In line with this hypothesis, we expect the powerful actors to have more access at all levels of the multigovernance system.

In addition, political actors in all European countries face a new strategic challenge: At which level, national or European, should they focus their efforts in order to influence public policy making most effectively?

Our general expectation is that all types of national political actors still privilege the national level when attempting to influence European politics, especially in the field of immigration. Only genuine supranational actors can be assumed to focus primarily on the EU level.

Among national actors, we expect political parties and SMOs to be less active at the EU level than are state actors, interest groups, and, following the persistence hypothesis, all actors whose political power has been increased by European integration. Furthermore, national actors from EU member states should choose to intervene at the EU level more frequently than actors from a non-EU member state such as Switzerland.

THE STRATEGIC CHALLENGE OF THE INCREASING IMPORTANCE OF THE PUBLIC SPHERE

Traditionally, and whatever the level of the multilevel governance structure, the default strategy for any political actor has been an inside strategy such as classical political lobbying. As is observed by Beyers (2004, p. 215), inside strategies are superior in terms of their efficiency with regard to information processing, and they avoid the costs of public strategies in terms of an actor's reputation as trustworthy interlocutor. But, as we have already observed for interest groups in particular, influence attempts are most effective when they involve multiple tactics. The expansion of the scope of conflict to a wider audience has always been a key political strategy in democratic polities. As Schattschneider (1960 [1988]) has famously observed, the result of political contests is determined by the scope of public involvement, and "conflicts are frequently won or lost by the success that the contestants have in getting the audience involved in the fight or in excluding it, as the case may be" (p. 4). The *agenda-setting approach* has elaborated this notion. It considers the struggle for the attention of the public as a key element of democratic representation and attention shifts as key mechanisms in the development of political conflicts (see Baumgartner and Jones 2002; Burstein 1998; Jones 1994). In the final analysis, the participants in the struggle for attention, of course, want not only public attention but also public *support* for their own issue-specific positions. The point of the agenda-setting approach is, however, that the road to support is decisively shaped by the management of public attention, which, in turn, can be decisively influenced by public-oriented strategies of political actors, most importantly by attempts to achieve news coverage in the media.

In general, public-oriented strategies are expected to be used primarily on the national level. While the mass-mediated public sphere is of increasing importance in present-day Western "audience democracies," there is, as has been argued in Chapter 2, no genuinely transnational public sphere at the EU level. Short of a fully fledged public sphere based on European-wide media, both European and national actors have no choice but to target the nationally based mass media to get news coverage and to attract the public's attention and support. Even in the most Europeanized policy domains, public-oriented strategies of all types of national actors are therefore expected to be mainly of a "domesticated" variant; in other words, they will primarily focus on national public spheres when addressing EU targets. The result of this development is a Europeanization of national public spheres, a phenomenon first noticed by Gerhards (1993) and confirmed by the empirical analyses in Chapter 3 of the present volume.

Under conditions of audience democracy, the struggle for public attention and, conversely, the use of public-oriented strategies is important for all types of actors, but to varying degrees. State actors are expected to regularly inform the citizen public about their projects, and they have established specific offices for public relations to do so (see Röttger, Hoffmann, and Jarren 2003). In addition, by "going public" (Kernell 1997), they may attempt to reinforce their own position in the policy-making process. Political parties constitute the main organizational channels linking the individual citizens to their representatives in the policy-making process. As such, public-oriented strategies are crucial for them: to seek public attention for electoral reasons, on the one hand, and to appeal to the public in order to impose their point of view in the policy-making process, on the other hand. Considering the various party families, we expect again the left to be particularly prone to go public, given its long tradition of protest mobilization, its roots in the labor movement, and its proximity to the new social movements of the 1970s and 1980s (Kriesi et al. 1995).

Interest groups are a more mixed case. Given their privileged access to policy makers, interest groups primarily try to defend their group-specific interests in the decision-making arenas above all by inside strategies. In case of failure, interest groups may use "outside lobbying" (Kollman 1998), too. SMOs, in contrast, typically lack routinized access to the decision-making arenas, and they can therefore be expected to primarily rely on public strategies. This expectation is a straightforward extension of Beyers' compensation hypothesis to the challenge of the audience democracy.

Regardless of what type of actors they are, we expect the strategy of collective political actors to also be determined by their political power. Powerful actors tend to have the resources to draw the attention of the media and to get their support, but they may not need to appeal to them. The default strategy of a powerful actor is likely to be an inside one. However, in an audience democracy, even powerful actors may increasingly use their resources to influence political processes in the public sphere, given that influence attempts are most effective when they involve multiple tactics. Applying Beyers' persistence hypothesis to the challenge imposed by the conditions of audience democracy, we expect powerful actors to simultaneously use elaborate inside strategies and elaborate public-oriented strategies. In line with the compensation hypothesis, weak actors may need to appeal to the public for lack of other means to influence the political process. However, due to their lack of prominence and prestige, such actors may find it difficult to gain access to the media (Wolfsfeld 1997). As a result of this predicament, weak actors such as SMOs tend to rely on a combination of two kinds of public-related strategies – a combination of "protest politics" (mobilizing for protest events) and "information politics" (the collection of credible information and their introduction into the public sphere as well as into strategically selected intervention points of the decision-making arenas).

The choice of public-oriented strategies further depends on the overall accessibility of the decision-making arenas at the domestic and the EU level. We expect the decision-making arenas to be less accessible in France, Spain, and Italy than in the other countries: France and Spain are majoritarian democracies in terms of Lijphart's (1999) typology, and all three are characterized by comparatively exclusive informal strategies. The remaining countries and the EU are either more consensual or, as in the case of the United Kingdom, characterized by more cooperative informal strategies. The relative lack of accessibility in the three Mediterranean states (France, Spain, and Italy) is likely to be especially consequential for interest groups and SMOs, whom we expect to be more public oriented in these three countries than in the others.

Finally, the choice of concrete action forms varies according to the phase of policy making in a given policy domain. Following Baumgartner and Jones (2002), we distinguish between an equilibrium phase of incremental change and a critical phase of rapid policy change. In a critical phase, serial shifts may occur; in other words, the general public and "macropolitics" may turn their attention to the policy subsystem in question and the dominant coalition in the subsystem may lose its control over the domain-specific policy making. In such phases, all actors are more likely to go public than in equilibrium phases of routine policy making. With regard to our three policy domains, the European Convention (2001–2003), producing a draft treaty establishing a Constitution for Europe, which took place during the period of our study, constituted one of those intermittent grand bargains or critical phases that establish the basic features of the EU's institutional design. The same applies to the negotiations for a bilateral treaty between Switzerland and the EU, at least as far as Switzerland is concerned. By contrast, the agricultural policy (Common Agricultural Policy) was in a rather steady state during the period of our study. Visa and asylum policy, finally, has become a highly politicized issue in domestic politics in most Western European countries. It has given rise to mobilizations by the radical-populist right in domestic politics. Accordingly, compared to agricultural policy, the domains of European integration and of asylum policies were high on the public agenda and of macropolitics during the period studied. This means that we expect the action repertoire of actors involved in European integration and immigration to be more public oriented than that of actors involved in agriculture.

In sum, as a result of the increased importance of the public sphere for politics, political actors in all European countries face a second strategic challenge: To what extent should they rely on public-oriented strategies to most effectively influence public policy making? Our general expectation is that all types of political actors still privilege inside strategies when attempting to influence politics – national actors at the domestic level and supranational actors at the EU level. In addition, we expect all actors to complement their inside strategies with public-oriented activities, especially when the decision-making arenas are largely inaccessible or when the policy domain is in a critical phase. Within these general constraints, state actors and especially parties and SMOs should be more public oriented than interest groups. With regard to the impact of power, the two competing hypotheses seem to us equally plausible at this point.

DATA AND OPERATIONALIZATION

The data for this chapter draw on semistructured interviews with key political actors in the seven European countries of our study and at the European level. In each location, 16 actors were selected in each one of the three policy domains – EU integration, agriculture, and immigration. Each set of 16 actors included the four most important organizations of each actor type – state actors, political parties, interest groups, and SMOs. Altogether we selected $8 \times 3 \times 4 \times 4 = 384$ actors. This selection procedure implies that we did not necessarily include all the most important actors in a given country-specific policy domain. It is, for example, possible that all of the SMOs in a given policy domain constitute marginal actors, while several additional state actors play a key role. In other words, this procedure may neglect some key actors, but it has the advantage of providing us with information about the action repertoires of all four types of actors. The interviews were held in 2003 by members of the different country teams of the joint project. They were based on semistructured questionnaires that were analogously organized for all interviews, but that were adapted to the specificities of the actor types, of the three policy domains and of the political level concerned. We completed 345 interviews, ranging between a minimum of 32 (France) and a maximum of 49 (Italy) actors per country. The response rate is close to 90%, which documents not only the effort that was put into these interviews by the country teams but also the exceptional degree of cooperation on the part of our interlocutors.

For the study of the action repertoires, we presented the respondents with a list of strategies (see Table 9.1) and asked them to indicate which of the strategies on this list they use to influence public policy, and whether they use them regularly or occasionally. We asked the question twice, once for the national level and a second time for the European level.[3] Based on the responses to this list, we constructed two types of indicators for each actor. The first set of indicators represents the extent to which an actor exploits the full range of a given repertoire, for example, the inside strategies. Each indicator in this set takes into account both the *scope* of the repertoire (by counting the number of activities of a given type used by an actor) and its *intensity* (by weighting regular activities twice as much as occasional ones). Each indicator has been standardized to the 0–1 range by dividing the actors' scores by the maximum possible value – a value that varies according to the type of actor, since the composition of the set of strategies is not the same for each actor. A resulting value of 0 means that an actor does not use the respective repertoire at all, while a value of 1 means that he exploits its full range intensively.

The second set of indicators represents the *relative importance* of a given component in an actor's repertoire. Given the expected effectiveness of multiple tactics, resourceful actors may exploit various kinds of strategies. However, the default strategy – the use of domestic inside interventions – may still be the most important one for any kind of actor. This will only become visible in an analysis of the relative importance of European or public strategies with regard to the default strategy. Accordingly, we use two types of indicators for the relative importance of a given strategic component. First, we measure the relative importance of activities at the European as compared to the national level – that is, the degree to which a component of an actor's repertoire is Europeanized. To obtain this indicator, we divide an actor's score at the European level by its corresponding score at the national level and standardize the resulting quotient in such a way that a value of -1 signifies a fully nationalized action repertoire, a value of $+1$ a fully Europeanized repertoire, and a value of 0 a repertoire evenly divided between the two levels.[4] Second, we construct an analogous

---

[3] For the precise labeling of the questions and the full interview schedule, see Kriesi (2003).

[4] To arrive at this standardized score, we add a minimal value to the denominator (to avoid divisions by 0), truncate the results of the divisions at a maximum value of 2, and subtract 1 from each resulting value.

TABLE 9.1. *Action Repertoire of Collective Political Actors: List of Strategies*

Inside strategies
   1. Administrative strategies
      Participating in governmental consultation procedures (all actors)
      Serving on governmental advisory commissions or boards (all actors)
      Supplying information to policy makers (nonstate actors)
      Direct personal contact with members of government or their staff (nonstate
        actors)
      Direct personal contact with public officials (nonstate actors)
      Negotiating with or informing branches of government (state actors)
      Negotiating with or informing interest groups (state actors)
   2. Parliamentary strategies
      Testifying in parliamentary committees or intervening in Parliament (all actors)
      Direct personal contact with members of Parliament or their staff (nonstate
        actors)
      Negotiating with or informing members of Parliament (state actors)
   3. Court-related strategies (all actors)
      Filing suit or engaging in some sort of litigation
Public-related strategies
   1. Media-related strategies (all actors)
      Giving interviews to the media
      Writing newspaper articles
      Distributing press releases
      Holding press conferences to announce policy positions
      Presenting yourself on the Web
   2. Informing or getting informed about the public ("information politics"; all actors)
      Making public speeches
      Hiring a public relations firm to assist you in your public activities
      Running ads in the media about your position on policy issues
      Polling the general public on policy issues of concern to you
      Polling your members on policy issues (only for nonstate actors)
   3. Mobilizing the public, incl. campaigning ("protest politics"; nonstate actors only)
      Making financial contributions to electoral campaigns
      Making public endorsements of candidates
      Contributing to other political campaigns
      Engaging in direct mail fund-raising for your organization
      Organizing letter campaigns in newspapers
      Organizing petitions or signature collections
      Launching or supporting referendum campaigns
      Holding public assemblies and meetings
      Protesting or demonstrating
      Organizing boycotts
      Striking

indicator for the degree to which an action repertoire is public instead of inside oriented. In addition, we also have a measure of the *subjective* importance of public strategies for a given actor. This indicator is based on two questions asking the respondents to evaluate the importance for their organization of media-related strategies and of strategies directly informing or mobilizing the public in comparison to working with policy makers. This subjective measure also ranges from a value of -1 (both types of public-related strategies are much less important than working with policy makers) to a value of $+1$ (both types are much more important than working with policy makers). With regard to the public orientation, we can also create a combined indicator that uses the subjective evaluations to weight the corresponding components of an actor's strategic repertoire.

The independent variables essentially consist of a set of dummy indicators for the actors' origins (for actors from the EU level and from EU member states, with the Swiss actors as reference category), the actor types (for parties, interest groups, and SMOs, with state actors as the reference category; for business interest groups; for interest groups or SMOs in the three Mediterranean countries), and for policy domains (EU Convention, immigration, with agriculture as reference category). Only two indicators are of a different type. The *power of an actor* is operationalized by reputational measures. These are based on a set of questions referring to a list of forty organizations, which included all the actors whom the country teams considered to be the most important ones in the respective domains based on media content analyses performed earlier in the project. The sixteen interviewed organizations constitute a subset of the forty organizations on the list. The interviewees were first asked to name all organizations on this list, which, from their point of view, have been particularly influential in the respective policy domain over the past five years. Next, they were asked to name the three most influential organizations, and, finally, the most influential one. For each actor on the list of forty, there are four measures of power, one for each question (level of power) and an overall measure corresponding to the sum of the three detailed measures, which has again been standardized to the 0–1 range: For each policy domain in each country, the maximum value has been set to 1 and the remaining values have been adjusted accordingly. The last independent variable refers to the parties' political orientation: parties have been placed on the *left–right continuum*, using the estimates of the party manifesto research group (Budge et al. 2001). These estimates are, however, hardly comparable across countries, which is why we have rescaled them in each country to the 0–1 range with the leftmost party taking the value of 0 and the rightmost party the value of 1.

RESULTS

Elaboration of the Action Repertoires at the Different Levels

First, we consider the overall level of activity by type of strategy and level of target. Figure 9.1 presents the relevant results for national actors only. The first

a) overall strategic orientation

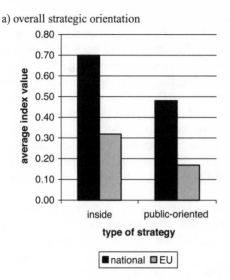

b) components of overall strategies

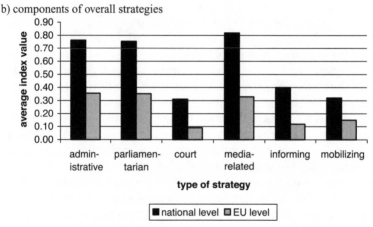

FIGURE 9.1. Overall level of activity by type of strategy and level of target: weighted averages for national actors only.

part of this figure confirms our two most basic assumptions. First, regarding the *level* of political intervention, the strategic repertoires of national political actors are still primarily focused on the national level. Compared to the national level, political actors are less active at the European level. However, in line with the multilevel governance perspective, the European level attracts a non-negligible range of activities on the part of domestic political actors: on average, both of the broadly defined types of repertoires are about half as elaborate at the European level as at the national one. Second, with regard to the *choice of a specific action form*, the default repertoire of domestic inside interventions is, as expected, the most fully exploited by our respondents. Virtually all actors

TABLE 9.2. *Determinants of the Action Repertoire at the National and EU Level: Unstandardized Ordinary Least Squares Regression Coefficients*

Determinant	National		EU	
	Inside	Outside	Inside	Outside
Constant (Swiss state actors in agriculture)	0.70***	0.31***	−0.53**	−0.23***
EU member states	−0.16***	−0.07**	0.37***	0.20***
EU	−0.57***	−0.11*	1.06***	0.61***
European integration	−0.06	0.04	0.09**	0.07**
Immigration	0.00	−0.01	0.06	0.02
Parties	−0.07	0.10*	0.14*	0.08*
Left–right parties (left = 0; right = 1)	0.03	−0.11*	−0.07	−0.11*
Interest groups	0.19***	−0.14***	0.08	−0.03
SMOs	0.09*	−0.07**	−0.06	−0.04
Persistence or compensation	—	0.35***	0.57***	0.34***
Power	0.15**	0.10**	0.13*	0.13***
R^2 adj.	0.34	0.44	0.44	0.41
N	(315)	(310)	(315)	(310)

Note: Persistence or compensation equals national-inside activities for the national-outside and EU-inside repertoire, and national-outside activities for the EU-outside repertoire.
*$p < 0.05$, **$p < 0.01$, ***$p < 0.001$.

have used at least one of the strategies involved and, on average, they reach roughly two-thirds of the maximum score. Our respondents' repertoire at the national level, however, is not exclusively composed of inside strategies, but also typically includes a public-oriented component: Virtually all actors have used at least one of the available outside strategies, and on average their public orientation reaches almost half of the maximum score.

The second part of the figure gives an impression of the extent to which the various components of the two broad strategies are used at both levels. The most important feature shown in this part of the figure is that today the action repertoires of national political actors are dominated by administrative, parliamentarian, and media-related strategies. At the national level, most actors fully exploit these three components of the action repertoire, while court action as well as informing and mobilizing the public are used much less frequently. In other words, at the national level, most political actors have added the full range of media-related activities to their classic action repertoire of intervening in the administrative and parliamentary arenas of decision making. At the EU level, administrative, parliamentarian, media-related activities, and mobilizing are about as frequently used as the overall average, whereas court actions and activities informing the public are, relatively speaking, relied on somewhat less frequently.

To explain the extent to which the different actors use the available action repertoire, we have performed a series of multiple ordinary least squares regression analyses. Table 9.2 presents the unstandardized regression coefficients, significance levels, and adjusted R^2 values for each one of the two broad components of the action repertoire at both the national and the EU level. Since all independent variables vary between 0 and 1, the sizes of the different regression coefficients can be directly compared. Origin and policy domain (i.e., political opportunity structure) and actor type and power (i.e., resources) are the relevant explanatory factors for the four broad components of the action repertoire considered here. Together they explain at least one-third of the variation in these components.

Let us look at the actors' *origin* first. The EU opportunity structure clearly exerts the expected effects: Supranational actors are much more active at the EU level and much less active at the domestic level than are domestic actors from the EU member states. More detailed analyses indicate that their strategic profile at the EU level largely corresponds to that of the domestic actors at the national level and vice versa. By contrast, Swiss actors, who form the reference category, are exceptionally active at the domestic level but highly significantly less active at the EU level – both inside and in the public sphere – than are actors from EU member states. In fact, Swiss actors hardly intervene at the EU level at all. The EU opportunity structure is clearly less relevant for them.

By contrast, *policy domains* are of little relevance for the determination of the action repertoires. The expectation that the political opportunity structure of a given policy domain (determined by the domain-specific phase of the decision-making process and by the domain-specific distribution of decision-making power over the different levels of governance) is influencing the strategies of political actors is only confirmed by the fact that actors in the domain of EU integration are somewhat more EU oriented (both inside and publicly) than those involved in the other two domains. This finding comes as somewhat of a surprise. As the reader will see, it contradicts the analyses of public claim making in Chapter 3, which shows that (a) the most important determinant of patterns of mass media coverage is simply where the decision-making power in a policy field is concentrated, and that (b) the degree of Europeanization of national public spheres reflects the actual distribution of power between the European and the national level. Figure 9.2 helps to clarify this unexpected result.[5] It suggests that, with respect to the multilayered EU polity, the power distribution of the selected set of actors for whom we have full interview information does not quite correspond to the power distribution among the set of the forty most important actors in the three policy domains. The figure presents the Europeanization of the power distribution in each policy domain, the extent of which is measured by the ratio of the power of supranational to the power of national actors. A ratio of 1 indicates that the two sets of actors have equal power in a given policy domain, a ratio greater than 1 indicates that supranational actors are more powerful, and a ratio of less than 1 indicates that national actors are more powerful. The first part of the figure refers to the set

[5] This figure only refers to EU member countries (including the EU level). Swiss actors are excluded from this calculation.

a) all 40 actors

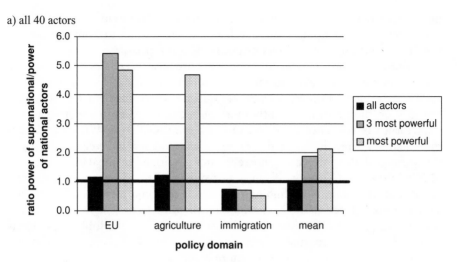

b) only selection of actors

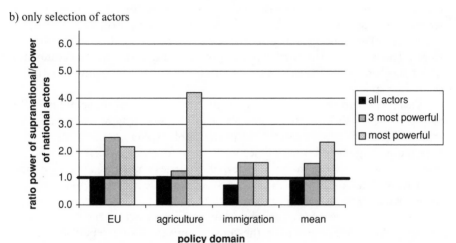

FIGURE 9.2. Europeanization of power distribution in the EU member countries, by issue: ratios (power of supranational actors to power of national actors).

of the forty most important actors, which serves as the standard of reference; the second part refers to our selected set of sixteen actors. In the reference set, supranational actors turn out to be much more powerful in the domains of EU integration and agriculture, while national actors are much more powerful in immigration. This is just what we would have expected, given the distribution of decision-making power in the three policy domains. In the restricted set of our sixteen actors, however, the power distribution does not as faithfully reflect the domain-specific distribution of decision-making power; in fact, supranational actors in our set are less powerful in the domain of EU integration, and they are more powerful in the domain of immigration than the corresponding actors are in the reference set. This relative equalization of power among supranational actors across policy domains may well explain at least part of our unexpected nonfinding with regard to domain-specific action repertoires.

Turning to *actor types*, we find that there are few differences at the national level. In line with our expectations, interest groups turn out to have the most elaborate inside and the least elaborate outside repertoires. Parties on the left (but not on the right) are slightly more public oriented than are state actors, who form the reference category. Our expectation that SMOs should have more elaborate public-oriented repertoires than actors with regular access to the decision-making process is, however, not confirmed by the data. In fact, the SMOs in our study use significantly less public-oriented strategies than state actors do. This surprising finding may again to some extent be due to our selection procedure. As the reader may recall, we selected the most important SMOs in a given policy domain – SMOs for whom inside lobbying is likely to be more important than for the more peripheral challengers. However, we find that powerful actors have more elaborate inside and more elaborate outside repertoires than their less resourceful competitors. Moreover, there is strong evidence that actors who, independently of their power, are more active inside the policy-making arenas also have more elaborate public-oriented repertoires. This supports the persistence hypothesis and undercuts the compensation hypothesis with respect to the challenge posed by the transformation of the public sphere.

With respect to the EU level, the results closely parallel those obtained for the domestic level: Powerful actors are again significantly more present than less powerful ones, both inside and in the public sphere, and the persistence hypothesis is again confirmed. Once we control for these two effects, there are few differences between the actor types; only parties appear as somewhat more EU oriented – all kinds of parties with respect to inside activities, and parties on the left with respect to public activities. Note that, in line with received notions, interest groups indeed have the most elaborate inside action repertoires at the EU level. Since they also have the most elaborate inside repertoires at the domestic level, this is taken into account by the persistence effect and does not show up in the corresponding direct effect.

Europeanization of the Action Repertoires

We now turn to the indicators for the relative importance of the repertoires' components. Table 9.3 presents the results of the regression analyses that explain the degree of Europeanization of the repertoires. These results largely confirm the previous ones. In line with the previous results, we find large differences concerning the actors' *origin*: The action repertoires of Swiss actors are almost entirely focused on the national level, while, obviously, the repertoires of supranational actors are primarily focused on the EU level. The repertoires of actors from EU member states remain generally also more nationally focused, although to a lesser extent than in the Swiss case. The corresponding effects

TABLE 9.3. *Determinants of Europeanization of Action Repertoire: Unstandardized Ordinary Least Squares Regression Coefficients*

Determinants	Inside Activities	Public-Oriented Activities
Constant (Swiss state actors in agriculture)	-1.06^{***}	-1.10^{***}
EU members	0.37^{***}	0.31^{***}
EU	1.50^{***}	1.55^{***}
European integration	0.15^{**}	0.14^{**}
Immigration	0.14^{**}	0.06
Parties	0.17	0.27^{***}
Left–right parties (left = 0; right = 1)	-0.16	-0.26^{*}
Interest groups	0.10	0.05
SMOs	-0.08	0.03
Power	0.23^{**}	0.23^{**}
R^2 adj.	0.57	0.65
N	(301)	(310)

* $p < 0.05$, ** $p < 0.01$, *** $p < 0.001$.

are virtually identical for inside and public-oriented activities, which means that the lack of a European public sphere does not seem to disadvantage public activities with respect to inside interventions at the EU level. As for policy domains, the action repertoire of actors in European integration and immigration appear to be somewhat more Europeanized than in agriculture. This is again surprising, but it is probably also a result of the selection bias among our collective actors.

As we have already observed, powerful actors generally have the most elaborate repertoires both at the national and at the EU level. It now turns out that, relatively speaking, their advantage at the EU level is even greater than domestically, both inside and in public. This is to say that the new opportunities at the EU level are opening up mainly for the select few. To paraphrase Schattschneider's (1960 [1988], pp. 34–35) famous quip, the flaw in the European heaven is that the heavenly chorus sings with a strong accent – the accent of the powerful national actors (as is also confirmed by our results in Chapter 4). There are few other actor-specific differences with regard to the Europeanization of the action repertoires. As we have seen earlier, domestic interest groups are heavily overrepresented in the inside arena at the national level and, because of the strong persistence effect, at the European level, too. However, in relative terms, their action repertoires are no more Europeanized than the repertoires of other domestic actors. The reason is precisely that they are also overrepresented in the inside arenas at the national level. The only other actor-specific difference we find is that the parties on the left (but not on the right) have a relatively Europeanized public-oriented repertoire. More detailed analyses, not shown here, indicate that this special focus of the left on Europe cannot be explained by an especially pro-European attitude. As suggested earlier, the internationalist tradition of the left and its more coherent organization at the EU level may, however, make it easier for its representatives to enlarge their action repertoire in the European direction.

When we compare the pattern of factors determining the Europeanization of inside strategies with the corresponding pattern for public-oriented strategies in Table 9.3, we hardly observe any differences between the two. This important result suggests that the opportunities and constraints for the Europeanization of the actors' strategies are the same for the two sides of the repertoire. The determinants of the relative neglect of public-oriented actions by national political actors to influence the political process at the EU level are in no way different from those of their relative neglect of inside-oriented actions to exert such influence.

The Relative Importance of Public and Inside Strategies

We have also analyzed the determinants of our two indicators for the relative importance of public-oriented as compared with inside-oriented strategies – a subjective measure and one based on the actual use of the available repertoire. For this analysis we only take into account an actor's privileged level of access, that is, the EU level for supranational actors and the national level for domestic actors. Table 9.4 presents the results. Let us first look at the determinants of the subjective preference for public-oriented activities. For the subjective measure, actor type is the key factor, while policy domain and power have hardly any effect here. Everywhere, state actors privilege inside strategies, while parties – whether left or right, in opposition or in government – evaluate public-oriented strategies as being more important.[6] For interest groups, we find the expected interaction with the political opportunity structures: In open systems, interest groups attribute as little importance to public strategies as state actors do. Business interest groups are even significantly less focused on public strategies than state actors are. It is only in closed systems that they value public strategies to a significantly greater extent. We also note that, independently from the political context, not all types of interest groups value public-oriented activities to the same extent. The groups with the easiest access to policy makers – business interest associations – differ from unions, farmers' associations and other groups (such as think tanks or churches) in that they put comparatively more value on inside activities. Finally, SMOs have a stronger preference for public strategies everywhere, but even more so in closed systems.

The two measures for the relative importance of public-oriented activities need not coincide. This is especially relevant for the operation of the persistence effect: as we have just seen, power has no effect on the subjective preference

---

[6] The distinction between government and opposition party has been introduced in additional analyses that are not shown in detail here. For the operationalization of this distinction, EU parties were not considered and, for the Swiss case, the Social Democrats and the Swiss People's party were considered to be "opposition parties," although they are members of government.

TABLE 9.4. *Determinants of Public Orientation of Action Repertoire: Unstandardized Ordinary Least Squares Regression Coefficients*

Determinants	Subjective Preference	Effective Repertoire	Weighted Effective Repertoire
Constant (Swiss state actors in agriculture)	−0.22	−0.17*	−0.06
EU	−0.28**	−0.01	−0.46***
EU member states	−0.09	0.09	−0.30**
European integration	0.11	0.10*	0.20*
Immigration	0.02	−0.08	0.03
Party	0.56***	0.14	1.05***
Left–right (left = 0; right = 1)	0.08	−0.30**	−0.14
Interest groups	0.13	−0.27***	0.43***
Business associations	−0.33**	−0.08	−0.63***
SMOs	0.32***	−0.14*	0.68***
Interest group or SMO in Spain, France, and Italy	0.33***	−0.06	0.42***
Subjective preference	—	0.43***	—
Power	−0.06	0.11	0.18
Subjective Preference × Power interaction	—	−0.44***	—
R^2 adj.	0.25	0.34	0.33
N	(281)	(274)	(274)

* $p < 0.05$, ** $p < 0.01$, *** $p < 0.001$.

of public strategies. But, as shown in Table 9.2, powerful actors heavily use public strategies. We now see that they do so, although they do not consider public strategies to be more important than do their less powerful competitors. In fact, if weaker actors do not exploit the range of public strategies to the same extent as their more powerful competitors, it is not necessarily because such strategies are not important for them. They may simply lack the resources to do so: Media-related strategies are relatively low-cost activities, but several of the components of the set of informing (e.g., running advertisements in the media, appointing a public relations agency or running opinion polls) and mobilizing strategies involve considerable costs. Weak actors who believe public strategies to be very important for their organization may face a trade-off between the two types of strategies. By contrast, strong actors may heavily use public strategies, although they consider them of secondary importance, because they have the resources and the opportunity to do so. We can test for this possibility by introducing the subjective importance of public activities as well as an interaction between the subjective importance and power into the regression model for the relative importance of public strategies in the effective repertoire.

The results presented in Table 9.4 indicate highly significant effects for the subjective importance and for its interaction with power on the effective use of public strategies. By contrast, the corresponding effect for power is not significant. This combination of effects can be interpreted as follows: for actors who have no power (power = 0), the subjective importance of public strategies has a sizeable impact on their effective use (an effect of 0.43), while its impact is very limited (0.10) for actors with maximum power (power = 1). In other words, powerful actors indeed make effective use of public strategies, even if they do not believe them to be crucial, while powerless actors only use them if they believe them to be very important.

Independently from their subjective importance, the relative importance of the effective use of public activities is hardly at all directly influenced by the available opportunities. There are no direct effects of origin, and policy domains again play a subordinate role. We conclude that the effective reliance on public strategies is a pervasive phenomenon, which is less conditioned by considerations of accessibility than we expected. While political actors appreciate public strategies as a function of accessibility, they seem to use them everywhere as much as they can, given the constraints of their resources and their preferences. The latter vary by actor type: Thus, relatively speaking, parties rely most on public-oriented strategies. This holds especially for parties on the left, regardless of whether they are in government or not (as is indicated by more detailed analyses not shown here). That is, the left's action repertoire is not only more Europeanized but also more public oriented than the action repertoire of the right. By contrast, interest groups rely most heavily on inside strategies. Surprisingly, SMOs also have a tendency to rely more heavily on inside than on public strategies, a result that we may again attribute, in part at least, to the particular selection of SMOs in our sample.

Weighting the effective repertoire by the subjective preference, as has been done in the third analysis in Table 9.4, leads to results that are similar to those for the subjective preference. But they accentuate the previous findings, indicating that the relative intensity of "going public" is, indeed, mainly determined by the type of actor, but not by the actor's power: Parties (all of them), but also SMOs and interest groups (especially in the Mediterranean countries, but not business associations), and Swiss actors generally are very significantly more likely to go public than the average state actor.

CONCLUSION

We started our chapter with the contention that, because of crucial transformations to the current political opportunities, political actors have to meet a double strategic challenge today: the challenge of Europeanization and the challenge of the increasing importance of the public arena in politics. Our attempt to trace and explain the strategic reaction of political actors to this double challenge has shown that the classic repertoire of inside interventions at the national level is still the most fully exploited by collective political actors of all stripes. In addition, the repertoires of all types of actors in all contexts are also heavily public oriented. In the audience democracies of Western Europe, where public opinion plays a crucial role in the political process, the public-oriented component of the domestic action repertoire is also heavily used. Today, the action repertoires of political actors are dominated by administrative, parliamentarian, *and* media-related strategies. At the national level, most actors fully exploit these repertoires, while court action as well as informing and mobilizing the public are used less frequently.

Compared to their involvement at the national level, domestic actors are clearly less involved in influencing the political process at the European level. The additional political opportunity structure of the EU is only predominant for the genuinely supranational actors who operate above all at this level. For the domestic actors, the salience and accessibility of the decision-making process of the EU is much lower than that at the national level, which explains why they are still predominantly focused on influencing the national political process. The neglect of the EU level is, however, a relative, not an absolute one: Only actors from a nonmember state such as Switzerland almost totally ignore the EU policy-making process. The actors from member states intervene in many ways to influence the policy-making process at the EU level. The relative neglect of both public-oriented as well as inside-oriented actions by domestic political actors at the EU level has been shown to be related to variations in institutionalized opportunities (EU membership, position of policy domain in the pillar structure, and phase of the decision-making process in a given domain), and endowment with resources (power and access at the domestic level). With regard to the Europeanization of the action repertoire, the persistence hypothesis has been confirmed.

The importance of national access for access at the EU level is linked to the lack of a European public sphere and to the remoteness of the political process at the EU level, which imply that the domestic actors' attempts to influence the European process are mainly of a domesticated variety: They heavily intervene in the national public sphere and in the national decision-making arenas to influence the decision making in Brussels. Domestic actors not only address EU issues in the national press but also try to influence them in the national decision-making arenas. The detailed comments of our respondents reveal that, short of genuine supranational interventions (such as participation in the elaboration of directives or in the negotiations of policy reforms), domestic actors tend to use their inside strategies in a way that is analogous to what was called "vertical" or "horizontal" Europeanization in the press in Chapter 2. In vertical forms of Europeanization, national actors refer to European institutions, issues, norms, and policies, whereas in horizontal forms they refer to those from other European countries. Thus, parties adopt positions with regard to the European Convention at their national Congress; they establish working groups at the national level to accompany the convention work; they elaborate motions that they submit to both the national and the European Parliament with regard to the Convention or the Common Agricultural Policy; they debate European issues in the national parliaments. State actors create working groups on the Future of Europe; they have contacts with other state actors to elaborate a common national position for the European Convention; they make proposals for national representatives in the Convention; they establish contact with governments of other EU member states or of accession states, possible partners with whom they could present common papers on the Convention. Interest groups and SMOs hold national conferences to develop their cata- logue of claims for the draft text of the European Convention, and they collect signatures to support their position papers.

Contrary to the Europeanization of the action repertoire, its public focus is much less influenced by institutional factors determining the opportunity structure. Public-oriented strategies play an important role in all countries and policy domains, and at both the national and the EU level. If there is contextual variation, it mainly concerns the subjective evaluation of such strategies by interest groups and SMOs. This evaluation depends on the openness of access to the domestic decision-making arenas. Power does not determine the degree to which public strategies are preferred, but it has an impact on their effective use: Contrary to their more powerful competitors, actors who lack power face a trade-off between inside and public strategies and are not always able to implement public strategies. They only use them relatively frequently, if they consider them very important. Political parties are generally the most public- oriented type of actors. They not only find public activities more important than working with decision makers, but they also use the public side of the action repertoire most intensively. Contrary to expectations, the SMOs that we studied here are less public oriented than parties, although they still are significantly more public oriented than the other types of actors. The persistence hypothesis has also been confirmed for the public orientation of the action repertoire.

Our presentation has been largely exploratory. It is limited in at least two ways. First, we have only provided a snapshot of the contemporary reper- toires. With our data we could not address questions concerning trends in the development of the action repertoires. To be able to document trends toward Europeanization and toward an increasing public orientation of the actors' repertoires, we would need longitudinal data. Second, our indicators for the action repertoires are, admittedly, rather crude and do not allow for a dif- ferentiated appreciation of the actors' strategies in a specific campaign. They have permitted us to explore an uncharted terrain and to draw a general map of the kind of strategies that political actors in Western Europe currently use to influence political decision making. To fully exploit the potential of this approach, we would need to have more detailed information about the strate- gies employed by the different actors in a given policy domain, on the purposes pursued by a given set of actors with these strategies, on the ways they react to each other's strategies, and on the direct and indirect effects each specific strategy has on both public opinion and political decision makers.

IO

Political Party Contestation

Emerging Euroscepticism or a Normalization of Eurocriticism?

Paul Statham, Ruud Koopmans, Anke Tresch,
and Julie Firmstone

INTRODUCTION

It is well known that party contestation over European integration and the European Union produces strange bedfellows, bringing together those who, as one activist candidly put it, "would not want to be seen dead in the same coffin" (Forster 2002, p. 60). Criticisms of Europe often come from the left and right poles, whereas center parties suspend normal hostilities advocating a generally pro-European line. At face value, this suggests that party behavior over Europe is exceptional and atypical. Over the past decade, however, the form and meaning of this relationship between party alignments over Europe and traditional ones, especially the left–right cleavage, and its consequences for party politics have become disputed. Questions arise over whether Europe is business as usual or transformative for party politics. For some, party contestation over Europe remains largely issue specific, with few "spillover" effects and limited impacts for national party politics (see, especially, Mair 2000b). For others, it constitutes part of an emerging cleavage, in the Rokkanian sense, that is transforming the political space in Western Europe (see, especially, Kriesi 2005, 2007; Kriesi et al. 2006b, 2008). Still others have made influential contributions standing between these poles.[1] This controversy has brought a renewed interest in questions about political parties' stances over Europe, and especially their critical ones: Is party contestation over Europe increasing? Is Euroscepticism on the rise? Does criticism of Europe come from the core or periphery, or from the left or right?

To address these important questions, we need to know more about where parties' campaigns over Europe fit within their patterns of party alignments in national party systems. In this chapter, we address these questions empirically. We aim to contribute to the understanding on political parties' European

---

[1] Among many, see, e.g., Hix and Lord (1997), Hooghe, Marks, and Wilson (2004), Marks (2004), Statham (2008), Steenbergen and Scott (2004), and Taggart (1998).

contestation by presenting the findings of a comparative study of parties' public statements. We apply our claim-making approach to study political parties' stances over European integration and the European Union that are visible in national media discourses. First, we examine the degree and form of parties' European contestation, its sources among party families, and whether patterns hold cross-nationally. Second, we study whether parties' mobilizations are more strategic or tactically or ideologically motivated, their substantive issue contents, and how their claims construct and frame a cleavage. On the basis of these findings, we try to assess the transformative potential of European contestation for national party politics in relation to the leading positions advanced in the literature.

There are sound theoretical reasons for focusing on how political parties compete over Europe by engaging in public debates carried by the mass media. As we argued in Chapter 2, in an era of mediated politics, when voters depend heavily on the mass media for access to political communication, news is a key location for party contestation (Bennett and Entman 2001; Swanson and Mancini 1996). It is through the news that issues are made publicly visible to citizens, and this is the forum where parties attempt to mobilize their campaigns and get their message across to voters. As a result of the media's limited carrying capacity and selection processes, not all parties' attempts to have their public statements reported are successful. However, from our perspective it is those which are reported by mass media that are important precisely because they are publicly visible and widely accessible. If they cannot be seen or heard, then a party's claims can have little impact in shaping the opinions of voters, public constituencies, their party competitors, policy elites, or governments.

From a methodological perspective, this also makes newspaper coverage a good potential data source for examining party contestation. News analysis has the advantage of retrieving data on parties' mobilization from the actual interactive "output" that is produced by all the different competing parties' efforts to communicate with voters and shape opinions in response to events, that is, mediated political discourse. Indeed, Peter Mair has identified precisely the type of public discourse analysis method that we have applied as a necessary development to move beyond some limitations he sees in analyses based on party manifestoes (e.g., Fligstein 2008, pp. 227–233, using Budge et al. 2001) and experts' opinions (e.g., Ray 1999, the Chapel Hill[2] group). Mair (2007b, p. 162) puts it in the following way:

What is really needed here, however, particularly given that this is a new and often exploratory avenue of research, is a much more systematic, inductive, and largely

---

[2] An important example of experts' opinions is the research by Gary Marks and Lisbet Hooghe and collaborators at the Chapel Hill Center for European Studies in North Carolina. Their research is based on a survey conducted in 2002, drawing on 238 country experts – scholarly specialists on political parties or European politics – to evaluate the ideological and policy locations of 171 political parties in Bulgaria, the Czech Republic, Hungary, Latvia, Lithuania, Poland, Romania, Slovakia, Slovenia, and all EU member states except Luxembourg.

bottom-up comparison of political discussions at the national level – whether as revealed in parliamentary debates, or in contests surrounding European referendums, or in the ebb and flow of the arguments used in national election campaigns. In other words, in addition to the imputed location of a party's core identity, and in addition to the evidence provided by the formal policies which it adopts or is obliged to adopt, we need to know more about how Europe actually plays in national political discourse, as well as about the way in which it is conceived: is Europe usually cited as a constraint by parties at the national level, for example, or is it seen as an opportunity, or do these parties scarcely cite it at all?

Media-retrieved data and party manifesto data are not mutually exclusive sources for studying parties; they demonstrate different aspects of political reality. Media data best show how parties successfully mobilize their positions in efforts to convince voters in response to real political events and circumstances that crop up often unpredictably. In contrast, manifestoes are an organizational statement of parties' positions prior to elections, but these may not become publicly mobilized or contested. Thus many policy positions expressed in manifestoes remain unseen by potential voters. Furthermore, parties may take up a different stance on a policy issue than that expressed in their manifesto when responding to real events or the campaigns of their political competitors. Manifesto data tell us little about the intensity with which a party campaigns on an issue. It is worth noting that in one of the few other newspaper-sourced studies, Hanspeter Kriesi (2005, p. 13) attempted to replicate his findings by using parties' election manifestoes, and in his own words "failed completely."[3] Regarding expert opinion data sets, these are derived from educated "guesstimates" rather than from data sources directly linked to parties' own actions. Indeed, experts' opinions are likely to be formed at least partly on the basis of perceptions of how party competition over Europe plays out in the mass media. By contrast, our approach analyzes this systematically.

Taking up Peter Mair's challenge, this chapter studies political parties' stances that are publicly visible in national media discourses. Given that supranational "Europarties" seem highly unlikely to replace the predominance of national parties, and that public spheres carrying political information remain predominantly nationally structured, we focus the study on national and regional parties' claims made in national media discourses. Our starting point for examining party contestation is parties' negative evaluations of European integration, or of the EU's actors, policies, or issues. We call these

---

[3] Within the political science community we have encountered a resistance to media data as sources for studying political parties. For example, it has been suggested to us that party manifesto data should be used to validate media data. We simply do not see why the validity of media data ought to be relegated in this way, when in fact they are more suited for capturing information on the intensity, focus, and direction of parties' public campaigns. The relevant data depend on the research question. Of course, one can attempt to correlate parties' mediated and manifesto positions, but this answers a different research question: Which aspects of their programs do parties select and successfully mobilize in their campaigns, and to what extent to their positions vary from those expressed in their programs?

Eurocriticisms. Since party politics has traditionally supported European integration, especially at the core of party systems, these negative evaluations are the most likely source of evidence for changes in party politics, including, for example, the possibility of mainstream Euroscepticism.

The seven Western European democracies covered by the study, that is, Britain, France, Germany, the Netherlands, Italy, Spain, and Switzerland, include six countries with long-standing participation in the European project, plus Switzerland, which remains outside the European Union but has held referenda over joining. Thus we have six countries whose parties have been contesting Europe from within the project for decades and one whose parties are contesting entry. In contrast to the newer democracies from Eastern Europe, these older democracies have more established party systems and patterns of contestation over Europe.

In line with the approach taken by several chapters in this book, our analysis is based on a large original sample of public claim-making acts by political parties that is retrieved systematically from newspapers (for method, see Chapter 2). For this chapter the key variables we use are the actor making the claim and the substance of the claim. First, the sample was constructed by selecting all claims by actors coded with a political party identity. As we have seen, each claim is coded at the general level for how it evaluates European integration or EU institutions, actors, and policies: for ($+1$), against (-1), or neutral (0). For the analyses here, we restricted the sample further to cases in which political parties took a clear stance over Europe by selecting only "evaluative claims" (i.e., $+1$ or -1). This approach allows us to produce a general picture by examining the location of negative claim making over Europe, that is, *Eurocriticisms*, across party families, countries, and time, by statistical analyses. Then, we are also able to select the actual language used in claims, and information on the event where it was mobilized, to conduct a qualitative analysis of the most negative parties' critiques and framing of Europe. The research design allows for cross-party and cross-national comparisons and combines quantitative and qualitative analyses. In addition, we use the sample's three time points, 1990, 1995, and 2000–2002, to assess whether parties' Eurocriticisms have increased along with advancing European integration.

In the next section, we unpack the main competing theoretical hypotheses over European party contestation. Then, we undertake descriptive and multivariate quantitative analyses of parties' mobilized Eurocriticisms to build a general picture of their patterns and determinants: across party families and countries, whether parties are in government or opposition, between subnational and national party organizations, and across time. From this, we select the most Eurocritical parties and undertake a detailed qualitative analysis of their claims' substantive contents to determine whether, and if so, on what basis, they produce a coherent critique placing Europe in a cleavage. Finally, we conclude by drawing on key findings to discuss the transformative impact of party contestation over Europe and the potential for emergent Euroscepticism.

EUROPEAN PARTISANSHIP: BEYOND AN INVERTED U?

A starting point for debates over European partisanship is the common observation of an "inverted U" pattern of support for Europe. Among many contributions on this, see Hix and Lord (1997), Hooghe et al. (2004), Marks (2004), Marks and Steenbergen (2004), Marks and Wilson (2000), Statham (2008), and Taggart (1998). Here parties' stances cross-cut the left–right divisions, so that center parties are largely pro-European, with opposition to Europe confined to the marginal poles of extreme left and right. Although many scholars observe this pattern for European contestation, there are several hypotheses about the substance of parties' mobilizations that produce the inverted U, the way it relates to the left–right cleavage, and its transformative prospects for realigning relationships within party systems. Here we outline the leading positions and different expectations they hold for the distribution of Eurocriticisms across the political system (core–periphery), party types (families), and for its substantive contents (claims).

A first set of explanations emphasizes the *strategic* or *tactical* dimension of parties' European mobilizations. Here a first position is represented by Steenbergen and Scott (2004, p. 166), who argue that the "issue salience of European integration across parties can be attributed to a considerable extent to the strategic behavior of those parties... parties that stand to gain from the issue, in whatever sense, try to emphasise the issue, while parties that stand to lose try to de-emphasise it." This "nothing new" view is supported by Mair's (2000b) general stance that Europe offers little as a new dimension for party contestation. For him, Eurosceptic parties cannot be reduced to their anti-European appeal. Europe constitutes only one element of their general oppositional stance. Like Taggart's (1998) study of Euroscepticism in which he calls European integration a "touchstone of domestic dissent," Europe is considered relatively "contentless" as a potential cleavage. It is a center-party pro-European consensus at the core that offers a mobilization potential for a politics of opposition by the usual malcontents from the periphery. This produces an inverted U. Hix and Lord (1997) complement this idea by adding that mainstream parties have interests in maintaining the status quo by pursuing a strategy that incorporates European integration issues into the left–right cleavage. They see European politics as an increasingly two-dimensional phenomenon, whereby parties' left–right contestation over economic and sociopolitical issues (functional interests), in the domestic arena, is largely independent from their contestation over national sovereignty (territorial interests). For them, major parties avoid contestation over European integration and adopt pro-European stances.

We can derive similar hypotheses about parties' strategic mobilization from a political opportunity approach (e.g., Kriesi et al. 1995; Tarrow 1994), which shows that closed political institutions provoke confrontational challenges, whereas open opportunity structures invite more consensual and cooperative strategies from collective actors. This view emphasizes that political actors' strategic choices depend on their degree and type of access to decision-making processes. European integration adds new channels of access, but access to these new channels is not equally distributed and favors, in particular, national governments, who have privileged access to decision making in the various European Councils, especially compared to national oppositions, regional political actors, and civil society actors (Koopmans 2007). This leads to the expectation that party actors with relatively limited access to European-level governance, such as opposition compared with governing parties, regional compared with national party branches, and marginal and excluded parties compared with mainstream ones, are likely to be more critical of European integration and institutions. Regarding the stances of opposition versus government and mainstream versus peripheral parties, this prediction deviates little from the prevalent views in the European integration literature. However, the prediction regarding subnational versus national party actors is less clear-cut. Some confirm that European integration is "more a danger to, than a liberator of, regions" (Bourne 2003, p. 597; see also Bache 1999), but within multilevel governance literature, the EU is often seen as improving the leverage of regions relative to national states by establishing direct contacts between European institutions and regional actors (e.g., Marks, Hooghe, and Blank 1996).

A second set of explanations places more weight on *ideological* contents as the basis for determining how parties compete over Europe. In these approaches, the inverted U is less of an empirical observation and more of a theoretically derived hypothesis, drawn from theses on the cleavage structure of the emergent European political space. Theories are advanced for how European issues constitute an ideological basis for party contestation that cross-cuts the traditional left–right cleavage. This transformation of the ideological space leads to new opportunities for mobilization and alignments among parties. However, there are important disagreements about the degree and nature of this transformation of the political space.

First, Hooghe et al. (2004) and Marks (2004) argue that specific aspects of parties' European contestation are absorbed into their left–right contestation, whereas others are not. This is partly because EU competences relative to nation-states do not penetrate all policy fields equally. For them, the basis for party contestation is over a *regulated capitalism versus neoliberalism* cleavage. This means that the two dimensions (more or less European integration; left or right) are not, as Hix and Lord claim, independent, and it leads to hypotheses about variations of center-parties' positioning over Europe. Hooghe and Marks argue that the more European integration focuses on market regulation as opposed to market making, then the more center-left social democratic parties, as supporters of *regulated capitalism*, become favorably disposed. This regulated capitalism stance is defined as a "project to build environmental, social, infrastructural, and redistributive policy" (Steenbergen and Marks 2004, pp. 9–10). By contrast, when economic and monetary union is largely completed, those on the political right become more opposed to European integration and pursue neoliberalism, defined as striving to provoke "regulatory competition among national governments within an encompassing market." Importantly, this explains opposition as a strategy defined by ideological commitment: "Euroskepticism of extreme parties arises... not only from their opposition to the EU's policies, but also because they reject the ideology of the EU's construction" (Hooghe et al. 2004, p. 125).

It is to the credit of Hooghe and Marks that their unexpected findings when they were testing their main thesis led to insights bringing the "new politics" cleavage dimension to the fore. Placing parties on a green-alternative-libertarian (GAL) versus a traditional-authoritarian-nationalist (TAN) cleavage, they conclude that (Marks 2004, p. 244) "a party's position on the new politics dimension is considerably more powerful than its position on the left/right dimension in predicting its support for integration." Here, the GAL parties are pro-EU parties, but the correlation is much stronger on the TAN Eurosceptic side, which drives the overall relationship, whereby the radical right and some traditional authoritarian conservative parties defend national sovereignty on an ideological rather than a strategic or tactical basis. However, Hooghe et al. (2004, p. 140) restrict their interpretation of this to the claim that "European politics is domestic politics by other means," calling for more research.

Kriesi (2005, 2007) and collaborators (Kriesi et al. 2006a, 2008) take this further. They advance a view in which European contestation restructures party politics by transforming its traditional left–right basis. Here, defense of national sovereignty is considered a response to globalization. According to Kriesi (2005, p. 1), "The mobilisation of the potential winners and losers of this new structural conflict between 'integration' (into the European or global community) and 'demarcation' (of the national community) by the political parties is expected to have a profound impact on the national party systems." Here party alignments are shaped by a new structural conflict whereby the winners and losers of globalization compete over its consequences in politics (a supranational authority challenge), economics (a market liberalization challenge), and culture (an immigration challenge). In contrast to Hooghe and Marks, Kriesi emphasizes the cultural and identity basis for Eurosceptic potentials: "I expect the *cultural* aspects of the opening up of the borders to be more important for the mobilisation of the 'losers' than the defence of their economic interests" (2005, p. 5). This brings a cultural defense of national sovereignty as a collective identity to the explanatory forefront. Importantly, opposition to Europe also comes from mainstream right parties who have redefined themselves in response to denationalization pressures. As a result, Kriesi's inverted U becomes significantly asymmetrical, with conservative and radical right parties making more efforts to mobilize against Europe, than parties dissenting against Europe on economic interests, namely, the classical "old" or radical left. Thus Kriesi sees (2005, p. 5) "conservative and new populist right parties, who most successfully appeal to the fears of the 'losers' to be the driving force of the current transformation of the Western European party systems." Lastly, Kriesi hypothesizes about the overall degree and direction of European party mobilization, (2005, p. 2): "I expect that the issue of European integration has generally become more salient for Western European parties and that the mobilisation concerning this issue has mainly been carried by the Eurosceptics who defend the losers' point of view."

From these competing positions it is possible to draw hypotheses about the distribution and contents of Eurocriticism across national party systems. Generally, those emphasizing the strategic or tactical dimension and "nothing new" substantially would expect Eurocriticism to be an eclectic and inconsistent critique mobilized at contingent times in response to specific opportunities. The inverted U would remain intact with anti-European challenges mobilized opportunistically from the radical poles as an antisystemic challenge to pro-European center parties. The political opportunity approach adds to this expectation that parties will be more inclined to make Eurocritical claims when they are further away from access to European decision making than governing parties and national party organizations are, that is, when they are in opposition or operate on the regional level.

Compared to this, Marks and Hooghe and Kriesi predict a more ideologically structured pattern, with an inverted U skewed on the right resulting from mobilized ideological critiques over Europe. If this view holds, one would expect to find evidence for these transformations across different national contexts. For Marks and Hooghe this is produced by parties' mobilization over a modified left–right cleavage (regulated capitalism vs. neoliberalism), where after the completion of the common market one would expect opposition to EU regulation from the right. For Kriesi, the skewed inverted U results from increasing party mobilization from the right based on traditional, authoritarian, and nationalist ideologies against Europe, and especially over the cultural (immigration challenge) consequences of globalization. This would be demonstrated by increasing European contestation as part of a "new politics" cleavage and by anti-Europeanism cutting across the core of the political system. We now look for evidence to support these competing hypotheses by analyzing parties' claim making.

POSSIBLE DETERMINANTS FOR EUROCRITICISMS

There are many attempts to group parties into families (see e.g., Taggart 1998). Here we distinguish between six families: three traditional party families that have representatives in all Western European countries, that is, social democrats, liberals, and conservatives (often Christian Democrats); a more recent competitor, that is, the greens; a radical right family including the old extreme right and newer populist right; and lastly the radical left, comprising the old and new radical left (often parties with communist or Marxist heritages). This effectively superimposes the "new politics" (green-alternative-libertarian versus traditional-authoritarian-nationalist) over the traditional left–right cleavage.[4] Table 10.1 places all parties appearing in our sample within these six party families.

At the radical left pole, we find unreconstructed Marxist and "old" far-left parties, including the French Ligue communiste révolutionnaire, along with "new" left-wing parties retaining communist heritages, the German Partei des Demokratischen Sozialismus and Italian Rifondazione. Next come the green parties at the Green-alternative-libertarian pole of the new politics axis. Back on the left–right continuum, the social democrat family covers the territory from the classical socialist left advancing labor interests to a Third Way emphasis on social justice while accepting some neoliberal free-trade ideas. This spans parties from the French Parti socialiste to the British Labour party, or New Labour as it has become known. At the center, liberals traditionally share an acceptance of free markets and social tolerance, but to differing degrees, which produces more-leftish and more-rightish parties. The distinction between Dutch liberal parties, the social-liberal Democraten 66 and the free-market Volkspartij voor Vrijheid en Democratie, captures this. The conservative family includes the Christian Democratic tradition plus parties that have adopted neoliberalism, including the British Conservative Party, and a strong national conservatism, sometimes with a populist orientation, like Schweizerische Volkspartei.[5] At the radical right pole, we find the unreconstructed extreme right, such as the French Front national, and their postfascist associates, including the Italian Alleanza nationale, along with anti-immigration and populist parties, from the right of the new politics axis, including the Lijst Pim Fortyn. Finally, we placed regionalist parties according to their ideological proximity within the families, rather than as a separate family. To examine the impact of the regional dimension in the analysis, we aggregate all regional-level actors from all parties. Like all categorizations, there is some arbitrariness in our placements. However, Table 10.1 makes our choices, made in consultation with national experts, transparent.

First, we analyze claims by party actors referring in someway to the European level (Europeanized claims) and containing a positive or negative evaluation of the integration process or of European-level actors, policies, or

---

[4] See Kriesi et al. (2008, pp. 69–70) for a categorization that is broadly similar; however, we keep the radical left parties together whereas they put the "new" radical left with the "Greens," we label the families at the right pole "radical right" whereas they prefer "populist right," and we call the center-right family "conservative" whereas they call it "Christian democratic/conservative."

[5] Perhaps the SVP fits best somewhere between the conservative and radical right families, which is why it is an interesting case. It has strong roots in national conservatism; it is a party of government; and it drew the largest share of the vote (29%) in 2007. Since the 1990s, the SVP has adopted a populist anti-immigration stance and neoliberalism. We included it as a conservative party as we think that its lack of extreme-right heritage and broader policy appeal than anti-immigration issues places it on the right wing of conservatism. Initially, this was the advice we received from our expert Hanspeter Kriesi, though we note that his own more recent categorization for the SVP is "populist right" (Kriesi et al. 2008, pp. 69). In any case, to avoid the inherent arbitrariness of this categorization unduly shaping our findings on party families, we have also analyzed the SVP as a separate party category, which allows us to show its specific effect. We also took this decision for the British Conservative Party (see analyses).

TABLE 10.1. *Political Parties from Our Sample within Party Families*

Country	Radical Left	Green	Social Democrat	Liberal	Conservative	Radical Right
Britain		Green Party	Labour Party Scottish National Party	Liberal Democrats	Conservative Party	UK Independence Party
France	Parti Communiste Français (PCF) Ligue communiste révolutionnaire Lutte ouvrière Parti Radical de Gauche Mouvement républicain et citoyen (MRC)	Les Verts (Verts)	Parti socialiste (PS)	Démocratie Libérale Union pour la Démocratie Française (UDF)	Rassemblement pour la République (RPR)	Front national (FN) Mouvement pour la France (MPF) Rassemblement pour la France et l'Indépendance de l'Europe (RPF)
Germany	Partei des Demokratischen Sozialismus (PDS)	Die Grünen/ Bündnis 90 (Grünen)	Sozialdemokratische Partei Deutschlands (SPD)	Freie Demokratische Partei (FDP –D)	Christlich Demokratische Union Deutschlands (CDU) Christlich-Soziale Union in Bayern (CSU)	Deutsche Volksunion (DVU) Nationaldemokratische Partei Deutschlands (NPD)
Netherlands	Socialistische Partij (SP)	GroenLinks (GL)	Partij van de Arbeid (PvdA)	Volkspartij voor Vrijheid en Democratie (VVD) Democraten 66 (D66)	Christen-Democratisch Appêl (CDA)	Lijst Pim Fortuyn (LPF)

Italy	Partito della Rifondazione Comunista (PRC)	Verdi	Democratici di Sinistra (Ds) l'Ulivo Socialisti Democratici (Sdi) Partito Socialista (PS)	Democrazia è Libertà – La Margherita Radicali Italiani (Lista Bonino) Partito Repubblicano Italiano (PRI)	Forza Italia (FI) Casa delle Libertà Centro Cristiani Democratici (CCD) Partito Popolare Italiano (PPI) Rinnovamento Italiano La Democrazia Cristiana (DC)	Alleanza nationale (An) Lega Nord
Spain	I Izquierda Unida Euskal (IU) Herritarrok/ Herri Batasuna (EH/HB)	Iniciativa por Cataluña Verdes (ICV)	Partido Socialista Obrero Español (PSOE) Bloque Nacionalista Galego (BNG)	Convergència i Unió (CiU) Partido Nacionalista Vasco (PNV)	Partido Popular Unión de Centro Democrático (UCD)	
Switzerland	Die Partei der Arbeit der Schweiz (PdA)	Grüne Partei der Schweiz (GPS)	Sozialdemokratische Partei der Schweiz (SPS)	Freisinnig-Demokratische Partei der Schweiz (FDP-CH) Liberale Partei der Schweiz (LPS)	Christlich Demokratische Volkspartei (CVP) Schweizerische Volkspartei (SVP) Evangelische Volkspartei der Schweiz (EVP) Christlich-soziale Partei (CSP)	Schweizer Demokraten (SD) Freiheits-Partei der Schweiz (FPS) Lega dei Ticinesi

Note: The criterion for inclusion is making a claim within our sample.

institutions. Table 10.2 shows the share among these Europeanized claims expressing negative evaluations of European integration or the EU, that is, Eurocriticisms.

First, the second-to-last column labeled Average shows that, measured across all seven countries, Eurocriticisms form a minority 37% of evaluative claims. The only country where Eurocriticism predominates in the party system is Britain (53%). The other countries range from 41% Eurocriticisms among Dutch to 31% among German parties. Second, the second-to-last row labeled Average shows that criticism over Europe is unevenly distributed across the various party families, conforming roughly to the inverted-U hypothesis. Eurocriticism is relatively low among two-party families situated at the political system's center, social democrats (28%) and liberals (26%). The same is true to a lesser extent for the greens (32%), but this is mainly due to the pro-European German Greens, who make up most of these cases. Greens in other countries tend to be more Eurocritical. Eurocriticism is more widespread among conservatives (44%) than social democrats and liberals, as Hooghe and Marks, and Kriesi, broadly suggest. However, closer inspection shows this to be largely due to two parties, the British Conservatives and Swiss Schweizerische Volkspartei (SVP; both 74%). We discuss their cases in detail in the subsequent text. Other conservatives display similar levels of Eurocriticism as most social democrats and liberals. In line with the inverted-U hypothesis, radical left (70%) and radical right (88%) parties display high levels of Eurocriticism.

Closer inspection of differences across party families per country reveals a number of patterns, which conform only partly to the inverted-U hypothesis. In Germany we find a combination of relatively low overall Eurocriticism with very little variation among parties across families. Germany seems to be the country where a broad pro-European consensus still holds. In the Netherlands, parties' positions also diverge very little, but Eurocriticism is clearly higher on average among Dutch than German parties. We examine this Dutch Eurocriticism in more detail below. In Switzerland we find a clear left–right divide with strong opposition to Europe among conservative (especially SVP) and radical right (mainly Schweizer Demokraten) parties, and a much more pro-European stance across the rest of the political spectrum, and especially the social democrats (7%). Left-wing Eurocriticism does not seem to be a force in Switzerland. In Britain, contestation over Europe extends to the political system's core, even more so than in Switzerland, pitching Labour (31%) and the Liberal Democrats (0%) against the strongly Eurocritical British Conservatives (74%). Spain also shows left–right opposition, but it is much less polarized, and, notably, this goes in a different direction than Britain and Switzerland. Spanish social democrats made more (41%) Eurocriticisms than conservative parties (28%) – we examine this in more detail in the qualitative part of the study. Finally, two countries display a fully inverted U pattern, France and to a lesser extent (given the radical left's low Eurocriticisms) Italy. In these countries, Eurocriticism is strong among radical right parties and green parties, and for France also the radical left.

TABLE 10.2. *Share of Eurocritical Claims within a Party Family's Evaluative Claim Making by Country*

Country	Radical Left	Green	Social Democrat	Liberal	Conservative	Radical Right	Average	N
Germany	–	28	29	18	38	–	31	572
France	76	50	26	28	20	88	32	458
Britain	X	X	31	0	74	–	53	383
Italy	–	67	16	25	36	81	36	180
Spain	–	–	41	–	28	X	32	92
Netherlands	–	–	40	37	50	–	41	107
Switzerland	–	–	7	28	46	100	37	199
Average	70	32	28	26	44	87	37	
N	37	112	739	210	830	63		1,991

Notes: Share of Eurocritical claims are shown as percentage figures. – dashes indicate that there were fewer than five cases; Xs indicate that there was no party from the family in the country's sample.

The low Eurocriticism among virtually all mainstream parties – except for the British Conservatives and Swiss SVP – may be due to such parties participating on a regular basis in government and profiting from the privileged access that national governments have to the European policy process. It is therefore important to control for whether a party is in government or opposition when criticizing Europe.

Our hypothesis is that party representatives will be more likely to make Eurocriticisms in opposition than in government.

For similar reasons, we need to control for whether a party actor is from the national level or speaks on behalf of a regional or local organization.

Here, we hypothesize on the basis of the political opportunity perspective that subnational party actors will be more Eurocritical because they have less access to European policy circles than national ones.

Table 10.3 presents a multivariate logistic regression with, as the dependent variable, whether or not a claim evaluates European integration or EU institutions negatively. The first regression includes party families, government incumbency, and whether a claim is made by a subnational party actor as the independent variables. Because of their deviant position within the conservative family, we include separate variables for the British Conservatives and Swiss SVP. Liberals are the omitted reference category, because they produce the lowest Eurocriticism among party families. The results confirm Table 10.2's descriptive findings: There are no significant differences in degrees of Eurocriticism between greens, social democrats, and various types of liberals. Conservative parties in Italy, Spain, Germany, the Netherlands, and France do not vary from this pro-European mainstream, but the British Conservatives and Swiss SVP stand out by their very strong Eurocritical voices. For Britain and Switzerland, contestation over Europe cuts right through the political system's core, pitching an anti-European right against a pro-European left, whereas elsewhere polarization over European integration is characterized by a Eurocritical periphery versus a pro-European center. As expected, the radical left, and even more so the radical right, are highly significant Eurocritics. These effects persist when we control for government incumbency, and subnational versus national party actors. This means that Eurocriticism from the political margins is explained neither by the fact that these parties seldom participate in governments, nor by the fact that some are more weakly represented on national than subnational levels.

Government incumbency has the predicted effect.[6] When parties form part of the government they are significantly less likely to make Eurocriticisms than when they are in opposition. This finding suggests that the often-heard complaint that Euroscepticism thrives because national governments claim

---

[6] Parties were assigned to government or opposition on the basis of exact dates of claims and government changes. For French *cohabitation* periods, the ruling President's party and parties participating in government were considered incumbents.

TABLE 10.3. *Possible Determinants for Eurocritical Claim Making*

Determinant	Negative Evaluation of European Integration or EU	
	First Analysis	Second Analysis
Party type (reference category: liberals)		
Radical left	5.742***	6.458***
Greens	1.564	1.028
Social Democrats	1.298	1.260
Conservatives	1.255	1.341
British Conservative Party	6.780***	7.699***
Swiss People's Party	6.671***	7.769***
Radical right	12.234***	13.287***
Government incumbency (ref. category: opposition parties)	0.560***	0.544***
Subnational party actors (ref. category: national-level party actors)	2.887***	2.838***
Country of party (ref. category: Switzerland)		
Germany	—	1.118
France	—	0.987
United Kingdom	—	1.257
Italy	—	1.115
Spain	—	1.106
Netherlands	—	1.966*
Issue field (ref. category: pensions and education)		
European integration	—	1.799
Monetary politics	—	1.969
Agriculture	—	6.202**
Immigration	—	1.854
Troop deployment	—	1.404
Time (ref. category: 1990)		
1995	—	1.622*
2000–2002	—	2.048***
Newspaper type (ref. category: center-right broadsheets)		
Center-left broadsheet	—	1.054
Regional	—	0.545*
Tabloid	—	1.221
N	1,991	1,991
Nagelkerke R^2	.209	.255

Note: Possible determinants are shown as odds ratios (only claims with European scope).
* $p < .05$, ** $p < .01$, *** $p < .001$.

all the good work for themselves, and blame all things bad on the European Union, has little empirical support. Table 10.3 shows that, in fact, national governments are the main political bulwarks for pro-Europeanism. We also find the effect predicted by the political opportunity structure perspective for subnational party actors, who are much more likely to be Eurocritical than their national counterparts. This result is remarkable given the emphasis in parts of the multilevel governance literature on the supposedly beneficial effects of European integration for the political leverage of regional actors. We therefore investigated it in more detail by adding interaction terms that allow us to investigate whether the finding holds in all countries (results available from the authors on request). In the three most centralized countries – France, the United Kingdom, and the Netherlands – there are so few claims by regional party organizations that nothing meaningful can be said about their stances toward European integration. In the four countries where we have sufficient cases, regional party representatives are consistently more Eurocritical than national party organizations. However, in line with the political opportunity structure argument, the effect is strongest and statistically significant in the two most strongly federalized countries, Germany and Switzerland, where regional actors have most to fear from a shift of decision-making power to Brussels where many crucial decisions are negotiated among national government representatives.

In the second regression, reported in the last column, we introduce further control variables. First, we include the countries of origin of party actors, with Swiss parties as the reference category. As we saw earlier, there are important cross-national differences in the distribution of Eurocriticism across the party spectrum. Moreover, not all party families are represented in all countries, or they are more strongly represented in some than others. By introducing the country of origin of claim makers, we are able to establish whether differences across party families are robust when we control for cross-national differences. In addition, we can investigate whether there are significant cross-national differences net of the differences in the composition of party systems. The results show that our findings for party families, government incumbency, and subnational actors hardly change when we control for national origin. Regarding cross-national differences, we find that when we control for differences in the composition of the party system, only the Netherlands deviates significantly from the reference category (Switzerland). This results from Dutch mainstream parties displaying comparatively high Eurocriticism (Table 10.2), which we investigate in more detail in the subsequent text. Our results also show that, taking into account the deviant British Conservatives and Swiss SVP within the conservative family, other British and Swiss parties do not differ significantly from members of the same party family in other countries.

Regarding differences across issue fields, Table 10.3 shows only parties' claims on agriculture are significantly more Eurocritical than those in the reference issue fields of pensions and education.[7] Given that 50% of the EU's budget

---

[7] Because the numbers were low, we combined these two issue fields as a reference category.

is spent on agriculture, this is one field where the supranational level attracts criticism from governmental and mainstream parties. However, we find no significant link for immigration as a source for Eurocriticism, although Kriesi sees this as such. Nor is monetary politics significant, again perhaps surprisingly, given the centrality that Hooghe and Marks attribute to neoliberalism versus regulated capitalism contestation.

Regarding variations across time, our data shows that parties have become more Eurocritical over the period 1990–2002, which on the surface supports a thesis for emergent Euroscepticism (Kriesi), or alternatively, the normalization of an increased party contestation over Europe.

Finally, we control for the type of newspaper reporting a claim. Here there are no significant differences between center-left and center-right broadsheets, or between broadsheets and popular or tabloid papers. Only regional newspapers tend to less frequently report parties' Eurocriticisms. Overall, this shows methodological robustness across newspaper types as a data source for retrieving claims.

In further quantitative analyses (not reported in the table, but available on request), we investigated whether these patterns differed across two basic types of Eurocriticism. As we will elaborate in the subsequent qualitative section, one can distinguish truly Eurosceptic claims that reject or criticize the European integration process from constructive criticisms that endorse the European integration process as such, while criticizing concrete steps or specific European institutions. Because we separately coded a claimant's stance with regard to the integration process (e.g., enlargement, institutional reform) and its evaluation of concrete European institutions (e.g., the European Commission, European Councils), we are able to distinguish these two types of Eurocriticism.[8] It turns out that the patterns underlying both types of Eurocriticism, when analyzed separately, are broadly similar to the ones reported in Table 10.3, and we therefore report only the deviations. Unlike the British Conservatives, the Swiss SVP is characterized only by strong Euroscepticism and not by significant levels of constructive Eurocriticism. Swiss party actors generally make significantly fewer constructive Eurocriticisms than those in any of the other countries, which is simply due to the fact that the Swiss debate is largely not about the concrete workings of European institutions or the implementation of particular policies, but about the pros and cons of European integration writ large. Further, we find that parties of government are especially less likely to make Eurosceptic claims, while they are only marginally significantly (at the 0.10 level) less likely to make constructive Eurocritical claims. Finally, we find that Eurocriticism in the agriculture issue field is only significantly pronounced when we consider its constructive variant, implying much criticism of the role

---

[8] The reference category in these additional analyses consists of what one might call "Europhile" claims: ones that evaluate neither the integration process nor European institutions negatively, and that evaluate at least one of them positively.

of European institutions and their concrete actions in the field, without calling into question the principal role of the EU in agricultural policy making.

To better understand the substance of their critiques, how they frame their criticisms of European integration and the EU's actors, policies, and issues, we now move to a detailed analysis of the most Eurocritical parties' claims.

THE SUBSTANCE AND FRAMING OF EUROCRITICISM

Generally, following those who emphasize the strategic or tactical dimension and predict "nothing new" in the ideological contents of Europe as a basis for party contestation (e.g., Mair), one would broadly expect Eurocriticism to be a set of somewhat eclectic and inconsistent beliefs mobilized at contingent times in response to opportunities for challenging the consensus. Against this, others emphasize that European integration is a substantive part of the ideological terrain that political parties contest in liberal democracies (e.g., Hooghe and Marks; Kriesi). In this view, parties' claims would define a more consistent, coherent, and identifiable ideological stance that places Europe within a cleavage. A first aim of our qualitative study is descriptive. We simply want to know how different parties criticize Europe, according to claims that they have successfully mobilized in the public domain. There is virtually no systematic evidence available about how parties criticize Europe through the mass media, although news is the main source of political information that confronts voters, and through which politicians gauge public opinion (Entman 2004). Second, by examining their mobilized Eurocriticisms, we try to assess whether parties' critiques are more ideologically motivated or tactical interventions.

It is important to move beyond the linear proversus anti-European axis and examine claims' substantive contents and the political events (context) that triggered their mobilization. This allows us to see what a party's Eurocriticisms consist of and whether they frame a coherent and consistent critique.[9] First, criticism is either dismissive, rejecting something, or it is constructive. Thus critical claims may be against, or for, European integration or the EU. Second, their mobilization may be more strategic or tactical, using Europe to challenge other parties, or more ideological, defining values and interests that place Europe within a cleavage. By combining these analytic dimensions, we identify four ideal types for Eurocriticism: *committed*

---

[9] Here we use framing from the social movement perspective pioneered by authors, including Snow and Benford (1992) and Gamson and Modigliani (1989), who study collective action frames from public discourse. In this view, frames are "action oriented sets of beliefs and meanings that inspire and legitimate . . . activities and campaigns" (Snow and Benford 1992, p. 136) by collective actors. This actor-oriented approach is suited to our inquiry, which retrieves data from news on parties' claims over Europe, made within their public campaigns. The other related approach to framing comes from a media perspective (e.g., Entman 2004), but this is less suitable to our present purposes because it examines how the media shapes and frames news contents. For a critical discussion of the differences in approach, see Gamson (2001).

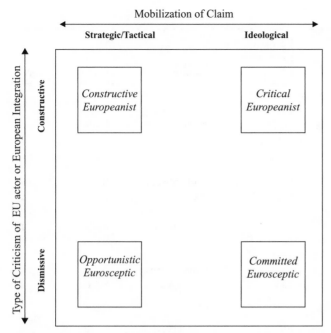

FIGURE 10.1. Types of Eurocriticism.

Euroscepticism; opportunistic Euroscepticism; critical Europeanism; and constructive Europeanism.

First, *committed Eurosceptic* claims reject the value and substance of Europe, ideologically, by mobilizing an anti-European critique that substantively politicizes a cleavage over advancing European integration. Second, and also in the bottom half of Figure 10.1, we find *opportunistic Eurosceptic* claims. These also reject Europe but without building a coherent anti-European critique that constructs a cleavage over the EU. Instead they are primarily tactical responses to perceived political opportunities to challenge other parties. Third, moving up to the more pro-European stances, we find *critical Europeanist* claims at the top right corner in Figure 10.1. These build a critique that rejects the existing value and substance of Europe, but from a commitment to a different pro-European belief, such as "federalism," thereby politicizing a cleavage over the EU. Lastly, *constructive Europeanist* claims do not mobilize a new ideological pro-European critique; they criticize aspects, or specify alternatives within the existing EU project. Such constructive claim making is largely pragmatic, treating the current European Union as normal and then making criticisms within it, rather than further politicizing its basis by mobilizing a challenge.

Our qualitative study uses these ideal types to examine the claims of the most "Eurocritical" parties revealed by the quantitative analyses. Table 10.4 lists our sample of fifteen parties for which we have at least ten claims in the sample, and that have shares of negative evaluative claims that exceed the

TABLE 10.4. *Eurocritical Parties*

Party	Eurocriticism: Evaluative Claims (%)	Family	Country	N
Hard Eurocritics from the periphery				
Front national (FN)	100	Radical right	France	11
Rassemblement pour la France et l'Indépendance del'Europe (RPF)	100	Radical right	France	11
Lega Nord (LN)	88	Radical right	Italy	16
Mouvement républicain et citoyen (MDC)	82	Radical left	France	11
Parti Communiste Français (PCF)	77	Radical left	France	13
Hard Eurocritics from the core				
Conservative Party	74	Conservative	Britain	204
Schweizerische Volkspartei (SVP)	74	Conservative	Switzerland	49
Soft Eurocritics				
Christlich-Soziale Union in Bayern (CSU)	60	Conservative	Germany	47
Christen-Democratisch Appèl (CDA)	50	Conservative	Netherlands	22
Les Verts	50	Green	France	10
Democraten 66 (D66)	47	Liberal	Netherlands	17
Partido Socialista Obrero Español (PSOE)	41	Social Democrat	Spain	29
Forza Italia (FI)	40	Conservative	Italy	30
Partij van de Arbeid (PvdA)	40	Social Democrat	Netherlands	40
Casa delle Libertà (CdL)	39	Conservative	Italy	39

overall mean of 37%. It includes parties from each family and each country. Table 10.4's ranking from top to bottom divides the sample into three groups. At the top, we find the strongest Eurocritics from radical right and left poles; we call these *hard Eurocritics from the periphery* (between 77% and 100% negative claims). In the middle, we have the two conservative parties who are *hard Eurocritics from the core* (74% negative claims). At the bottom, we find *soft Eurocritics* who make some criticisms but also have positive things to say about Europe (between 39% and 60% negative claims). Our analysis is based on the actual language and contents of the claims and descriptions of their mobilizations coded from newspapers. All quotations come directly from the source material (translated into English).

Hard Eurocritics from the Periphery

Starting with the Front national (FN), we see that its entire evaluative claim making is against Europe. The FN's claims build a coherent and consistently mobilized critique that characterizes it as a committed Eurosceptic. The party defines itself as France's defender against a loss of sovereign national autonomy imposed by the EU and collaborating French governments. This advocacy against the European Union constructs a territorial cleavage of France versus the EU: "European integration is bad for France." It opposes European enlargement, calling for treaty renegotiations "to improve national independence." Likewise the euro is criticized for being "against national, economic, social, and political independence." Instead of Europe, the FN proposes strong sovereign independent nations. As Marine Le Pen puts it, "We want a Europe of sovereign nations. France can't be like Nebraska in the US." French governments are criticized for "selling France and its sovereignty cheaply to the EU." In addition, the EU is criticized for its "totalitarian" treatment of Austria over the Haider affair and for wanting to "integrate millions of immigrants over the next 20 years." However, the FN's Euroscepticism addresses the national consequences of globalization in economic and political terms much more than mobilizing a cultural threat of immigration.

Charles Pasqua's Rassemblement pour la France et l'Indépendance de l'Europe (RPF) is also entirely against Europe. Its critique has similarities to the FN, being territorial, but its nationalism criticizes the substance of Europeanization processes even more. Pasqua calls on the French government to organize a referendum on the euro, arguing in populist tones that "France will sacrifice its destiny, and that the French people has a different ambition." He asks President Chirac "not to sacrifice national cohesion for Europe's sake." The euro is depicted as potentially "weak," leading to a doomsday scenario of inflation, unemployment, social crisis, and "national identity" problems. Monetary union is dismissed as a "federalist vocation," leading to a situation in which the European Central Bank would be able to "dominate democratic states." The RPF's nationalist critique is consistently committed Eurosceptic; however, in contrast to the FN, it also takes pragmatic policy stances in response to political opportunities, such as demanding the euro's postponement or to avoid the convergence criteria. This indicates also a more strategic engagement within the party system over Europe.

The Italian regionalist Lega Nord exhibits a different form of Euroscepticism. Its critique of Europe mobilizes antistatist claims, but it is eclectic and superficial in addressing the political and economic substance of European integration. Thus Umberto Bossi considers the European Union as a source of "supercentralist philosophy" and a "new form of Statism." However, the Lega mobilizes virtually no economic or political arguments against Europe. Instead it depicts the consequences of an advancing EU as cultural threats. Thus, the EU Charter of Rights is criticized for being "communist, a little bit Nazi, a little bit Jacobin, and a little bit Social Democratic," whereas Bossi argues, "we want a Europe of the people against the superstate of freemasons." It describes

EU intervention in the Haider Affair as a plot by "big businessmen, who are often Jewish, wanting to impose immigration." This high eclecticism defines the Lega as an opportunistic Eurosceptic. The Lega uses Europe's salience as an opportunity for mobilizing its populist antistatist world view within its anti-systemic opposition. It does not engage in substantive politics over European integration.

Turning to the left, we see that Jean Pierre Chevènement's Mouvement républicain et citoyen (MDC) has strong similarities with the RPF. It actually has little to say about the social consequences of European integration and its critique is basically a territorial nationalist defense of sovereignty. Like the RPF, its committed Euroscepticism coherently focuses on the substance and perceived consequences of Europeanization processes. Monetary union is criticized for its technical unfeasibility: "A strong euro will bring high interest rates, deflation, a tight national budget and tight salaries." The European Central Bank is depicted as incapable of serving France's economic needs. Politically, the MDC opposes the loss of national sovereignty implied by "the idea of a European Constitution that would turn France into a German 'Land'." This antifederalism becomes anti-German when Chevènement claims that Joschka Fischer's federalist propositions "were the sign that Germany wasn't cured from its Nazi past." Like the FN and RPF, the main cleavage it constructs over Europe is territorial, that is, a political and economic, and occasionally cultural, nationalism against Europe.

By contrast, the cornerstone of the Parti Communiste Français' (PCF) critique of Europe is not nationalism but emphasizes the EU's social deficits. The PCF defends national social welfare and labor interests against the EU's perceived neoliberalism. Its General Secretary criticizes the French EU Presidency "for having done nothing on social policy at the European level." Likewise, the PCF sees the attempt to make the euro rival the dollar as "dropping the European social model and promoting financial markets." The party also criticizes the EU's immigration policies for their "repressive and restrictive" consequences for third-country nationals. Overall, the PCF's committed Euroscepticism constructs a critique that fits within the modified left–right cleavage over Europe identified by Hooghe and Marks, that is, regulated capitalism versus neoliberalism: It defends France's national social model against the EU's neoliberal market making. Here the territorial nationalist dimension is not decisive, which is demonstrated by the PCF's support for nonnationals in France in its criticisms of EU immigration policies.

Hard Eurocritics from the Core

The British Conservative Party is the only mainstream EU member state party that is strongly critical of Europe. Its mobilization produced four times as many negative evaluations of Europe than its nearest rival in any of the other countries. The British Conservatives use the regular opportunities presented by EU summits, proposals, and treaties to politicize European integration and the EU, thereby carrying the cleavage over Europe to the core of the British political system. The British Conservatives are committed Eurosceptics *par excellence* and their substantive rejection of Europe is a coherent ideological critique. Like the radical right, they emphasize the territorial dimension by advocating national sovereignty and independence over political union, but at the core of the Conservative party's Euroscepticism is a strong commitment to the free market against any possible regulation or intervention by the EU. Politically, the advancing European Union is seen as a threat to the Westminster Parliament's sovereignty. Economically, the EU is depicted as potentially reintroducing state interventionism into a deregulated economy. Conservatives oppose the EU's political substance, which is depicted as an interventionist "Federal EU superstate," a "United States of Europe," "anti-American, big government Europe," and criticized for fraud, mismanagement, high cost, and incompetence. All EU regulatory intervention is firmly rejected. However, this vision is not reducible to antiglobalist nationalism, but specifies an alternative international world order: Economically, the British Conservatives propose Europe as a "free-trade area," and politically, they advocate international relations between strong sovereign nation-states, promoting Britain within NATO and the Commonwealth. For the British Conservatives, it is not clear why internationalism stops at the EU's borders; they want free markets between sovereign states everywhere. We find a few cases in which Euroscepticism drifts into "little Englander" xenophobia, for example, Minister Nicholas Ridley claiming that Monetary Union was a "German trick to gain power," or giving sovereignty to Brussels was "tantamount to giving it to Adolf Hitler." However, the vast majority of Eurosceptic claims are reasoned arguments against the perceived threats of declining political sovereignty and increasing market regulation. Conservative Euroscepticism is only to a limited extent populist or cultural (xenophobia–ethnic nationalism–parochialism). Mostly, it addresses core political (prosovereignty–civic nationalist) and economic (pro-free market) substantive issues with reasoned alternatives. The driving force of conservative Euroscepticism is a commitment to market-oriented neoliberalism and defense of national sovereignty, much more than cultural opposition to Europe.[10] However, it is not just reducible to opposition to "regulated capitalism" a la Hooghe and Marks; the nationalist component is also salient in its strong defense of political sovereignty, but mostly this is an expression of civic nationalism, that is, "conservatism" in the face of change, not xenophobia.

Since Switzerland is not an EU member, many of the SVP claims are mobilized within the specific political opportunity presented by referenda over EU entry and bilateral agreements. The SVP campaigns strongly against the "Oui à l'Europe" initiative. Faced by opportunities to politicize Europe, the SVP mobilizes a committed Eurosceptic critique. It galvanizes a populist appeal to

---

[10] This limited "cultural/historical" framing within conservative Euroscepticism is supported by Statham and Gray's study (2005, p. 75), who found that it made up a sixth.

a loss of the individual Swiss citizen's power with a defense of national interests, while rejecting so-called superstatist EU interventionism. Interventionist
EU statism is presented as a substantive threat to the political and economic
freedoms and liberties of Swiss citizens. The party's leader, Christoph Blocher,
argues "one should search for one's national salvation in oneself not within
a bigger supranational building." The threat to national independence is symbolically depicted by potential consequences for farmers: "EU agriculture regulations will corner small Swiss farmers and hinder the independence of the
food supply." According to the SVP, the EU will remove Swiss direct democracy, it demonstrated its antidemocratic credentials in the Haider Affair, and
joining the Monetary Union will make the Swiss (especially farmers) poorer.
Nor does the continental security argument resonate with the SVP, for whom
"Europe can live in peace without the EU." Overall, the SVP's nationalist critique emphasizes the territorial cleavage over Europe. It is more populist than
the British Conservatives and lacks their strong commitment to neoliberalism,
which places it closer to the RPF, MDC, and FN parties.

Soft Eurocritics

The remaining parties in Table 10.4 are above-average Eurocritics. However,
except for the German Christlich-Soziale Union in Bayern (CSU), negative
evaluations form a minority of their claims. Nonetheless, if criticizing Europe
is an emergent phenomenon – Table 10.3 showed significant increases over
time – then these parties are its likeliest source. It is therefore important to know
what type of critiques they present. To gauge this potential for Euroscepticism,
we start on the right, where it is most present, and move across the political
spectrum.

The CSU, the junior partner of Germany's Christian Democracy, mobilizes
against Europe almost exclusively around one issue: the EU's sanctions against
Austria over Haider. The CSU's criticism is not a coherent critique over the
substance of European integration, but a single-issue campaign. It argues, "the
EU may not interfere in the government of a member state." A few additional
cases criticize the euro's weakness and oppose Turkey's proposed membership;
however, the CSU has no consistent substantive political or economic stance
against the EU. It is basically a one-issue opportunistic Eurosceptic.

The Italian conservatives in Berlusconi's Casa delle Libertà (CdL) coalition,
led by his Forza Italia (FI), show more evidence than the CSU of critiques
similar to the British Conservatives. The CdL's opposition to the EU focuses
on neoliberal, antiregulatory, antistate elements. Berlusconi "dreams of a more
free market-oriented Europe," arguing for less centralized government and
regulation and praises Mrs. Thatcher's approach to Europe. The EU's Stability
and Growth Pact is presented as "against the interests of Italian citizens" and
the euro is criticized for raising prices. The CdL is sceptical of EU enlargement
on grounds of national interest, arguing that Southern Italy's development
ought to take precedence. However, the CdL advocates neoliberalism within

Europe, not as an ideology against it. Its stances are pragmatic and not consistently pitched against Europe's political substance. Eurocriticisms appear on an ad hoc basis, depending on whether Italy stands to benefit or lose from a proposed integration measure. Such eclecticism combining market rhetoric and nationalist populism is perhaps the hallmark of Berlusconi politics, leading to opportunistic Euroscepticism.

The Dutch Christen-Democratisch Appèl (CDA) criticizes aspects of the EU's performance and efficiency, but without politicizing or questioning its value and substance. For example, the CDA demands that the European Commission stick to the Stability and Growth Pact rather than make concessions to other states, because "the credibility of the euro is at stake." Likewise, a CDA Minister says adjusting market policies for special categories of farmers "is a threat to the foundations of the common agricultural politics." Such criticisms are made from an acceptance of the Netherlands' inclusion within a European framework. There is no nationalist challenge. They support the European project and carry no ideological opposition to it. The CDA's Eurocriticisms are constructive Europeanism that aims to keep common European standards high by specifying pragmatic alternatives within the existing project.

This type of Eurocriticism seems prominent at the Dutch center, because constructive Europeanism also characterizes the claim making of the liberal Democraten 66 (D66) and social democratic Partij van de Arbeid (PvdA). For example, on immigration, D66 wants a "charitable and open position" on asylum so that it is "first of all a matter for the EU," while demanding that the EU makes other member states do their duty for Bosnian refugees too. The PvdA's criticisms defend the Netherlands' status within the EU. Thus the Prime Minister demands the Netherlands receives a greater share of EU votes than Belgium, Greece, and Portugal, and the Secretary of State for European Affairs intends to protest over any proposed reduction of EU "official languages" to the detriment of Dutch. This is pro-European nationalism. Far from Euroscepticism, this strong constructive Europeanism is evidence for a Dutch party politics that sees Europeanized governance as normalized. It explains the high level of Dutch Eurocriticism (see Table 10.3) to actually be the product of an impatiently Europhile party politics.[11]

The Spanish social democratic Partido Socialista Obrero Español (PSOE) demonstrates that constructive Europeanism is not just Dutch. On German Unification, the PSOE criticizes "certain members of the European Community for

---

[11] Note that our data stop in 2002. After the failed referendum on the European Constitutional Treaty in 2005, Dutch party politics has transformed considerably, so this situation no longer holds to the full extent. Subsequent developments suggest this Dutch party consensus for European governance proved to be "too cozy," and that from the Dutch public's viewpoint did not give sufficient representation to national interests over Europeanized ones. Former Prime Minister Ruud Lubbers recognized this long before subsequent events made it a fashionable thesis; speaking to British journalist Hugo Young (1998, p. 510) in 1996, he stated that "If I and others went on television for a few nights, to make a case against the integration of Europe, I think the Dutch people could easily turn round."

using these events as an excuse for not progressing with the European Union."
There is even a protest against the euro for not being sufficiently included: San
Sebastián de la Gomera's Mayor launches his own currency, the "Gomeuro,"
against the exclusion of small Canaries islands from the currency's distribution. Again this supports, not challenges, the existing context of European
governance.

Finally, the French Greens, Les Verts, are pro-European, but unlike the
Dutch center parties and PSOE, their claims reject the existing European Union
for not advancing far enough. The party is against the Nice Treaty, because "it
does not stand for political responsibility and tends to re-nationalise common
policies." Its leaders demand that Laeken "must be the occasion to re-launch
European integration" and promote sustainable development. Les Verts' radical federalism advocates a social, political, and federal Europe to replace the
current EU. Opposing the nationalist Eurosceptic challenge from the right, Les
Verts present a postnationalist challenge on the territorial dimension by rejecting nation-states' dominance over the EU through a commitment to federalism.
In addition, they want a greening and more emphasis on social aspects within
the EU's substance. This critical Europeanism politicizes the EU's substance
and value by demanding a more radical Europeanization.

WHITHER EUROCRITICISM: TOWARD NORMALIZATION?

This chapter examined Eurocriticism across seven party systems to test
hypotheses about the degree and nature of European party contestation. Our
multivariate analysis showed that, generally, a party's country of origin has
little explanatory power, once differences between the compositions of party
systems are taken into account. Even British parties are not significantly more
Eurocritical than similar ones elsewhere, when the great exception of the British
Conservative Party is taken into account. This implies an ideological dimension to European mobilization. However, there was also support also for the
strategic or tactical dimension. First, regardless of differences between party
families, we found that all parties are more pro-European when they are government incumbents. Second, we found that subnational party representatives
take up more Eurocritical stances. This was particularly the case in the two
most strongly federalized countries, Switzerland and Germany, where regional
actors stand to lose most from transfers of power to the EU level, where
national actors have privileged access to core decision-making forums. These
findings on political parties follow those on subnational actors in Chapter 4,
by confirming expectations from the political opportunity approach that those
more excluded from participating within European-level governance – opposition parties, regional actors – are significantly more critical regardless of their
political colors.

Another important general point is that party contestation in the public domain remains strongly pro-European (cross-country average: 63% pro-
European evaluative claims), especially at the core among liberals and social

democrats. In contrast, the radical right and radical left are clear opponents. The conservatives (56% pro-European) come in between. They are divided between the statistically significant exceptions of the Eurocritical British Conservatives and the Swiss SVP (both 74% Eurocritical), and the remaining parties, who do not vary significantly from the pro-European center consensus. Thus, overall we find a lop-sided inverted U on the right of the political spectrum, but this is generated almost entirely by the mobilization of the British Conservatives and the Swiss SVP.

Our detailed qualitative study put flesh on the bones of this pattern. On the Eurocritical periphery, the French radical right were committed Eurosceptics contesting an ideological cleavage over Europe that is territorial, constructing different brands of mostly political or economic nationalism in opposition to the advancing EU. In contrast, the French Communists mobilized against neoliberal Europe by defending social welfare and labor interests. The Italian Lega was different again, an opportunistic Eurosceptic mobilizing little meaningful critique over Europe's substance within its antisystemic opposition. Among Europe's soft critics, we witnessed little evidence for latent ideological Euroscepticism at the party system's core. The CSU and Berlusconi parties used Europe tactically – opportunistic Euroscepticism – to oppose Europe, whereas the Dutch parties' criticisms and those of the PSOE were actually evidence for Europhilia, constructive Europeanism. In addition, the French Greens mobilized a critical Europeanist case, opposing the existing Europe through an ideological commitment to a greener federal one. The most developed committed Eurosceptic critiques came from the British Conservative and Swiss SVP cases: For them, Europe is a new threat of statist interventionism, against national political sovereignty and neoliberal market and individual freedoms.

First, from this, it is clear that mobilized opposition to Europe is not reducible to "contentless" antisystemic challenges (Taggart). Only the Lega at the periphery were opportunistic Eurosceptics in this pure sense. Against those emphasizing parties' tactical positioning (Steenbergen and Scott) and a broadly "no change" thesis (Mair), we found that most criticism from core and periphery actually constructed critiques over the substance of Europe. When parties make the effort to take a clear stance against Europe, they mostly have something to say politically and economically about Europeanization. Nonetheless, it is worth repeating that party contestation is for the most part still dominated by parties saying positive things about Europe, especially those in government. Thus, we are still some considerable way from an "all change" thesis (Kriesi). Even if we found a significant increase in Eurocriticism over time, our evidence showed that committed Euroscepticism at the core of party systems is basically limited to two conservative parties in Britain and Switzerland. Thus, it remains questionable to what extent there is a transformation of party politics driven by an anti-European right, especially if this is conceived as a new cleavage in a fundamental sense (Kriesi). As an emergent trend, Euroscepticism still has a lot of emerging to do to reach that status, especially considering the overall prominence of pro-Europeanism among parties.

What we are perhaps witnessing is the beginning of a process in which criticism of Europe becomes normalized within national party politics. Europe is a key issue in the transformation of a national politics dealing with the consequences of globalization, and the repositioning of parties over this. We could be at the stage where there are clear but smallish groups of "winners" and "losers" of Europeanization, who politically see themselves as such, whereas the rest of the population remain increasingly aware of the issues but undecided (for a similar view, see Fligstein 2008). Parties increasingly step forward to test the water over Europe with the majority of the population, as the field is increasingly publicly visible and politicized by those who have clear stakes. As parties start to say more about Europe, critiques and ideological divisions emerge over the benefits and disadvantages of Europeanization. This means that Europe is becoming part of the way that parties address the challenges of globalization and translate this into political choices. When it is normal to have something to say about Europeanization, purely tactical opposition to Europe has relatively little to offer, because to enter a debate, even tactically, one has to say something of substance. So Europe is part of a changing national party politics, but whether it will become central to transforming party politics remains an open question.

Second, regarding the nature of mobilized cleavages over Europe, our findings are also mixed. We consider that party contestation over Europe is, as Hooghe and Marks suggest, linked within a modified left–right cleavage (regulated capitalism vs. neoliberalism). However, not all party critiques of Europe can be placed within this framework. It fits the French Communists from the radical left and the neoliberalism of the British Conservatives. But Eurosceptic nationalism, including that of the British Conservatives, SVP, RPF, MDC, and Front national, opposes most reductions in the political sovereignty of the nation-state, not just those relating to market regulation. It is also difficult to place the Greens' critical Europeanism or the SVP's populism. Superimposed over a modified left–right cleavage, we consider, like Kriesi, "new politics" themes (TAN or traditional-authoritarian-nationalist vs. GAL or Green-alternative-libertarian) important. However, in contrast to Kriesi, we see the key sources of rightist TAN Euroscepticism to be grounded in civic-political rather than cultural responses to Europeanization, especially when they are expressed at the core of the political system. For Kriesi, the cultural aspect of TAN is fundamental and explanatory (2005, p. 13): "the relevance of Euroscepticism for the restructuring of the national political space depends on the deep cultural roots referred to by Díez Medrano (2003). It is only in countries where Euroscepticism, as in Britain and Switzerland, resonates with deep-seated national anxieties that it serves as the key for the restructuring of the party system – with conservatives or new populist right becoming the decisive restructuring force."

However, Kriesi's thesis misses important elements. First, this brand of Eurosceptic nationalism cannot be reduced to cultural nationalism, that is, "deep cultural" threats and xenophobia. It is highly questionable, and not empirically proven, that the British and Swiss are more beset by "deep seated national anxieties" over globalization issues, such as immigration, than others, such as the French and Dutch. We found only limited cases of populist cultural nationalist and xenophobic Euroscepticism, even among the radical right. Actually, most Eurosceptic nationalism finds expression as civic-nationalist claims about sovereignty. Defense of sovereignty is not necessarily a product of "deep-seated national anxieties," nor is it logically linked to "immigration threats" and "fear of foreigners." Instead nationalism can be a form of "constitutional patriotism" (*Verfassungspatriotismus*) located in advancing interests of the national community of citizens and belief in core political institutions. This stands for more than addressing a constituency of denationalization "losers." Civic nationalism can also appeal across internal divides (e.g., class, sectoral interests), standing for a cohesive national civic community sharing common values. This is literally "conservatism" and need not drift into xenophobia. Indeed, the more Euroscepticism exists at the political mainstream, the less likely it is to be based on the appeal of ethnic nationalism. To succeed at the core, Euroscepticism has to be made appealing to the political classes, which is more likely on the basis of civic nationalism and sovereignty than xenophobia.

Overall, then, it is clear that there are ideological positions over Europe being mobilized within national party systems, but core Euroscepticism is limited to nonmember Switzerland, where it is an issue for competition in referendum campaigns, and an EU member, Britain, which is exceptional in retaining elite divisions and competition over Europe since its entry to the project. However, the possibility of the British experience transferring across the Channel remains unlikely, even if Eurocriticism is increasing. First, growing criticism of Europe is not coterminous with emerging Euroscepticism. Significantly high Eurocriticisms among Dutch center parties in our sample were actually indicative of a normalized Europhile party politics. Criticizing Europe can be part of its normalization and integration within national politics. Second, few European conservative parties have the same degree of commitment to neoliberalism as the British, who more often than not draw inspiration from across the Atlantic. In this sense, perhaps Britain's party elites' "deep cultural roots" are rooted in different political soil than those of continental Europe, which goes some way to explaining their exceptional behavior.

PART V

CONCLUSION

11

What Kind of Europeanized Public Politics?

Paul Statham

From the outset, the aim in conducting this research was to address the unanswered questions and myths about the emergence and performance of a European public sphere by recourse to systematic empirical evidence. To examine the impact of European integration on public debate, our research effort was necessarily substantial in size and wide ranging across countries, policies, actors, time, and different media. This concluding chapter synthesizes the main findings on the transformation of political communication into a narrative covering where we have come from, what form of Europeanized public politics has emerged, and what consequences this holds for democratic performance.

The first section outlines a road map for an emergent European public sphere by defining a conceptual space for the possible routes that may have been taken after the erosion of the "permissive consensus." This draws from the historical-theoretical discussion of the European public sphere and its conceptual definition, specification, and operationalization (see Chapters 1 and 2), to specify four possible paths to a Europeanized public politics. It provides an interpretive framework for synthesizing the overall findings. The subsequent sections discuss the empirical findings on the visibility of, inclusiveness of, and contestation over European public politics, respectively. This provides our answer to the question: What kind of Europeanized public politics has emerged? Finally, the chapter draws overall lessons from our collaborative study in relation to important recent developments, to propose a thesis for public legitimacy that sustained European politics prior to the failure of the European Constitution in 2005, and to speculate about the most realistic way forward for mediated politics afterward.

WHICH ROAD TO EUROPEANIZED PUBLIC POLITICS?

These days, most people agree about the need for a European public sphere in response to advancing institutional integration. However, scholars and politicians arrive at this common conclusion by applying different normative and empirical standards for democratic and media performance. Mapping out this range of different perspectives allows us to gain insight into the different understandings of, and disputes over, what constitutes an adequate Europeanized public politics. Moreover, it provides a road map for interpreting our own empirical findings on the actual development of the European public sphere, in relation to where it has come from and where it might possibly go to.

To design this map of public sphere development, we use two analytic dimensions that are central to this study: the public *visibility* and *inclusiveness* of European policy decision making. First, a necessary condition for a public sphere to exist at all in a meaningful sense is that the decision-making process is made sufficiently and adequately visible to citizens. This occurs primarily through mass media communication. Second, the public legitimacy of decision making depends on whether citizens and civil society organizations are adequately included and empowered to voice their preferences in the policy process. At stake here are the channels of access between the polity and citizens to represent and include the popular will. The primary mechanisms are political party representation and collective action. By combining the two dimensions, the degree of public visibility and the degree of public inclusiveness of European policy making, we arrive at four possible types of *Europeanized public politics*.

Figure 11.1 shows a two-by-two model depicting a conceptual space for four ideal types of Europeanized public politics: executive bargaining, corporatist interest group politics, elite-dominated public politics, and inclusive public politics. Moving from top to bottom, European decision making becomes more mediated and publicly *visible*. Positions on the vertical axis are an output of the mass media system. Obviously, media performance in giving attention to the European level of actors, issues, and policies is crucial here. Positions on the horizontal axis are an output of the political system, in particular the structure of political opportunities for gaining access to the multilevel European polity. Moving from left to right, European policy decision making becomes less dominated by executive, state, and party elites and more *inclusive* of collective action by actors from civil society and social movements. All liberal democracies have party systems representing citizens. Therefore, we assume the European policy process to be more inclusive, the more it additionally provides open access for, and responsiveness to, collective actors from civil society.[1] At stake here is democratic performance of the polity. A third analytic dimension *contestation* over Europe derives from the degree of visibility and inclusiveness. The more publicly visible the European level of politics becomes, the more it is likely to

[1] The difference between the left and right sides of Figure 11.1 has similarities to the distinction by Ferree et al. (2002a, Chapter 10) between *elite dominance* – restricted access, top down, representative – and *popular inclusiveness* – open, egalitarian, public participatory – norms for types of public sphere. For them, the elite dominance public sphere is drawn from classical representative liberal theory (e.g., Schumpeter 1942), and the popular inclusiveness sphere is drawn from participatory liberal and discursive traditions (e.g., Barber 1984; Habermas 1984), respectively.

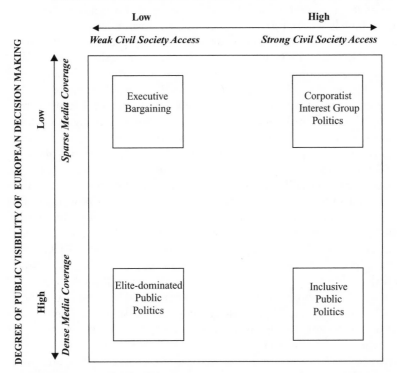

DEGREE OF PUBLIC INCLUSIVENESS OF EUROPEAN DECISION MAKING

FIGURE 11.1. A two-dimensional conceptual space for types of Europeanized public politics.

be subject to party competition and challenges by civil society organizations in the public domain. Thus increasing visibility is likely to lead to an increasing contestation over Europeanized public politics mobilized by demands for more inclusion. If realized, these mutually reinforcing dynamics of increasing visibility, political contention, and demands for inclusion could lead to an inclusive Europeanized public politics, which is shown in the bottom-right corner of Figure 11.1.

Although the ideal types in Figure 11.1 do not exist in pure form in the real world, this conceptual space provides a heuristic framework for bringing our findings together, to answer what type of Europeanized public politics has emerged. The distinctions serve to guide different expectations for how the components of a European public sphere – policy makers, citizens, parties, interest groups, social movements, and mass media – work effectively. It is first necessary, however, to flesh out the four possibilities for Europeanized public politics.

The logical starting point is *executive bargaining*, shown in the top-left corner of Figure 11.1, where European policy making has low public visibility and low civil society inclusion. Here European decision making is not public: It proceeds in the elite-dominated world of political institutions and state bureaucracies, largely without party competition, without collective action, and away from the media spotlight. This situation closely approximates Europe's "permissive consensus" era from the early 1950s to the late 1980s. In the immediate postwar period and for a considerable time afterward, European integration was neither politically salient, contested, nor publicly visible in the participating countries. State elites were largely free to act on behalf of the people. Europe-building took on a functional logic orchestrated by state elites and bureaucracies as a series of common foreign policy acts. European integration was driven by a politics of interstate diplomacy as national and the emerging European-level political elites built Europe in the absence of Europeans. Citizens were not called on to directly ratify the international treaties through which integration advanced and European institutions' powers grew.[2] Major left and right political parties supported the project, saving competition for domestic affairs. Before 1979, Europeans were not called on to vote for a European Parliament. When it came on the scene, the European Parliament remained an impotent talking-shop that Europeans could hardly see or hear, but nor did they show any desire to do so. If at all, national media reported Europe through a lens of foreign affairs and international relations. As Albert Weale puts it (2005, p. 2), "For most citizens, for most of the time while integration was occurring, Europe was merely a geographical expression."

In this permissive consensus era, the European Commission and its bureaucracy established itself as a supranational actor in the interstate game adopting federalist aspirations. However, the closest contact of the European elite to people came through its Eurobarometer opinion polling, which served as an ersatz indicator for public preferences and as a quasi-test to see whether Europe's citizens had reached a stage of evolution from which they could appreciate the benefits bestowed on them from on high. The Eurobarometer was the EU-level technocratic solution *par excellence* to Europe's missing public. Paradoxically, policy makers at the supranational level started to act as if citizens with national loyalties no longer existed, whereas the citizens of member states acted as if the European level of politics and administration had not come into being. The more evident and irreversible the substantive impact of European policy decision making became, however, the more this contradiction came to the fore as a political issue. Only then did talk of "democratic deficits" begin.

It should be pointed out, however, that there are still those in academia, the so-called intergovernmentalists, for whom Europe has "no deficit" (see, especially, Moravcsik 2002) and is still largely located conceptually in the top-left hand corner of Figure 11.1. These scholars see the European Union principally

---

[2] The exceptions are cases of national referenda in which countries contemplated joining or leaving the common project, for example, Denmark and Ireland in 1972 and the United Kingdom in 1975. Even in these cases, however, the peoples of existing member countries were not asked to directly ratify the inclusion of potential newcomers.

as an intergovernmental organization in which national governments have decided to pool their sovereignty in a limited number of policy fields to gain mutual benefits. For them, a European public sphere is unnecessary because European Union institutions derive their political legitimacy from nationally elected governments that, for the most part, shape European policy decisions. The EU has no "democratic deficit," since citizens, if they wish, can vote out governments in national elections. In this view, national political elites and parties dominate the public sphere while the media remain relatively inattentive to the European level.

Moving across the top of Figure 11.1, from left to right, we see that another possible development is the inclusion of collective actors from civil society in the European policy-making process, but without this receiving media attention. This takes us toward a situation of *corporatist interest group politics*. Indeed, an important growth area within the European multilevel system of administration has been the inclusion of lobby groups. In the policy fields that are the most Europeanized – for example, environment, agriculture, trade – there has been a proliferation of lobby groups in Brussels and in national capitals (see contributions to Featherstone and Radaelli 2003; Greenwood and Aspinwall 1998). For some researchers, this increasing access to the European-level policy process and insider treatment for specialist collective actors constitutes the emergence of a latent or restricted semipublic sphere (Lahusen 2004). In this optimistic view, the Brussels cocktail circuit and its national-level counterparts serve as forums for lobbyists and social movements to adapt, gain influence, and deliberate within the European policy game. Europe's lack of visibility to the general public is not considered an obstacle to collective actors mobilizing on behalf of groups who are directly affected by European policy decisions.

Against such optimism, however, it is well documented in social movement research that weak and marginal collective actors often need media attention and a public discourse to exert credible and effective pressure on an issue (e.g., Ferree et al. 2002a; Gamson and Modigliani 1989). Without media attention for Europe, this route is effectively blocked for many actors. By contrast, the absence of public visibility may be less harmful to, and even sometimes even beneficial for, the efforts of more powerful lobbies. So far, the interest groups and NGO sectors that have mushroomed in Brussels strongly represent powerful institutional interests, such as state quangos (quasi-autonomous nongovernmental organizations), multinational business corporations, professions, and labor unions (Aspinwall and Greenwood 1998). In addition, plenty of think tanks and consultants are on hand to be co-opted and supply technocratic expertise. There is relative little "demos" in evidence. Sabine Saurugger's (2008, p. 1274) review of empirical research conducted on European interest groups concludes that "the elite characteristics of these actors question their capacity to increase democratic legitimacy." For the most part, efforts by the supranational European administration to introduce a wider civil society inclusion, or to enhance the say of weaker groups, have been initiated from the top down as a form of co-optation. For example, in the migration field, European migrants' organizations are unrepresentative of migrant communities, undemocratic in structure, and almost wholly dependent on EU subsidies for their survival (Guiraudon 2001; Koopmans et al. 2005). Overall, it seems that there are barriers to overcoming a civil society participation deficit, when European policy making lacks public visibility. Nonetheless, Europeanized corporatist interest groups politics remains a possible path of development.

Starting again from Europe's permissive consensus, but moving down the left-hand side of Figure 11.1, we reach a situation of *elite-dominated public politics*. How can European executive bargaining transform to this? An obvious answer is that increasing media attention for the European level erodes the basis for a permissive consensus by bringing European actors, policies, and issues more centrally into public view, that is, mediatization, leading to a public politicization of Europe. Another answer, related to this development, is that as the EU takes on more competences, adopts features of a supranational polity, and increasingly wields powers that directly affect citizens, the substance of European politics also changes from the permissive consensus era. This latter point is the stance of the critics of intergovernmentalism within political science (see especially Hix 2008). For these authors the EU is already a supranational polity whose decisions directly affect citizens, but without providing adequate institutional channels for their representation. In this view, the European Commission's lack of direct accountability combined with the European Parliament's limited powers constitutes a "democratic deficit." However, this is an institutional "democratic deficit" located in the EU's inadequate representative political architecture, in particular its inability to replicate anything resembling a national party system on the European level.

For Simon Hix (2008), the solution is an institutional fix for the European Union polity, and in particular a European Parliament worthy of the name, in which parties vote along ideological rather than national lines. Surprisingly, however, Hix makes no systematic reference to mass-mediated communication as a possible mechanism for enhancing the transparency of European policy decision making to citizens. If mentioned at all, it is assumed that media coverage will simply result automatically from the implementation of institutional reforms. There is little consideration of possible barriers to a transnational European mediated politics from the supply side of the media system, or, alternatively, of the possibility that the media is sufficiently autonomous to provide attention to European politics before it is institutionally fixed. Hix's concluding chapter to *What's Wrong with the European Union and How to Fix It* contains only one short reference to the media, stating that (2008, p. 185), "More [EU-level] open contestation and coalition-building would increase the stakes, which in turn would also encourage the media to cover the Brussels soap opera for the first time." Furthermore, his shopping list of reforms (2008, p. 186) makes no direct reference to a central role for the media. Against this, we saw earlier that the media already cover the "Brussels soap opera" where the EU is powerful (Chapter 3). Thus we do not have to wait for this proposed EU-level political institutional fix for the media to enter the equation; the media have already put themselves on the Brussels and Strasbourg scene. Moreover, adequate media attention and public visibility for the competing elites and political parties – at either the national level or EU level or both – is an essential ingredient for an effective representative politics. If voters cannot see executive and party elite stances over European policy making to make informed electoral choices, then democratic control cannot be exerted adequately.

In the situation of Europeanized elite-dominated public politics, legitimacy is based on citizens' trust in effective representation by political elites and parties. The politicization of elite decision making and its public visibility depends to a large extent on the degree to which parties compete over European policy issues. Media attention largely follows the agenda set by elites and parties, with high levels of party competition generating high levels of coverage. Hence, the public sphere is dominated by political elite actors. The news is full of political elites – national governments, EU institutions and administrations, national political parties, Europarties, and the occasional expert or technocrat – and their claims and counterclaims over European policy decisions. Civil society inclusion is underdeveloped, with elites co-opting professional groups and interest groups mostly for their technical expertise, not to widen participation. The media's role remains largely descriptive, limited to naming and shaming incompetent and corrupt political elites and supplying sufficient information for the electorate to make informed choices. In this view, media interpretation and opinion leading can distort issues and choices by shifting the focus away from the opinions of competing elites. Generally, the citizen is passive and minimally informed under these conditions. European policy making is mediated through institutionalized political channels – voting and co-opted lobbying – with the public sphere largely downgraded to a monitoring function. In a sense, this type of Europeanized public politics has a public sphere "lite."

Finally, the participatory potential of a mass-mediated public discourse and enhanced opportunities for collective action are more fully realized as we move across to the bottom-right corner of Figure 11.1 to an *inclusive Europeanized public politics*.[3] In this stance, which is depicted in the related positions on Europeanized contentious politics and social movements (see, especially, Imig and Tarrow 2001a) and a European political public sphere (see, especially, Habermas 2006), more public participation is required than party representation to overcome Europe's democratic deficit. This can come in the form of a deliberative European policy discourse, in which people use mass media reporting to form and mobilize opinions. In Jürgen Habermas' words (2006, p. 102), "the democratic deficit can only be redressed by the simultaneous emergence of a European political public sphere in which the democratic process is embedded. In complex societies, democratic legitimacy results from the interplay of institutionalised consultation and decision-making processes, on the one hand, and informal public processes of communication in which

---

[3] This could also result from an increasing mediatization and public politicization of the corporatist interest group variant, as one moves down the right-hand side of Figure 11.1.

opinions are formed via the mass media, on the other." It can also come from the increasing participation of "contentious Europeans" in the European policy process, the bottom-up mobilization of social movements to challenge and engage with the state and institutional power holders of the multilevel polity (Tarrow 2001, pp. 250–251): "Democracy, if it evolves at the European level will grow out of the capacity of social movements, public interest groups, and other non-state actors to make alliances with combinations of national government actors, supranational institutions, and with each other in Europe's increasingly composite polity."

In this view, the mass-mediated public discourse is a vital field for interaction that extends politics from institutional arenas to wider public forums and provides opportunities for the mobilization of collective actors and social movements, allowing alternative viewpoints to be heard. Mediated political discourse becomes an interface for deliberative exchanges between policy makers and their challengers, under the gaze of an informed and active public. Mass media discourse is seen as a public forum. It allows individual members of the public to see, be informed about, and have access to European policy decision-making processes. From one side, it gives policy makers the chance to respond to expressed public preferences, and from the other, it gives collective actors, including marginal ones, the chance to participate in public policy debates and voice alternative viewpoints. Through all this Europeanized politics becomes legitimate. In this perspective, the media's role is to represent all significant interests in society, facilitate their participation in the public domain, and enable them to contribute to public debate and have an input in the framing of public policy. In some cases, the media actively open and expand the public discourse and participation that is vital to democracy, even becoming advocates. As a result, the public sphere is populated by a wide range of state and civil society actors, including those from the EU level and other European countries, as well as domestic ones. When relevant, policies, issues, and discourses have Europeanized frames of reference. Through this, the seeds are sown for an active European citizenry to identify with a common European political culture, even if this does not require becoming a culturally thick "European," but a secondary form of identification, that is, Europe as an "identity-lite" (Risse 2003, forthcoming).[4] As Imig and Tarrow suggest (2001, p. 23), "it is the struggle over European policy making that may, in the long run, create European citizens."

So far, the section has characterized a conceptual space for types of Europeanized public politics. This analytic tool allows us to distinguish between competing theoretical positions and to construct possible trajectories for

---

[4] Cris Shore's cultural analysis of the EU underlines the so-far weak impact of supranational efforts to build a common culture and identity, concluding (2000, p. 222) that "The European Commission has invented a new repertoire of 'post-nationalist' symbols, but these are pale imitations of nationalist iconography and have so far failed to win for the EU the title deeds upon which national loyalties and allegiances are claimed."

European public sphere development. The following sections evaluate the main empirical findings from our book by referring to this model.

A VISIBLE EUROPEANIZED PUBLIC POLITICS?

Our first set of empirical findings answer questions about European public sphere development by examining what is visible in media discourse: Is there sufficient political communication and interaction across borders and political levels? What are the prevalent forms of Europeanized communication? Does Europeanized communication vary across countries and policy fields, and is it growing over time? How do journalists perform in making Europe visible? This cumulative evidence on the public visibility of the European political level shows how far we have moved down the conceptual space of Figure 11.1, from top to bottom. Perhaps the single most significant finding is that the European level *is* publicly visible in fields in which it is influential. In policy fields in which the EU level has competences, EU actors appear frequently as speakers or as addressees of claims, and issues are frequently discussed in a European frame of reference. At least when viewed quantitatively, this contradicts the often heard thesis that the EU's perceived democratic deficit derives from a "communication deficit." Against the claim that European-level politics remains invisible and unmediated – see, for example, the position of Hix (2008) discussed earlier – our findings clearly show that important Europeanization trends are evident and that these serve to make European politics visible to general publics.[5] Importantly, this means that European public sphere development has moved significantly toward the bottom half of Figure 11.1, where the European level receives relatively denser media coverage.

In support of the opportunity approach advanced by this project, we find that the degree and form of this emergent Europeanized political communication is best explained by the structures of access provided by the multilevel polity (Chapter 3). Crucially, the clearest determinant for the Europeanization of claim making is the extent to which competences in a policy field have shifted up to the EU level. Thus, EU-level actors have a visible say in European integration, monetary politics, and agriculture debates, in which decision making is more supranational, but very little in debates over immigration, troop deployment, education, and pensions, in which national sovereignty remains powerful.

Distinct from communication flows that remain within the national domestic public sphere, we identified vertical and horizontal Europeanized communication. These indicate the degree of openness or closure of a national public sphere, up to the EU level (vertical), or across to other European countries (horizontal). Here we find significant evidence for the emergence of vertical Europeanized communication flows. The general rule is that the more a policy

---

[5] Hans-Jörg Trenz's media contents analysis of eleven quality newspapers from six EU countries in 2000 supports the general idea that Europe has a significant visibility in national media. He finds that (2004, p. 311) "one out of three articles in a European quality newspaper makes political reference to Europe, and one out of five directly reports on at least on European issue."

field is supranationalized, the more it has a debate including the EU level, and the more vertical communication flows occur. For the emergence of horizontal communication flows across countries, the story is less straightforward. As the opportunity approach leads us to expect, the more intergovernmentalized policy fields – European integration, troop deployment, immigration – do indeed host a significant presence of claim makers from other European countries. However, the supranationalized fields – monetary, agriculture – also witness similar levels of claim making from other European countries. This is most likely due to the increasing cross-national interdependence that results from common supranational institutions and approaches to policy making. Turning to trends across time, we find that the visibility of EU actors has grown markedly as integration has advanced. For example, in monetary policy it has trebled. However, the increase in vertical communication flows is not matched by increased horizontal flows, as the frequency of claims by actors from foreign European countries remains stable across the period.

Overall, domestic claim making remains prominent. It seems that the deepening of European integration has led to a rise in vertical Europeanization within national public spheres but not to increased horizontal flows. Detailed analyses show that the total amount of attention for Europe remains at a relatively stable level, but the form of communication transforms in a way that makes the EU level more present. We are not witnessing a European transnationalization of claim making to an extent in which mutual interpenetration across countries is transforming national public spheres potentially into a common entity. Instead, the change is limited to incorporating supranational EU-level politics within national debates. Rather than Europe supplanting domestic claim making, or increasing mutual cross-national observation, it seems that news about "Europe as foreign affairs" is replaced by "EU-level news."

These general trends largely hold across countries, which again supports the idea that the transformation of political communication has been shaped by the degree and form of competences transferred to the EU. However, it is still possible to divide experiences into distinct camps. Among the six EU members, the dividing line is between Germany, France, the Netherlands, Spain, and Italy, who experience significant amounts of the Europeanization we outlined earlier, and Britain, which is highly exceptional and exhibits much weaker trends and forms. The French lead the way among the five, whereas the Brits stand alone. British debates give the lowest attention to EU and foreign European actors, and supranational claim making (EU on EU) is less present than elsewhere. However, the British do not ignore Europe; they just discuss it differently. British claim making is Europeanized in a very parochial way. National actors give high attention to European issues, but as a national domestic affair. Europe is a contested issue within British politics, but the debate is relatively closed and noninclusive toward other Europeans.[6] The Swiss trajectory is also distinct, reflecting its status as a non-EU member with national debates over whether to

---

[6] For a detailed analysis of the specificity of the British case, see Statham and Gray (2005); for a comparison with France, see Statham (2007a).

join the club. Swiss debates make the EU level visible and give high attention to European countries, but unsurprisingly produce fewer substantive vertical flows up to the EU level.

Interestingly, one of the few other large-scale empirical attempts to study the Europeanization of media discourse, led by Bernhard Peters and others (Peters et al. 2005; Wessler et al. 2008; Sifft et al. 2007), produces similar general findings. On the vertical dimension, their impressive study finds a robust increase in articles where EU policy making is the major topic from 1982 to 2003, from 2% to 9%. In addition, the share of articles mentioning EU institutions more than doubles, reaching 29%, of which 14% have EU institutions as their main topic (Sifft et al. 2007, p. 136). On the horizontal dimension, they find that the share of speakers from other European countries remains relatively stable at about 17%. France leads the way, with the United Kingdom hanging back.

It is necessary to distinguish our position from that of the Peters group, however, because in contrast to us they interpret their broadly similar findings as evidence for a public sphere "deficit." We consider their claims for a deficit to be overstated. A source of their pessimism comes from setting the normative barrier for finding adequate Europeanization very high indeed. They define two variants of Europeanization: a weaker one, labeled "monitoring governance," that rests on the public visibility of the EU (vertical); and a stronger one, labeled "discursive integration," that is based on "a more profound transformation characterised by intensified discursive interaction among EU Member States and the emergence of a *common European discourse*" (Sifft et al. 2007, p. 130; emphasis in the original), in which (horizontal) "discursive exchanges" between Europeans would lead to a "collective identification" carried by a sense of belonging to a common European discourse. A problem here is that it is not the case that horizontal exchanges necessarily imply a stronger variant of Europeanization. The adequacy of vertical versus horizontal linkages depends on what the institutional architecture of the EU looks like: If it is more supranational, then it requires more vertical communication; if it is more intergovernmental, then it requires more horizontal. In addition, crucially, the Europeanization of public discourse is necessary in those instances in which policy decision-making power is Europeanized, not generally across the board. A further problem is that the normative standard applied is so high that even positive findings fall short. Effectively, the requirement for "discursive integration" raises the standards to Habermas' ideal for the emergence of a common transnational "community of communication" (see Sifft et al. 2007, p. 131), or approaching what we call an inclusive Europeanized public politics. Since political discourses that remain national struggle to reach such standards, it is unfair to place the bar so high for emerging Europeanized ones. Also the search for Habermasian ideal-type communication in real newspapers' discourses is always likely to lead to negative findings. We prefer a more realist approach for evaluating discourses in relation to their relevant institutional frameworks.

A further validation for our general view on the degree and form of the emergent field of Europeanized communications is that it is corroborated by our study of another medium, the Internet (Chapter 7). The European public debate thrown up by Internet search engines and hyperlinks is largely the same one we see when we open newspapers. First, search engines structure the supply of political information to Internet users looking for it, so that one-seventh of claim makers come from the EU and one-twelfth from other European countries. Again, like in conventional news, the EU is significantly visible, with vertical forms more evident than horizontal ones. Second, on whether Web sites' hyperlinks lead us to a political level above or beyond the host nation-state, we find that European supranational actors receive strong links, which contrasts to strikingly little horizontal linking. Hyperlinks direct users much more upward to the EU than across to neighboring EU countries. Once more, this triangulates our finding from the newspaper analysis that vertical Europeanization trends appear more robust than horizontal ones. Overall, the Internet study shows that the Internet is no more a motor for transnationalization than conventional media. This goes against the common myth and self-image of the World Wide Web as an alternative forum that allows individual members of the public access to a political world that is less directly shaped by conventional institutional mass media. On the contrary, one of the reasons why Europeanization on the Web looks like Europeanization in the press is the strong presence of broadcasters and online versions of newspapers.

Furthermore, the distinction between the exceptional British experience and that of other EU members plus the Swiss distinction as a non-EU member were corroborated by our findings on framing (Chapter 8) and on journalists' claim making in editorials and commentaries (Chapter 6). The salient ways of viewing and interpreting the political world appear to be broadly similar across our countries, indicating the potential for common shared understandings, except in Britain, where European integration is framed from the perspective of national interest. The study of the media's own claim making through editorials underlines this British exceptionalism. In the five continental EU countries, media commentating over European integration refers much more strongly to EU supranational actors and those from other EU states. The media's claim making opens up and geographically expands the European policy debate by inviting readers to include the EU, and other EU countries, in their perceptions of issues. It introduces multileveling and transnationalizing communicative linkages into the national story, leading to a more Europeanized elaboration. In these countries, commentators select issues that emphasize contributing to and shaping the form of integration, whether power within the EU should be more supranational or intergovernmental, and whether deepening integration or expanding the EU is a more pressing concern. Journalists emphasize a supranational EU and deepening integration as the important concerns. By contrast, British editorials depict European integration as a national domestic affair. This shrinks the scope of the European story to the competing activities of national domestic actors and brackets out the EU as a purposeful actor. Readers are encouraged to view European politics through a national lens. Topically, British commentators push EU intergovernmentalism and focus on expanding the EU to new members as a more pressing concern than deepening integration. British editorials also focus strongly on monetary and foreign policies, topics of less interest elsewhere, advocating the retention of policies based on national sovereignty over a common European approach. Finally, the Swiss case was different again. Press commentating in Switzerland focuses like Britain on national actors, but with opinion leading focusing overwhelmingly on the issue of joining the EU or not. Overall, our findings provide clear evidence that Britain's press stands in a discursive world apart from colleagues in the other EU member states. In this way the British press' opinion leading follows the same degrees and forms of exceptionalism that are apparent generally in British political debates.

How to explain these distinctions in trajectories for Europeanization, and especially British exceptionalism? One factor is that it appears that a country has greater incentives to maintain and extend common institutions, regulatory systems, and markets, the more its economy is dependent on intra-EU trade. Britain's relatively low dependency on EU trade is a factor in its politics – and its elites – standing back and weighing up the pros and cons of integration steps on a case-by-case basis. Low intra-EU trade also gives a clue for the relatively low Europeanization trends in Italy, a founder EU member. By contrast, relatively high Swiss – horizontal – Europeanization can be derived from Switzerland's high dependency on markets in the European region. This type of argument fits with the general stance advanced by Neil Fligstein, like ours inspired by Karl W. Deutsch (see Chapter 2), that social communication is generated across national borders through increasing economic interaction, which has "woven new interests and interdependence together to cause people in governments, those involved in businesses, and ordinary citizens to recognize that they need each other" (2008, p. 3). Another related explanatory factor is more explicitly political. It seems that the degree of formal European integration and elite commitment to it matters. Among our EU members this places Britain, with its history of opt-outs from substantive integrative common policies, in contrast to the other five, among whom France, Germany, and the Netherlands have strongly pioneered a deeper EU.

For France and Germany, European integration was a way to build and maintain their regional influence in the postwar period. The German nation rebuilt itself especially economically, but also politically, through European integration, after the catastrophe of the Nazi period and WWII. France obscured its Vichy shame and imperial decline by salvaging national pride in taking a political lead in Europe. Compare this to Britain, which was pardoned the need for immediate national self-reflection as a victor in 1945. Europe only mattered later, in the 1970s, as an opt-in designed to offset severe domestic economic failure, after the harsh reality of postcolonial decline and national delusions of grandeur hit home. Europe was the only option for Britain, but it has remained only an option ever since. Over time these distinct visions and trajectories for Europeanization have been institutionalized and subject to dynamics of "path dependency" (Pierson 2000, 2004) within national politics, especially among elites, with the result that the gap between the British and the other EU member states has become mutually reinforcing. This makes it unlikely that the British will become unexceptional over Europe in the near future, but it also means that British parochialism and scepticism do not serve as blueprints for the other EU countries, even if their politics starts to generate more contentious European public debates.

So if Europe is now visible, then what of the performance of the journalists who make it so? Media performance is central to any debate about a European public sphere, since media actors are entrusted with making the European level visible and accessible to citizens. Overall, our findings on journalism (Chapter 5) indicate that the press operates within a difficult context for providing political information over Europe, but has nonetheless adapted to take on this role effectively. There is a common experience of adapting to the challenges of reporting the European level. Journalists of all types and from all countries identified many similar problems. The restricted market generated by low readership demand plus the dominance of information flows from national sources do not provide an encouraging context. We can add to this the EU's own feeble public communication efforts – at least according to journalists – to address its citizens through the primary medium that people use to engage with politics, that is, mass media. The lack of news values of technocratic EU politics is a factor, too. Journalists face high barriers to make Europe news. Nonetheless, Europe is visible. This implies that the members of the press have not been pushed by external factors, but have largely taken the initiative to incorporate Europe within their news coverage. Mostly, journalists see their goals to be raising awareness, informing, and opening up spaces for Europe within their readerships' understandings. Most of their advocacy is strongly educational, rather than partisan or ideological. They largely follow and represent the opinions expressed by political actors. This does not mean that journalists are reticent in mobilizing opinions but rather that their primary aim is strongly informative. Indeed, public knowledge deficits and professional duty motivate journalists to cover Europe, not that they have a political ax to grind.

The findings summarized in this section have identified that the mass media – print and the Internet – can be seen as performing adequately in giving public visibility to the EU level where it holds power, and where it is most important. Actors have responded and adapted to advancing European integration, and the institutional form and degree of this integration process have importantly shaped how, where, and how much Europeanized political communication has emerged. This has carried us into an era of mediated Europeanized public politics (shown in the bottom half of Figure 11.1). Thus, whatever the basis of the European Union's perceived democratic deficit, it is no longer caused primarily by a lack of public communication.

AN INCLUSIVE EUROPEANIZED PUBLIC POLITICS?

While the public sphere dimension of Europe's perceived democratic deficit is not that Europe is insufficiently visible, it could result from qualitative aspects regarding who has a voice in Europeanized political communication. A second set of empirical findings addresses the important question of who participates in Europeanized public debates: Who wins and loses in discursive power as a result of advancing European integration? The question of inclusiveness turns the focus onto collective actors. It should be noted that an advantage of the claim-making method over its content analysis rivals – such as, those by Trenz (2004) and by Sifft et al. (2007) – is precisely that it allows a sophisticated examination of the relationships of collective actors on the basis of their claim making in public discourses. The degree of inclusiveness shows whether we are situated more toward an elite-dominated Europeanized public politics (bottom-left corner of Figure 11.1), or an inclusive Europeanized public politics (bottom-right corner).

The European Union is a governance structure with unique characteristics combining a variety of authoritative institutions at supranational, national, and subnational levels of decision making. This presents a transformed structure of political opportunities for collective actors to attempt to gain access to and influence policy decision making. European integration inevitably implies a redistribution of power, but it is disputed whether this favors or disadvantages civil society actors compared with those from the state and executive. So, the question is this: Does advancing European integration lead to public debates that are more or less inclusive than national ones?

The findings on the inclusiveness of Europeanized public debates are unequivocal (Chapter 4). Strikingly, the only actors who are systematically overrepresented in Europeanized claim making are government and executive actors. Executive actors mobilize about one-half of Europeanized political communication, compared to one-third in domestic debates. This holds across forms of Europeanized claim making. Generally, it seems that Europeanization enhances the discursive power of the already powerful: national and EU executive elites. The evidence strongly supports the idea that after the permissive consensus, we are well on the road to an elite-dominated Europeanized public sphere (Figure 11.1).

In contrast to executive actors, legislative and political party actors are less well represented in Europeanized discourses. At face value this seems problematic from the view of democratic legitimacy. Apart from the executive, media actors are the only ones overrepresented in Europeanized compared to national debates. This shows that the media are ahead of the game compared to other nonstate actors in adapting to raise a European voice, and it again goes against the idea that the media have little to say about Europe. The big-time losers are civil society actors, who mobilize only one-eighth of Europeanized claims, compared to more than one-third nationally. Even among civil society actors, less resourceful groups, such as consumers' associations, environmentalists, and pensioners, are even more strongly underrepresented in Europeanized public politics than the powerful interest groups representing capital and labor. Against the view that the supranational level offers opportunities through legitimating discourses and norms for NGOs to enhance their voice, we find no indication that Europeanization has been accompanied by inclusiveness for civil society actors that even closely approximates their empowerment in national discourses. This relative exclusion of civil society is especially acute among actors from the EU level. For example, claims by European Commission President Romano Prodi were present in the public debate 2.5 times more often than claims by the whole of the EU-level civil society combined. The virtual invisibility and lack of representation of EU civil society actors in public discourses is problematic from the viewpoint of democratic legitimacy.

It is often claimed that civil society actors may circumvent the restrictions of conventional media by mobilizing claims, interacting, and networking on the World Wide Web. However, our Internet findings on inclusiveness once more replicate those from the newspaper discourses (Chapter 7). Thus NGOs and social movements make about one-tenth of claims on Web sites supplied by search engines, compared with two-thirds by state and party actors. State and party actors are 2.5 times more likely to receive hyperlinks from other actors than NGOs and social movements. EU-level civil society actors are extraordinarily marginal and isolated in this virtual network of self-selected organizational links. This provides strong counterevidence against a possible interpretation of our newspaper-based data, that which attributes the low presence of EU-level civil society groups to the fact that they do not need to mobilize media attention because they are well integrated in nonpublic and semipublic forms of EU-level policy deliberation. If this were correct, one would expect it to be reflected in the fact that national-level actors provide frequent hyperlinks to these organizations. However, while actors from the national level underline the importance of European executive and legislative institutions by providing dense network links to them, they virtually ignore European civil society groups. This is true even for national-level NGOs, which do not seem to attribute much importance to their supposed European-level representatives. This is not because of a general lack of interest in transnational NGOs, as national actors do provide frequent links to NGOs with a global reach beyond Europe. European civil society is therefore not only marginal compared with national civil society and with the European executive, but also compared with globally operating NGOs. From these corroborated findings, we surmise that the substance of the European Union's public sphere "deficit" consists in the overdomination by elite actors of Europeanized debates.

So far, we have assumed that the publicly visible world is what matters. However, the study also looks at collective actors' action repertoires to access different levels of the European polity, and whether they use insider or public-oriented strategies to gain influence (Chapter 9). The analysis of collective actors strongly supports the view on elite dominance of Europeanized public politics. An important finding is that the degree of Europeanization of action repertoires is mainly determined by institutional factors and by an actor's power. To gain access to the EU-level policy process, it seems that first you must be able to access and be powerful in the national one. Of course, this means that state elites who hold power nationally have the key to the door of the EU level. This national elite dominance also importantly shapes the opportunities for other actors to gain access. There are especially high barriers against the inclusion of actors who are already weak at the national level. The evidence goes completely against the thesis that "boomerang effects" (Keck and Sikkink 1998) exist, whereby weaker actors, such as SMOs, enhance their power nationally by accessing a political level above the nation-state.

On the contrary, it seems that powerful actors are advantaged at the EU level, even more than they are nationally, and importantly, *because* they are dominant nationally. Overall, the new opportunities at the EU level are opening up mainly for the select few, that is, powerful national state actors. This crucial finding confirms those of the claim-making analyses of news discourse and Internet discourse, that is, that Europeanization leads to an empowerment of the already powerful national elites.[7]

We also see that powerful elites are not shy about entering the public domain. Our findings lend support to the mediatization thesis, because powerful actors heavily use public-oriented strategies, even though they do not consider them to be crucial in gaining access and influence. Against this, weak actors, such as social movement organizations, consider public strategies to be very important for them, but they only use them if they consider it to be highly necessary. This low usage of public strategies by weak actors is due to their limited resources. The weak, it seems, face a trade-off between the high costs of going public and the dependency of going through insider channels. In contrast, the powerful state actors are dominant in the insider policy domain, but they are also able to swamp the public domain, even if this is viewed as of secondary importance.

This dominance of state power within policy communities is further underlined by additional findings that use the same data set. Hanspeter Kriesi, Silke Adam, and Margit Jochum from our team undertook a block-model network analysis to examine the compositions of domestic coalitions across three policy fields – EU, immigration, and agriculture – for our seven countries. On the actor composition and power of blocks, they find that (2006a, p. 354), "Independently of the policy domain or the country, the first block is typically dominated by state actors and it is typically the most powerful block. Roughly two-thirds of the actors in the first block are state actors, and their average power is almost twice as high as that of the next two blocks. The second block is dominated by parties, but it also includes an important share of state actors. The remaining two blocks are typically composed of interest groups and SMOs-NGOs – with the former dominating the third block and the latter dominating the fourth block." This reinforces the evidence for dominant executive power in public policy making. Regarding the shift of power above the nation-state, they find that a few supranational EU elite actors have become the most important actors in their specific policy fields, but when viewed more widely, national elites also come into play as power holders. Again, this underlines the prominence of national and EU-level elites.

---

[7] Tanja Börzel's (2006) study of actors' attempts to gain influence by using the EU-level judiciary draws similar conclusions, from a completely different approach and method.

Our findings make especially grim reading for social movements. It is clearly not the case that civil society actors are relatively invisible in mediated European policy discourse because their demands are met through insider channels. Their weakness is compounded in the insider policy world too. For SMOs, public strategies are vital for mobilizing a challenge because their institutional route to power is often blocked. However, their public-oriented action repertoires are not more elaborated than those of state actors. A plausible explanation for this is that the type of SMO that is able to survive in this political context is relatively powerless and depends almost entirely on its close contacts with powerful state actors to achieve any influence. In this view, Europeanization leads to a pattern of adaptation for social movements, where, on one side, some SMOs are largely co-opted clients dependent on national state or EU-level patronage, and, on the other, if they exist at all, the SMOs that mobilize an independent voice are extremely weak. For example, such tendencies have been observed in studies on the Europeanization of the promigrant NGO sector within the immigration policy field in Britain (Gray and Statham 2005; Statham and Geddes 2006). In an empirical study using data sets from this book, Della Porta and Caiani (2007b) confirm the weakness of SMOs and NGOs within Europeanization.

Generally, our study finds little evidence for social movements addressing Europe of the type commonly depicted in participatory theory (e.g., Habermas 2006). For example, Chapter 8 finds few such emergent frames from civil society. In Britain, there are some ideological anti-European SMOs that emerge to compete with pro-European SMOs over whether the country should join the Monetary Union or hold a referendum on the Constitutional Treaty. However, such movements are produced by the national context of elite divisions over Europe. They tend to be loose alliances that appear when a single issue arises and then wither away afterward.[8] In other countries, there are some cases of "critical Europeanist" SMOs that advocate an alternative path to Europeanization (Della Porta and Caiani 2007b). The findings here show, however, that their claims remain for the most part publicly inaudible and substantially lacking in power and influence compared to the policy elites they challenge.

The relative weakness of civil society, relative to elites within Europeanization processes, raises questions about the performance of media actors and their perceived role in adequately representing political debates (Chapter 5). Although we find the media to be an overrepresented voice in Europeanized

---

[8] On civil society claim making in Britain, using this book's data, see Statham and Gray (2005). Statham and Gray (2005, p. 71) find that pro- and anti-European campaign organizations account for 8.1% of claim making by British actors over Europe in the domestic public sphere. Virtually all other claim making by nonstate actors (which is 27% of all claim making) is mobilized by organized interests of capital and labor (employers and trade unions) and scientific and economic experts. Apart from the pro- and anti-European campaigns, there is virtually no sign of a "social movement" type of organization. For a detailed study on the European campaign movements in Britain, see the doctoral thesis by Emily Gray (2005) written within the broader context of this project.

debates, an active commentator, and strongly present in the Web discourse, we find very little evidence for journalists who feel motivated to initiate and lead an inclusive and deliberative public debate over Europe. They consider it the job of politicians to make a case for Europe and address any perceived democratic deficits. The journalism that has emerged seeks to prod general readerships into seeing Europeanized power, but it largely disseminates information about the political competition between elite actors over Europe – national governments, political parties, and EU institutions – and holds back from politicizing the cleavages itself. The media have taken up the difficult task of telling a story that its publics – at least according to journalists' perceptions of readership demand – are not particularly interested in hearing. This is a considerable achievement. Of course, media performance is regularly criticized by politicians and some academics. However, journalists can only mediate the political world that they are given. The strong elite dominance that our study shows is not an artefact of media reporting but an accurately drawn assessment by journalists of the current political reality of European multilevel governance, which is corroborated by our interviews with collective actors and the Internet study. There is nothing to suggest that journalists would be unable to adapt if politicians made European policy making more inclusive. Hence we consider that the democratic deficit in inclusiveness is a product of the political system, not the media system that largely follows it.

Overall, the imbalances we find on inclusiveness are problematic from the viewpoint of the democratic quality of public debates. Europe's public sphere deficit is one of gaining access. The onset of Europeanization has clearly enhanced executive discursive power, but without adequately including non-state actors and especially civil society actors. Actual European public sphere development remains a long way from an emergent civil society mobilization that would carry it at least some way from right to left across the bottom of Figure 11.1. Europeanization has led to an empowerment of the already powerful executive actors and an elite-dominated public politics.

A CONTESTED EUROPEANIZED PUBLIC POLITICS?

A third set of empirical findings addresses how actors evaluate and contest European integration and EU institutions. Is criticism of Europe increasing as integration advances? Does it vary across countries? What is the substance of this "Eurocriticism", and what interests does it represent? Are the winners and losers of Europeanization starting to contest its perceived outcomes?

Importantly, we find that the more decision-making power shifts to the European level for a policy field, or over time, the more attention for and criticism of the European Union rise (Chapters 3 and 4). In general, claim making remains supportive of the integration process across policy fields, but criticism of European institutions has become significantly more frequent as integration has advanced. It should be noted, however, that actors still criticize EU institutions less than their domestic ones. Furthermore, negative evaluations of Europe are not equivalent to Euroscepticism; in many cases they are demands for better performing EU institutions or a better form of integration, that is, a constructive or critical Europeanism (Chapter 10). Hence we interpret the increasing criticism as evidence for the "normalization" of the EU as a visible and powerful actor, one that is increasingly drawn into political debates and contested, both as a subject and object. The future of Europe is not under threat from a potential tidal wave of negative Euroscepticism, but increasing criticism and contestation is more a sign of political maturity that results from an increased visibility through mass mediation.

Across countries, we find a distinction between those which have experienced deeper and stronger Europeanization trends that are more favorable to the EU, and Britain, which has not and is more critical. France is Europe's clearest supporter; Germany and the Netherlands come out as critical supporters; but Britain stands alone as the undisputed Eurosceptic opponent. Thus British "path-dependent" exceptionalism not only consists in the parochial way Europe is discussed but is confirmed by a stronger oppositional propensity toward Europe. From our study, as the analysis of framing underlines (Chapter 8), France comes out as a "pace setter" at the vanguard of the EU bloc, whereas Britain is a clear "foot dragger" in the Europeanization stakes.[9] Given the elite dominance of Europeanized communication, it is clear that British elites view the European project differently from their EU counterparts, and that this has had an impact on Britain's exceptional trajectory in its relationship to European integration and the EU.[10] Even with increasing contestation, it is not at all likely that the continental European countries will "turn British." British elites are distinct. They have always measured themselves against colleagues and drawn inspiration from across the Atlantic, not the British Channel. Nothing demonstrated that alignment more clearly than the British Government's support for U.S. President George W. Bush's War on Iraq, against widespread continental European opposition, and despite being led by the supposedly pro-European Prime Minister Tony Blair.

Crucially, the main findings on actors support an opportunity structure interpretation. Basically, those who lose access to decision-making power as a result of European integration are critical of Europe, and those who see themselves gaining in influence are supportive. Tellingly, government and executive actors are the most favorable of all to the EU integration process and among the least critical of EU institutions (Chapter 4). Contrary to the popular perception that national governments claim all the good news for themselves and blame the EU for all the bad, national executives are actually the EU's prime public cheerleaders. We attribute this to their enhanced discursive power and greater access to power relative to other national actors within European multilevel governance. By contrast, the big losers in discursive power and access are civil

---

[9] Börzel (2002) introduces a terminology of "pace-setters," "fence-sitters," and "foot-draggers" for her analysis of national variants of Europeanization in the environmental policy field.
[10] For a detailed comparison of France and Britain, see Statham (2007a).

society actors, who are less favorable to the integration process and much more critical in their evaluations of EU institutions.

The media come between the favorable executive and critical civil society. Press commentating is on aggregate favorable toward European integration (Chapter 6). In this way, its stance largely follows the elite-dominated political world that it reports. In the EU countries with a favorable elite consensus, the press tells a story that carries the European project forward, whereas in Britain with its elite divisions and the most Eurosceptic mainstream political party, the press wonders, often sceptically, what Europe can do for Britain. In Switzerland, where referenda politicize the EU, the press witnesses some partisanship and, like Britain, depicts Europe as a national affair. However, the outsider view of the EU presented by the Swiss press appropriately reflects the country's status as a nonmember country, whereas the Brits' discussing Europe from an outsider perspective stands in contradiction to their EU membership of more than 30 years. In all cases, it seems that the national politicization of Europe has shaped the way that the press takes up the issue. This implies that the scope for autonomy within media commentating is delimited by the elite divisions over Europe within a country's political system.

So far, all findings point toward an elite-dominated public politics shown in the bottom-left corner of Figure 11.1, in which national and European executive actors strongly wield the decision-making and discursive power. These executive actors swamp Europeanized communication and favor more integration. As the supportive media look on, civil society struggles to raise a voice, and when it does, it either tries to apply the brakes to the current form of Europeanization, where its influence is withering away, or it advocates a different Europeanization. Because civil society actors face very high barriers in their attempts to expand inclusiveness, we think that at present the most realistic source for a more inclusive, representative, and pluralistic Europeanized public politics comes from among the elites themselves, through political party competition. So what are the prospects for resolving the "deficit" through party competition?

This requires political parties that start mobilizing different visions for the European integration process. Such a development would indicate the onset of a more mature European public politics, whereby public contestation between parties is aligned to perceived differences in the consequences of Europeanization, whose impacts are experienced differentially across groups within society. In this view, the consequences of globalization transform the social and political basis of relationships among people across the European region, leading to winners and losers who are starting to have their interests politically represented and find a political voice. It presents a realist view for a European politics that is generated by collective actors from within nation-states, but that mediates substantive issues that impact upon people and their relationships across the region that result from globalization processes. Europe is integrated within a national politics, which itself has been transformed by globalization. The question of European integration can no longer be viewed as yes or no for national societies, because globalization effects have happened and are largely irreversible. Contestation arises over what kind of Europeanized country (e.g., social welfare versus neoliberal market) is preferable and over the distribution of the costs and gains of this regional globalization process.

In this respect, our perspective is like that of Hanspeter Kriesi, Edgar Grande et al. (2008) – discussed in Chapter 10 – which focuses on the political mechanisms for mediating cleavages over the impacts of globalization at the national level, that is, party competition that is mediated through public discourses. From their highly innovative research, the group's (Grande 2008, p. 322), "main *conclusion* is that globalisation has not only been (at least partly) the result of political decisions and is the object of an increasing amount of political decision making, but is at the same time also *transforming the very basis of politics*" (emphasis in the original). So what evidence do we find for political party competition filling the gap in democratic performance that derives from the elite dominance of Europeanized politics?

Generally, we find some transformation of party politics beyond the inverted-U pattern of center party consensus and marginal party opposition over Europe, but there is still some way to go before one can declare an era of Europeanized party politics (Chapter 10). Just less than two-thirds of all party actors' evaluations remain favorable toward Europe, though negative evaluations increase significantly over time, indicating growing party contestation. All parties are more pro-European when they are in government, which again underlines the relationship between support for Europe and access to power in the multilevel polity. However, party family differences are more robust than country ones, which implies a basis for competition.

At the core of party systems, liberal and social democratic parties remain pro-European, whereas conservative parties divide between the highly exceptional British Conservatives and Swiss Schweizerische Volkspartei (SVP) and the rest who are pro-European. The exceptional British and Swiss parties turn out to be committed Eurosceptics, who depict Europeanization as a new threat of state interventionism that challenges national political sovereignty and the perceived benefits of neoliberal market and individual freedoms. Most of their arguments against Europe remain civic-political ones, however, with relatively few appeals to xenophobia. In the Swiss case, elite divisions have been spurred by the specific political opportunities of public referendum campaigns over joining the EU. In Britain, elite divisions and their politicization of Europe are long-standing and specific issues. This makes the British Conservatives an unlikely forerunner for continental Europe. Just as few center-right parties share the same deep commitment to neoliberalism as the British Conservatives, who have a heritage closer to the U.S. Republicans than European Christian Democracy, there is no reason for other parties' politicization of Europe to follow British Conservative Euroscepticism. Apart from the British Conservatives and the SVP, there is relatively little Euroscepticism to find in the political mainstream.

In most countries, anti-European dissent still largely comes from the margins, and especially from radical right parties. Radical right parties advocate political and economic nationalism and territorial autonomy against Europe, whereas the radical left opposes the neoliberal basis of Europeanization. It is interesting to note that even from the margins, however, Euroscepticism as a form of anti-systemic protest is rare. Most marginal parties mobilize critiques against Europe in a way that says something substantive – politically and economically – about Europeanization, and its potential consequences for people. This is indicative of a maturing and real party-political debate about Europeanization and its consequences.

We interpret our findings as evidence for the onset of the normalization of party competition over Europe. Now that Europe is publicly visible in media discourse, parties are increasingly prepared to discuss the issue in a way that is starting to present choices to voters. Perspectives on the winners and losers of Europeanization indicate that the structural transformation resulting from Europeanization is producing new groups with new identifiable stakes in the European project. The extent to which this confrontation moves to the forefront of party politics depends on the degree to which and how the consequences of globalization in the European region become publicly articulated. At the very least, our findings show the onset of a more mature party political public debate over Europe. The center parties of government and opposition no longer hide Europe under a blanket of consensus, and Europe's critics not only speak out more but more substantively about European integration and the EU institutions, and sometimes constructively. To what extent Europe will become central to transforming party politics, and whether the traditional cleavages of left–right will be modified or replaced, at present remains an open question. Resolving such issues is beyond this project's scope, but – following the important lead of Kriesi et al. (2008) – is an important field for future research. However, on public sphere development, we think our study shows that the most likely effective mechanism for carrying this normalization of Europe forward, in a way that allows greater inclusiveness and representation, is through a competitive national party politics.

POST-CONSTITUTION EUROPEANIZED PUBLIC POLITICS: A REALISTIC WAY FORWARD

The findings give a clear picture of the emergent Europeanized public politics: European policy debates are publicly visible but not very inclusive. The transformation of political communication and collective action in response to advancing European integration has led to the empowerment of the already powerful. How did this politics receive sufficient resources of public legitimacy to be sustainable? What are the most likely paths that it may take in the post-Constitution era, after a public rejection in the 2005 referenda by the French and Dutch people of the European project?

In its assessment of the public dimension of Europeanized politics, our study examines only the supply side of public debates. We have not addressed general public demand for, and reception of, mediated politics and opinion-formation processes. However, the public demand side is important for assessing the performance of media and politics. Existing studies based on public opinion polls show that the general public has a low level of knowledge about and interest in the European Union, plus "only a small proportion of the public holds strong affective supranational attachments" (Gabel 1998, p. 112). Commenting on the Commission's own Eurobarometer figures, Shore notes that they (2000, pp. 223–224) "provide grim reading for advocates of ever closer union. Support for EU membership across the Union has plummeted from 72% in 1991 to only 46% – fewer than at any time in the past twenty years – while eight out of ten Europeans admit to being 'not very well informed' or 'not informed at all' about the EU." By 2009, when pressed to express an opinion over Europe, although a majority of citizens (56%) believed that membership of the EU had benefited their country, a significant minority (31%) believed that their country had not benefited.[11] Overall, these findings suggest that relatively few people across Europe have sufficient knowledge to form a meaningful political opinion about the European level, compared to their understandings of national politics, and that when they do focus on Europe their support cannot be taken for granted. Perhaps at most about 15% know enough to be for or against issues, whereas the rest simply do not know, and many may not be interested at all.

It is worth recalling that our research shows that the general public's apparent lack of interest in Europe does not result from low media attention. On the contrary, the media report significantly about the European level, despite perceiving few commercial incentives to do so because of low readerships' demand. Apart from the executive, media actors were the only other actors more present in Europeanized debates compared to purely national ones. Moreover, the media find plenty to say about Europe in editorials and opinion articles. Thus, the media produce a European public debate, even if for the most part this elicits little public interest. This also means that media discourse – which in most countries and at most times has been on aggregate supportive – becomes an important resource of public legitimacy for political elites to push the integration project forward. In this sense, we think that mass media discourse over Europe has served a "proxy" role for Europe's absent general public by supplying a degree of legitimacy that allowed the elite dominance of the European project to be sustainable.

To illustrate the point, we use Gabriel Almond's (1960) classic distinction that there are broadly three types of public opinion on policy making: a "general public," an "attentive public," and a "policy and opinion elite." In this view, the general public do not know or care about much beyond their immediate concerns except at times of crisis; the attentive public are an educated minority who follow more abstract concerns, whom the elite plays to, and who also pass on views to the general public; and the policy and opinion elite are a small group of highly influential people, officials, politicians, and top journalists who devise policies and articulate them largely for attentive publics. Applying this

---

[11] Standard Eurobarometer 71 (fieldwork June–July 2009). European Commission, September 2009 (available at http://ec.europa.eu/public_opinion/archives/eb/eb71/eb71_std_part1.pdf).

formula to Europeanized politics,[12] we think that the "attentive public" has been very much smaller than it usually is in domestic politics. This is supported by our findings that civil society mobilization is weak in discursive influence. A consequence of this very small attentive public from civil society over Europe is that the mass media has taken center stage as *the* actor representing the public. This occurred more by default than by intention. Our study shows that media attention for Europe arises more from professional norms for reporting – journalists recognizing the growing location of power at the European level – than partisanship. The media's generally supportive stance for this version of the European project is contingent, not absolute. However, the weak presence of civil society has meant that the media have tended to look much more to elites for views to disseminate about Europe than to nonstate actors. To some extent the media have filled the gap for the missing attentive public through its own opinion mobilization, though it seems that such messages, if they have made any impact on the views of the general public at all, have largely induced passivity for the elite-dominated project. Overall, the policy and opinion elite has effectively been able to play to its own image of the European project represented in the mass media discourse, which has reinforced its legitimacy, while Europe has largely remained off the radar of the general public. In this way, the elite-led European integration project gains a degree of legitimacy by being made publicly visible, and exposed to some media scrutiny, even if this mediated public discourse remains dominated by elite voices. We think this was the normal state of affairs that sustained the stages of advancing European integration prior to the European Constitution's rejection in 2005.

Although sustainable when European integration is not at a critical juncture, the flaw in this model is that the proxy public legitimacy supplied to elites by media discourse is trumped by direct calls on the people that result in an expression of popular will. Nothing exposed this more than the failed referenda for the 2005 Constitution Treaty. Required to give a voice on a topic about which they had shown little previous inclination to do so, the French and Dutch publics responded with a protest vote against the elite consensus supported by all the main parties and conventional media. Of course, the French and Dutch had not been transformed en masse over night from uninformed to informed attentive publics over Europe. It is likely that they voted for domestic political concerns and interests – including opposition to perceived elite dominance – rather than on the substantive policy contents of European Constitutional Treaty, even if, as in the French case, a copy of the 500-plus page document was posted to each voter.[13] Regardless of whether referenda are considered good or bad for democratic politics, the Constitution case nonetheless demonstrates that, by seeking a popular mandate, the French and Dutch governments effectively

---

[12] Almond's *The American People and Foreign Policy* (1960) is especially pertinent because European policy decision making has traditionally been as remote and distant for the general public as foreign policy.

[13] Even the Convention's President Giscard d'Estaing complained about the folly of sending a 500-page document comprising 446 articles and 36 supplementary protocols to every French voter (Anderson 2007).

undermined their own normal basis for legitimating European politics. By contrast, the German approach was to manage the Constitution in the normal way. The treaty was ratified by the national parliament, the Bundestag, with the legitimacy for the "yes" flowing from the elected parties, and mass media discourse giving prominence to supportive elite voices including their own. This approach provoked few signs of popular opposition from the general public, at least not prior to the French and Dutch "no."

The failed 2005 Constitution attempt stands as a watershed moment, because it brought to public attention and politicized the elite dominance of the European project to an unprecedented extent across the whole European region. Initially, many academics hailed the constitutional process enthusiastically as a potential midwife for the birth of a European popular will and political community driven by an emerging European civil society. On this, Habermas was especially prominent: "The generation of a European public opinion depends on the vital inputs of actors within a European civil society. At the same time, a European-wide public sphere needs to be embedded in a political culture shared by all." (2005, p. 29); and "we should not underestimate the symbolic importance of the sheer fact that a constitutional debate is now underway. The euro alone is not sufficient to inspire enthusiasm for Europe as a political community in the minds of Europeans. The intergovernmental agreement in Maastricht lacks the symbolic power which can only be generated by a political founding act" (2006, p. 90). Some academics were overenthusiastic in translating this normative vision into a prediction for the forthcoming reality. For example, Bruter claimed (2005, p. 171) that, "without a doubt, a mass European identity has emerged and progressively grown.... [T]he average level of European identity of citizens...can be expected to progress even further as the European Union is going through the symbolic stage of giving itself its first Constitution."

On one side, however, the EU's consultation processes remained strongly top down and for insiders. On the other, the available evidence indicates that the impacts of the constitution opportunity structure on broader civil society mobilization were very limited. An empirical study using similar methods to this one – claim making and semi-structured interviews – specifically geared to examining civil society participation in debates over the Constitution produced negative findings.[14] Debates became more national and internally focussed and elites dominated public debates over the European Constitution. In interviews, NGOs emphasized their lack of resources and dependency on executive actors for funding. They largely saw themselves as clients of national governments, dependent on what their patrons succeeded in bargaining for within their policy

---

[14] Claim-making analyses were undertaken on mediated debates over the Constitution in France, Germany, Britain, and Spain (see contributions to Trenz et al. 2008). In addition, structured interviews were undertaken with national NGOs in the fields of consumer protection, women's rights, and religion in Britain (Firmstone 2008a; Statham 2009) and Germany (Trenz et al. 2008).

sector at the EU level and waiting for a trickle-down effect. Importantly, NGOs did not see themselves or act like "civil society" in the sense understood by democratic theory. From this, it seems that civil society over Europe remains very weak, and not of a type that is likely to expand the ranks of the attentive public to any great extent soon.

Nonetheless, our own findings point to an increasingly critical public debate over Europe, even prior to 2005. It is a matter for future research to determine the long-term impact of the exceptional Constitution event on Europeanized debates and whether this may after all stimulate the growth of an attentive public for Europe. However, we consider it unlikely that an emergent attentive public will take the form of the Europe-friendly bottom-up mobilized civil society depicted in Habermas' normative theory, because the substantive conditions for such a development remain absent, and civil society is likely to produce as many opponents as supporters. In the meantime, the mass media remains an important actor. After the European Constitution, at the very least, media debates are likely to be more critical, given that the public has shown itself not to be unidimensionally in favor of European integration, and that one of the media's roles is to represent public opinion. Indeed, the Lisbon Treaty (2007), the watered-down attempt by political elites to rehash the technical aspects of the Constitutional Treaty, was rebuffed by an Irish referendum in 2008, which is indicative of this heightened public critical environment. Even when the Lisbon Treaty was adopted by all member states, finally staggering into existence on December 1, 2009, national governments had remained careful to keep their decisions behind closed doors, not least their deliberations over the selection of Herman Van Rompuy as the first full-time President of the European Council. Overall, it seems that the failed European Constitution has contributed to the normalization of a critical mediated public debate over Europe, but has not supplied the compliant version of a European political community of citizens that was envisaged by its elite architects and promoted by some academics.

Another possible way forward in the postconstitutional era is through an enhanced performance for party politics linking citizens to the European level. Simon Hix (2008) claims that Europe's perceived democratic deficit should be addressed by an institutional fix of the EU's political architecture, largely by increasing the powers of the European Parliament and voting for a President, leading to a more effective supranational party politics characterized by "Europarties" working across national borders. Earlier, we pointed out the absence of mediated politics in the Hix thesis. For elites to introduce such a radical measure without it appearing as an authoritarian act requires public legitimacy, for which mediated discourse is an important source. Without such minimum resources of public legitimacy, the new political system could not even begin to perform. Indeed its introduction would most likely repeat the European Constitution debacle. In addition, regardless of the difficulty of publicly legitimating this institutional fix, others have pointed out that the envisaged EU-level political parties would still lack many of the governance–populace linkages performed by national ones. As Albert Weale (2005, p. 140) states, "From the point of view of citizens, strengthening parliament is not the same as strengthening democratic input, when the line of connection between voters and legislators is a long one." Furthermore, without a substantive transfer of executive power to the EU-level polity, its politics will continue to be perceived as "second order" by the public (van der Eijk and Franklin 1996). Perhaps the strongest argument for not reinforcing the power of the EU-level political system, however, is that there is no evidence for a popular will to do so.

Voters obviously do not rate European elections anywhere close to the importance of national ones, judging by their low levels of turnout, plus their willingness to use them to register protests against national governments over domestic issues. Turnout has dropped in every European election since they started in 1979. The June 2009 European Parliament elections produced a record low turnout of 43.4% across the twenty-seven countries, and the turnout was especially low in Germany (42.2%) and France (40.5%), two of Europe's largest countries who have carried the torch for advancing integration. This occurred despite the fact that the European Parliament's advertising campaign cost 18 million euros, encouraging people to vote and publicizing its increased powers in key policy fields. "How much shall we tame financial markets?" boasted one slogan. There were also joint initiatives by the European Parliament, the Commissioner for Institutional Relations and Communication Strategy Margot Wallström, national broadcasters, and the European Broadcasting Union in an effort to focus media coverage of the election more on the EU level than national domestic issues. Nonetheless, the 2009 election results show few signs of emerging pan-European understandings, at least from the side of the voters. The net effect of European elections is to undermine the EU's public legitimacy by making the EU level appear far more meaningless to people than it is, when judged by the actual decision-making power it wields over them. On European election day, voters have no idea how their members of European Parliament (MEPs) performed in Brussels and Strasbourg in the last Parliament, no idea about the programs of the European People's Party (EPP) and Party of European Socialists (PES), and no idea which issues will be coming up in the European Parliament. Whatever the good intentions, in its search for legitimacy through the ballot box, the EU hoists itself by its own petard by demanding a direct input from a still strongly inattentive and disinterested general public.

To some degree, European parliamentarians seem to have internalized this understanding of their second-rate status and general public indifference to their performance. As the global crisis started heralding the potential collapse of international financial markets, in 2008, the *Guardian*, a pro-European British newspaper, published a double-page photograph with the simple title: '18.11.08 EU debate on the global financial crisis, Strasbourg'. Among the rows and rows of empty seats sit a few lost souls – members of the European Parliament – one sending a text message. So much for taming financial markets! It was largely national governments and politicians that addressed the financial crisis, sometimes competitively against their counterparts from other countries, even when calling for common actions across borders. National politicians knew they would be held accountable by their national publics.

Making people vote at the European level, when for the most part they lack the knowledge to form opinions about preferences, simply demonstrates to them that European voting is meaningless, compared to the values and understandings of democratic practice to which they are accustomed at the national level. Journalists and other small informed public elites, such as academics, think tanks, and public intellectuals, know the truth that considerable power is held at the supranational level and have some idea of how the EU works. However, no amount of indirect legitimacy provided by supportive media discourses, plus self-validation by policy and opinion elites, can challenge the outcomes of calls on the people to participate directly at the ballot box. Like the case of the constitutional referenda, European elections are self-defeating in achieving their public legitimacy aims. People are asked from on high to vote at a political level where there has never been a popular demand for suffrage. This actually detracts from the normal sources of support and public legitimation for policy and elite opinion, which is derived from receiving at least some degree of attention and scrutiny by journalists and informed public elites in the media discourse.

If implementing a European public from the top down is self-defeating, then perhaps the emergent critique these efforts stimulate is a source for carrying a more legitimate Europeanized public politics forward. Allowing the national politics that people understand to do the job of providing legitimacy to the EU is much more likely to be sustainable, meaningful, and effective. For this reason, we see mediated political party competition at the national level as the most realistic starting point for generating a Europeanized public politics. This is not simply the old national party politics, but one addressing the structural changes resulting from globalization identified by the "winners and losers" perspective. In looking for a fix from within national party politics, we agree with Kriesi, Grande et al. (2008, p. 3) that globalization impacts need to be studied at the national level: "paradoxically, the political reactions to economic and cultural globalisation are bound to manifest themselves above all at the national level: given that the democratic political inclusion of citizens is still mainly a national affair, nation states still constitute the major arenas for political mobilization."

The basic conclusion is that the transformation of party competition within national politics in response to advancing European integration offers the best realistic chance for a legitimate Europeanized public politics. We think there is still some way to go before we can say that national Europeanized party politics has arrived, though the process has started. Although party consensus for Europe remains strong, and Europeanized debates are dominated by the executive, we also think that a more mature critique of Europe is emerging through mediated party competition. As the "credit crunch" and financial crisis from autumn 2008 have already started to demonstrate, the politics for managing the consequences of globalization (and Europeanization) is likely to come increasingly to the fore. As Almond's thesis on American foreign policy and public opinion noted, crises are the rare moments when even general publics start to pay attention. Perhaps the increasingly self-evident impacts of economic globalization will start to shape perceptions of the European Union's role in that story and as a possible way of managing its consequences. This makes an effective party competition and media performance vital for translating interpretations of the consequences of globalization into voting choices for the people who are living with them. We think that, in the future, choices about different paths to Europeanization (including negative options) will be mobilized increasingly by parties in the media discourse. This locates Europe within national mediated politics, which is not a bad thing given that political will remains expressed through nationally elected governments. In such a Europe, election results in neighboring European countries – especially the larger ones – hold greater consequences for shaping the direction of EU policies than those of the European Parliament. This suggests that the supranational European institutions holding power would be better off strengthening their communicative links to citizens and seeking public legitimacy through national parliaments and media, rather than engaging in another round of top-down efforts to engage a remote and inattentive citizenry. It would also offer a way for legitimating the EU on the basis of performance on policies that concern people about globalization – climate change, immigration, market regulation – instead of focusing public attention on institutional procedural changes that are little wanted or understood, and that seem remote from everyday life.

References

Adam, Silke. 2007a. *Symbolische Netzwerke in Europa. Der Einfluss der nationalen Ebene auf europäische Öffentlichkeit. Deutschland und Frankreich im Vergleich.* Köln: Halem.

Adam, Silke. 2007b. "Domestic Adaptations of Europe. A Comparative Study of the Debates on EU Enlargement and a Common Constitution in the German and French Quality Press." *International Journal of Public Opinion Research* 19: 409–433.

Agre, Philipp E. 2002. "Real-Time Politics: The Internet and the Political Process." *The Information Society* 18: 311–331.

AIM Research Consortium (Ed.). 2007. *Reporting and Managing European News: Final Report of the Project "Adequate Information Management in Europe," 2004–2007.* Bochum and Freiburg: Projekt Verlag.

Alexander, Janet, John Powell, and Marsha Tate. 2001. Evaluating Internet Resources. Retrieved April 15, 2007, from http://med-libwww.bu.edu/library/introwww/index .htm.

Almond, Gabriel A. 1960. *The American People and Foreign Policy.* New York: Praeger.

Anderson, Perry. 2007. "Depicting Europe." *London Review of Books.* September 20, 2007. LRB online. Retrieved October 15, 2007, from http://www.lrb.co.uk/v29/n18/ andeo1_.html.

Anderson, Peter J. and Antony Weymouth. 1999. *Insulting the Public?: The British Press and the European Union.* London: Longman.

Archibugi, Daniele. 2005. "The Language of Democracy." *Political Studies* 53: 537–555.

Aspinwall, Mark and Justin Greenwood. 1998. "Conceptualising Collective Action in the European Union: An Introduction," pp. 1–30 in Justin Greenwood and Mark Aspinwall (Eds.), *Collective Action in the European Union.* London: Routledge.

Bache, Ian. 1999. "The Extended Gatekeeper: Central Government and the Implementation of EC Regional Policy in the UK." *Journal of European Public Policy* 6: 28–45.

Baisnée, Olivier. 2002. "Can Political Journalism Exist at the EU Level?," pp. 108–128 in Raymond Kuhn and Erik Neveu (Eds.), *Political Journalism: New Challenges, New Practices.* London: Routledge.

Barber, Benjamin R. 1984. *Strong Democracy: Participatory Politics for a New Age.* Berkeley: University of California Press.

Bartolini, Stefano. 2005. *Restructuring Europe. Centre Formation, System Building and Political Structuring between the Nation-State and the European Union.* Oxford: Oxford University Press.

Bartolini, Stefano. 2006. "Should the Union Be 'Politicized'?," pp. 28–50 in Simon Hix and Stefano Bartolini (Eds.), *Politics: The Right or the Wrong Sort of Medicine for the EU?* Notre Europe, Policy Paper No. 19. Retrieved October 15, 2007, from http://www.unizar.es/euroconstitucion/library/working%20papers/Hix,%20Bartolini%202006.pdf.

Baumgartner, Frank R. and Bryan D. Jones. 2002. "Positive and Negative Feedback in Politics," pp. 3–28 in Frank R. Baumgartner and Bryan D. Jones (Eds.), *Policy Dynamics.* Chicago: University of Chicago Press.

Baumgartner, Frank R. and Beth L. Leech. 1998. *Basic Interests: The Importance of Groups in Politics and in Political Science.* Princeton: Princeton University Press.

Bennett, W. Lance and Robert M. Entman. 2001. "Mediated Politics: An Introduction," pp. 1–29 in W. Lance Bennett and Robert M. Entman (Eds.), *Mediated Politics. Communication in the Future of Democracy.* Cambridge: Cambridge University Press.

Bentham, Jeremy. 1830 [1983]. *Constitutional Code.* Oxford: Clarendon Press.

Beyers, Jan. 2002. "Gaining and Seeking Access: The European Adaptation of Domestic Interest Associations." *European Journal of Political Research* 41: 585–612.

Beyers, Jan. 2004. "Voice and Access. Political Practices of European Interest Associations." *European Union Politics* 5: 211–240.

Bleich, Erik. 2003. *Race Politics in Britain and France: Ideas and Policymaking since the 1960s.* Cambridge: Cambridge University Press.

Blondel, Jean, Richard Sinnott, and Peter Swenson (Eds.). 1998. *People and Parliament in the European Union.* Oxford: Clarendon Press.

Blumler, Jay G. and Michael Gurevitch (Eds.). 1995. *The Crisis of Public Communication.* London: Routledge.

Blumler, Jay G. and Dennis Kavanagh. 1999. "The Third Age of Political Communication: Influences and Features." *Political Communication* 16: 209–230.

Börzel, Tanja A. 2002. "Pace-Setting, Foot-Dragging, and Fence-Sitting. Member State Responses to Europeanization." *Journal of Common Market Studies* 40: 193–214.

Börzel, Tanja A. 2006. "Participation through Law Enforcement. The Case of the European Union." *Comparative Political Studies* 39: 128–152.

Bourne, Angela K. 2003. "The Impact of European Integration on Regional Power." *Journal of Common Market Studies* 41: 597–620.

Brin, Sergey and Lawrence Page. 1998. The Anatomy of a Large-Scale Hypertextual Web Search Engine. Retrieved June 12, 2007, from http://infolab.stanford.edu/~backrub/google.html.

Bruter, Michael. 2005. *Citizens of Europe? The Emergence of a Mass European Identity.* Houndmills: Palgrave Macmillan.

Bücker, Nicola. 2008. "Returning to Where? 'Images' of Europe and Support for the Process of European Integration in Poland," pp. 265–294 in Ireneusz Pawel Karolewski and Viktoria Kaina (Eds.), *European Identity: Theoretical and Empirical Perspectives.* Berlin: LIT Verlag.

Budge, Ian, Hans-Dieter Klingemann, Andrea Volkens, Judith Bara, Eric Tanenbaum et al. 2001. *Mapping Policy Preferences. Estimates for Parties, Electors, and Governments 1945–1998.* Oxford: Oxford University Press.

Burstein, Paul. 1998. *Discrimination, Jobs, and Politics. The Struggle for Equal Employment Opportunity in the United States since the New Deal.* With a New Introduction. Chicago: The University of Chicago Press.

Calhoun, Craig. 2003. "The Democratic Integration of Europe: Interests, Identity, and the Public Sphere," pp. 243–274 in Mabel Berezin and Martin Schain (Eds.), *Europe without Borders: Remapping Territory, Citizenship and Identity in a Transnational Age.* Baltimore: Johns Hopkins University Press.

Calleo, David P. 2001. *Rethinking Europe's Future.* Princeton: Princeton University Press.

Christin, Thomas and Alexander H. Trechsel. 2002. "Joining the EU? Explaining Public Opinion in Switzerland." *European Union Politics* 3: 415–443.

Cohen, Jean and Andrew Arato. 1992. *Civil Society and Political Theory.* Cambridge, MA: MIT Press.

Crouch, Colin. 1999. *Change in Western Europe.* Oxford: Oxford University Press.

Dahlberg, Lincoln. 2001. "Computer-Mediated Communication and the Public Sphere: A Critical Analysis." *Journal of Computer-Mediated Communication* 7. Retrieved June 12, 2007, from http://jcmc.indiana.edu/vol7/issue1/dahlberg.html.

Dahlberg, Lincoln. 2004. "Internet Research Tracings: Towards Non-Reductionist Methodology." *Journal of Computer-Mediated Communication* 9. Retrieved June 12, 2007, from http://jcmc.indiana.edu/vol9/issue3/dahlberg.html.

Davies, Norman. 1996. *Europe: A History.* Oxford: Oxford University Press.

de Swaan, Abram. 1993. "The Evolving European Language System: A Theory of Communication Potential and Language Competition." *International Political Science Review* 14: 241–255.

de Swaan, Abram. 2001. *Words of the World: The Global Language System.* Oxford: Blackwell.

de Swaan, Abram. 2007. "The Language Predicament of the EU since the Enlargements." *Sociolinguistica* 21: 1–21.

de Vreese, Claes H. 2001. "Europe in the News: A Cross-National Comparative Study of the News Coverage of Key EU Events." *European Union Politics* 2: 283–307.

de Vreese, Claes H. 2003. *Framing Europe. Television News and European Integration.* Amsterdam: Aksant.

de Vreese, Claes H. 2007. The EU as a Public Sphere. Living Reviews in European Governance 2. Retrieved January 20, 2008, from http://europeangovernance.livingreviews.org/Articles/lreg-2007-3/.

de Vreese, Claes H. and Hajo G. Boomgaarden. 2006. "Media Message Flows and Interpersonal Communication. The Conditional Nature of Effects on Public Opinion." *Communication Research* 33: 19–37.

de Vreese, Claes H., Jochen Peter, and Holli A. Semetko. 2001. "Framing Politics at the Launch of the Euro: A Crossnational Comparative Study of Frames in the News." *Political Communication* 18: 107–122.

Delanty, Gerard. 1995. *Inventing Europe.* Basingstoke: MacMillan.

Delanty, Gerard and Chris Rumford. 2005. *Rethinking Europe.* London: Routledge.

Della Porta, Donatella. 2003. Dimensions of Political Opportunities and the Europeanisation of Public Spheres. Report Workpackage 1. Retrieved February 20, 2006, from http://europub.wzb.eu/Data/reports/WP1/wp1%20integrated%20report.pdf.

Della Porta, Donatella and Manuela Caiani. 2006. *Quale Europa? Europeizzazione, identità e conflitti*. Bologna: Il Mulino.

Della Porta, Donatella and Manuela Caiani. 2007a. "Eurosceptics or Critical Europeanists? Social Movements and Europe," pp. 363–400 in Claes de Vreese and Herrmann Schmitt (Eds.), *A European Public Sphere: How Much of It Do We Have and How Much Do We Need? CONNEX Report Series No 2*. Mannheim: University of Mannheim.

Della Porta, Donatella and Manuela Caiani. 2007b. "Europeanization from Below? Social Movements and Europe." *Mobilization: An International Quarterly* 12: 1–20.

Deutsch, Karl W. 1953. *Nationalism and Social Communication. An Inquiry into the Foundations of Nationality*. Cambridge, MA: MIT Press.

Díez Medrano, Juan. 2003. *Framing Europe. Attitudes to European Integration in Germany, Spain and the United Kingdom*. Princeton: Princeton University Press.

Dinan, Desmond. 2005. *Ever Closer Union*. Basingstoke: Palgrave Macmillan.

Donati, Pierpaolo. 1992. "Political Discourse Analysis," pp. 136–167 in Mario Diani and Ron Eyerman (Eds.), *Studying Collective Action*. London: Sage.

Donsbach, Wolfgang and Thomas E. Patterson. 2004. "Political News Journalists: Partisanship, Professionalism, and Political Roles in Five Countries," pp. 251–270 in Frank Esser and Barbara Pfetsch (Eds.), *Comparing Political Communication: Theories, Cases and Challenges*. Cambridge: Cambridge University Press.

Downey, John and Natalie Fenton. 2003. "New Media, Counter Publicity and the Public Sphere." *New Media and Society* 5: 185–202.

Downey, John and Thomas Koenig. 2006. "Is There a European Public Sphere? The Berlusconi-Schulz Case." *European Journal of Communication* 21: 165–187.

Duchêne, Francois. 1994. *Jean Monnet*. New York: Norton.

Duchesne, Sophie and Virginie von Ingelgom. 2008. "Chantiers de recherche comment les discussions deviennent politiques, lorsque des français, des anglais ou des belges francophones parlent de l'Europe?" *Politique européenne* 24: 145–149.

Duff, Andrew. 2005. *The Struggle for Europe's Constitution*. London: I.B. Tauris.

Earl, Jennifer, Andrew Martin, John D. McCarthy, and Sarah A. Soule. 2004. "The Use of Newspaper Data in the Study of Collective Action." *Annual Review of Sociology* 30: 65–80.

Eder, Klaus, Kai-Uwe Hellmann, and Hans-Jörg Trenz. 1998. "Regieren in Europa jenseits öffentlicher Legitimation? Eine Untersuchung zur Rolle von politischer Öffentlichkeit in Europa." *Politische Vierteljahresschrift* 29: 321–344.

Eder, Klaus and Cathleen Kantner. 2000. "Transnationale Resonanzstrukturen in Europa. Eine Kritik der Rede vom Öffentlichkeitsdefizit." *Kölner Zeitschrift für Soziologie und Sozialpsychologie* 40: 306–331.

Eder, Klaus, Cathleen Kantner, and Hans-Jörg Trenz. 2000. Transnationale Öffentlichkeit und die Strukturierung politischer Kommunikation in Europa. Antrag auf Förderung eines Forschungsvorhabens im Rahmen des DFG-Schwerpunkts Regieren in Europa. Retrieved January 12, 2002, from http://www2.rz.hu-berlin.de/struktur/forschung/transoeff/Euro-DFG-Antrag.pdf.

Egloff, Daniel. 2002. *Digitale Demokratie: Mythos oder Realität? Auf den Spuren der demokratischen Aspekte des Internets und der Computerkultur*. Wiesbaden: Westdeutscher Verlag.

Eilders, Christiane, Friedhelm Neidhardt, and Barbara Pfetsch (Eds.). 2004. *Die Stimme der Medien. Pressekommentare und politische Öffentlichkeit in der Bundesrepublik*. Wiesbaden: VS – Verlag für Sozialwissenschaften.

Entman, Robert. 2004. *Projections of Power. Framing News, Public Opinion and US Foreign Policy*. Chicago: University of Chicago Press.

Erbring, Lutz (Ed.). 1995. *Kommunikationsraum Europa*. Konstanz: U.K. Medien.

Ernst, Andreas. 1998. "Vielsprachigkeit, Öffentlichkeit und politische Integration: schweizerische Erfahrungen und europäische Perspektiven." *Swiss Political Science Review* 4: 225–240.

Esser, Frank and Barbara Pfetsch. 2004. "Meeting the Challenges of Global Communication and Political Integration: The Significance of Comparative Research in a Changing World," pp. 384–410 in Frank Esser and Barbara Pfetsch (Eds.), *Comparing Political Communication: Theories, Cases, and Challenges*. New York: Cambridge University Press.

Etzioni, Amitai. 2001. *Political Unification Revisited*. Lanham, MD: Lexington Books.

European Commission. 2001. Allocation of 2000 EU operating expenditure by Member State. Retrieved May 17, 2008, from http://www.ukie.gov.pl/14powodow/ile/2000_en.pdf.

European Commission. 2006a. Time to Move up a Gear. Annual Progress Report on Growth and Jobs. Retrieved January 21, 2008, from http://ec.europa.eu/growthand jobs/european-dimension/200601-annual-progress-report/index_en.htm.

European Commission. 2006b. White Paper on a European Communication Policy. Retrieved January 21, 2008, from http://europa.eu/documents/comm/white_papers/pdf/com2006_35_en.pdf.

European Commission. 2009. Standard Eurobarometer 71 (fieldwork June–July 2009). Retrieved September 18, 2009, from http://ec.europa.eu/public_opinion/archives/eb/eb71/eb71_std_part1.pdf.

Evans, Peter B., Harold K. Jacobson, and Robert D. Putnam (Eds.). 1993. *Double-Edged Diplomacy*. Berkeley: University of California Press.

Everett, Rogers M. and James W. Dearing. 1988. "Agenda Setting Research: Where Has It Been and Where Is It Going?," pp. 555–594 in James A. Anderson (Ed.), *Communication Yearbook 11*. Beverly Hills, CA: Sage.

Featherstone, Kevin and Claudio M. Radaelli (Eds.). 2003. *The Politics of Europeanization*. Oxford: Oxford University Press.

Ferree, Myra Marx, William A. Gamson, Jürgen Gerhards, and Dieter Rucht. 2002a. *Shaping Abortion Discourse. Democracy and the Public Sphere in Germany and the United States*. Cambridge: Cambridge University Press.

Ferree, Myra Marx, William A. Gamson, Jürgen Gerhards, and Dieter Rucht. 2002b. "Four Models of the Public Sphere in Modern Democracies." *Theory and Society* 31: 289–324.

Firmstone, Julie. 2007. *The Editorial Opinions of the British Press on European Integration*. PhD dissertation. Leeds: University of Leeds.

Firmstone, Julie. 2008a. Mediating the Economic, Cultural and Socio-political Interests of Citizens in the EU: A Research Report. European Political Communication Working Paper Series 17/08. University of Leeds. Retrieved September 30, 2009, from http://www.eurpolcom.eu/exhibits/paper_17.pdf.

Firmstone, Julie. 2008b. "Approaches of the Transnational Press to Reporting Europe." *Journalism. Theory, Practice and Criticism* 9: 423–442.

Fisher, Diana R. and Larry M. Wright. 2001. "On Utopias and Dystopias: Toward an Understanding of the Discourse Surrounding the Internet." *Journal of Computer-Mediated Communication* 6. Retrieved June 12, 2007, from http://jcmc.indiana.edu/vol6/issue2/fisher.html.

Fittkau & Maass Internet Marktforschung. 2000. Ergebnisse für Teilnehmer der 10. W3B-Umfrage. Retrieved June 12, 2007, from http://www.w3b.org/ergebnisse/w3b10/.

Fligstein, Neil. 2008. *Euro-Clash. The EU, European Identity, and the Future of Europe.* Oxford: Oxford University Press.

Follesdal, Andreas and Simon Hix. 2005. Why There Is a Democratic Deficit in the EU. European Governance Papers No. C-05-02. Retrieved January 21, 2007, from http://www.connex-network.org/eurogov/pdf/egp-connex-C-05-02.pdf.

Forster, Anthony. 2002. *Euroscepticism in Contemporary British Politics.* London: Routledge.

Fossum, John Erik and Philip Schlesinger (Eds.). 2007. *The European Union and the Public Sphere: A Communicative Space in the Making?* London: Routledge.

Franzosi, Roberto. 2004. *From Words to Numbers. Narrative, Data and Social Science.* Cambridge: Cambridge University Press.

Gabel, Matthew J. 1998. *Interests and Integration. Market Liberalization, Public Opinion, and European Union.* Ann Arbor: University of Michigan Press.

Galbraith, John Kenneth. 1954 [1975]. *The Great Crash 1929.* Reprint with revisions. London: Penguin Books.

Galtung, Johan and Mari Holmboe Ruge. 1965. "The Structure of Foreign News: The Presentation of the Congo, Cuba and Cyprus Crises in Four Norwegian Newspapers." *Journal of Peace Research* 2: 64–91.

Gamson, William A. 2001. "Forward," pp. ix–xi in Stephen D. Reese, Oscar H. Gandy, Jr., and August E. Grant, *Framing Public Life.* Mahwah, NJ: Erlbaum.

Gamson, William A. and Kathryn E. Lasch. 1983. "The Political Culture of the Social Welfare Policy," pp. 397–415 in Shimon E. Spiro and Ephraim Yuchtman-Yaar (Eds.), *Evaluating the Welfare State: Social and Political Perspectives.* New York: Academic Press.

Gamson, William A. and Andre Modigliani. 1989. "Media Discourse and Public Opinion on Nuclear Power: A Constructionist Approach." *American Journal of Sociology* 95: 1–38.

Gamson, William A. and Gadi Wolfsfeld. 1993. "Movements and Media as Interacting Systems." *Annals of the American Academy of Political and Social Science* 528: 114–126.

Gans, Herbert J. 1979. *Deciding What's News: A Study of CBS News, NBC Nightly News, Newsweek, and Time.* New York: Pantheon Books.

Garrido, Maria and Alexander Halavais. 2003. "Mapping Networks of Support for the Zapatista Movement: Applying Social Networks Analysis to Study Contemporary Social Movements," pp. 165–184 in Martha McCaughey and Michael Ayers (Eds.), *Cyberactivism: Online Activism in Theory and Practice.* London: Routledge.

Garton Ash, Timothy. 2004. *Free World.* London: Allen Lane.

Gerhards, Jürgen. 1993. "Westeuropäische Integration und die Schwierigkeiten der Entstehung einer europäischen Öffentlichkeit." *Zeitschrift für Soziologie* 22: 96–110.

Gerhards, Jürgen. 2000. "Europäisierung von Ökonomie und Politik und die Trägheit der Entstehung einer europäischen Öffentlichkeit." *Kölner Zeitschrift für Soziologie und Sozialpsychologie* 40: 277–305.

Gillingham, John. 2003. *European Integration, 1950–2003.* Cambridge: Cambridge University Press.

Gimmler, Antje. 2001. "Deliberative Democracy, the Public Sphere and the Internet." *Philosophy and Social Criticism* 27: 21–40.

Gleissner, Martin and Claes H. de Vreese. 2005. "News about the EU Constitution. Journalistic Challenges and Media Portrayal of the European Union Constitution." *Journalism* 6: 221–242.

Goulard, Sylvie. 2002. "Frankreich und Europa: die Kluft zwischen Politik und Gesellschaft," pp. 173–195 in Michael Meimeth and Joachim Schild (Eds.), *Die Zukunft von Nationalstaaten in der europäischen Integration. Deutsche und französische Perspektiven*. Opladen: Leske + Budrich.

Gowan, Peter and Perry Anderson (Eds.). 1997. *The Question of Europe*. London: Verso Books.

Grande, Edgar. 2008. "Globalizing West European Politics: The Change of Cleavage Structures, Parties and Political Systems," pp. 320–344 in Hanspeter Kriesi et al., *West Europe Politics in the Age of Globalization*. Cambridge: Cambridge University Press.

Grant, Charles. 1994. *Delors*. London: Nicholas Brealey.

Graphics, Visualisation & Usability Center. 1998. GVU's WWW User Survey: How Users Find Out about WWW Pages. Retrieved June 12, 2007, from http://www.gvu .gatech.edu/user_surveys/survey-1998-10/graphs/use/q52.htm.

Gray, Emily. 2005. *The Politics of Pressure: Group Campaigning for and against European Integration in Britain*. PhD dissertation. Leeds: University of Leeds.

Gray, Emily and Paul Statham. 2005. "Becoming European? The Transformation of the British Pro-Migrant NGO Sector in Response to Europeanization." *Journal of Common Market Studies* 43: 877–898.

Green Cowles, Maria, James Caporaso, and Thomas Risse (Eds.). 2001. *Transforming Europe. Europeanization and Domestic Change*. Ithaca: Cornell University Press.

Greenwood, Justin and Mark Aspinwall (Eds.). 1998. *Collective Action in the European Union*. London: Routledge.

Guiraudon, Virginie. 2001. "Weapons of the Weak? Transnational Mobilization around Migration in the European Union," pp. 163–183 in Doug Imig and Sidney Tarrow (Eds.), *Contentious Europeans. Protest and Politics in an Emerging Polity*. Oxford: Rowman & Littlefield.

Haas, Ernst B. 1958. *The Uniting of Europe. Political, Economic and Social Forces, 1950–1957*. London: Stevens.

Habermas, Jürgen. 1962. *Strukturwandel der Öffentlichkeit*. Neuwied: Luchterhand.

Habermas, Jürgen. 1984. *The Theory of Communicative Action*. Boston: Beacon Press.

Habermas, Jürgen. 2001. *Zeit der Übergänge. Kleine Politische Schriften IX*. Frankfurt am Main: Suhrkamp.

Habermas, Jürgen. 2004. *Der gespaltene Westen*. Frankfurt am Main: Suhrkamp.

Habermas, Jürgen. 2005. "Why Europe Needs a Constitution," pp. 19–34 in Erik O. Eriksen, John E. Fossum, and Agustín José Menéndez (Eds.), *Developing a Constitution for Europe*. London: Routledge.

Habermas, Jürgen. 2006. *Time of Transitions*. Cambridge: Polity Press.

Hallin, Daniel C. and Paolo Mancini. 2004. *Comparing Media Systems: Three Models of Media and Politics*. Cambridge: Cambridge University Press.

Heikkilä, Heikki and Risto Kunelius. 2006. "Journalists Imagining the European Public Sphere. Professional Discourses about the EU News Practices in Ten Countries." *Javnost – The Public* 13: 63–80.

Held, David, Anthony McGrew, David Goldblatt, and Jonathan Perraton. 1999. *Global Transformations*. Cambridge: Polity Press.

Henzinger, Monika. 2001. "Hyperlink Analysis for the Web." *IEEE Internet Computing* 5: 45–50.

Héritier, Adrienne. 1999. *Policy-making and Diversity in Europe*. Cambridge: Cambridge University Press.

Hilgartner, Stephen and Charles S. Bosk. 1988. "The Rise and Fall of Social Problems: A Public Arenas Model." *American Journal of Sociology* 94: 53–78.

Hitchcock, William H. 2003. *The Struggle for Europe*. New York: Doubleday.

Hix, Simon. 2005. *The Political System of the European Union*. Houndmills: Palgrave Macmillan.

Hix, Simon. 2006. "Why the EU Needs (Left-Right) Politics?," pp. 1–27 in Simon Hix and Stefano Bartolini, *Politics: The Right or the Wrong Sort of Medicine for the EU?* Notre Europe, Policy Paper No.19. Retrieved October 15, 2007, from http://www .unizar.es/euroconstitucion/library/working%20papers/Hix,%20Bartolini% 202006.pdf.

Hix, Simon. 2008. *What's Wrong with the EU and How to Fix It*. Cambridge: Polity Press.

Hix, Simon and Christopher Lord. 1997. *Political Parties in the European Union*. New York: St. Martin's Press.

Hix, Simon and Klaus H. Goetz. 2000. "Introduction: European Integration and National Political Systems." *West European Politics* 23: 1–26.

Hoffmann, Stanley. 1995. *The European Sisyphus*. Boulder: Westview Press.

Hooghe, Liesbet and Gary Marks. 2001. *Multi-level Governance and European Integration*. Lanham, MD: Rowman & Littlefield.

Hooghe, Liesbet and Gary Marks. 2004. "Does Identity or Economic Rationality Drive Public Opinion on European Integration?" *PS: Political Science and Politics* 37: 415–420.

Hooghe, Liesbet and Gary Marks. 2005. The Neofunctionalists Were (Almost) Right. conWEB. Webpapers on Constitutionalism and Governance 5. Retrieved October 18, 2006, from http://www.arena.uio.no/events/papers/HoogeMarks.pdf.

Hooghe, Liesbet, Gary Marks, and Carole J. Wilson. 2004. "Does Left/Right Structure Party Position on European Integration?," pp. 120–140 in Gary Marks and Marco R. Steenbergen (Eds.), *European Integration and Political Conflict*. Cambridge: Cambridge University Press.

Huber, Claudia K. 2007. *Meeting in the Middle. German and British EU Correspondents' Interplay with Sources of Information in Brussels*. Paper to 4th ECPR General Conference, Pisa, Italy.

Huntington, Samuel P. 1968. *Political Order in Changing Societies*. New Haven: Yale University Press.

Imig, Doug and Sidney Tarrow (Eds.). 2001a. *Contentious Europeans*. Lanham, MD: Rowman & Littlefield.

Imig, Doug and Sidney Tarrow. 2001b. "Political Contention in a Europeanising Polity," pp. 73–93 in Klaus H. Goetz and Simon Hix (Eds.), *Europeanized Politics? European Integration and National Political Systems*. London: Frank Cass.

Jachtenfuchs, Markus and Beate Kohler-Koch. 2003. *Europäische Integration*. Stuttgart: UTB.

Jackson, Michele. 1997. "Assessing the Structure of Communication on the World Wide Web." *Journal of Computer-Mediated Communication* 3. Retrieved June 12, 2007, from http://jcmc.indiana.edu/vol3/issue1/jackson.html.

Jones, Bryan D. 1994. *Reconceiving Decision-Making in Democratic Politics*. Chicago: The University of Chicago Press.

Jönsson, Christer, Sven Tägil, and Gunnar Törnqvist. 2000. *Organizing European Space*. London: Sage.

Judt, Tony. 2005. *Postwar*. London: Heinemann.

Kantner, Cathleen. 2004. *Kein modernes Babel. Kommunikative Voraussetzungen europäischer Öffentlichkeit*. Wiesbaden: Verlag für Sozialwissenschaften.

Katzenstein, Peter. 1987. *Policy and Politics in West Germany: The Growth of a Semi-Sovereign State*. Philadelphia: Temple University Press.

Katzenstein, Peter J. 2005. *A World of Regions*. Ithaca: Cornell University Press.

Kaufmann, Bruno, Alain Lamassoure, and Jürgen Meyer. 2004. *Transnational Democracy in the Making*. Amsterdam: Initiative & Referendum Institute Europe.

Keck, Margaret and Kathryn Sikkink. 1998. *Activists beyond Borders*. Ithaca: Cornell University Press.

Kepplinger, Hans Mathias. 1998. *Die Demontage der Politik in der Informationsgesellschaft*. Freiburg and München: Karl Alber.

Kernell, Samuel. 1997. *Going Public. New Strategies of Presidential Leadership*. Washington, DC: CQ Press.

Kevin, Deidre. 2003. *Europe in the Media: A Comparison of Reporting, Representation, and Rhetoric in National Media Systems in Europe*. London: Erlbaum.

Key, Valdimer Orlando Jr. 1961. *Public Opinion and American Democracy*. New York: Knopf.

Kielmansegg, Peter Graf. 1996. "Integration und Demokratie," pp. 47–71 in Markus Jachtenfuchs and Beate Kohler-Koch (Eds.), *Europäische Integration*. Opladen: Leske + Budrich.

Kitschelt, Herbert. 1986. "Political Opportunity Structures and Political Protest." *British Journal of Political Science* 16: 57–85.

Kleinberg, Jon Michael. 1999. "Authoritative Sources in a Hyperlinked Environment." *Journal of ACM* 46: 604–632.

Kohler-Koch, Beate. 1994. "Changing Patterns of Interest Intermediation in the European Union." *Government and Opposition* 29: 166–180.

Kohler-Koch, Beate (Ed.). 2003. *Linking EU and National Governance*. Oxford: Oxford University Press.

Kollman, Ken. 1998. *Outside Lobbying. Public Opinion and Interest Group Strategies*. Princeton: Princeton University Press.

Koopmans, Ruud. 2002. Codebook for the Analysis of Political Mobilisation and Communication in European Public Spheres. Retrieved October 17, 2005, from http://europub.wzb.eu/Data/Codebooks%20questionnaires/D2-1-claims-codebook.pdf.

Koopmans, Ruud. 2004. "Movements and Media: Selection Processes and Evolutionary Dynamics in the Public Sphere." *Theory and Society* 33: 367–391.

Koopmans, Ruud. 2007. "Who Inhabits the European Public Sphere? Winners and Losers and Opponents in Europeanised Political Debates." *European Journal of Political Research* 46: 183–210.

Koopmans, Ruud and Jessica Erbe. 2004. "Towards a European Public Sphere? Vertical and Horizontal Dimensions of Europeanised Political Communication." *Innovation* 17: 97–118.

Koopmans, Ruud and Susan Olzak. 2004. "Discursive Opportunities and the Evolution of Right-Wing Violence in Germany." *American Journal of Sociology* 110: 198–230.

Koopmans, Ruud and Barbara Pfetsch. 2003. Toward a Europeanised Public Sphere? Comparing Political Actors and the Media. ARENA Working Paper 23/03. Oslo: Center for European Studies.

Koopmans, Ruud and Paul Statham. 1999. "Political Claims Analysis: Integrating Protest Event and Public Discourse." *Mobilization* 4: 203–222.

Koopmans, Ruud and Paul Statham. 2002. The Transformation of Political Mobilisation and Communication in European Public Spheres: A Research Outline. Europub.com. Retrieved October 7, 2008, from http://europub.wzb.eu/Data/reports/Proposal.pdf.

Koopmans, Ruud, Paul Statham, Marco Giugni, and Florence Passy. 2005. *Contested Citizenship. Immigration and Cultural Diversity in Europe*. Minneapolis: University of Minnesota Press.

Kopper, Gerd G. 1997. *Europäische Öffentlichkeit: Entwicklung von Strukturen und Theorie*. Berlin: Vistas.

Kreppel, Amie. 2002. *The European Parliament and the Supranational Party System*. Cambridge: Cambridge University Press.

Kriesi, Hanspeter. 1993. *Political Mobilization and Social Change*. Aldershot: Avebury.

Kriesi, Hanspeter. 2003. Interview Questionnaire for Collective Actors in Claims-making and Political Mobilization. Retrieved October 18, 2005, from http://europub.wzb.eu/codebooks.en.htm.

Kriesi, Hanspeter. 2004. "Strategic Political Communication: Mobilizing Public Opinion in 'Audience Democracies'," pp. 194–212 in Frank Esser and Barbara Pfetsch (Eds.), *Comparing Political Communication: Theories, Cases and Challenges*. Cambridge: Cambridge University Press.

Kriesi, Hanspeter. 2005. *How National Political Parties Mobilize the Political Potentials Linked to European Integration*. Unpublished manuscript. Zurich: University of Zurich.

Kriesi, Hanspeter. 2007. "The Role of European Integration in National Election Campaigns." *European Union Politics* 8: 83–108.

Kriesi, Hanspeter, Silke Adam, and Margit Jochum. 2006a. "Comparative Analysis of Policy Networks in Western Europe." *Journal of European Public Policy* 13: 341–361.

Kriesi, Hanspeter, Edgar Grande, Romain Lachat, Martin Dolezal, Simon Bornschier, and Timotheos Frey. 2006b. "Globalization and the Transformation of the National Political Space: Six European Countries Compared." *European Journal of Political Research* 45: 921–956.

Kriesi, Hanspeter, Edgar Grande, Romain Lachat, Martin Dolezal, Simon Bornschier, and Timotheos Frey. 2008. *West European Politics in the Age of Globalization*. Cambridge: Cambridge University Press.

Kriesi, Hanspeter, Ruud Koopmans, Jan Willem Duyvendak, and Marco G. Giugni. 1995. *New Social Movements in Western Europe: A Comparative Analysis*. Minneapolis: University of Minnesota Press.

Kriesi, Hanspeter, Anke Tresch, and Margit Jochum. 2007. "Going Public in the European Union. Action Repertoires of Western European Collective Political Actors." *Comparative Political Studies* 40: 48–73.

Kupchan, Charles. 2002. *The End of the American Era*. New York: Knopf.

Lahusen, Christian. 2004. "Joining the Cocktail Circuit: Social Movement Organizations at the European Union." *Mobilization* 9: 55–71.

Lamont, Michèle and Laurent Thévenot. 2000. *Rethinking Comparative Cultural Sociology: Repertoires of Evaluation in France and the United States*. Cambridge: Cambridge University Press.

Lavenex, Sandra. 2001. "The Europeanization of Refugee Policies: Normative Challenges and Institutional Legacies." *Journal of Common Market Studies* 39: 851–874.

Leibfried, Stephan and Paul Pierson (Eds.). 1995. *European Social Policy*. Washington, DC: Brookings Institution.

Leonard, Mark. 2005.*Why Europe Will Run the 21st Century*. London: Fourth Estate.

Levy, Daniel, Max Pensky, and John Torpey (Eds.). 2005. *Old Europe, New Europe, Core Europe*. London: Verso Books.

Lichtheim, George. 1972 [2000]. *Europe in the 20th Century*. London: Phoenix Press.

Lijphart, Arend. 1968 [1975]. *The Politics of Accommodation*. Berkeley: California University Press.

Lijphart, Arend. 1968. *Verzuiling, pacificatie en kentering in de Nederlandse politiek*. Amsterdam: De Bussy.

Lijphart, Arend. 1984. *Democracies*. New Haven: Yale University Press.

Lijphart, Arend. 1999. *Patterns of Democracy. Government Forms and Performance in Thirty-six Countries*. New Haven: Yale University Press.

Lijphart, Arend. 2008. *Thinking about Democracy*. London: Routledge.

Lindberg, Leon and Stuart Scheingold. 1970. *Europe's Would-Be Polity*. Englewood Cliffs, NJ: Prentice-Hall.

Lippmann, Walter. 1922 [2007]. *Public Opinion*. Sioux Falls, SD: NuVision Publications.

Lipset, Seymour and Jason Lakin. 2004. *The Democratic Century*. Norman: University of Oklahoma Press.

Ludlow, Peter. 2002. *The Laeken Council*. Brussels: EuroComment.

Machill, Marcel, Markus Beiler, and Corinna Fischer. 2006. "Europe-Topics in Europe's Media. The Debate about the European Public Sphere: A Meta-Analysis of Media Content Analyses." *European Journal of Communication* 21: 57–88.

Magnette, Paul and Yannis Papadopoulos. 2008. On the Politicization of the European Consociation. European Governance Papers No. C-08–01. Retrieved March 18, 2009, from http://www.connex-network.org/eurogov/pdf/egp-connex-C-08–01.pdf.

Mair, Peter. 1997. *Party System Change. Approaches and Interpretations*. Oxford: Clarendon Press.

Mair, Peter. 2000a. "Partyless Democracy. Solving the Paradox of New Labour?" *New Left Review* 2: 21–35.

Mair, Peter. 2000b. "The Limited Impact of Europe on National Party Systems." *West European Politics* 23: 27–51.

Mair, Peter. 2002. "Populist democracy vs. party democracy," pp. 81–98 in Yves Mény and Yves Surel (Eds.), *Democracies and the Populist Challenge*. Basingstoke: Palgrave.

Mair, Peter. 2007a. "Political Opposition and the European Union." *Government and Opposition* 42: 1–17.

Mair, Peter. 2007b. "Political Parties and Party Systems," pp. 154–166 in Paolo Graziano and Maarten P. Vink (Eds.), *Europeanization. New Research Agendas*. Houndmills, Basingstoke: Palgrave Macmillan.

Majone, Giandomenico. 1996. *Regulating Europe*. London: Routledge.

Majone, Giandomenico. 1998. "Europe's 'Democratic Deficit'." *European Law Journal* 4: 5–28.

Majone, Giandomenico. 2002. "The European Commission: The Limits of Centralization and the Perils of Parliamentarization." *Governance* 15: 375–392.

Mak, Jeannette. 2001. *Selling Europe: Communicating Symbols or Symbolic Communication?* PhD dissertation. Florence: European University Institute.

Manin, Bernard. 1995. *Principes du gouvernement représentatif.* Paris: Flammarion.

Manin, Bernard. 1997. *The Principles of Representative Government.* Cambridge: Cambridge University Press.

Mansfield, Edward D. and Jack Snyder. 2005. *Electing to Fight.* Cambridge, MA: MIT Press.

Marks, Gary. 2004. "Conclusion: European Integration and Political Conflict," pp. 235–259 in Gary Marks and Marco R. Steenbergen (Eds.), *European Integration and Political Conflict.* Cambridge: Cambridge University Press.

Marks, Gary, Liesbet Hooghe, and Kermit Blank. 1996. "European Integration from the 1980s: State-Centric v. Multi-level Governance." *Journal of Common Market Studies* 34: 341–378.

Marks, Gary and Doug McAdam. 1996. "Social Movements and the Changing Structure of Political Opportunity in the European Union." *West European Politics* 19: 249–278.

Marks, Gary and Doug McAdam. 1999. "On the Relationship of Political Opportunities to the Form of Collective Action: The Case of the European Union," pp. 97–111 in Donatella Della Porta, Hanspeter Kriesi, and Dieter Rucht (Eds.), *Social Movements in a Globalizing World.* London: Macmillan.

Marks, Gary and Marco R. Steenbergen (Eds.). 2004. *European Integration and Political Conflict.* Cambridge: Cambridge University Press.

Marks, Gary and Carole J. Wilson. 2000. "The Past in the Present: A Cleavage Theory of Party Response to European Integration." *British Journal of Political Science* 30: 433–459.

Maurer, Andreas, Jürgen Mittag, and Wolfgang Wessels. 2003. "National Systems' Adaptation to the EU System: Trends, Offers, and Constraints," pp. 53–81 in Beate Kohler-Koch (Ed.), *Linking EU and National Governance.* Oxford: Oxford University Press.

Mazzoleni, Gianpietro. 1987. "Media Logic and Party Logic in Campaign Coverage: The Italian General Election of 1983." *European Journal of Communication* 2: 81–103.

Mazzoleni, Gianpietro and Winfried Schulz. 1999. "'Mediatization' of Politics: A Challenge for Democracy?" *Political Communication* 16: 247–262.

McAdam, Doug, John D. McCarthy, and Mayer N. Zald (Eds.). 1996. *Comparative Perspectives on Social Movements: Political Opportunities, Mobilizing Structures, and Cultural Framings.* New York: Cambridge University Press.

McCombs, Maxwell E. and Donald L. Shaw. 1972. "The Agenda-Setting Function of the Mass Media." *Public Opinion Quarterly* 36: 176–187.

McQuail, Denis. 1994. *Mass Communication Theory.* London: Sage.

Menéndez-Alarcón, Antonio V. 2004. *The Cultural Realm of European Integration: Social Representations in France, Spain, and the United Kingdom.* Westport: Praeger.

Merton, Robert K. 1973. *The Sociology of Science. Theoretical and Empirical Investigations.* Chicago: University of Chicago Press.

Meyer, Christoph O. 1999. "Political Legitimacy and the Invisibility of Politics: Exploring the European Union's Communication Deficit." *Journal of Common Market Studies* 37: 617–639.

Meyer, Christoph O. 2002. *Europäische Öffentlichkeit als Kontrollsphäre: Die Europäische Kommission, die Medien und politische Verantwortlichkeit.* Berlin: Vistas.

Meyer, Christoph O. 2005. "The Europeanization of Publicised Debates: A Study of Quality Press Coverage of Economic Policy Coordination since Amsterdam." *Journal of Common Market Studies* 43: 119–146.

Meyer, Christoph O. 2007. The Constitutional Treaty Debates as Revelatory Mechanisms: Insights for Public Sphere Research and Re-Launch Attempts. Recon-Online Working Paper 2007/4. Retrieved October 7, 2008, from http://www.reconproject.eu/projectweb/portalproject/Publications.html.

Meyer, Christoph O. 2009. "Does the European Union Become Mediatized? The Case of the European Commission." *Journal of European Public Policy* 16: 1047–1064.

Meyer, Martin F. 2010. "Public Visibility and Citizen Participation: The Europeanization of Foreign Policy Debates in the British and German Public Spheres," in Sonia Lucarelli, Furio Cerutti, and Vivien Schmidt (Eds.), *Debating Political Identity and Legitimacy in the European Union: Interdisciplinary Views.* London: Routledge (on press).

Michailidou, Asimina. 2007. The Impact of 'Constitutionalisation' on the EU Public Communication Strategy: EU Official Rhetoric and Civil Society. European Political Communication Working Paper Series 14/07. University of Leeds. Retrieved November 8, 2008, from http://www.eurpolcom.eu.

Middlemas, Keith. 1995. *Orchestrating Europe.* London: Fontana.

Milward, Alan. 1984. *The Reconstruction of Western Europe 1945–1951.* London: Routledge.

Milward, Alan. 1992. *The European Rescue of the Nation State.* London: Routledge.

Mittag, Jürgen and Wolfgang Wessels. 2003. "The 'One' and the 'Fifteen'? The Member States between Procedural Adaptation and Structural Revolution," pp. 413–457 in Wolfgang Wessels, Andreas Maurer, and Jürgen Mittag (Eds.), *Fifteen into One? The European Union and its Member States.* Manchester: Manchester University Press.

Moravcsik, Andrew. 1993. "Preferences and Power in the European Community: A Liberal Intergovernmentalist Approach." *Journal of Common Market Studies* 31: 473–524.

Moravcsik, Andrew. 1994. Why the European Community Strengthens the State: Domestic Politics and International Cooperation. Working Paper 52. Cambridge, MA: Harvard University Press.

Moravcsik, Andrew. 1998. *The Choice for Europe.* Ithaca: Cornell University Press.

Moravcsik, Andrew. 2002. "In Defence of the 'Democratic Deficit': Reassessing Legitimacy in the European Union." *Journal of Common Market Studies* 40: 603–644.

Moravcsik, Andrew. 2004. "Is There a 'Democratic Deficit' in World Politics?" *Government and Opposition* 39: 336–363.

Moravcsik, Andrew. 2005a. *Europe without Illusions. The Paul-Henri Spaak Lectures 1994–1999.* Lanham, MD: University Press of America.

Moravcsik, Andrew. 2005b. "Europe without Illusions." *Prospect* 112 (July): 1–10.

Moravcsik, Andrew. 2006. "What Can We Learn from the Collapse of the European Constitutional Project?" *Politische Vierteljahresschrift* 47: 219–241.

Morgan, David. 1995. "British Media and European News. The Brussels News Beat and Its Problems." *European Journal of Communication* 10: 321–343.

Morgan, Glyn. 2005. *The Idea of a European Superstate.* Princeton: Princeton University Press.

Münkler, Herfried. 2005. *Imperien.* Berlin: Rowohlt.

Neidhardt, Friedhelm, Christiane Eilders, and Barbara Pfetsch. 2004. "Einleitung: Die 'Stimme der Medien' – Pressekommentare als Gegenstand der Öffentlichkeitsforschung," pp. 11–38 in Christiane Eilders, Friedhelm Neidhardt, and Barbara Pfetsch (Eds.), *Die Stimme der Medien: Pressekommentare und politische Öffentlichkeit in der Bundesrepublik.* Wiesbaden: VS – Verlag für Sozialwissenschaften.

Neuman, W. Russell, Marion R. Just, and Ann N. Crigler. 1992. *Common Knowledge. News and the Construction of Political Meaning.* Chicago: University of Chicago Press.

Norman, Peter. 2003. *The Accidental Constitution.* Brussels: EuroComment.

Norris, Pippa. 2000a. *A Virtuous Circle.* Cambridge: Cambridge University Press.

Norris, Pippa. 2000b. "The Internet in Europe: A New North-South Divide?" *The Harvard International Journal of Press/Politics* 5: 1–12.

Nugent, Neill. 2001. *The European Commission.* Basingstoke: Macmillan.

Olson, Mancur. 1982. *The Rise and Decline of Nations.* New Haven: Yale University Press.

Pagden, Anthony (Ed.). 2002. *The Idea of Europe.* Cambridge: Cambridge University Press.

Page, Benjamin I. 1996. "The Mass Media as Political Actors." *Political Science and Politics* 29: 20–24.

Page, Benjamin, Robert Y. Shapiro, and Glenn R. Dempsey. 1987. "What Moves Public Opinion?" *American Political Science Review* 81: 23–43.

Park, Han Woo. 2003. "Hyperlink Network Analysis: A New Method for the Study of Social Structure on the Web." *Connections* 25: 49–61.

Park, Han Woo and Mike Thelwall. 2003. "Hyperlink Analyses of the World Wide Web: A Review." *Journal of Computer-Mediated Communication* 8. Retrieved June 12, 2007, from http://jcmc.indiana.edu/vol8/issue4/park.html.

Patterson, Thomas E. 1997. "The News Media: An Effective Political Actor?" *Political Communication* 14: 445–455.

Patterson, Thomas E. 1998. "Political Roles of the Journalist," pp. 17–32 in Doris Graber, Denis McQuail, and Pippa Norris (Eds.), *The Politics of News. The News of Politics.* Washington, DC: CQ Press.

Patterson, Thomas E. and Wolfgang Donsbach. 1996. "News Decisions: Journalists as Political Actors." *Political Communication* 13: 455–468.

Pedler, Robin H. and Marinus C.P.M. van Schendelen. 1994. *Lobbying in the European Union.* Aldershot: Dartmouth.

Pennock, David M., Gary W. Flake, Steve Lawrence, Eric J. Glover, and Lee Cn. Giles. 2002. "Winners Don't Take All: Characterizing the Competition on the Web." *Proceedings of the National Academy of Science* 99: 5207–5211.

Peter, Jochen. 2003. *Why European TV News Matters.* Amsterdam: University of Amsterdam.

Peter, Jochen and Claes H. de Vreese. 2004. "In Search of Europe. A Cross-National Comparative Study of the European Union in National Television News." *The Harvard International Journal of Press/Politics* 9: 3–24.

Peter, Jochen, Edmund Lauf, and Holli Semetko. 2004. "Television Coverage of the 1999 European Parliamentary Elections." *Political Communication* 21: 415–433.

Peters, Bernhard, Steffanie Sifft, Andreas Wimmel, Michael Brüggemann, and Katharina Kleinen von Königslöw. 2005. "National and Transnational Public Spheres: The Case of the EU." *European Review* 13: 139–160.

Pfetsch, Barbara. 2008a. "Editorial," pp. 1437–1439 in Wolfgang Donsbach (Ed.), *International Encyclopedia of Communications*. Oxford: Blackwell.

Pfetsch, Barbara. 2008b. "Agents of Transnational Debate across Europe. The Press in Emerging European Public Sphere." *Javnost – The Public* 15: 21–40.

Pfetsch, Barbara and Silke Adam. 2008. "Die Akteursperspektive in der politischen Kommunikationsforschung – Fragestellungen, Forschungsparadigmen und Problemlagen," pp. 9–26 in Barbara Pfetsch and Silke Adam (Eds.), *Massenmedien als politische Akteure. Konzepte und Analysen*. Wiesbaden: VS – Verlag für Sozialwissenschaften.

Pfetsch, Barbara, Silke Adam, and Barbara Eschner. 2008. "The Contribution of the Press to Europeanization of Public Debates. A Comparative Study of Issue Salience and Conflict Lines of European Integration." *Journalism. Theory, Practice & Criticism* 9: 465–492.

Pierson, Paul. 2000. "Increasing Returns, Path Dependency, and the Study of Politics." *American Political Science Review* 94: 251–267.

Pierson, Paul. 2004. *Politics in Time. History, Institutions, and Social Analysis*. Princeton: Princeton University Press.

Pisani-Ferry, Jean and André Sapir. 2006. Last Exit to Lisbon. Bruegel Policy Contribution. Retrieved February 21, 2008, from http://www.pisani-ferry.net/base/papiers/re-06-lisbonpaper.pdf.

Plake, Klaus, Daniel Jansen, and Birgit Schuhmacher, 2001. *Öffentlichkeit und Gegenöffentlichkeit im Internet. Politische Potenziale der Medienentwicklung*. Wiesbaden: Westdeutscher Verlag.

Poor, Nathaniel. 2005. "Mechanisms of an Online Public Sphere: The Website Slashdot." *Journal of Computer-Mediated Communication* 10(2). Retrieved June 15, 2008, from http://jcmc.indiana.edu/vol10/issue2/poor.html.

Putnam, Robert D. 1988. "Diplomacy and Domestic Politics." *International Organization* 42: 427–460.

Radaelli, Claudio M. 2003. "The Europeanization of Public Policy," pp. 27–56 in Kevin Featherstone and Claudio M. Radaelli (Eds.), *The Politics of Europeanization*. Oxford: Oxford University Press.

Radaelli, Claudio M. and Vivien A. Schmidt (Eds.). 2005. *Policy Change and Discourse*. London: Routledge.

Raeymaeckers, Karin, Lieven Cosjin, and Annelore Deprez. 2007. "Reporting the European Union." *Journalism Practice* 1: 102–119.

Ray, Leonard. 1999. "Measuring Party Orientations towards European Integration. Results from an Expert Survey." *European Journal of Political Research* 36: 283–306.

Resnick, David. 1997. "Politics on the Internet: The Normalization on Cyberspace." *New Political Science* 41–42: 47–67.

Rifkin, Jeremy. 2004. *The European Dream*. New York: Tarcher.

Risse, Thomas 2002. *How Do We Know a European Public Sphere When We See One? Theoretical Clarifications and Empirical Indicators*. IDNET Workshop 'Europeanization and the Public Sphere'. Florence: European University Institute.

Risse, Thomas. 2003. An Emerging European Public Sphere? Theoretical Clarifications and Empirical Indicators. Paper presented to the Annual Meeting of the European Union Studies Association (EUSA), Nashville, TN, March 27–30.

Risse, Thomas. 2010. *A Community of Europeans? Transnational Identities and Public Spheres*. Ithaca: Cornell University Press.

Robyn, Richard (Ed.). 2005. *The Changing Face of European Identity*. London: Routledge.

Ross, George. 1995. *Jacques Delors and European Integration*. Cambridge: Polity Press.

Röttger, Ulrike, Jochen Hoffmann, and Otfried Jarren. 2003. *Public Relations in der Schweiz. Eine empirische Studie zum Berufsfeld Öffentlichkeitsarbeit*. Konstanz: U.K.Verlag.

Rucht, Dieter. 2000. "Zur Europäisierung politischer Mobilisierung." *Berliner Journal für Soziologie* 10: 185–202.

Rucht, Dieter, Ruud Koopmans, and Friedhelm Neidhardt (Eds.). 1999. *Acts of Dissent: New Developments in the Study of Protest*. Lanham, MD: Rowman & Littlefield.

Saguy, Abigail C. 2003. *What Is Sexual Harassment? From Capitol Hill to the Sorbonne*. Berkeley: University of California Press.

Sapir, André (Ed.). 2004. *An Agenda for a Growing Europe*. Oxford: Oxford University Press.

Sapir, André. 2005. Globalization and the Reform of European Social Models. Bruegel Policy Brief. Retrieved October 25, 2007, from http://aei.pitt.edu/8336/01/PB200501_SocialModels.pdf.

Saurugger, Sabine. 2008. "Interest Groups and Democracy in the European Union." *West European Politics* 31: 1274–1291.

Sbragia, Alberta, et al. 2006. "The EU Constitution: RIP?" *Political Science and Politics* 39: 237–272.

Scharpf, Fritz W. 1997. *Games Real Actors Play*. Boulder: Westview.

Schattschneider, Elmer Eric. 1960 [1988]. *The Semi-Sovereign People. A Realist's View of Democracy in America*. London: Wadsworth.

Schlecht, Tobias. 2002. *Europa in den deutschen Fernsehnachrichten. Eine Analyse des Nachrichtenmagazins Tagesthemen*. Master's thesis. Berlin: Free University, Institut für Publizistik und Kommunikationswissenschaft.

Schlesinger, Philip R. 1995. Europeanisation and the Media: National Identity and the Public Sphere. ARENA Working Paper 95–07. Oslo: The Norwegian Research Council.

Schlesinger, Philip R. 1999. "Changing Spaces of Political Communication: The Case of the European Union." *Political Communication* 16: 263–279.

Schlesinger, Philip R. and Howard Tumber. 1994. *Reporting Crime. The Media Politics of Criminal Justice*. Oxford: Clarendon Press.

Schmidt, Vivien A. 2006. *Democracy in Europe*. Oxford: Oxford University Press.

Schmitter, Philippe C. 1969. "Three Neo-functional Hypotheses about European Integration." *International Organization* 23: 161–166.

Schmitter, Philippe C. 2000. *How to Democratize the European Union... and Why Bother*. Lanham, MD: Rowman & Littlefield.

Schneider, Steven M. 1997. Expanding the Public Sphere Through Computer-mediated Communication: Political Discussion about Abortion in a Usenet Newsgroup. Retrieved June 12, 2007, from http://people.sunyit.edu/~steve/main.pdf.

Schudson, Michael. 1995. *The Power of News*. Cambridge, MA: Harvard University Press.

Schudson, Michael. 2007. "The Concept of Politics in Contemporary U.S. Journalism." *Political Communication* 24: 131–142.

Schulz, Winfried. 1997. *Politische Kommunikation. Theoretische Ansätze und Ergebnisse empirischer Forschung zur Rolle der Massenmedien in der Politik.* Opladen: Westdeutscher Verlag.

Schumpeter, Joseph A. 1942. *Capitalism, Socialism, and Democracy.* New York: Harper.

Scott, John 1991. *Social Network Analysis. A Handbook.* London: Sage.

Semetko, Holli A., Claes de Vreese, and Jochen Peter. 2001. "Europeanised Politics – Europeanised Media? European Integration and Political Communication." *West European Politics* 23: 121–141.

Sen, Amartya. 2005. *The Argumentative Indian.* London: Allen Lane.

Seymore-Ure, Colin. 1974. *The Political Impact of the Mass Media.* Beverly Hills, CA: Sage.

Shoemaker, Pamela and Stephen Reese. 1996. *Mediating the Message: Theories of Influence on Mass Media Content.* White Plains, NY: Longman.

Shore, Cris. 2000. *Building Europe.* London: Routledge.

Siedentop, Larry. 2000. *Democracy in Europe.* London: Allen Lane.

Sifft, Steffanie, Michael Brüggemann, Katharina Kleinen-von Königslöw, Bernhard Peters, and Andreas Wimmel. 2007. "Segmented Europeanization: Exploring the Legitimacy of the European Union from a Public Discourse Perspective." *Journal of Common Market Studies* 45: 127–155.

Smith, Andy (Ed.). 2004. *Politics and the European Commission.* London: Routledge.

Snow, David A. and Robert D. Benford. 1992. "Master Frames and Cycles of Protest," pp. 133–155 in Aldon D. Morris and Carol McClurg Mueller (Eds.), *Frontiers in Social Movement Theory.* New Haven: Yale University Press.

Snyder, Jack. 2000. *From Voting to Violence.* New York: Norton.

Soysal, Yasemin. 1994. Limits of Citizenship. *Migrants and Postnational Membership in Europe.* Chicago: University of Chicago Press.

Spinelli, Altiero. 1966. *The Eurocrats.* Baltimore: Johns Hopkins University Press.

Splichal, Slavko. 1999. *Public Opinion.* Lanham: Rowman & Littlefield.

Statham, Paul. 2007a. "Political Communication, European Integration and the Transformation of National Public Spheres: A Comparison of Britain and France," pp. 110–134 in John Erik Fossum and Philip Schlesinger (Eds.), *The European Union and the Public Sphere: A Communicative Space in the Making?* London: Routledge.

Statham, Paul. 2007b. "Journalists as Commentators on European Politics: Educators, Partisans, or Ideologues?" *European Journal of Communication* 22: 461–477.

Statham, Paul. 2008. "Making Europe News: How Journalists View Their Role and Media Performance." *Journalism. Theory and Praxis* 9: 395–419.

Statham, Paul. 2009. The Impact of EU 'Constitutionalisation' on Public Claims-making over Europe. Final Report to the Economic and Social Research Council (RES-000-23-0886-A). Retrieved October 18, 2009, from http://www.eurpolcom.eu/research_projects_const.cfm.

Statham, Paul, Julie Firmstone, and Emily Gray. 2003. Interview Schedule for Journalists. Workpackage 6. Retrieved June 18, 2006, from http://europub.wzb.eu/codebooks.en.htm.

Statham, Paul and Andrew Geddes. 2006. "Elites and Organized Publics: Who Drives British Immigration Politics and in Which Direction?" *West European Politics* 29: 245–266.

Statham, Paul and Emily Gray. 2005. "The Public Sphere and Debates about Europe in Britain." *Innovation* 18: 61–81.

Steenbergen, Marco R. and Gary Marks. 2004. "Introduction: Models of Political Conflict in the European Union," pp. 1–10 in Gary Marks and Marco R. Steenbergen (Eds.), *European Integration and Political Conflict*. Cambridge: Cambridge University Press.

Steenbergen, Marco R. and David J. Scott. 2004. "Contesting Europe? The Salience of European Integration as a Party Issue," pp. 165–192 in Gary Marks and Marco R. Steenbergen (Eds.), *European Integration and Political Conflict*. Cambridge: Cambridge University Press.

Steinberg, Marc W. 1999. "The Talk and Back Talk of Collective Action." *American Journal of Sociology* 105: 736–780.

Streeck, Wolfgang. 1995. "Neo-Voluntarism: A New European Social Policy Regime?" *European Law Journal* 1: 31–59.

Swanson, David L., and Paolo Mancini. 1996. "Patterns of Modern Electoral Campaigning and Their Consequences," pp. 247–276 in David L. Swanson and Paolo Mancini (Eds.), *Politics, Media, and Modern Democracy. An International Study of Innovations in Electoral Campaigning and Their Consequences*. London: Praeger.

Taggart, Paul. 1998. "A Touchstone of Dissent: Euroscepticism in Contemporary Western European Party Systems." *European Journal of Political Research* 33: 363–388.

Tarrow, Sidney. 1994. *Power in Movement. Social Movements, Collective Action and Politics*. Cambridge: Cambridge University Press.

Tarrow, Sidney. 2001. "Contentious Politics in a Composite Polity," pp. 233–252 in Doug Imig and Sidney Tarrow (Eds.), *Contentious Europeans. Protest and Politics in an Emerging Polity*. Oxford: Rowman & Littlefield.

Taylor, Paul. 2008. *The End of European Integration. Anti-Europeanism Examined*. London: Routledge.

Therborn, Göran. 1995. *European Modernity and Beyond*. London: Sage.

Tilly, Charles. 2005. *Trust and Rule*. Cambridge: Cambridge University Press.

Trenz, Hans-Jörg. 2000. "Korruption und politischer Skandal in der EU. Auf dem Weg zu einer europäischen politischen Öffentlichkeit?," pp. 332–359 in Maurizio Bach (Ed.), *Die Europäisierung nationaler Gesellschaften*. Sonderheft 40 der Kölner Zeitschrift für Soziologie und Sozialpsychologie. Opladen: Westdeutscher Verlag.

Trenz, Hans-Jörg. 2004. "Media Coverage on European Governance: Exploring the European Public Sphere in National Quality Newspapers." *European Journal of Communication* 19: 291–319.

Trenz, Hans-Jörg. 2005. *Europa in den Medien. Die europäische Integration im Spiegel nationaler Öffentlichkeit*. Frankfurt am Main: Campus.

Trenz, Hans-Jörg. 2007. "Quo Vadis Europe? Quality Newspapers Struggling for European Unity," pp. 89–109 in John Erik Fossum and Philip Schlesinger (Eds.), *The European Union and the Public Sphere: A Communicative Space in the Making?* London: Routledge.

Trenz, Hans-Jörg, Agustín José Menéndez, and Fernando Losada (Eds.). 2008. *¿Y por fin somos europeos? La comunicación política en el debate constituyente europeo*. Madrid: Dykinson.

Trif, Maria and Doug Imig. 2003. *Demanding to be Heard*. Paper for The Europeanization of Public Spheres? International Conference, Wissenschaftszentrum Berlin, June 20–23.

Tsaliki, Liza. 2002. "Online Forums and the Enlargement of Public Space: Research and Findings from a European Project." *Javnost – The Public* 9: 95–112.

Tsoukalis, Loukas. 2003. *What Kind of Europe?* Oxford: Oxford University Press.

Tuchman, Gaye. 1978. *Making News: A Study in the Construction of Reality.* New York: The Free Press.

Tumber, Howard. 1995. "Marketing Maastricht: The EU and News Management." *Media, Culture and Society* 17: 511–519.

Tumber, Howard and Marina Prentoulis. 2005. "Journalism and the Making of a Profession," pp. 58–76 in Hugo de Burgh (Ed.), *Making Journalists*. London: Routledge.

Tversky, Amos and Daniel Kahneman. 1981. "The Framing of Decisions and the Psychology of Choice." *Science* 211: 453–458.

Van Der Eijk, Cees and Mark N. Franklin (Eds.). 1996. *Choosing Europe? The European Electorate and National Politics in the Face of Union.* Ann Arbor: University of Michigan Press.

Van Der Steeg, Marianne. 2002. "Rethinking the Conditions for a Public Sphere in the European Union." *European Journal of Social Theory* 5: 499–519.

Van Der Steeg, Marianne. 2005. *The Public Sphere in the European Union.* PhD dissertation. Florence: European University Institute.

Van Der Velden, Ben. 2005. *De Europese onmacht.* Amsterdam: Meulenhoff.

Van Gerven, Walter. 2005. *The European Union.* Stanford: University of California Press.

Vetters, Regina, Erik Jentges, and Hans-Jörg Trenz. 2009. "Whose Project Is It? Media Debates on the Ratification of the EU Constitutional Treaty." *Journal of European Public Policy* 16: 412–430.

Voltmer, Katrin. 1998–1999. *Medienqualität und Demokratie. Eine empirische Analyse publizistischer Informations- und Orientierungsleistungen in der Wahlkampfkommunikation.* Baden-Baden: Nomos.

Voltmer, Katrin and Christiane Eilders. 2003. "The Media Agenda. The Marginalization and Domestication of Europe," pp. 173–197 in Kenneth Dyson and Klaus H. Goetz (Eds.), *Germany, Europe and the Politics of Constraint.* Proceedings of the British Academy 119. Oxford: Oxford University Press.

Wagner, Peter (Ed.). 2006. *The Languages of Civil Society.* New York: Berghahn Books.

Walgrave, Stefaan, Stuart Soroka, and Michiel Nuytemans. 2008. "The Mass Media's Political Agenda-Setting Power." *Comparative Political Studies* 41: 814–836.

Wallace, Helen. 2000. "The Institutional Setting: Five Variations on a Theme," pp. 3–36 in Helen Wallace and William Wallace (Eds.), *Policy-Making in the European Union.* Oxford: Oxford University Press.

Ward, David. 2004. *The European Union Democratic Deficit and the Public Sphere. An Evaluation of EU Media Policy.* Amsterdam: IOS Press.

Weale, Albert. 2005. *Democratic Citizenship and the European Union.* Manchester: Manchester University Press.

Weiler, Joseph H.H. 1999. *The Constitution of Europe.* Cambridge: Cambridge University Press.

Wessels, Wolfgang. 1997. "An Ever Closer Fusion? A Dynamic Macropolitical View on Integration Processes." *Journal of Common Market Studies* 35: 267–99.

Wessler, Hartmut Bernhard Peters, Steffanie Sifft, Michael Brüggemann, and Katharina Kleinen von Königslöw. 2008. *Transnationalization of Public Spheres.* Houndmills, Basingstoke: Palgrave Macmillan.

Wiener, Antje. 1998. *European Citizenship Practice. Building Institutions of a Non-State*. Boulder: Westview Press.

Wiener, Antje and Thomas Diez (Eds.). 2004. *European Integration Theory*. Oxford: University Press.

Wilkinson, David, Mike Thelwall, and Xuemei Li. 2003. "Exploiting Hyperlinks to Study Academic Web Use." *Social Science Computer Review* 21: 340–351.

Wolfsfeld, Gadi. 1997. *Media and Political Conflict: News from the Middle East*. Cambridge: Cambridge University Press.

Young, Hugo. 1998. *This Blessed Plot. Britain and Europe from Churchill to Blair*. London: Macmillan.

Zaret, David. 2000. *Origins of Democratic Culture*. Princeton: Princeton University Press.

Zielonka, Jan. 2006. *Europe as Empire*. Oxford: Oxford University Press.

Zürn, Michael. 1998. *Regieren jenseits des Nationalstaats. Globalisierung und Denationalisierung als Chance*. Frankfurt am Main: Suhrkamp.

Zürn, Michael. 2000. "Democratic Governance beyond the Nation State: The EU and Other International Institutions." *European Journal of International Relations* 6: 183–221.

Index

Titles in the series (continued from page iii)